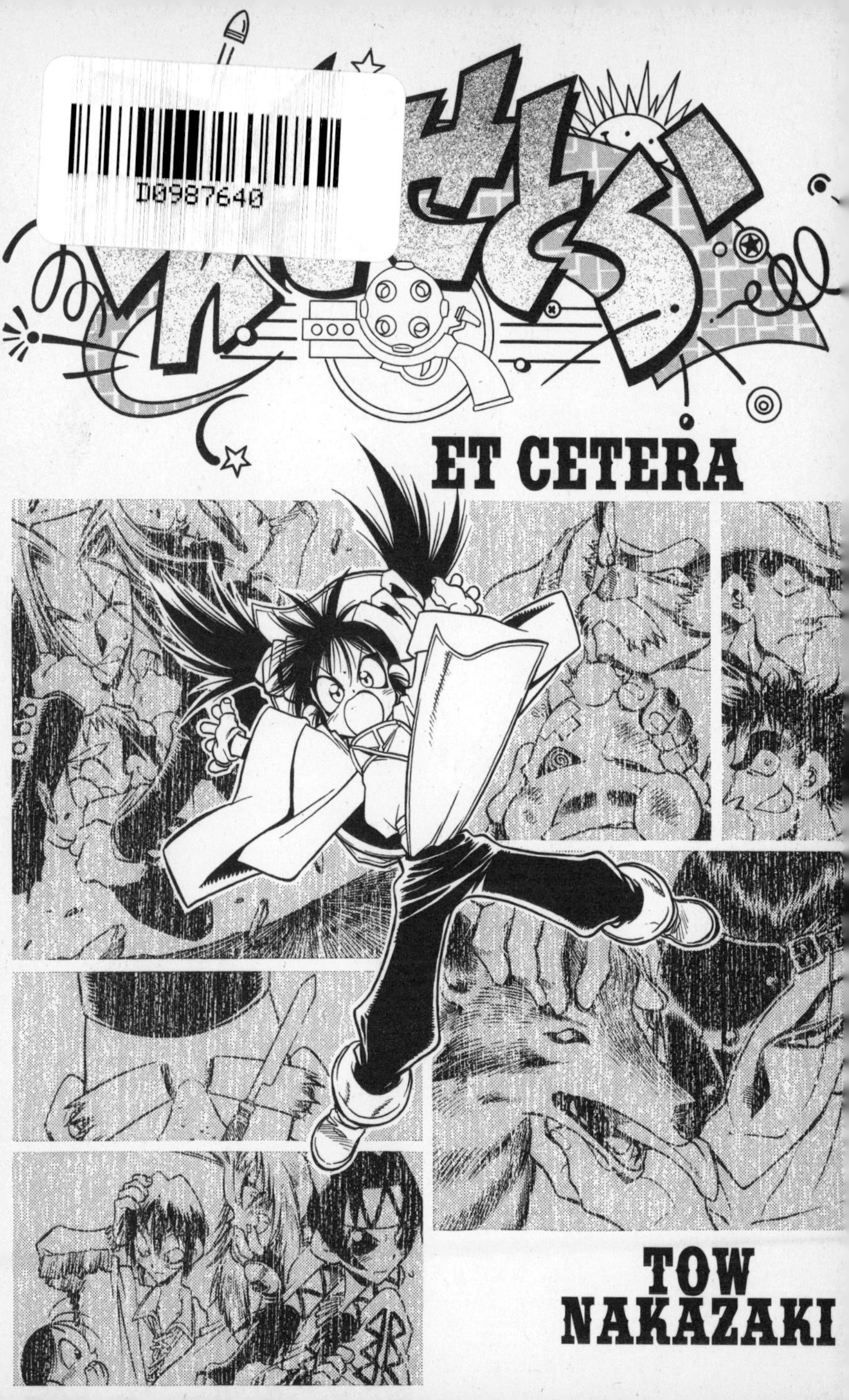
ET CETERA
TOW
NAKAZAKI

Translation - Katherine Schilling
English Adaptation - Jake Forbes
Associate Editor - Peter Ahlstrom
Retouch and Lettering - Jennifer Carbajal
Cover Design - Al-Insan Lashley

Editor - Aaron Suhr
Digital Imaging Manager - Chris Buford
Production Manager - Jennifer Miller
Managing Editor - Lindsey Johnston
VP of Production - Ron Klamert
Publisher and E.I.C. - Mike Kiley
President and C.O.O. - John Parker
C.E.O. and Chief Creative Officer - Stuart Levy

A  Manga

TOKYOPOP Inc.
5900 Wilshire Blvd. Suite 2000
Los Angeles, CA 90036

E-mail: info@TOKYOPOP.com
Come visit us online at www.TOKYOPOP.com

ISBN: 1-59532-136-5

First TOKYOPOP printing: April 2006
10 9 8 7 6 5 4 3 2 1
Printed in the USA

VOLUME 7

STORY AND ART BY
TOW NAKAZAKI

HAMBURG // LONDON // LOS ANGELES // TOKYO

STORY SO FAR

THE WILD WEST... A DANGEROUS FRONTIER WHERE THE ONLY LAW IS THE GUN. MINGCHAO ISN'T ABOUT TO LET A FEW OUTLAWS KEEP HER FROM HER HOLLYWOOD DREAMS! SHE HAS THE ETO GUN, A MYSTERIOUS WEAPON THAT USES THE SPIRITS OF THE ZODIAC ANIMALS TO FIRE UNSTOPPABLE BULLETS. TOGETHER WITH AN UNLIKELY BUNCH OF TRAVELING COMPANIONS, MINGCHAO IS HEADING WEST TO BECOME A STAR!

FUTURA THE MAGICIAN STIRS UP TROUBLE WITH HIS MAGIC SHOW AND REUNITES MINGCHAO WITH BASKERVILLE. HOWEVER, SPARKS FLY AS A FIGHT WITH BLUSH ABRUPTLY INTERRUPTS THE REUNION. THE THREE OF THEM END UP IN THE SHIP'S BOILER ROOM. THINGS GET TOO HOT TO HANDLE WHEN THE ETO GUN GETS DROPPED INTO THE BOILER AND BASKERVILLE STICKS HIS HAND IN TO RETRIEVE IT!

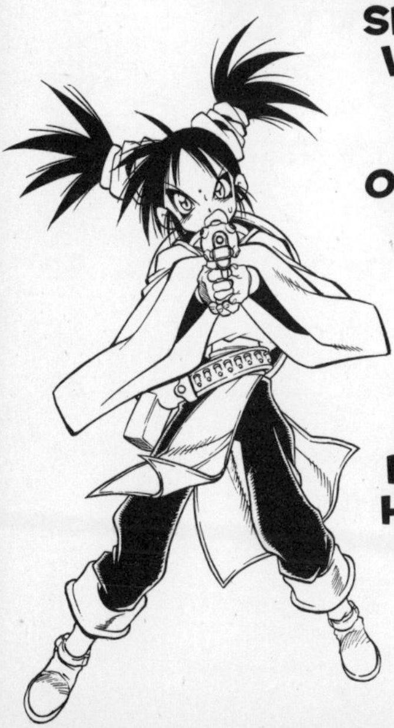

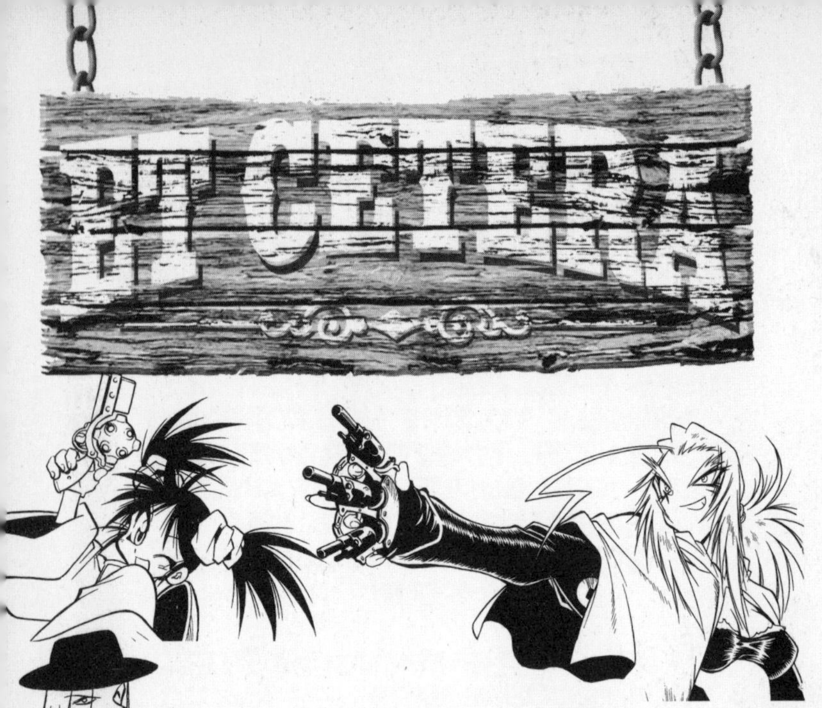

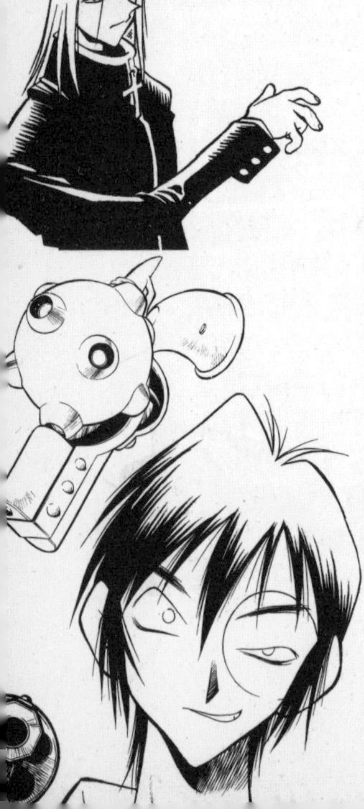

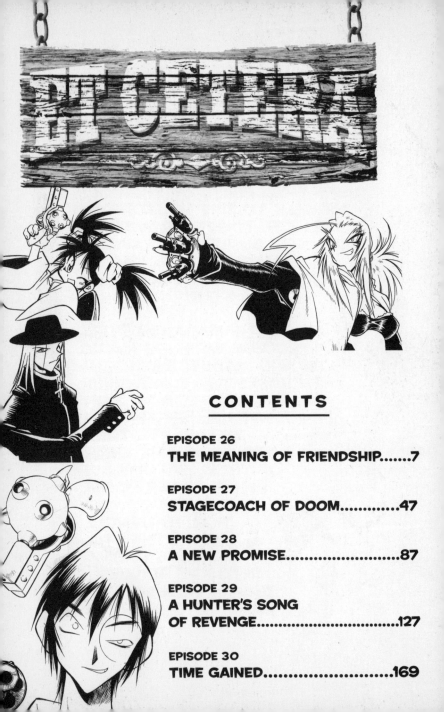

CONTENTS

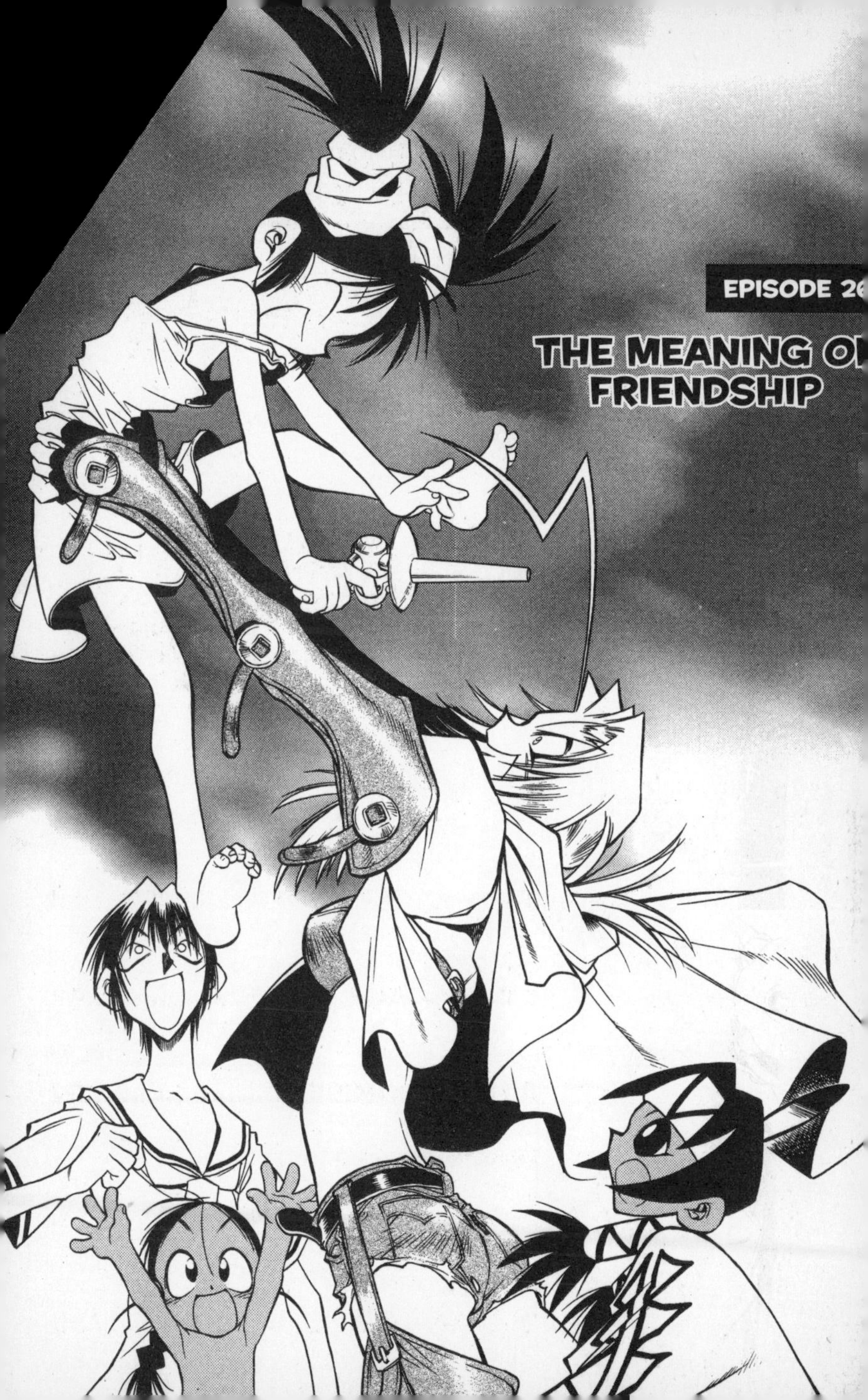
EPISODE 26
THE MEANING OF
FRIENDSHIP

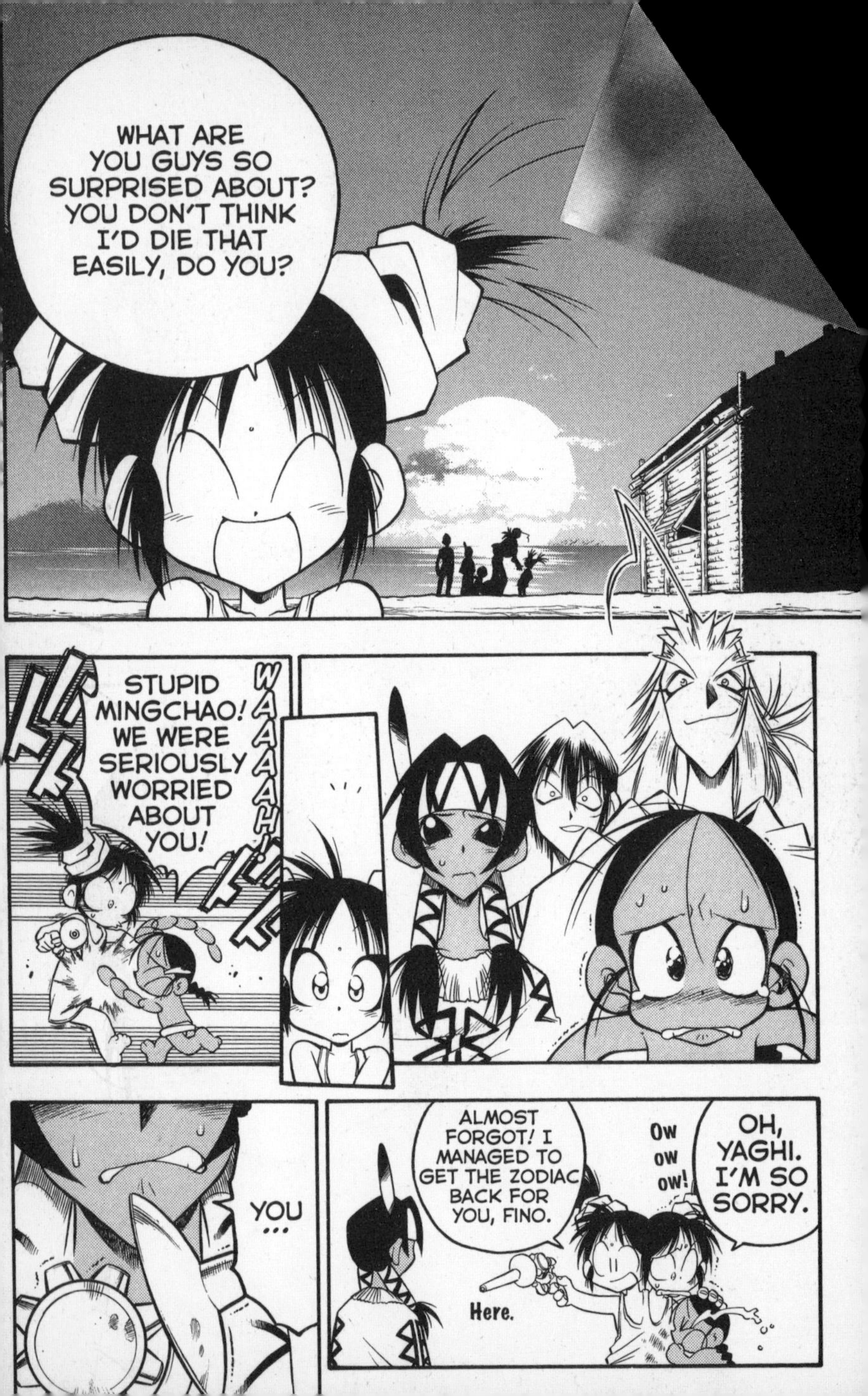
WHAT ARE YOU GUYS SO SURPRISED ABOUT? YOU DON'T THINK I'D DIE THAT EASILY, DO YOU?
STUPID MINGCHAO! WE WERE SERIOUSLY WORRIED ABOUT YOU!
WAAAAAH!
OH, YAGHI. I'M SO SORRY.
Ow ow ow!
ALMOST FORGOT! I MANAGED TO GET THE ZODIAC BACK FOR YOU, FINO.
Here.
YOU...

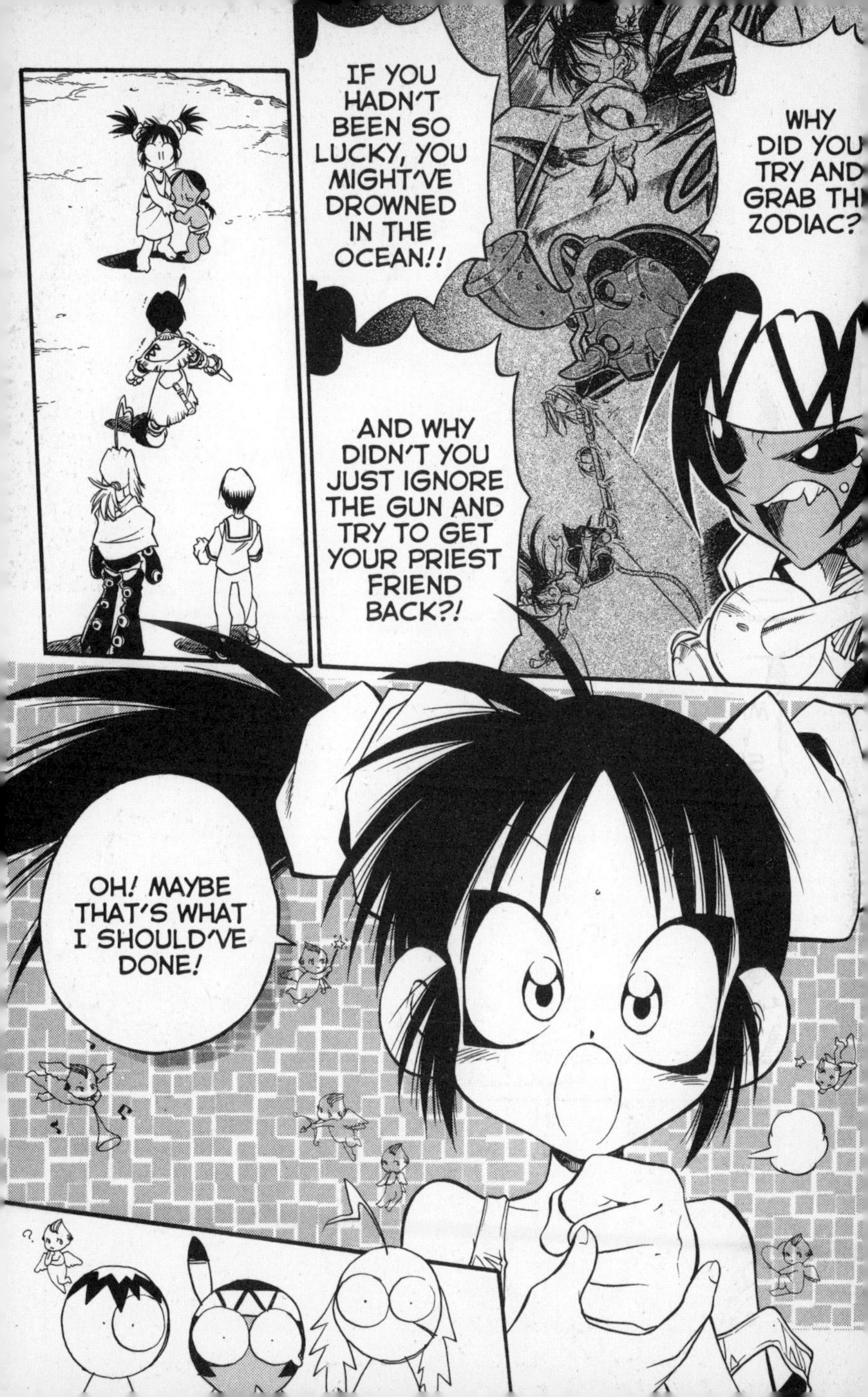
WHY DID YOU TRY AND GRAB TH ZODIAC?
IF YOU HADN'T BEEN SO LUCKY, YOU MIGHT'VE DROWNED IN THE OCEAN!!
AND WHY DIDN'T YOU JUST IGNORE THE GUN AND TRY TO GET YOUR PRIEST FRIEND BACK?!
OH! MAYBE THAT'S WHAT I SHOULD'VE DONE!

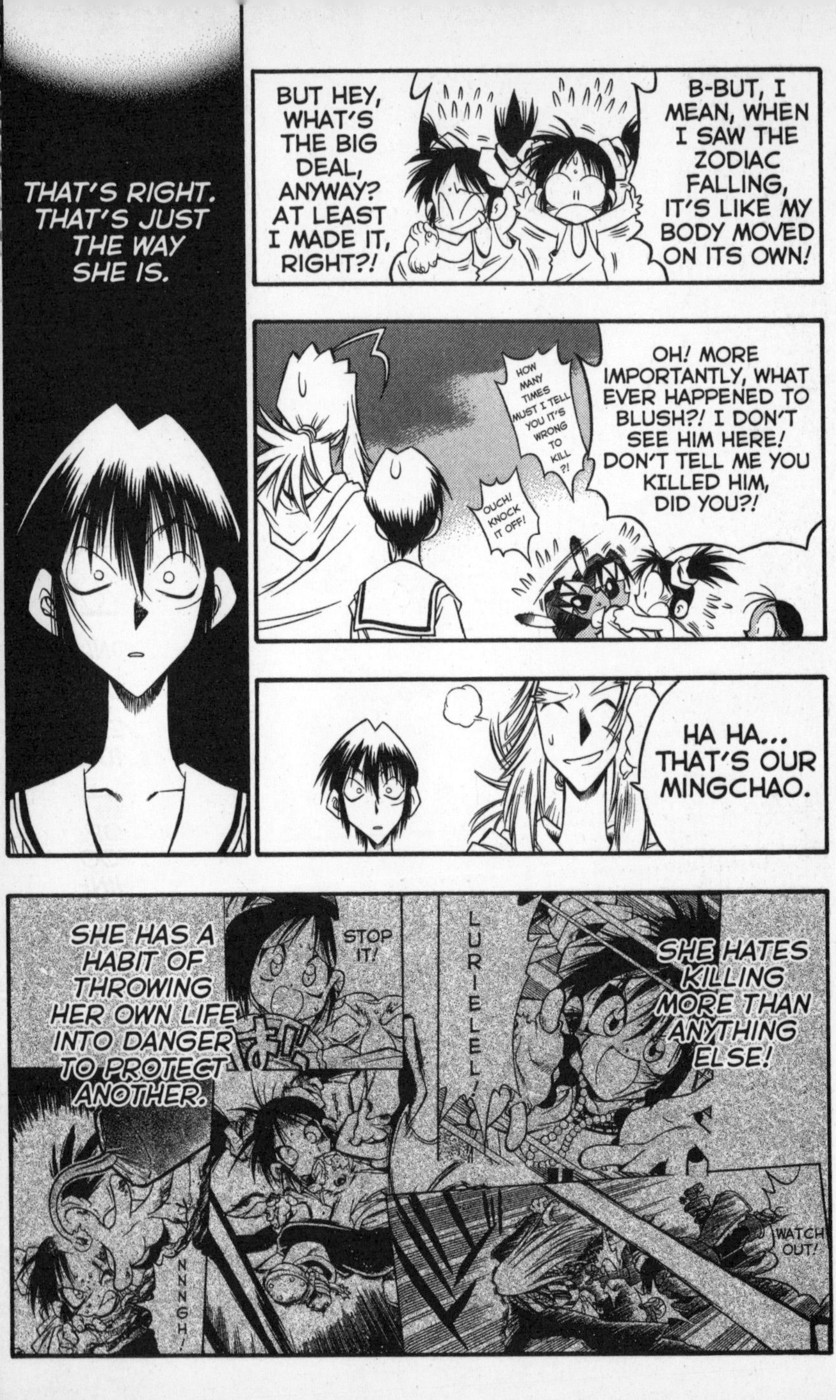
B-BUT, I MEAN, WHEN I SAW THE ZODIAC FALLING, IT'S LIKE MY BODY MOVED ON ITS OWN!
BUT HEY, WHAT'S THE BIG DEAL, ANYWAY? AT LEAST I MADE IT, RIGHT?!
OH! MORE IMPORTANTLY, WHAT EVER HAPPENED TO BLUSH?! I DON'T SEE HIM HERE! DON'T TELL ME YOU KILLED HIM, DID YOU?!
HOW MANY TIMES MUST I TELL YOU IT'S WRONG TO KILL?!
OUCH! KNOCK IT OFF!
HA HA... THAT'S OUR MINGCHAO.
THAT'S RIGHT. THAT'S JUST THE WAY SHE IS.
SHE HATES KILLING MORE THAN ANYTHING ELSE!
LURIELEL!
STOP IT!
SHE HAS A HABIT OF THROWING HER OWN LIFE INTO DANGER TO PROTECT ANOTHER.
WATCH OUT!
NNNGH!

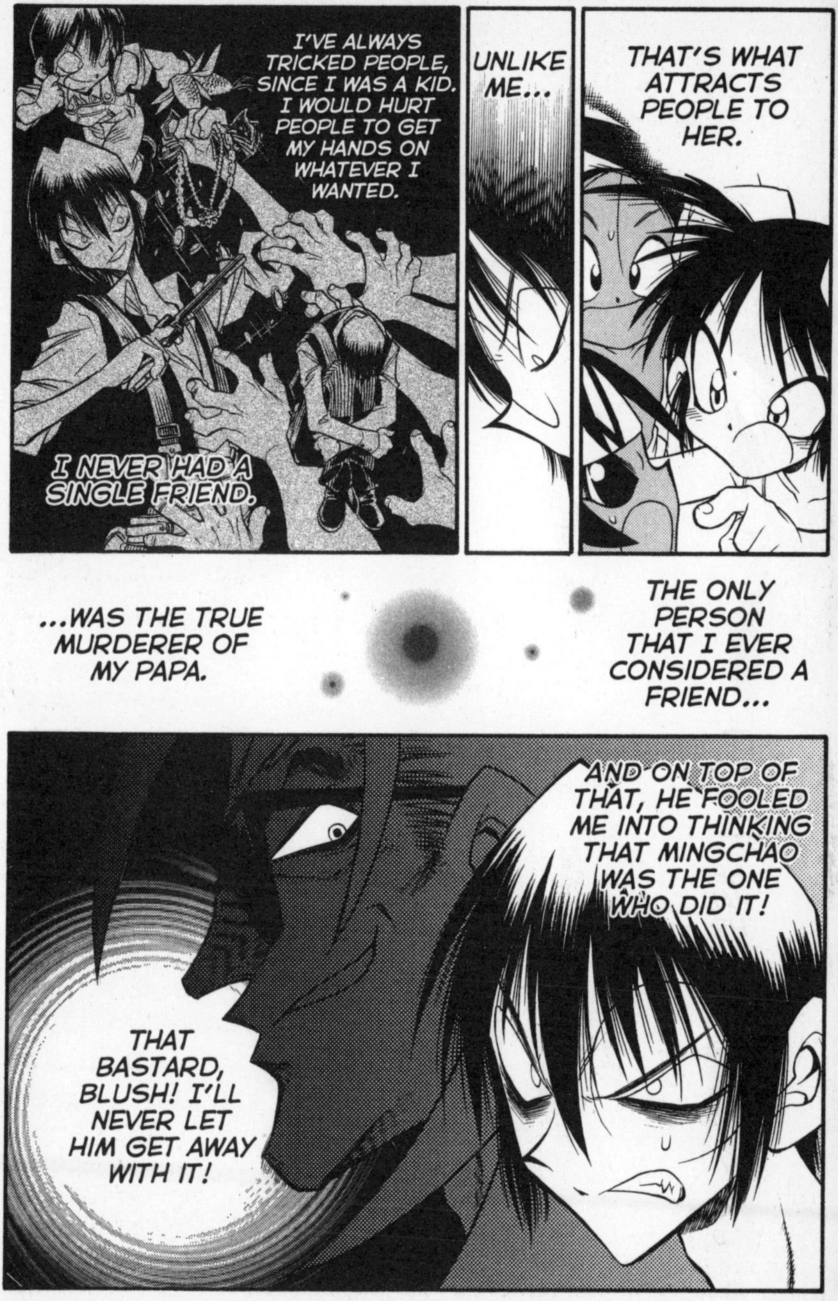
THAT'S WHAT ATTRACTS PEOPLE TO HER.
UNLIKE ME...
I'VE ALWAYS TRICKED PEOPLE, SINCE I WAS A KID. I WOULD HURT PEOPLE TO GET MY HANDS ON WHATEVER I WANTED.
I NEVER HAD A SINGLE FRIEND.
THE ONLY PERSON THAT I EVER CONSIDERED A FRIEND...
...WAS THE TRUE MURDERER OF MY PAPA.
AND ON TOP OF THAT, HE FOOLED ME INTO THINKING THAT MINGCHAO WAS THE ONE WHO DID IT!
THAT BASTARD, BLUSH! I'LL NEVER LET HIM GET AWAY WITH IT!

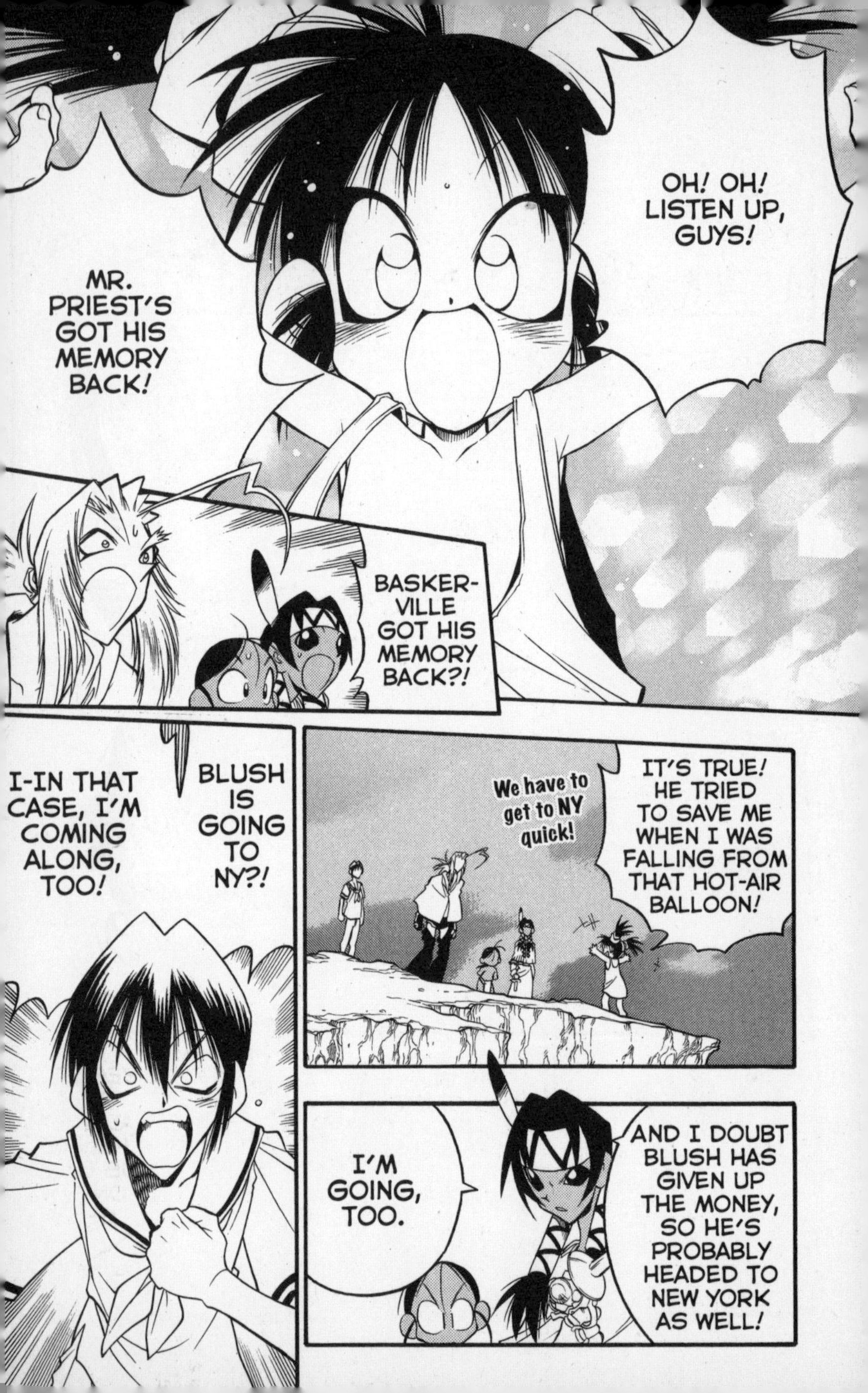
OH! OH! LISTEN UP, GUYS!
MR. PRIEST'S GOT HIS MEMORY BACK!
BASKER-VILLE GOT HIS MEMORY BACK?!
IT'S TRUE! HE TRIED TO SAVE ME WHEN I WAS FALLING FROM THAT HOT-AIR BALLOON!
We have to get to NY quick!
AND I DOUBT BLUSH HAS GIVEN UP THE MONEY, SO HE'S PROBABLY HEADED TO NEW YORK AS WELL!
I'M GOING, TOO.
BLUSH IS GOING TO NY?!
I-IN THAT CASE, I'M COMING ALONG, TOO!

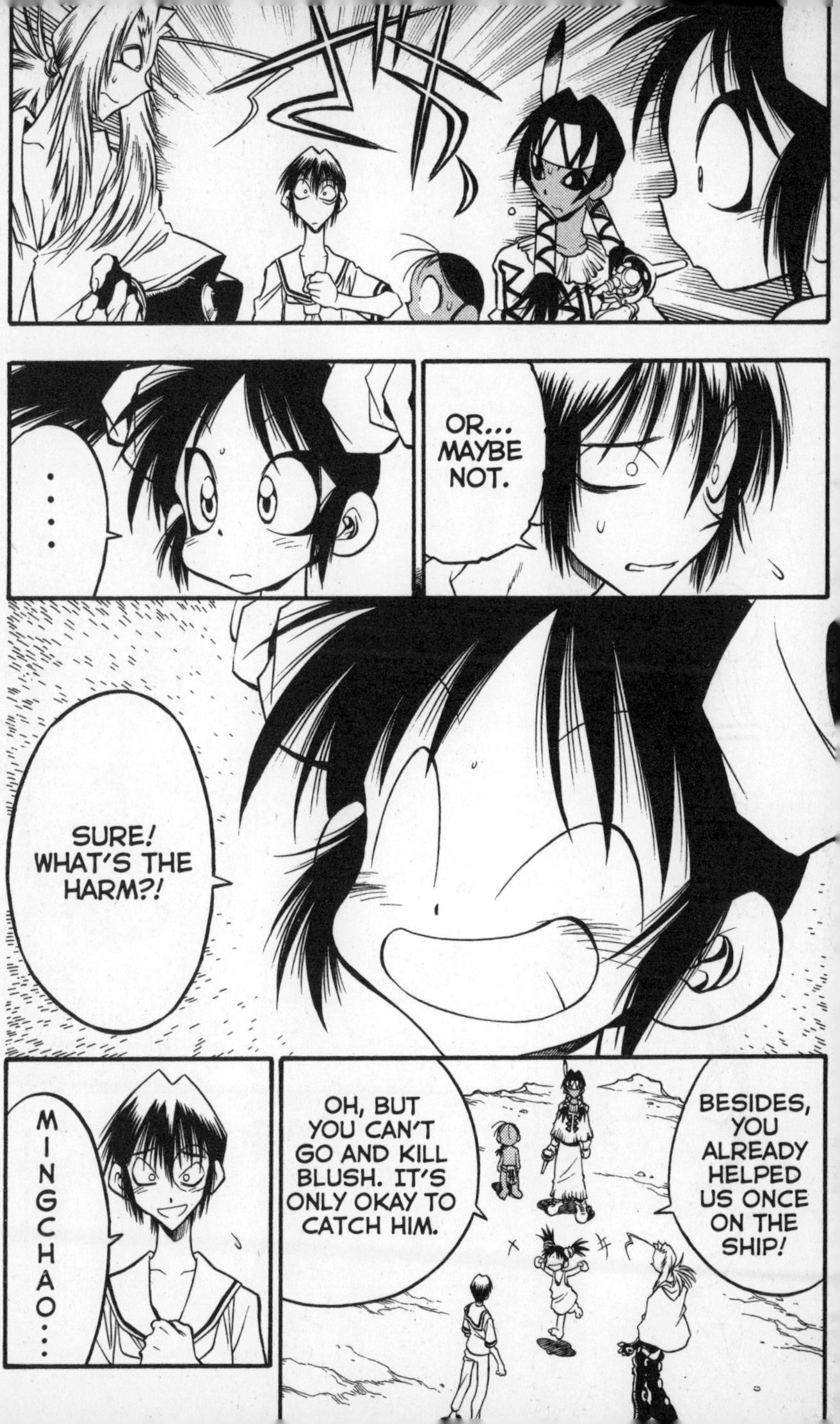
OR... MAYBE NOT.
....
SURE! WHAT'S THE HARM?!
BESIDES, YOU ALREADY HELPED US ONCE ON THE SHIP!
OH, BUT YOU CAN'T GO AND KILL BLUSH. IT'S ONLY OKAY TO CATCH HIM.
MINGCHAO...

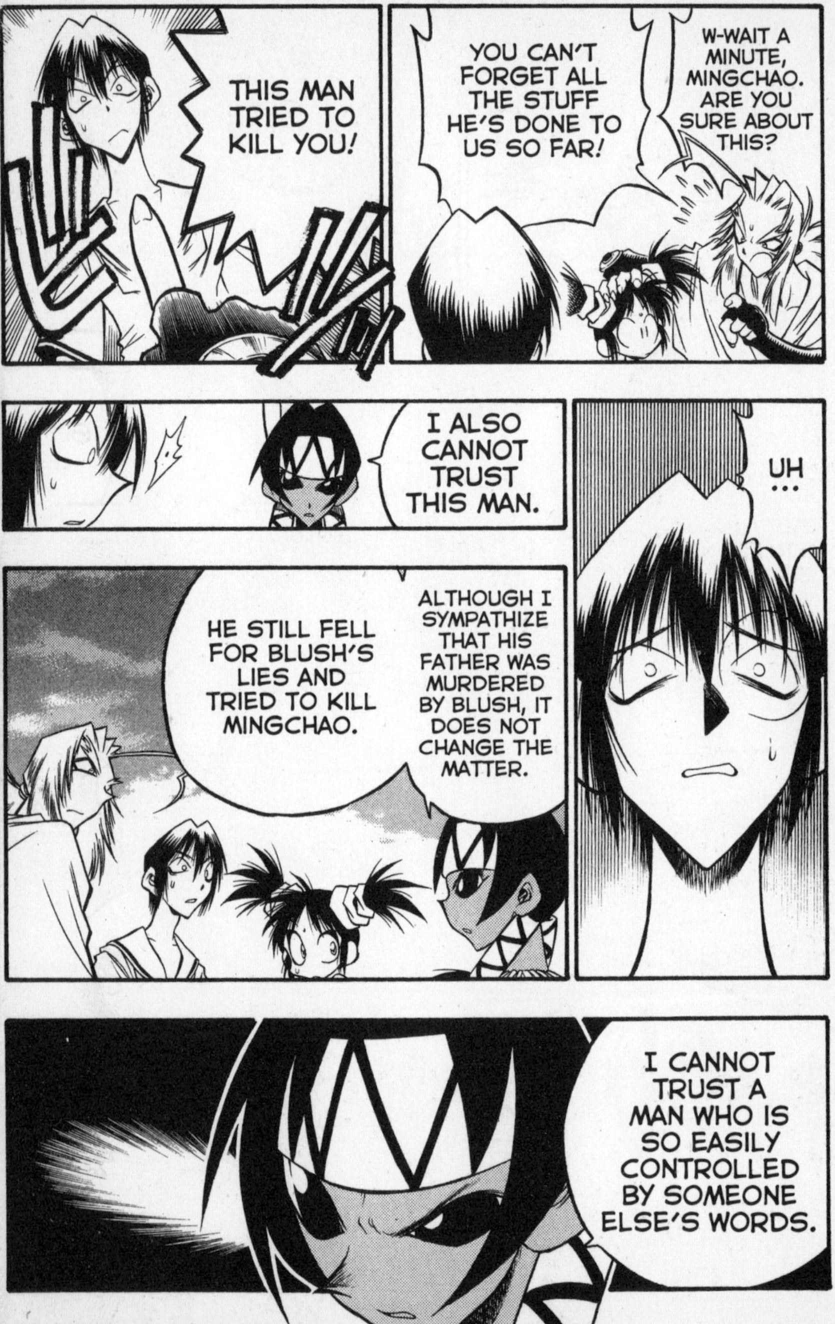
W-WAIT A MINUTE, MINGCHAO. ARE YOU SURE ABOUT THIS?
YOU CAN'T FORGET ALL THE STUFF HE'S DONE TO US SO FAR!
THIS MAN TRIED TO KILL YOU!
UH...
I ALSO CANNOT TRUST THIS MAN.
ALTHOUGH I SYMPATHIZE THAT HIS FATHER WAS MURDERED BY BLUSH, IT DOES NOT CHANGE THE MATTER.
HE STILL FELL FOR BLUSH'S LIES AND TRIED TO KILL MINGCHAO.
I CANNOT TRUST A MAN WHO IS SO EASILY CONTROLLED BY SOMEONE ELSE'S WORDS.

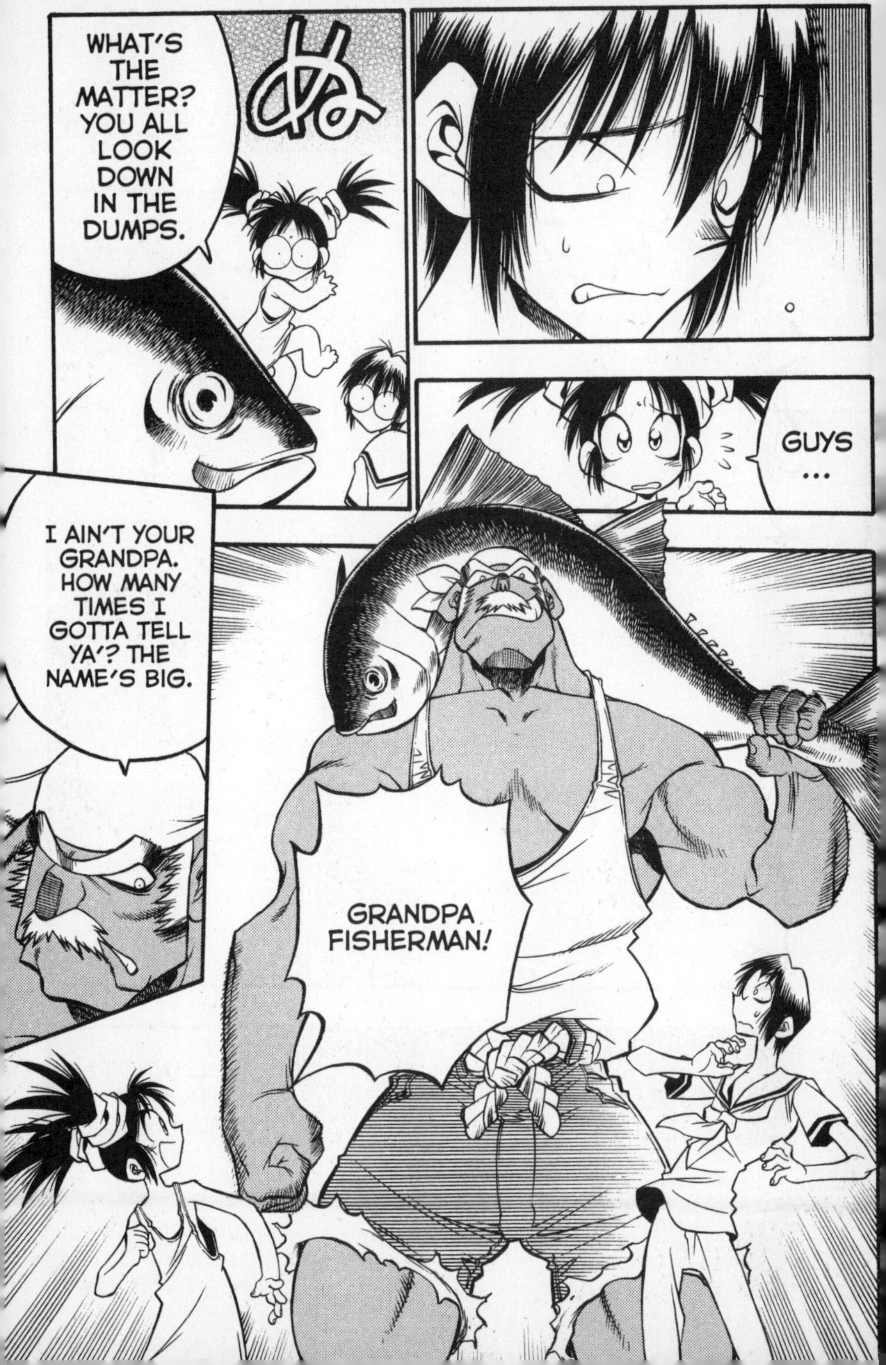
ぬ
WHAT'S THE MATTER? YOU ALL LOOK DOWN IN THE DUMPS.
GUYS ...
GRANDPA FISHERMAN!
I AIN'T YOUR GRANDPA. HOW MANY TIMES I GOTTA TELL YA'? THE NAME'S BIG.

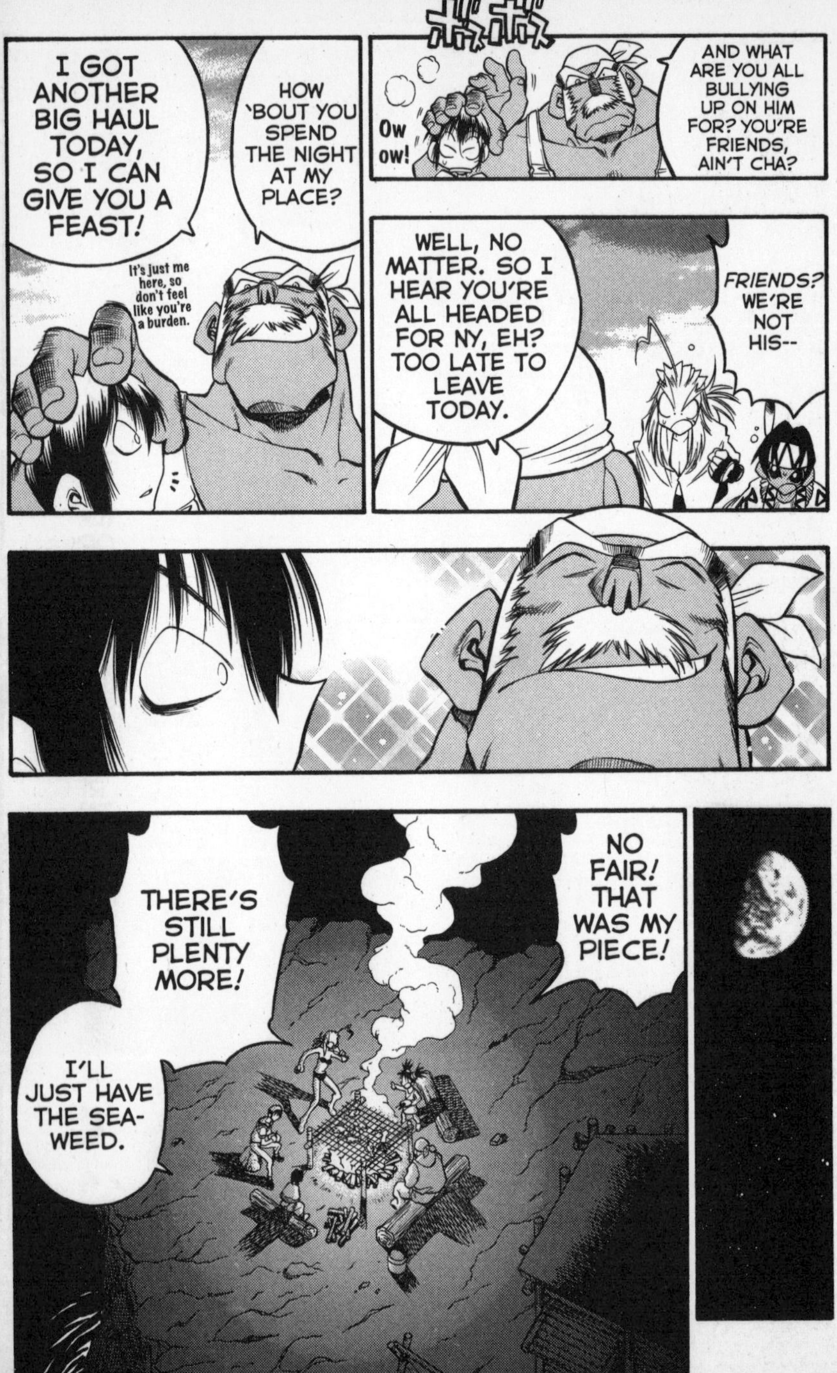
AND WHAT ARE YOU ALL BULLYING UP ON HIM FOR? YOU'RE FRIENDS, AIN'T CHA?
Ow ow!
FRIENDS? WE'RE NOT HIS--
WELL, NO MATTER. SO I HEAR YOU'RE ALL HEADED FOR NY, EH? TOO LATE TO LEAVE TODAY.
HOW 'BOUT YOU SPEND THE NIGHT AT MY PLACE?
I GOT ANOTHER BIG HAUL TODAY, SO I CAN GIVE YOU A FEAST!
It's just me here, so don't feel like you're a burden.
NO FAIR! THAT WAS MY PIECE!
THERE'S STILL PLENTY MORE!
I'LL JUST HAVE THE SEA-WEED.

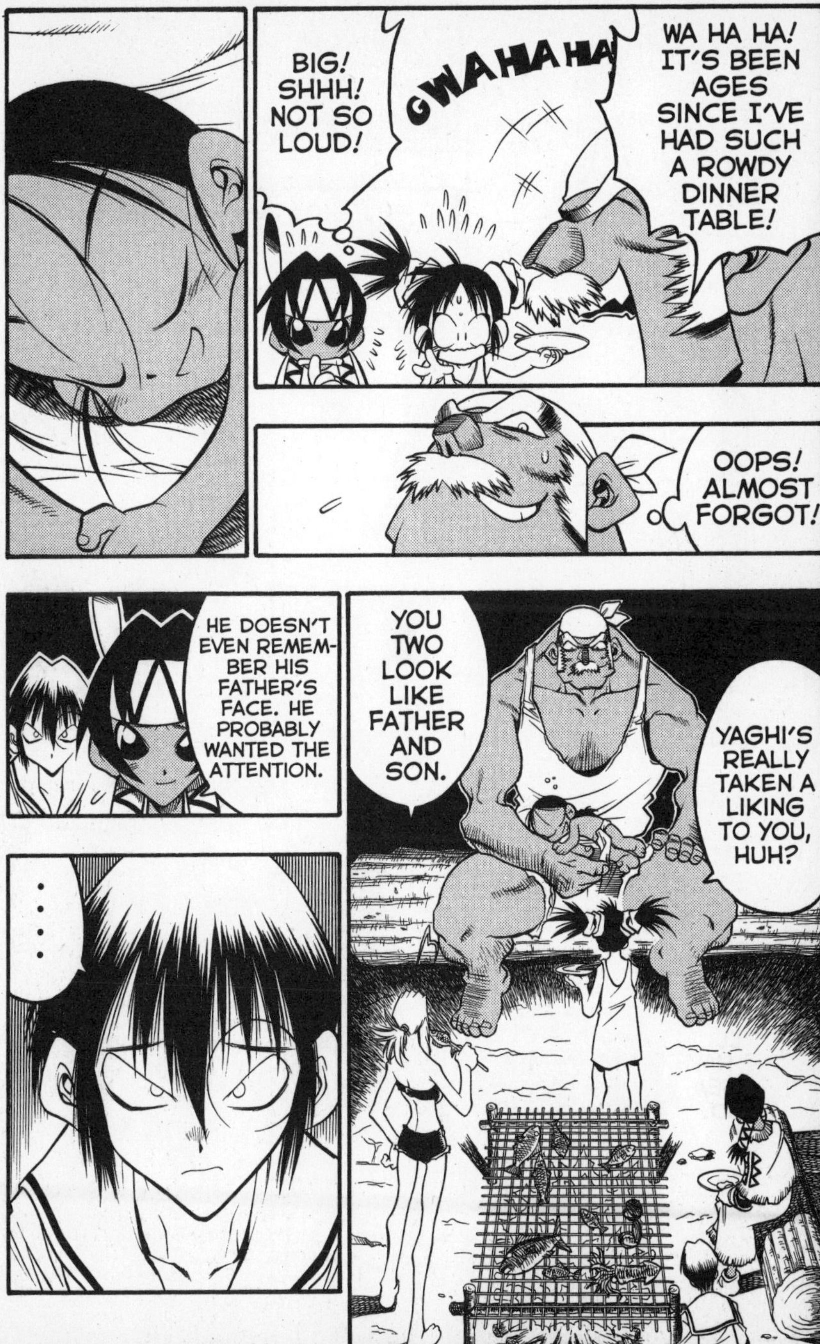
WA HA HA! IT'S BEEN AGES SINCE I'VE HAD SUCH A ROWDY DINNER TABLE!
GWAHAHAHA
BIG! SHHH! NOT SO LOUD!
OOPS! ALMOST FORGOT!
YAGHI'S REALLY TAKEN A LIKING TO YOU, HUH?
YOU TWO LOOK LIKE FATHER AND SON.
HE DOESN'T EVEN REMEMBER HIS FATHER'S FACE. HE PROBABLY WANTED THE ATTENTION.
.....

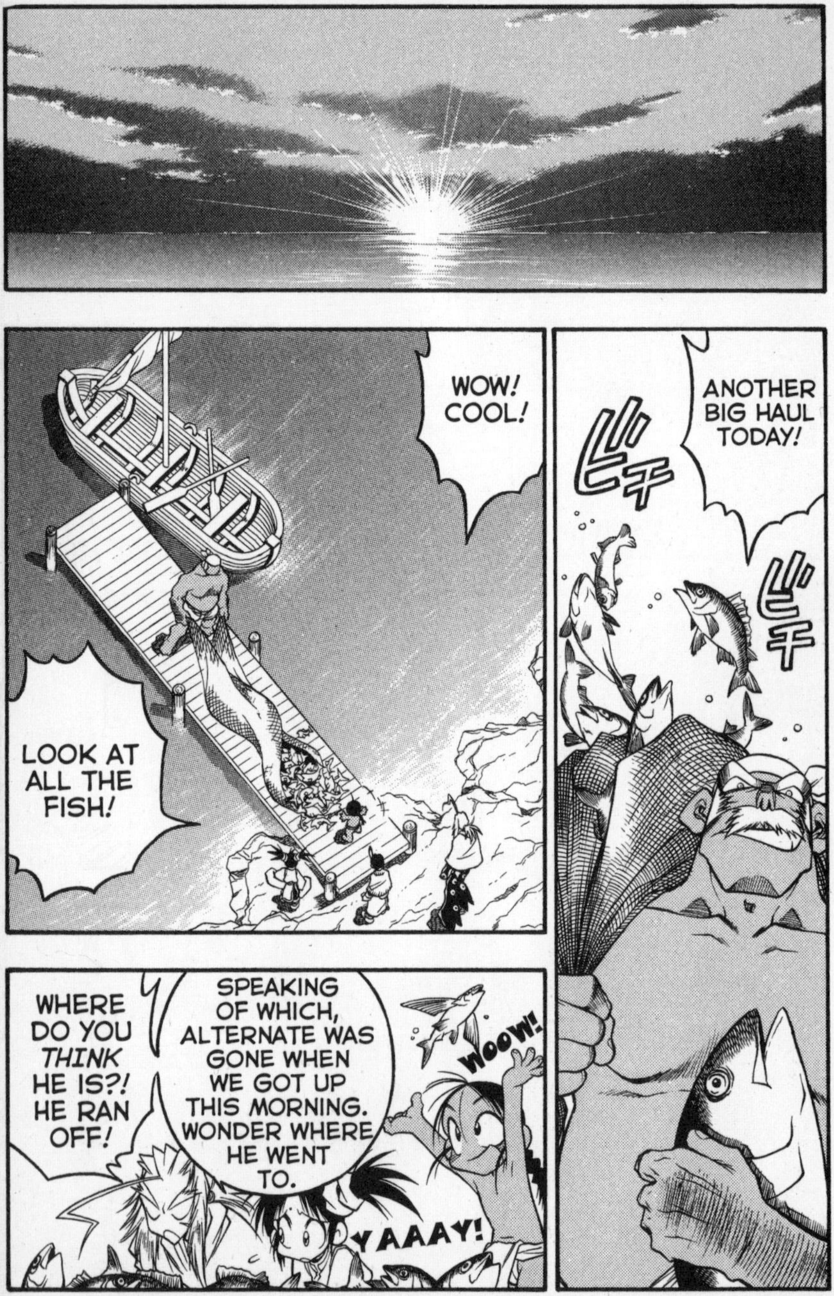
ANOTHER BIG HAUL TODAY!
ビチ
ビチ
WOW! COOL!
LOOK AT ALL THE FISH!
WOOW!
SPEAKING OF WHICH, ALTERNATE WAS GONE WHEN WE GOT UP THIS MORNING. WONDER WHERE HE WENT TO.
WHERE DO YOU *THINK* HE IS?! HE RAN OFF!
YAAAY!

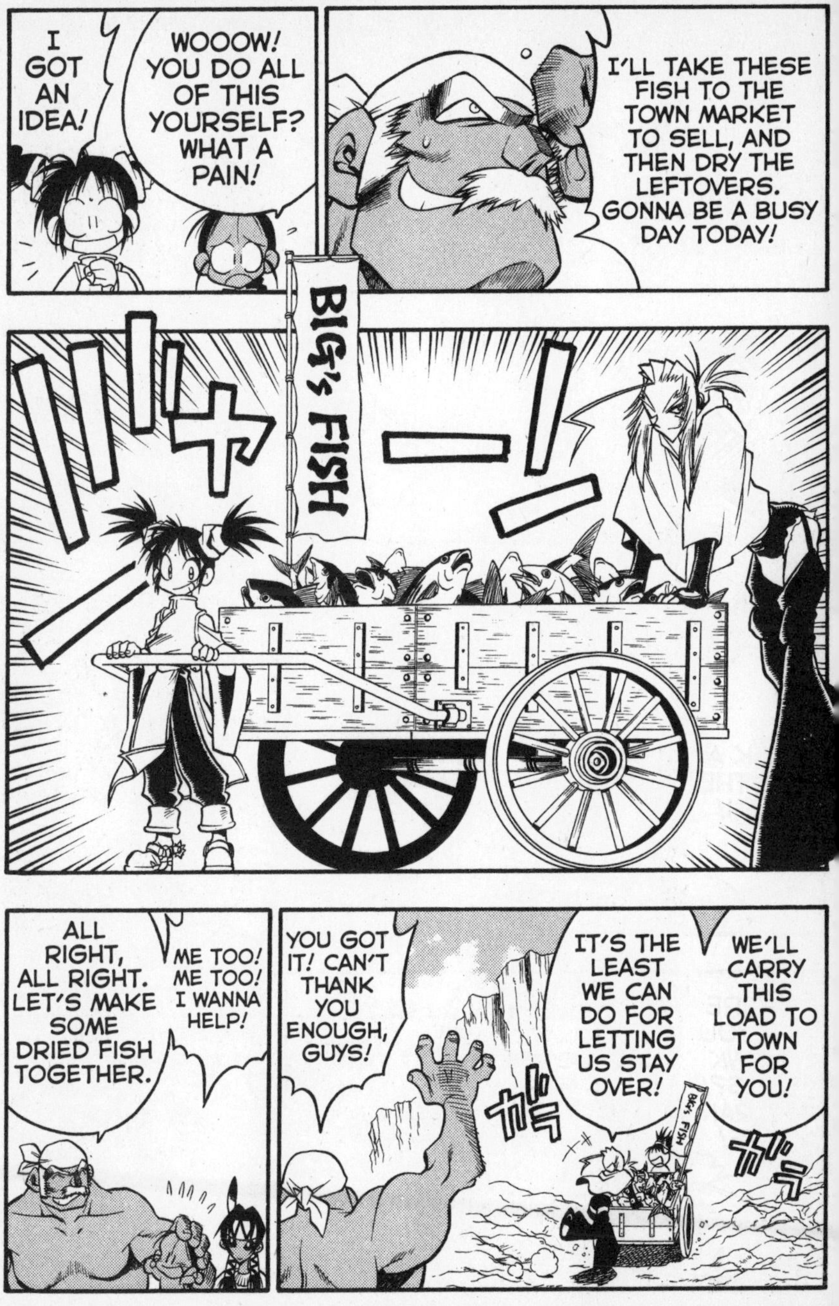
I'LL TAKE THESE FISH TO THE TOWN MARKET TO SELL, AND THEN DRY THE LEFTOVERS. GONNA BE A BUSY DAY TODAY!
WOOOW! YOU DO ALL OF THIS YOURSELF? WHAT A PAIN!
I GOT AN IDEA!
BIG's FISH
WE'LL CARRY THIS LOAD TO TOWN FOR YOU!
IT'S THE LEAST WE CAN DO FOR LETTING US STAY OVER!
YOU GOT IT! CAN'T THANK YOU ENOUGH, GUYS!
ME TOO! ME TOO! I WANNA HELP!
ALL RIGHT, ALL RIGHT. LET'S MAKE SOME DRIED FISH TOGETHER.

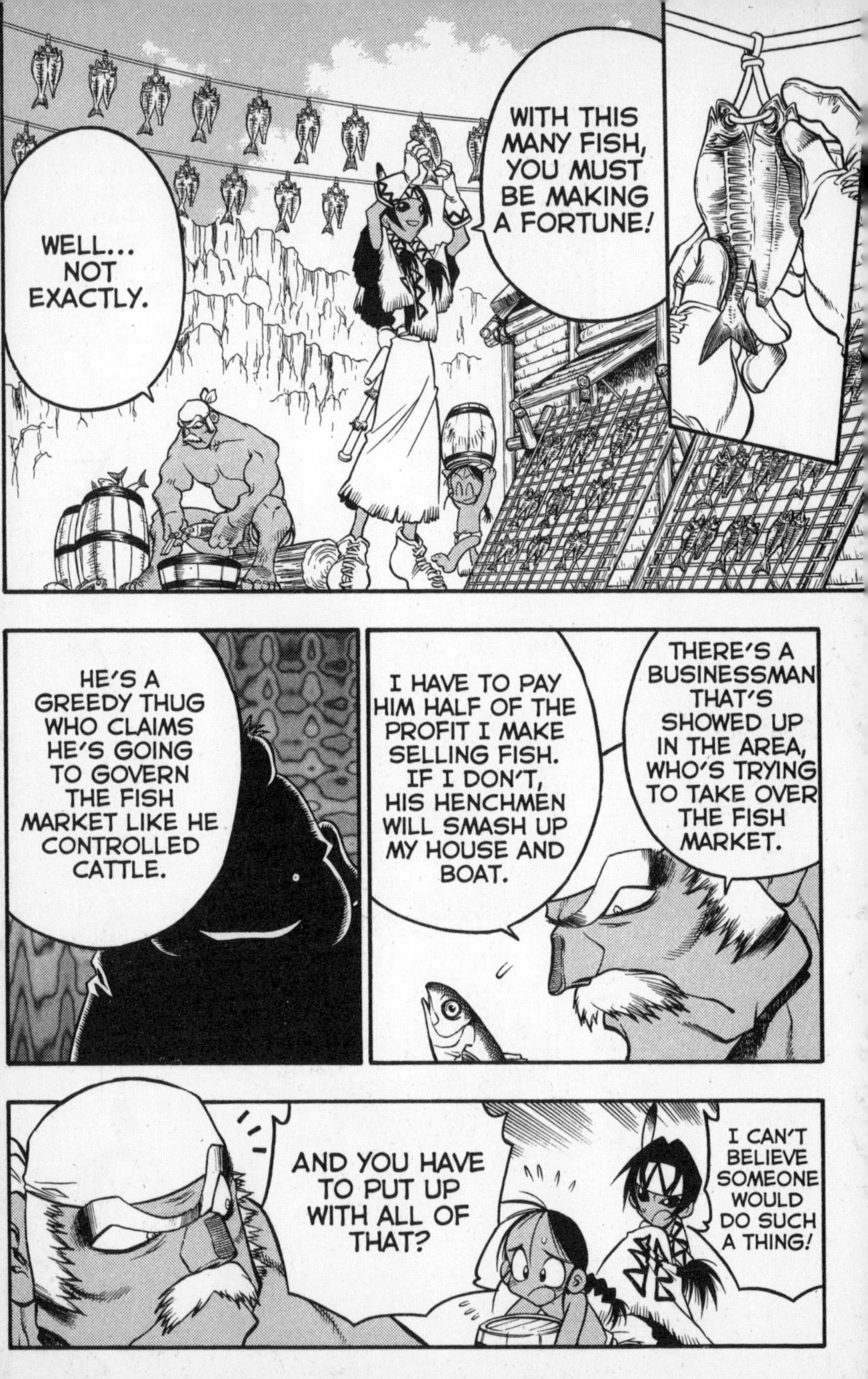
WITH THIS MANY FISH, YOU MUST BE MAKING A FORTUNE!
WELL... NOT EXACTLY.
THERE'S A BUSINESSMAN THAT'S SHOWED UP IN THE AREA, WHO'S TRYING TO TAKE OVER THE FISH MARKET.
I HAVE TO PAY HIM HALF OF THE PROFIT I MAKE SELLING FISH. IF I DON'T, HIS HENCHMEN WILL SMASH UP MY HOUSE AND BOAT.
HE'S A GREEDY THUG WHO CLAIMS HE'S GOING TO GOVERN THE FISH MARKET LIKE HE CONTROLLED CATTLE.
I CAN'T BELIEVE SOMEONE WOULD DO SUCH A THING!
AND YOU HAVE TO PUT UP WITH ALL OF THAT?

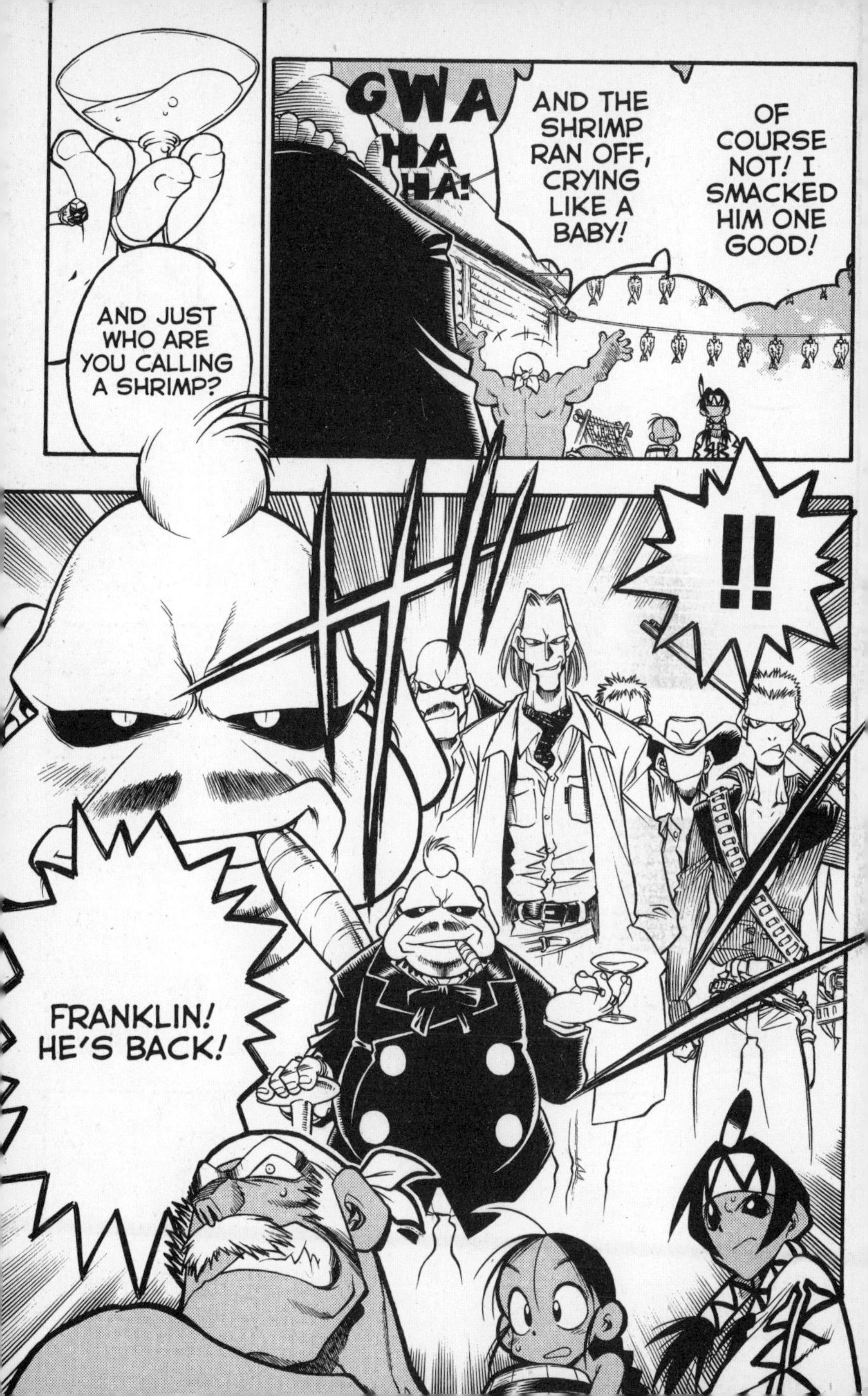
OF COURSE NOT! I SMACKED HIM ONE GOOD!
AND THE SHRIMP RAN OFF, CRYING LIKE A BABY!
GWA HA HA!
AND JUST WHO ARE YOU CALLING A SHRIMP?
!!
FRANKLIN! HE'S BACK!

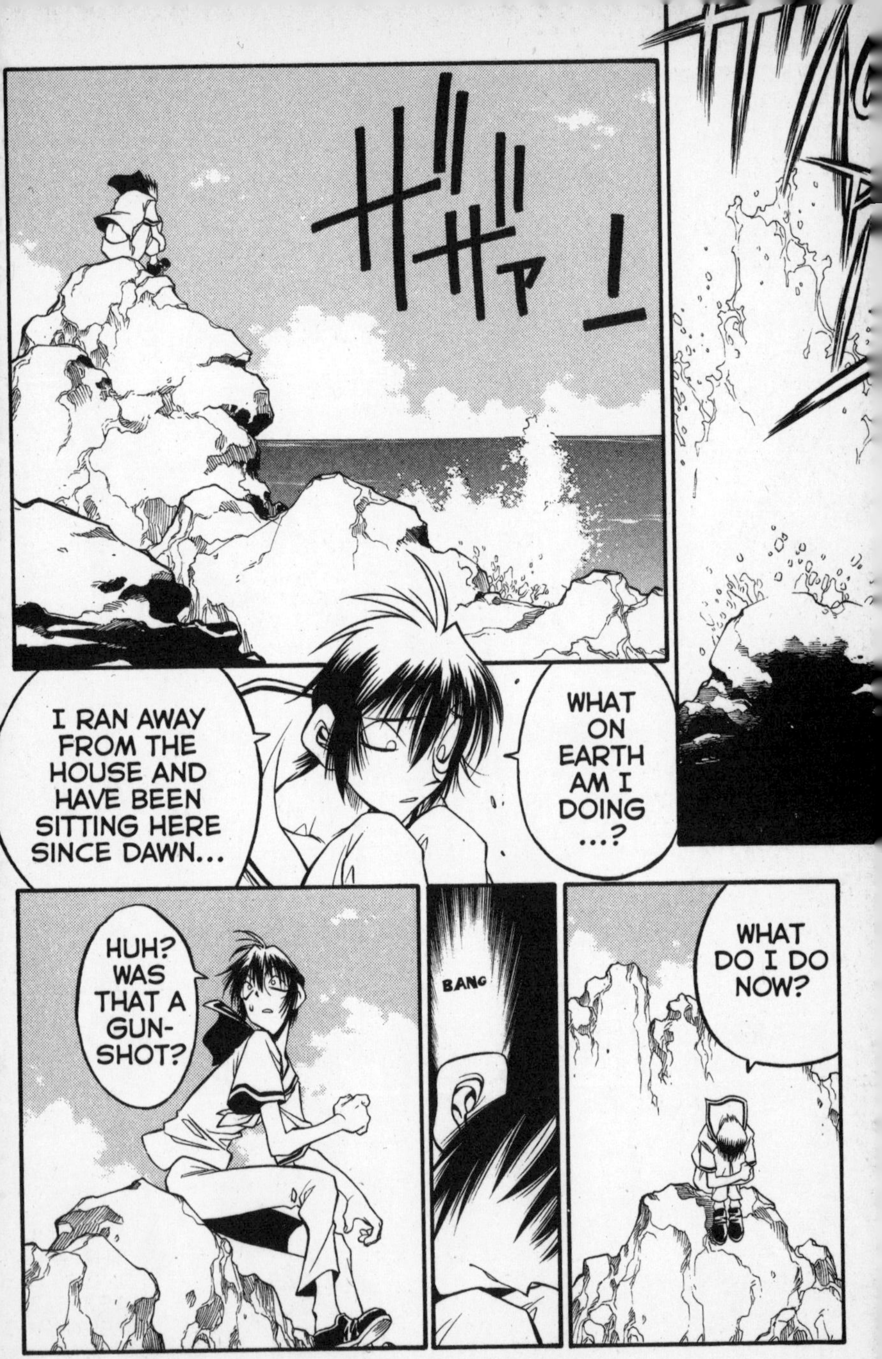
ザザァー
WHAT ON EARTH AM I DOING ...?
I RAN AWAY FROM THE HOUSE AND HAVE BEEN SITTING HERE SINCE DAWN...
WHAT DO I DO NOW?
BANG
HUH? WAS THAT A GUN-SHOT?

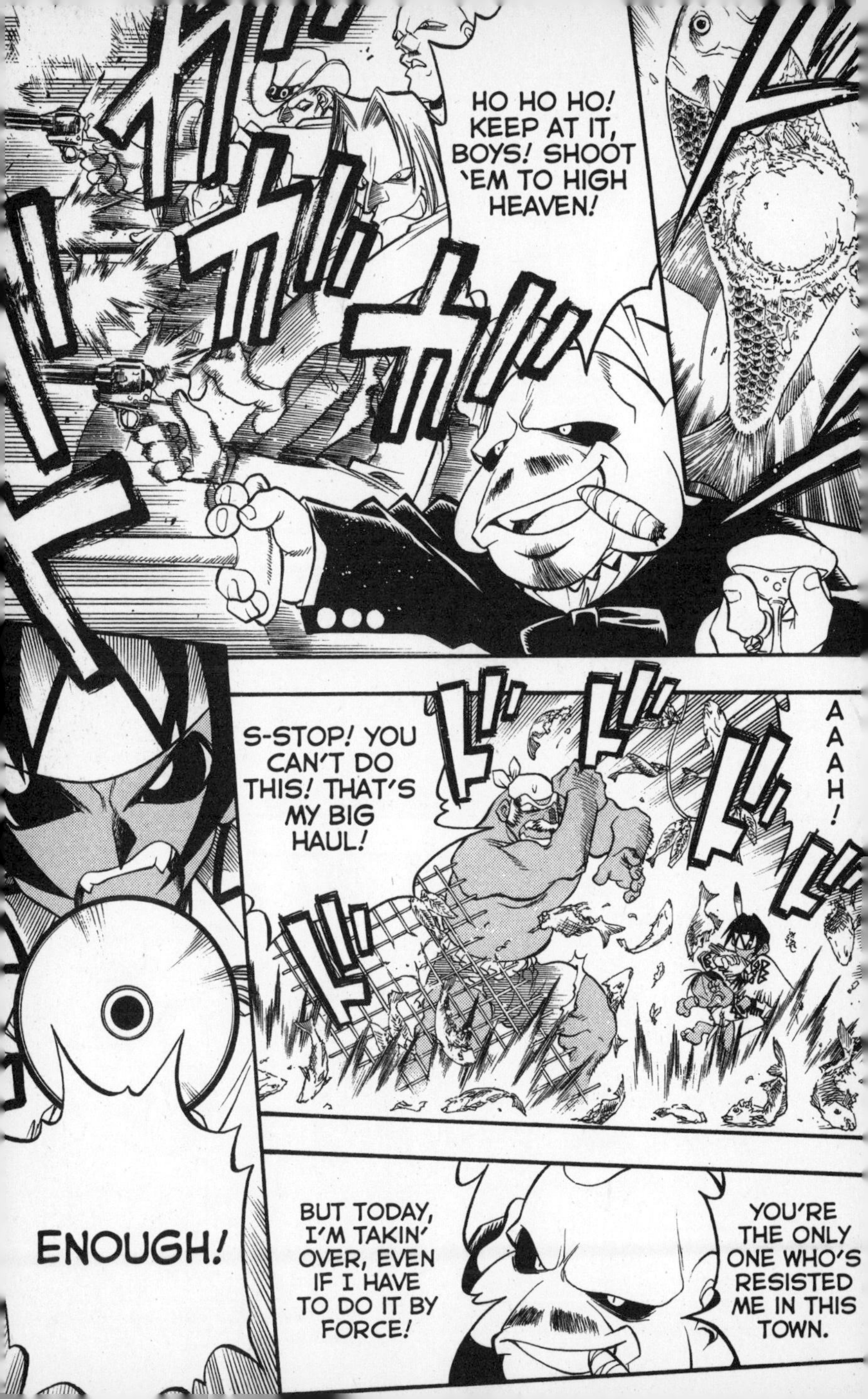
HO HO HO! KEEP AT IT, BOYS! SHOOT 'EM TO HIGH HEAVEN!
AAAH!
S-STOP! YOU CAN'T DO THIS! THAT'S MY BIG HAUL!
YOU'RE THE ONLY ONE WHO'S RESISTED ME IN THIS TOWN.
BUT TODAY, I'M TAKIN' OVER, EVEN IF I HAVE TO DO IT BY FORCE!
ENOUGH!

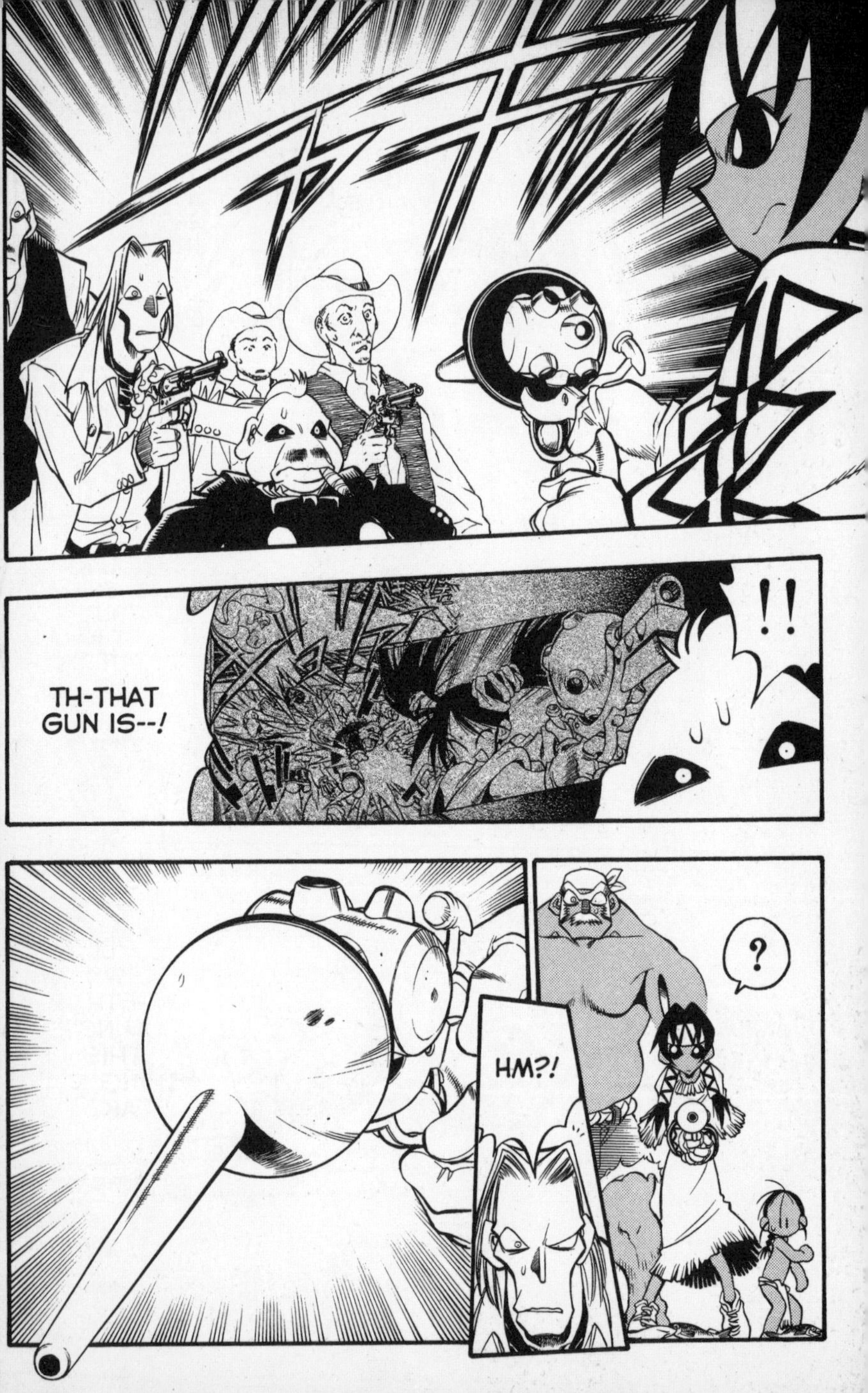
!!
TH-THAT GUN IS--!
?
HM?!

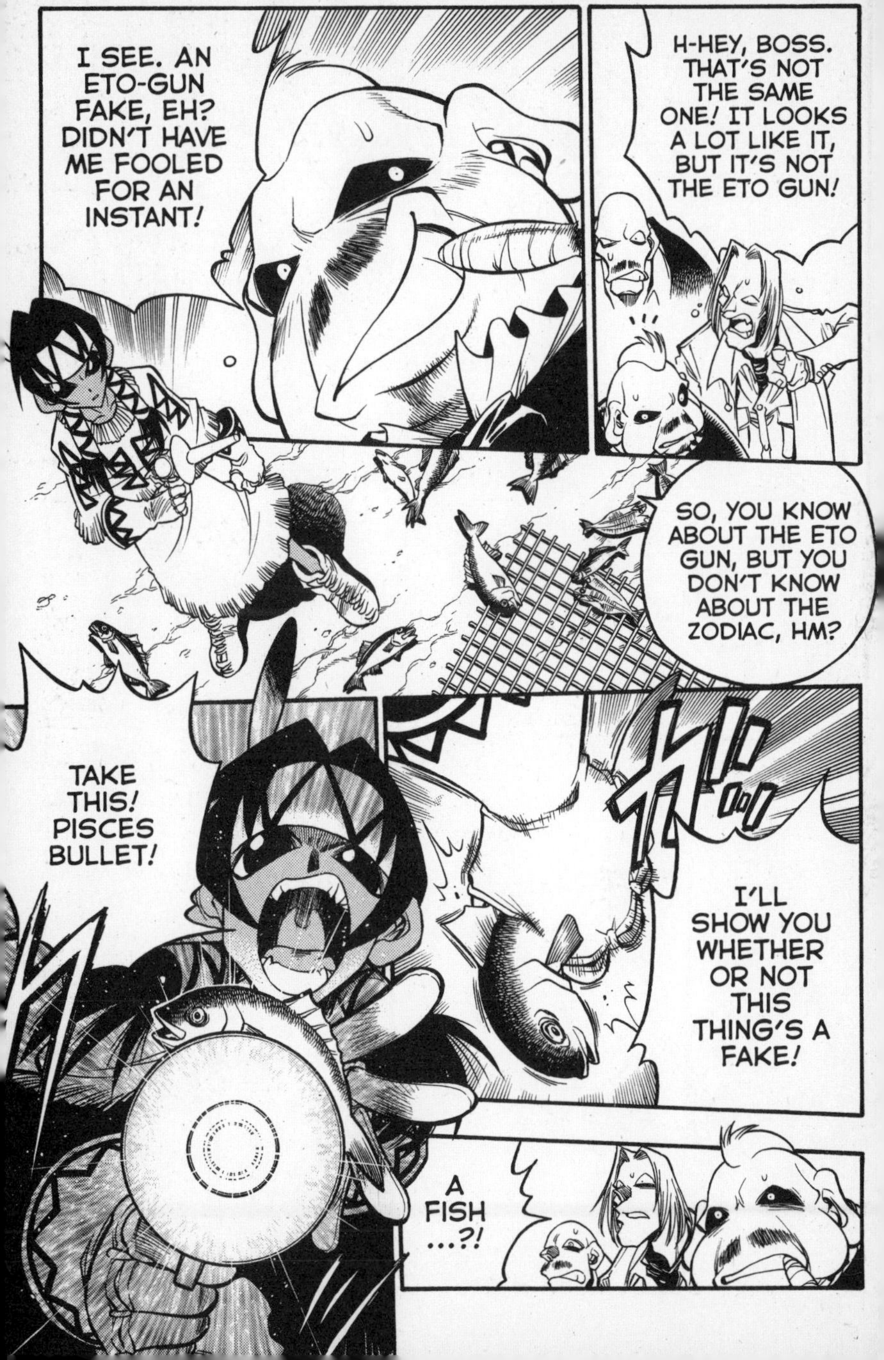
H-HEY, BOSS. THAT'S NOT THE SAME ONE! IT LOOKS A LOT LIKE IT, BUT IT'S NOT THE ETO GUN!
I SEE. AN ETO-GUN FAKE, EH? DIDN'T HAVE ME FOOLED FOR AN INSTANT!
SO, YOU KNOW ABOUT THE ETO GUN, BUT YOU DON'T KNOW ABOUT THE ZODIAC, HM?
I'LL SHOW YOU WHETHER OR NOT THIS THING'S A FAKE!
A FISH ...?!
TAKE THIS! PISCES BULLET!

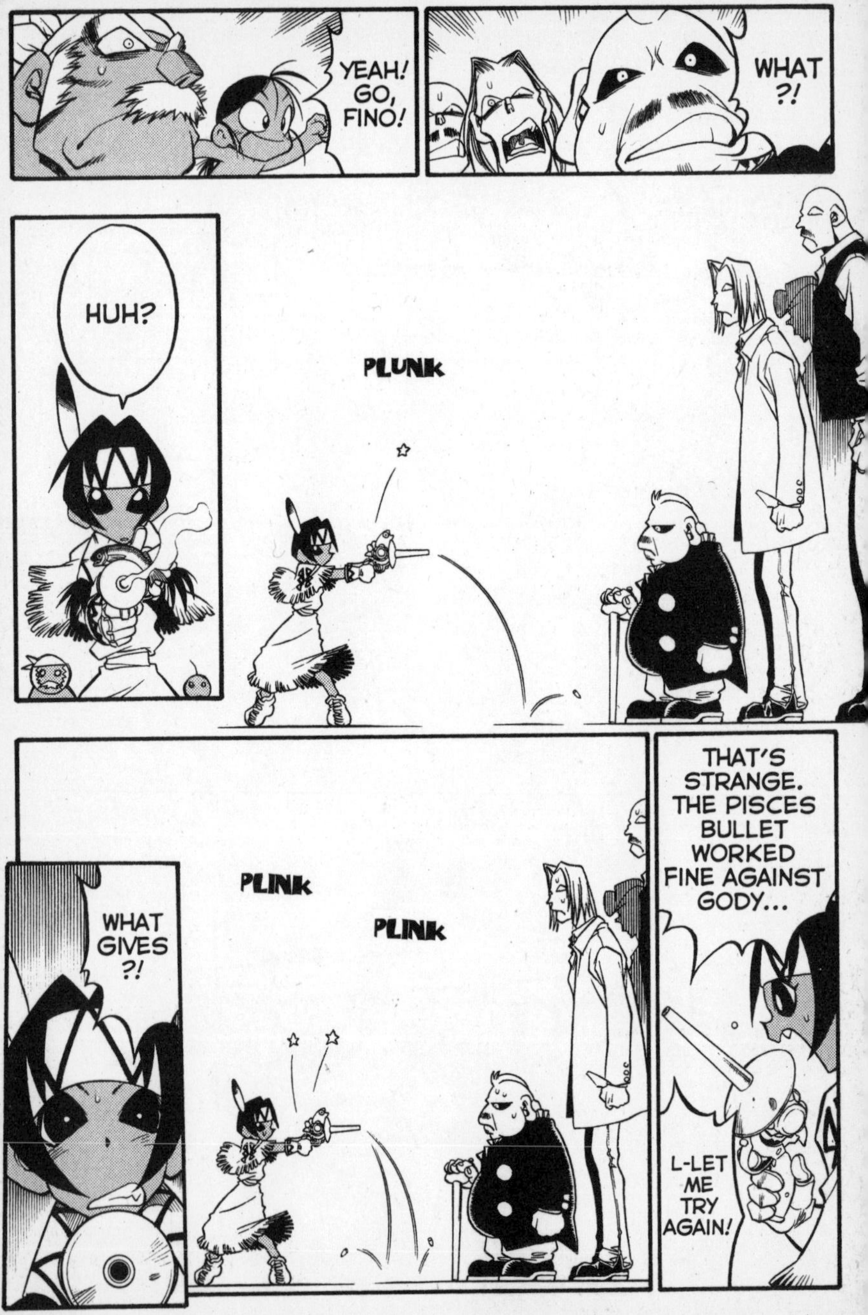
WHAT ?!
YEAH! GO, FINO!
PLUNK
HUH?
THAT'S STRANGE. THE PISCES BULLET WORKED FINE AGAINST GODY...
L-LET ME TRY AGAIN!
PLINK
PLINK
WHAT GIVES ?!

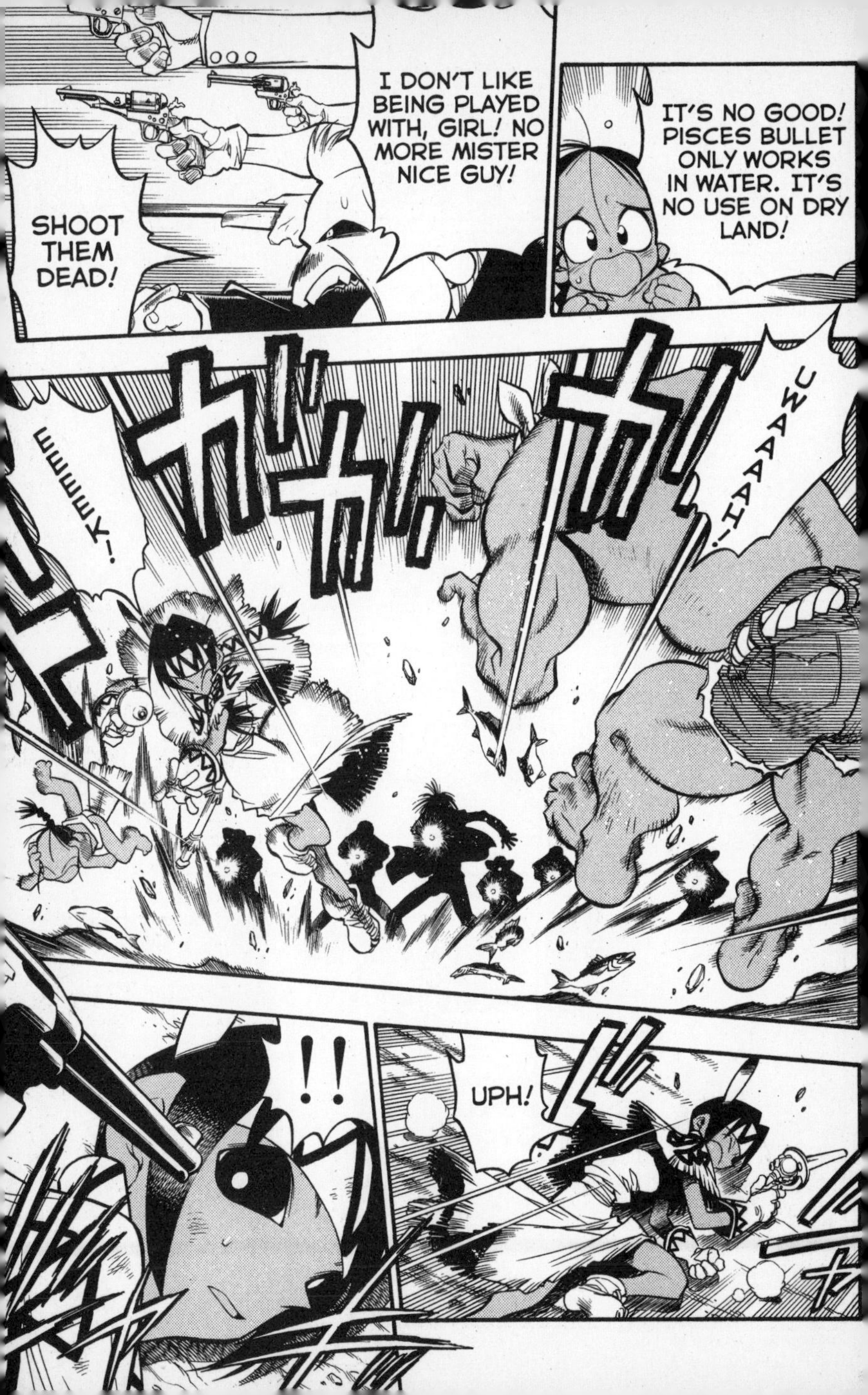
IT'S NO GOOD! PISCES BULLET ONLY WORKS IN WATER. IT'S NO USE ON DRY LAND!
I DON'T LIKE BEING PLAYED WITH, GIRL! NO MORE MISTER NICE GUY!
SHOOT THEM DEAD!
UWAAAAAH!
EEEEEK!
UPH!
!!

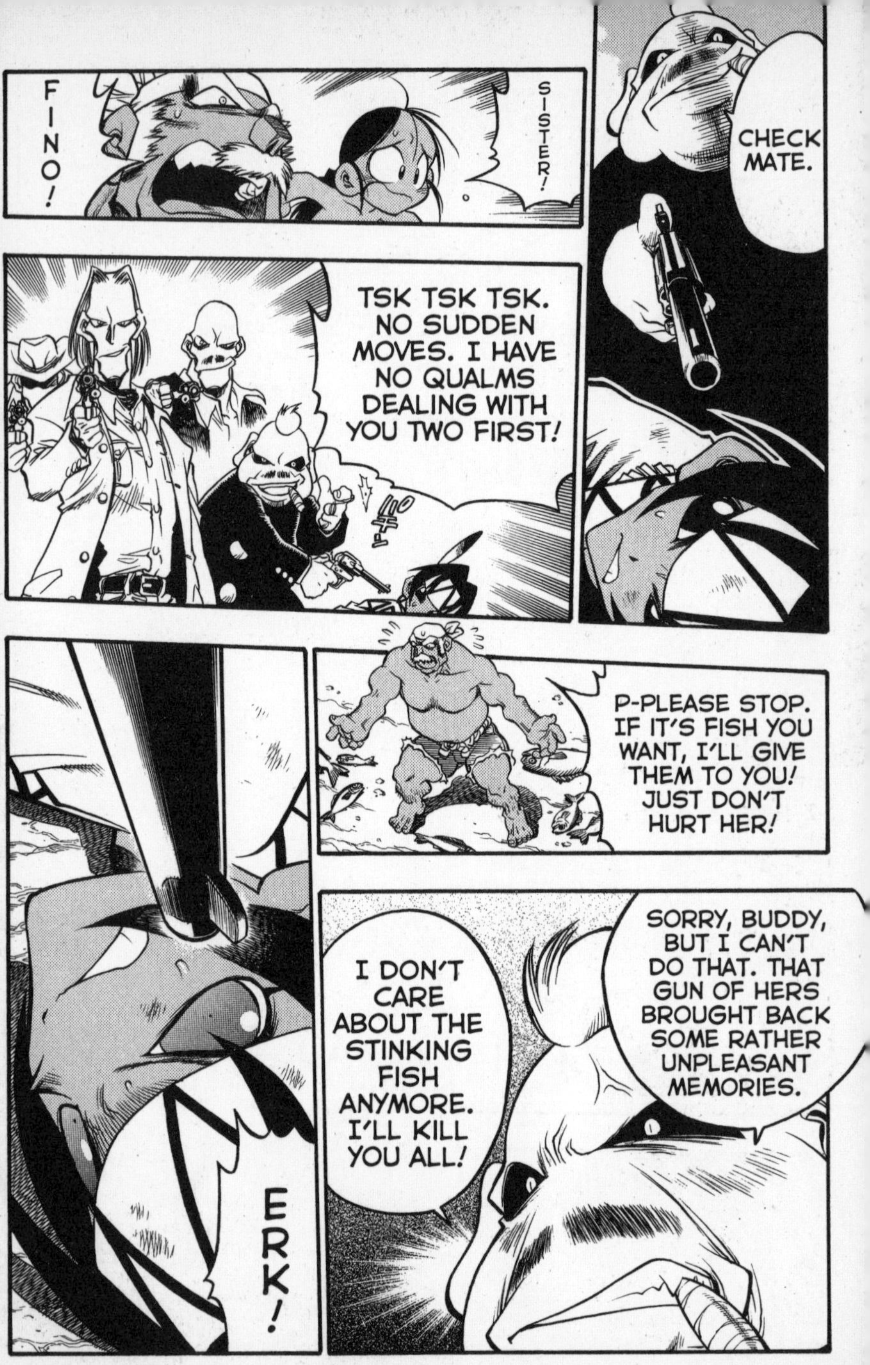
CHECK MATE.
SISTER!
FINO!
TSK TSK TSK. NO SUDDEN MOVES. I HAVE NO QUALMS DEALING WITH YOU TWO FIRST!
P-PLEASE STOP. IF IT'S FISH YOU WANT, I'LL GIVE THEM TO YOU! JUST DON'T HURT HER!
SORRY, BUDDY, BUT I CAN'T DO THAT. THAT GUN OF HERS BROUGHT BACK SOME RATHER UNPLEASANT MEMORIES.
I DON'T CARE ABOUT THE STINKING FISH ANYMORE. I'LL KILL YOU ALL!
ERK!

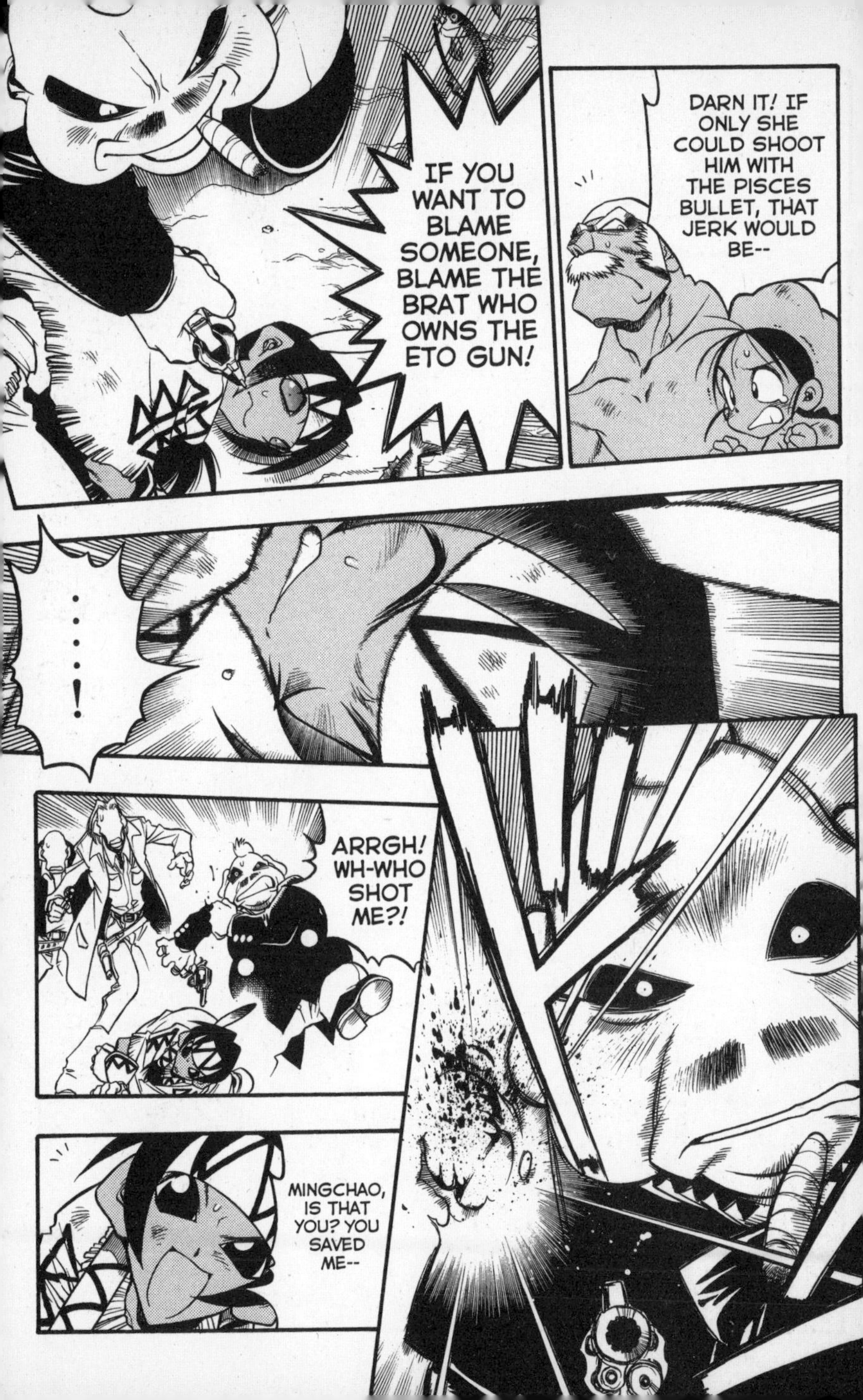
DARN IT! IF ONLY SHE COULD SHOOT HIM WITH THE PISCES BULLET, THAT JERK WOULD BE--
IF YOU WANT TO BLAME SOMEONE, BLAME THE BRAT WHO OWNS THE ETO GUN!
...!
ARRGH! WH-WHO SHOT ME?!
MINGCHAO, IS THAT YOU? YOU SAVED ME--

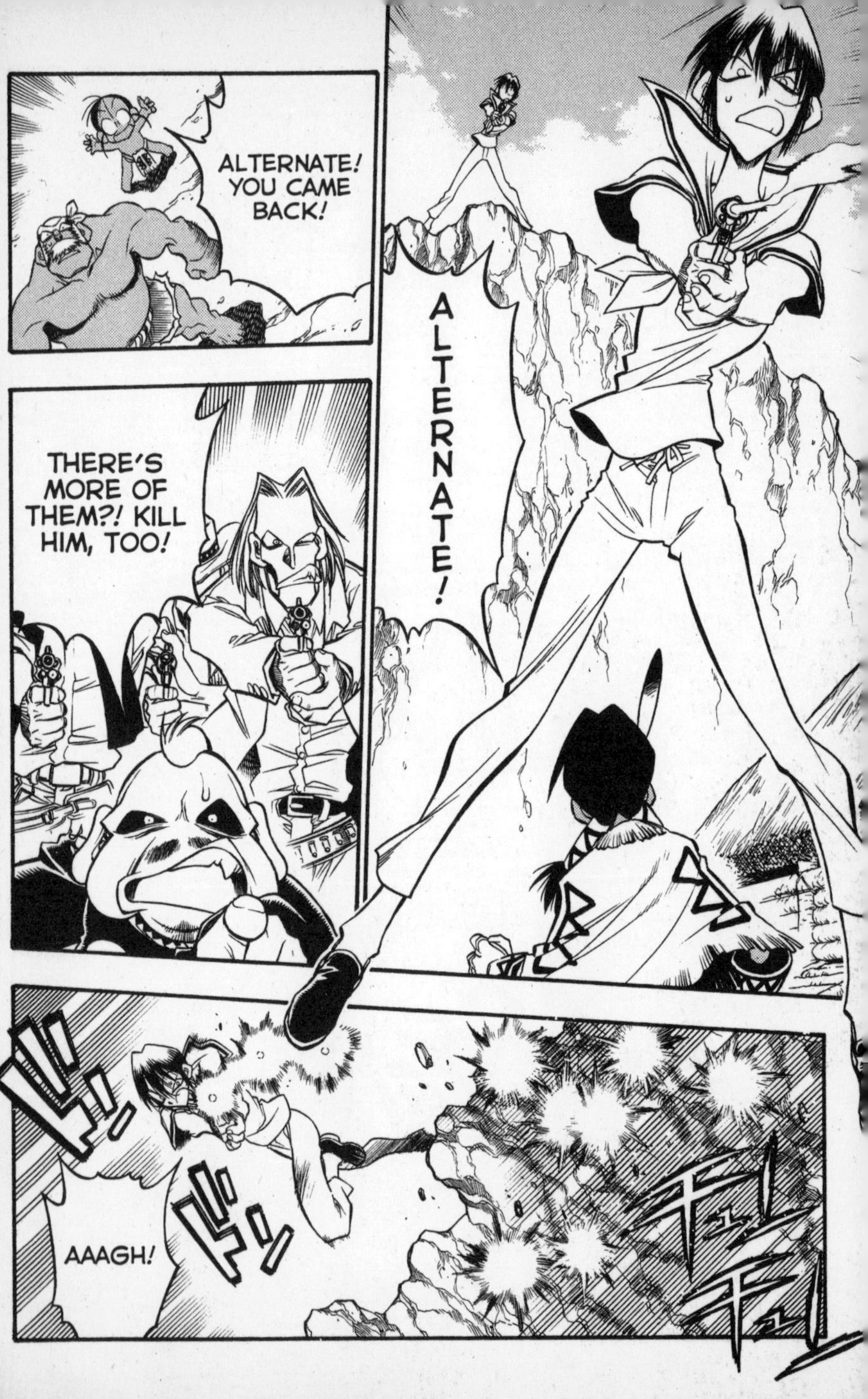
ALTERNATE!
ALTERNATE! YOU CAME BACK!
THERE'S MORE OF THEM?! KILL HIM, TOO!
AAAGH!

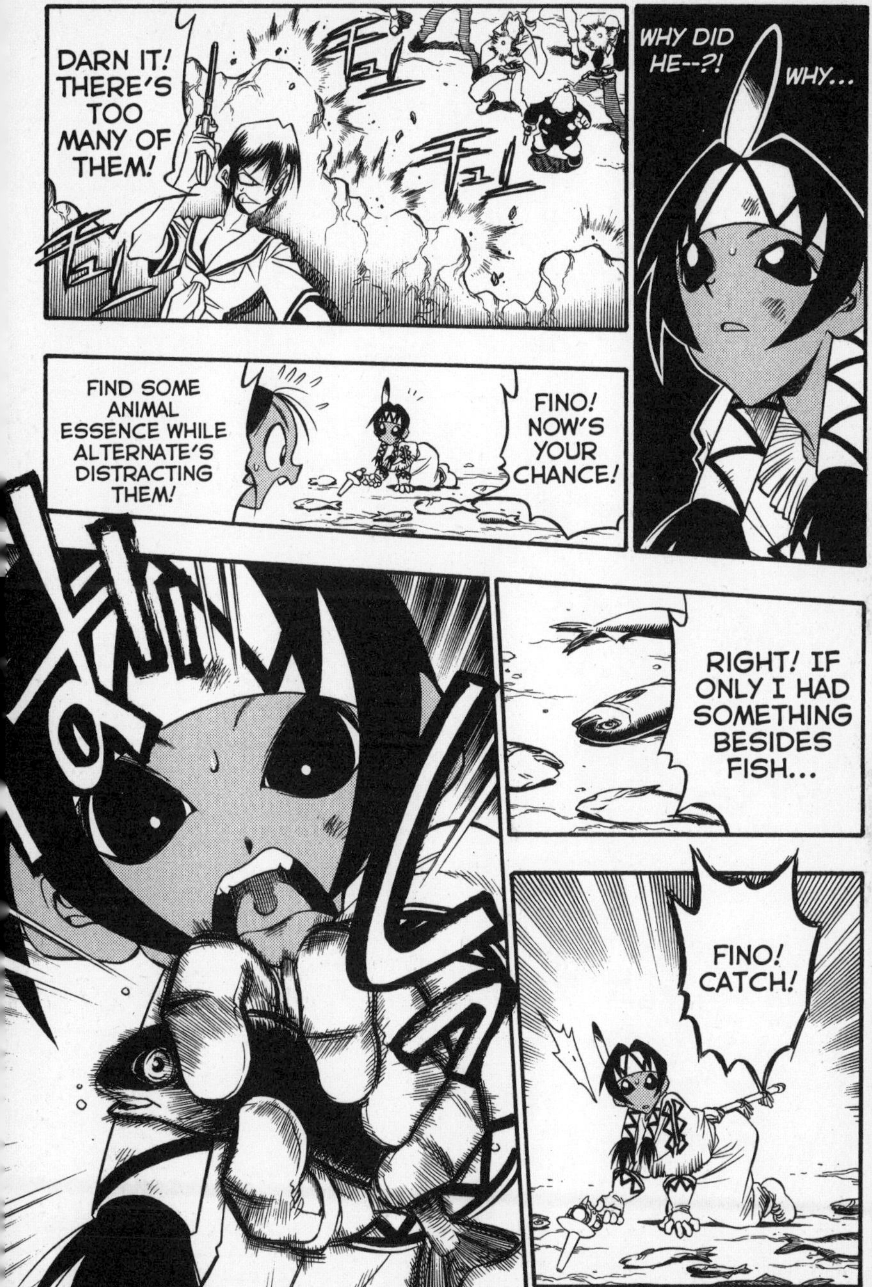
WHY DID HE--?!
WHY...
DARN IT! THERE'S TOO MANY OF THEM!
FINO! NOW'S YOUR CHANCE!
FIND SOME ANIMAL ESSENCE WHILE ALTERNATE'S DISTRACTING THEM!
RIGHT! IF ONLY I HAD SOMETHING BESIDES FISH...
FINO! CATCH!

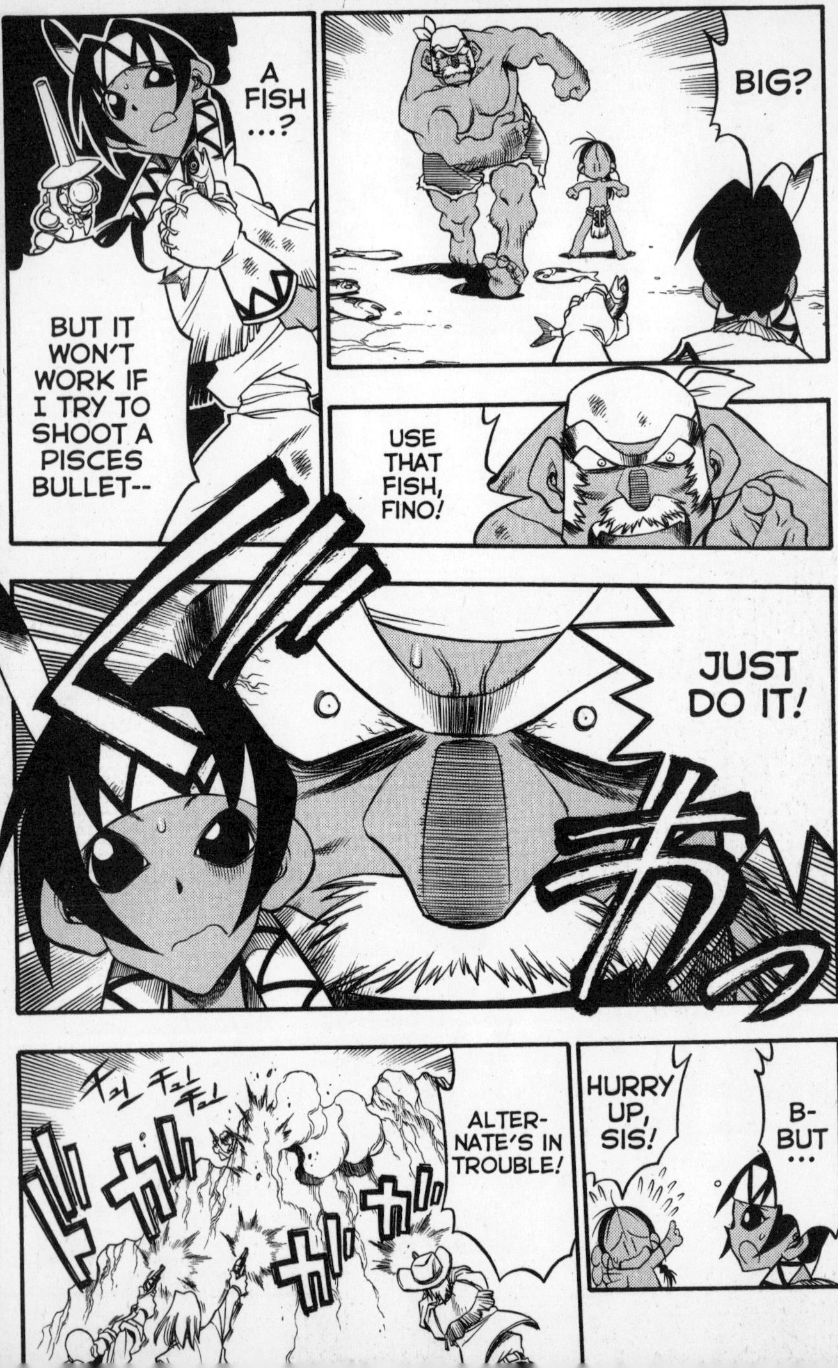
BIG?
USE THAT FISH, FINO!
A FISH ...?
BUT IT WON'T WORK IF I TRY TO SHOOT A PISCES BULLET--
JUST DO IT!
B-BUT ...
HURRY UP, SIS!
ALTER-NATE'S IN TROUBLE!

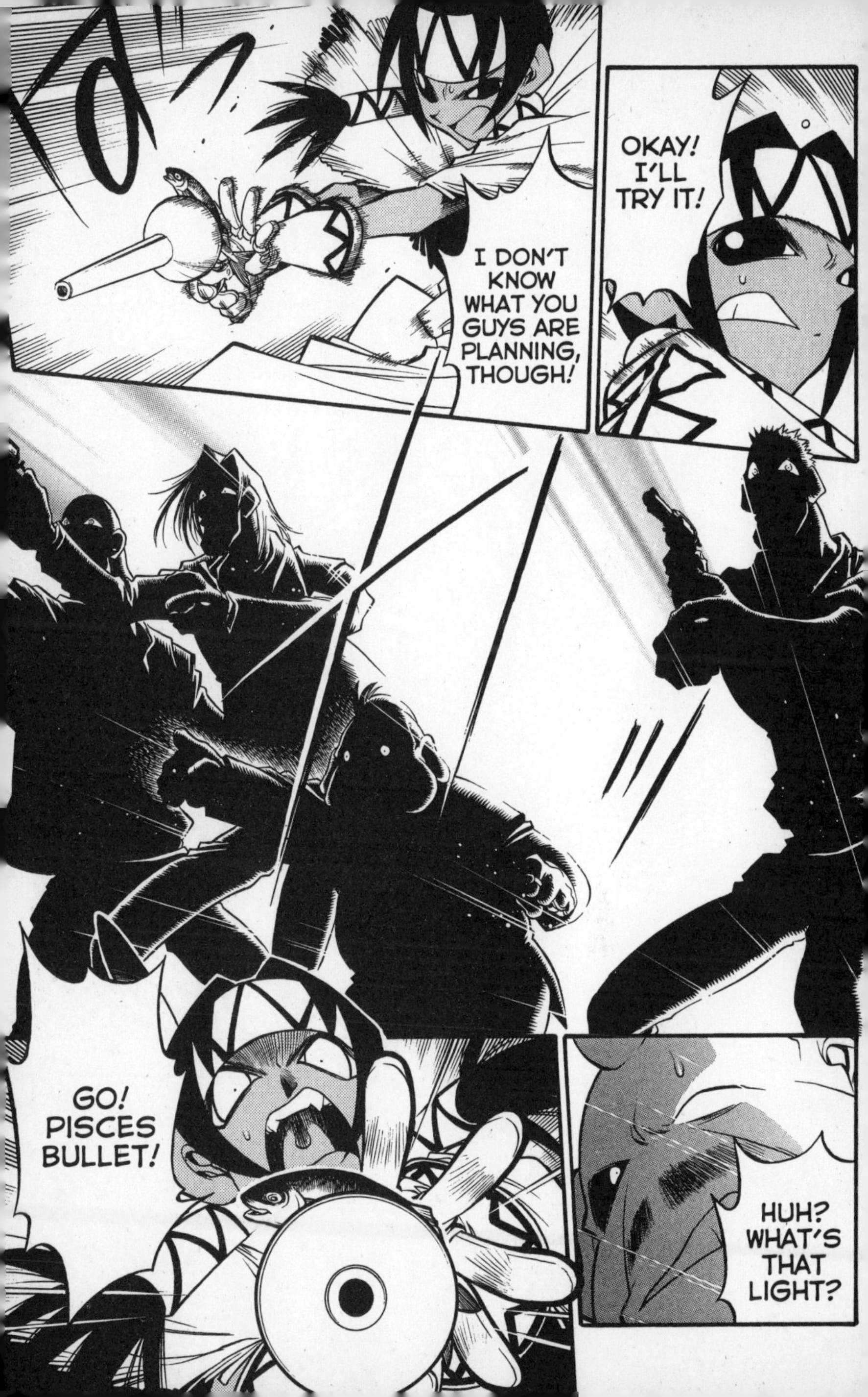
OKAY! I'LL TRY IT!
I DON'T KNOW WHAT YOU GUYS ARE PLANNING, THOUGH!
HUH? WHAT'S THAT LIGHT?
GO! PISCES BULLET!

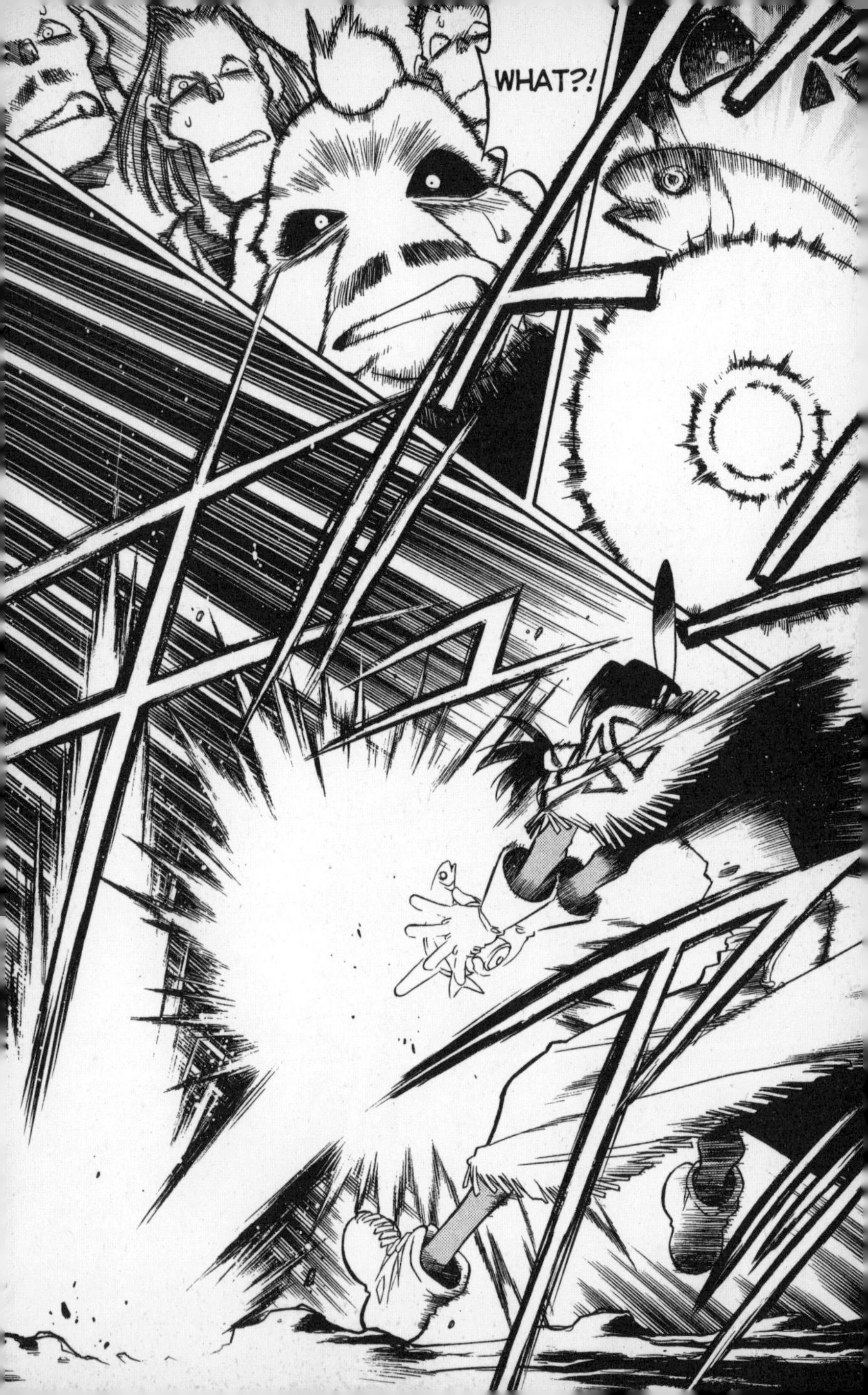
WHAT?!

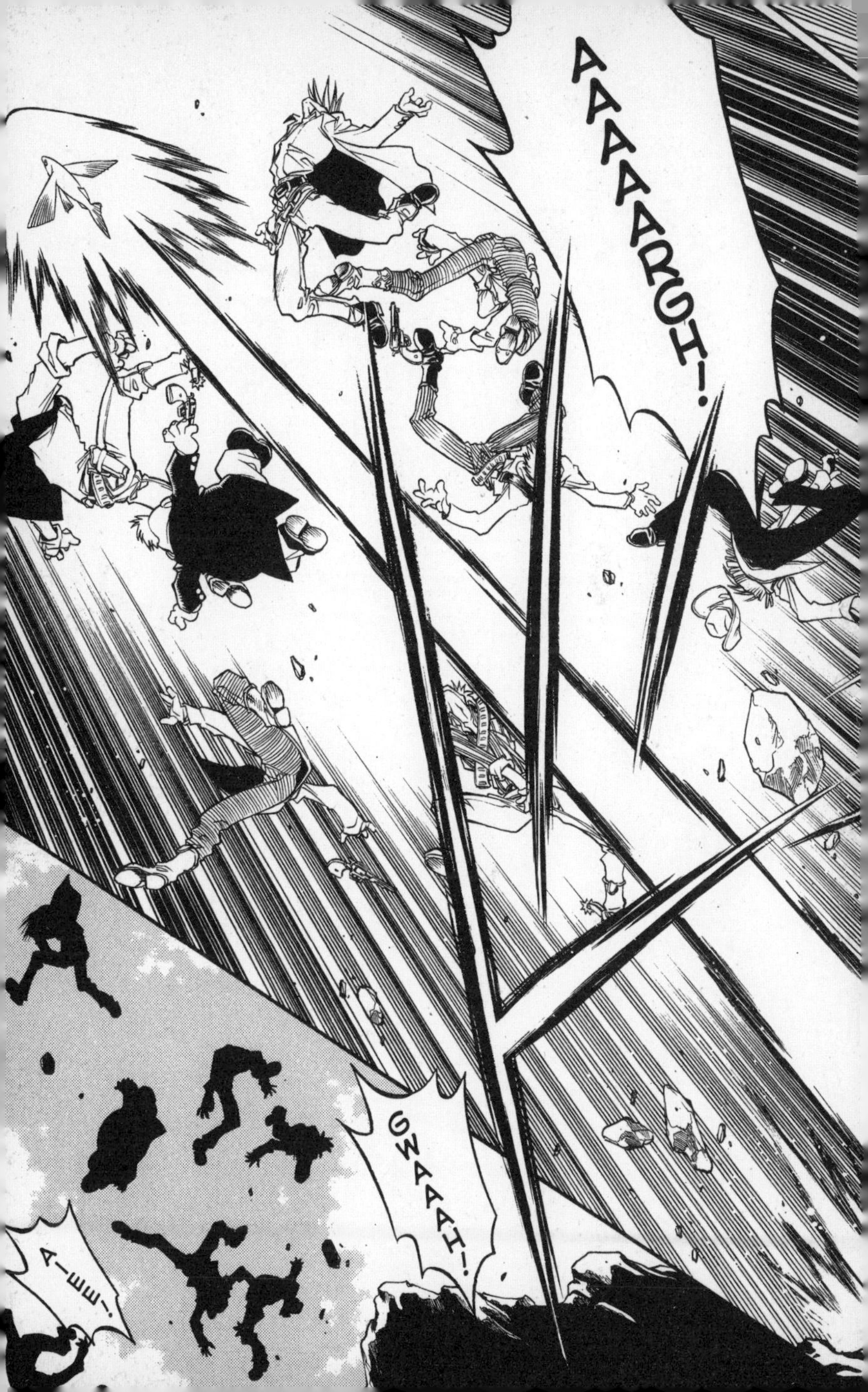
AAAAARGH!
GWAAAH!
A—EE—!

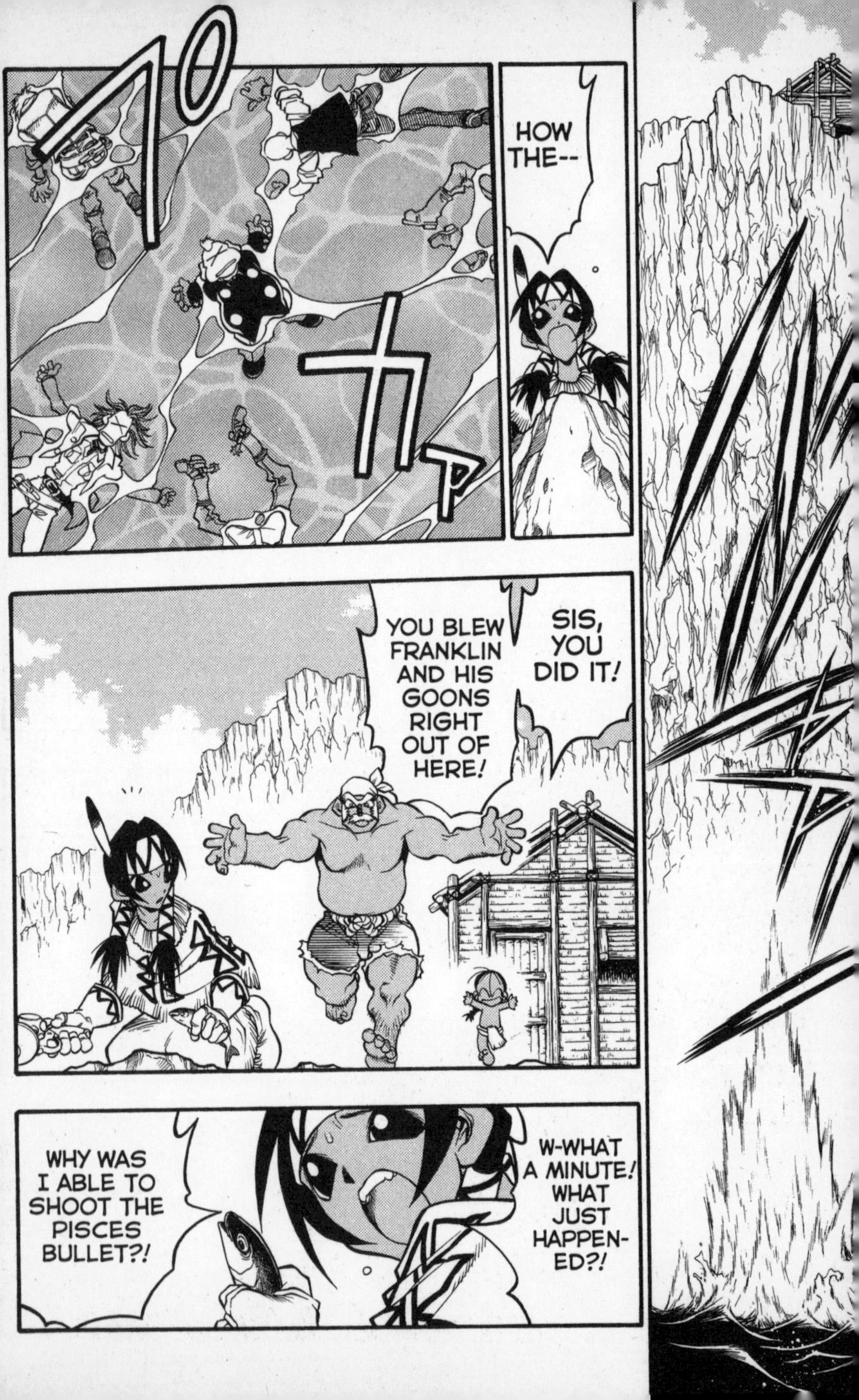
HOW THE--
SIS, YOU DID IT!
YOU BLEW FRANKLIN AND HIS GOONS RIGHT OUT OF HERE!
W-WHAT A MINUTE! WHAT JUST HAPPENED?!
WHY WAS I ABLE TO SHOOT THE PISCES BULLET?!

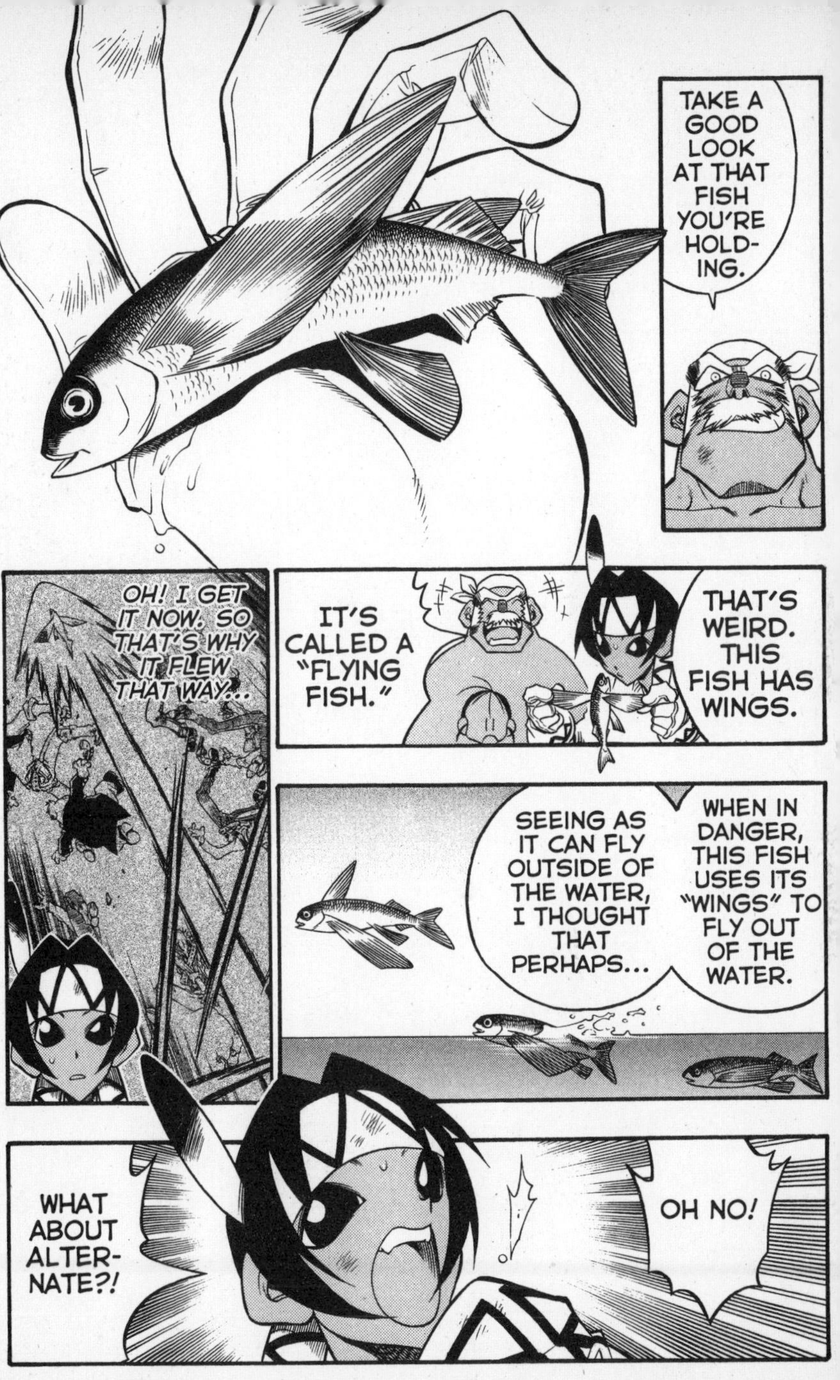
TAKE A GOOD LOOK AT THAT FISH YOU'RE HOLD-ING.
THAT'S WEIRD. THIS FISH HAS WINGS.
IT'S CALLED A "FLYING FISH."
WHEN IN DANGER, THIS FISH USES ITS "WINGS" TO FLY OUT OF THE WATER.
SEEING AS IT CAN FLY OUTSIDE OF THE WATER, I THOUGHT THAT PERHAPS...
OH! I GET IT NOW. SO THAT'S WHY IT FLEW THAT WAY...
OH NO!
WHAT ABOUT ALTER-NATE?!

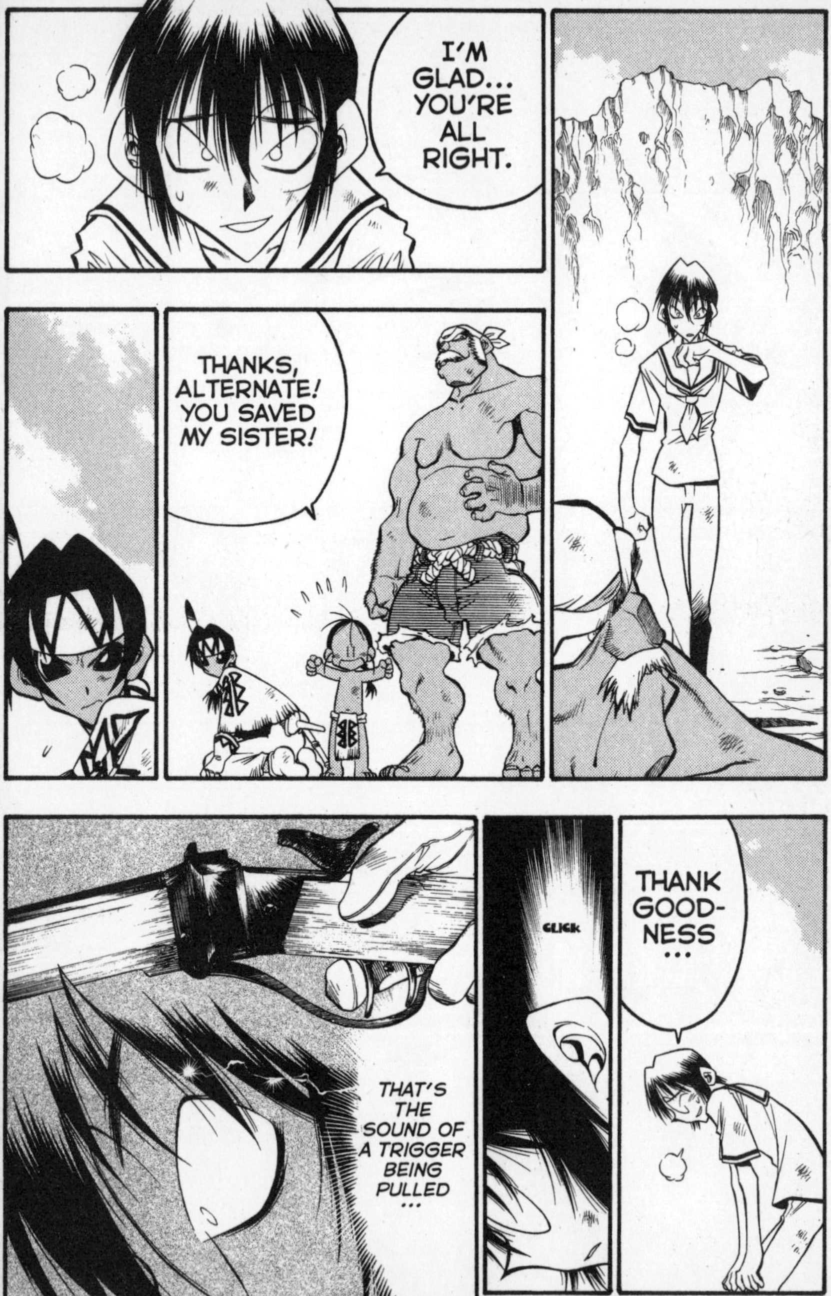
I'M GLAD... YOU'RE ALL RIGHT.
THANKS, ALTERNATE! YOU SAVED MY SISTER!
THANK GOODNESS...
CLICK
THAT'S THE SOUND OF A TRIGGER BEING PULLED...

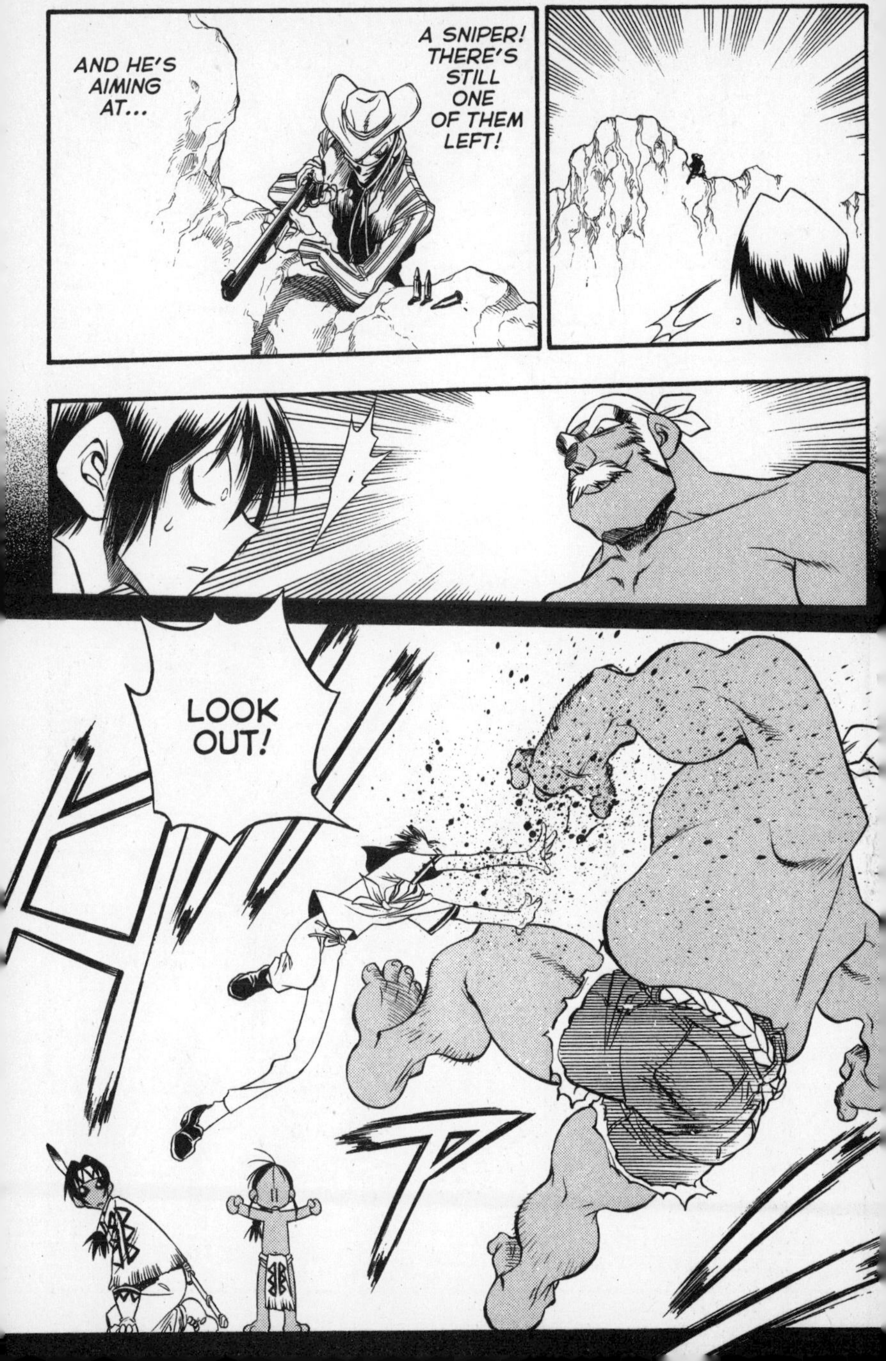
A SNIPER! THERE'S STILL ONE OF THEM LEFT!
AND HE'S AIMING AT...
LOOK OUT!

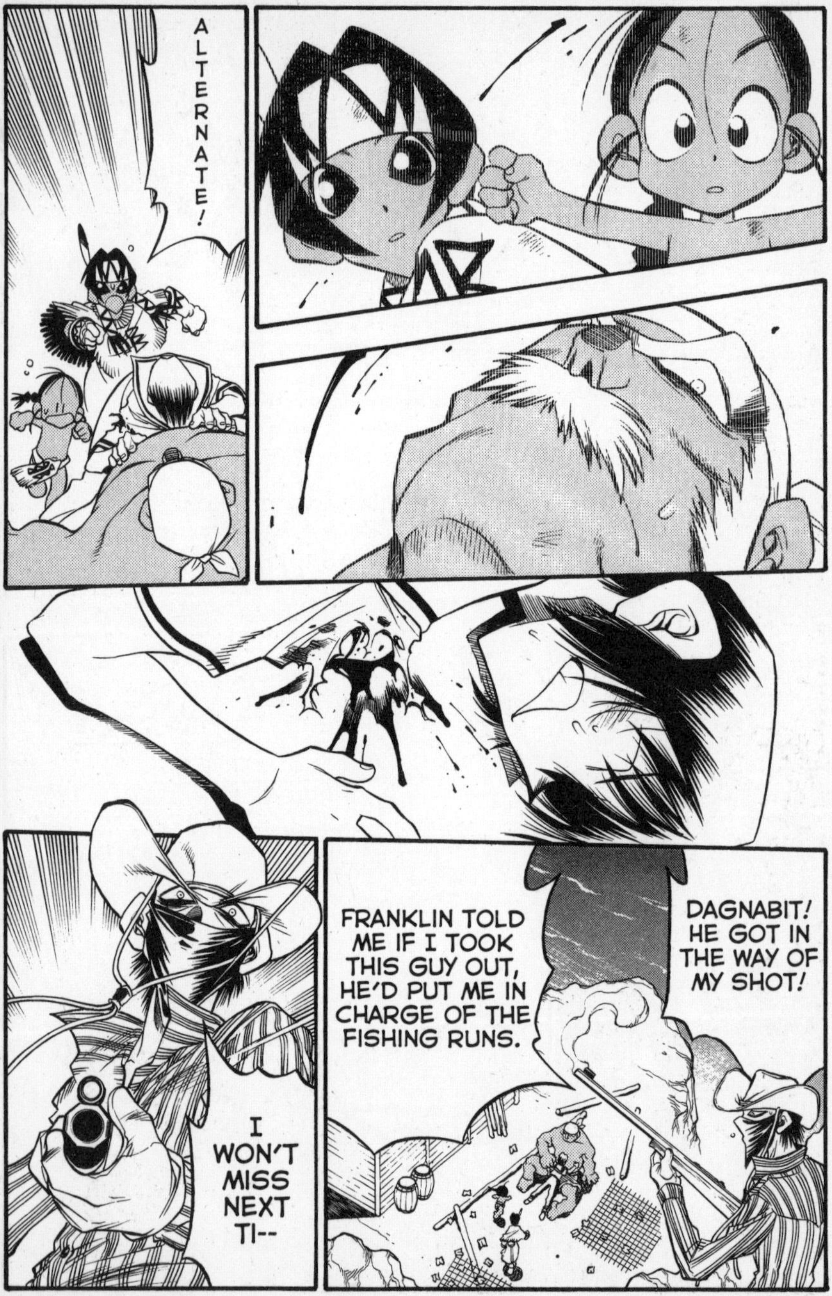
ALTERNATE!
DAGNABIT! HE GOT IN THE WAY OF MY SHOT!
FRANKLIN TOLD ME IF I TOOK THIS GUY OUT, HE'D PUT ME IN CHARGE OF THE FISHING RUNS.
I WON'T MISS NEXT TI--

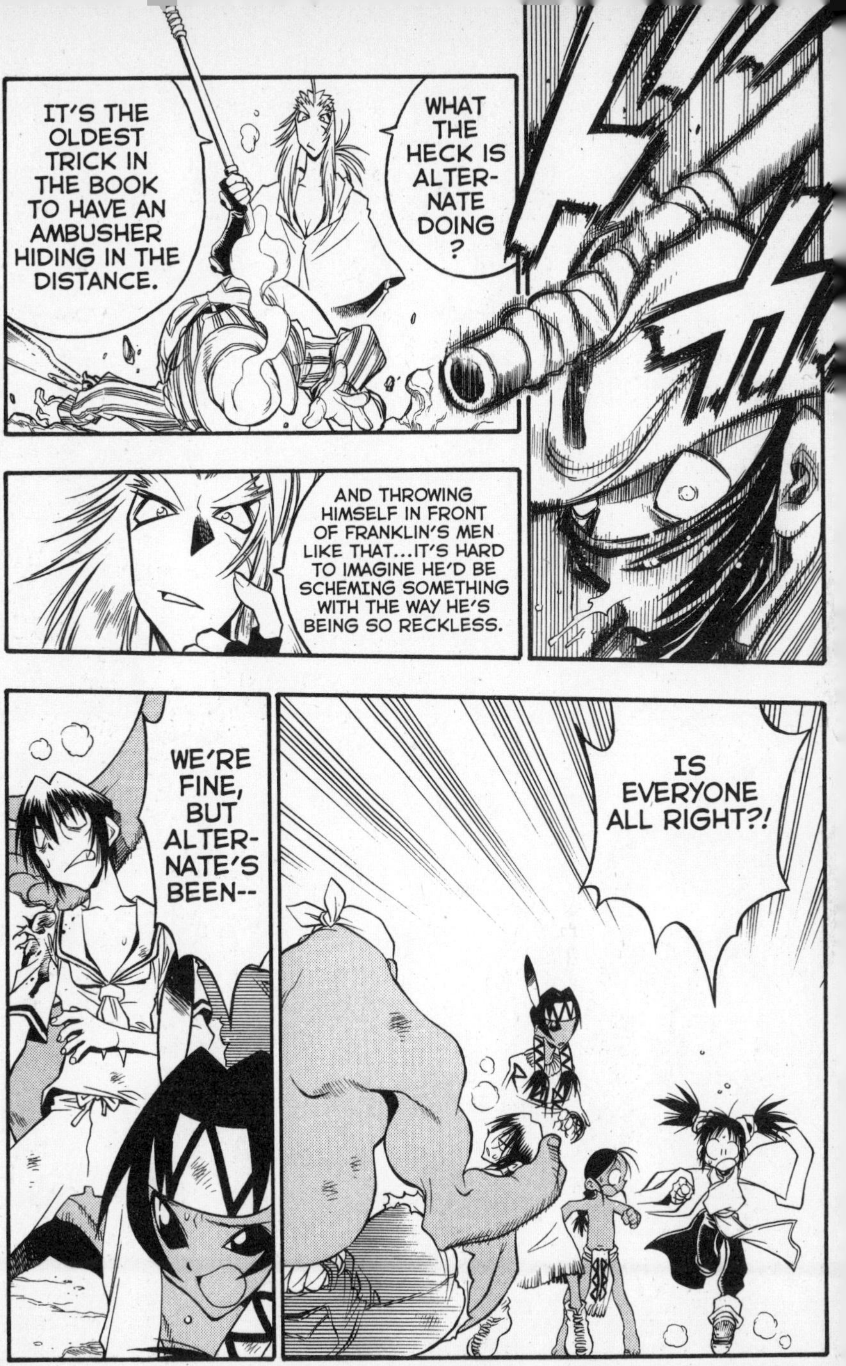
WHAT THE HECK IS ALTER-NATE DOING?
IT'S THE OLDEST TRICK IN THE BOOK TO HAVE AN AMBUSHER HIDING IN THE DISTANCE.
AND THROWING HIMSELF IN FRONT OF FRANKLIN'S MEN LIKE THAT...IT'S HARD TO IMAGINE HE'D BE SCHEMING SOMETHING WITH THE WAY HE'S BEING SO RECKLESS.
IS EVERYONE ALL RIGHT?!
WE'RE FINE, BUT ALTER-NATE'S BEEN--

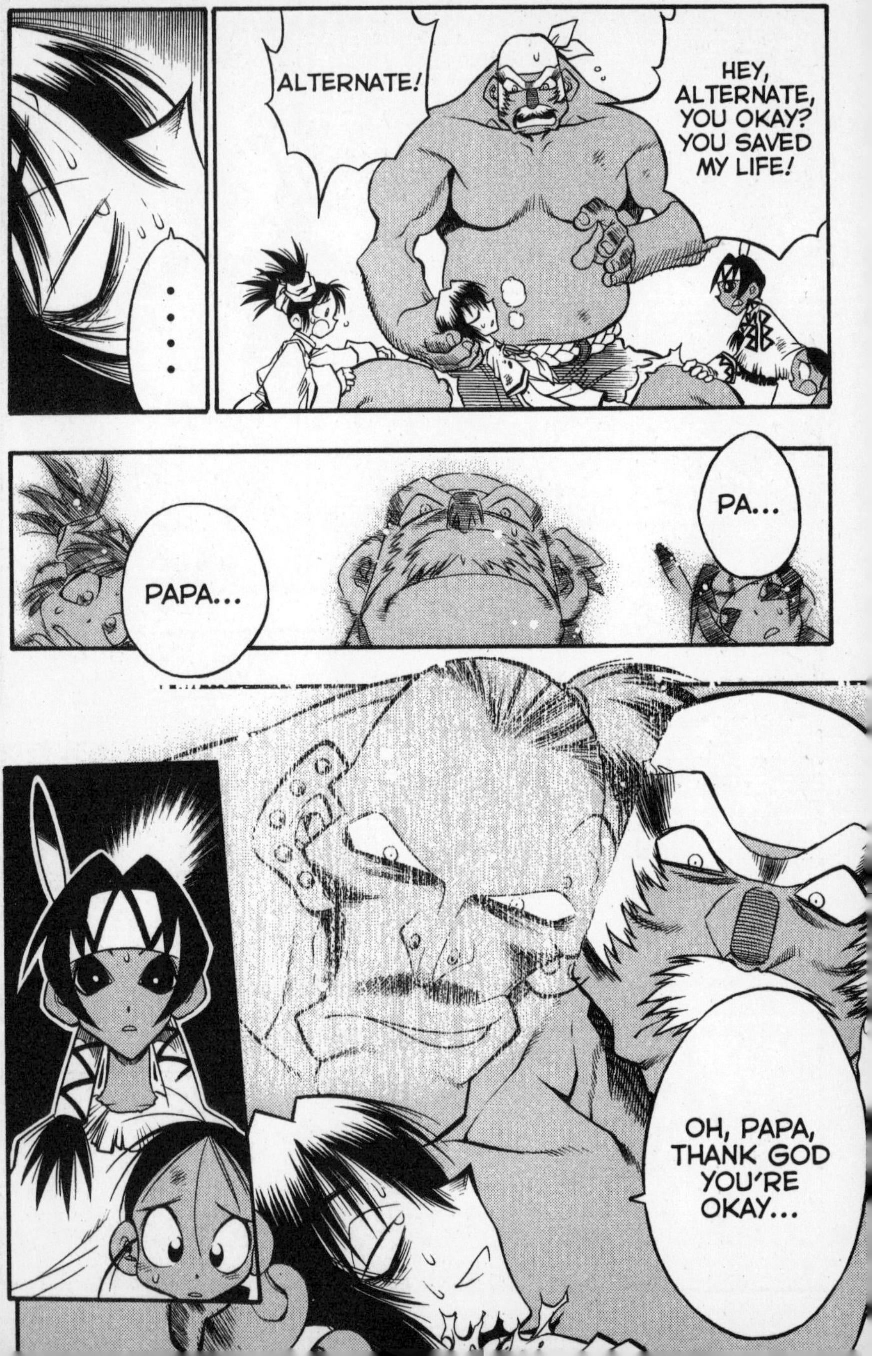
HEY, ALTERNATE, YOU OKAY? YOU SAVED MY LIFE!
ALTERNATE!
....
PA...
PAPA...
OH, PAPA, THANK GOD YOU'RE OKAY...

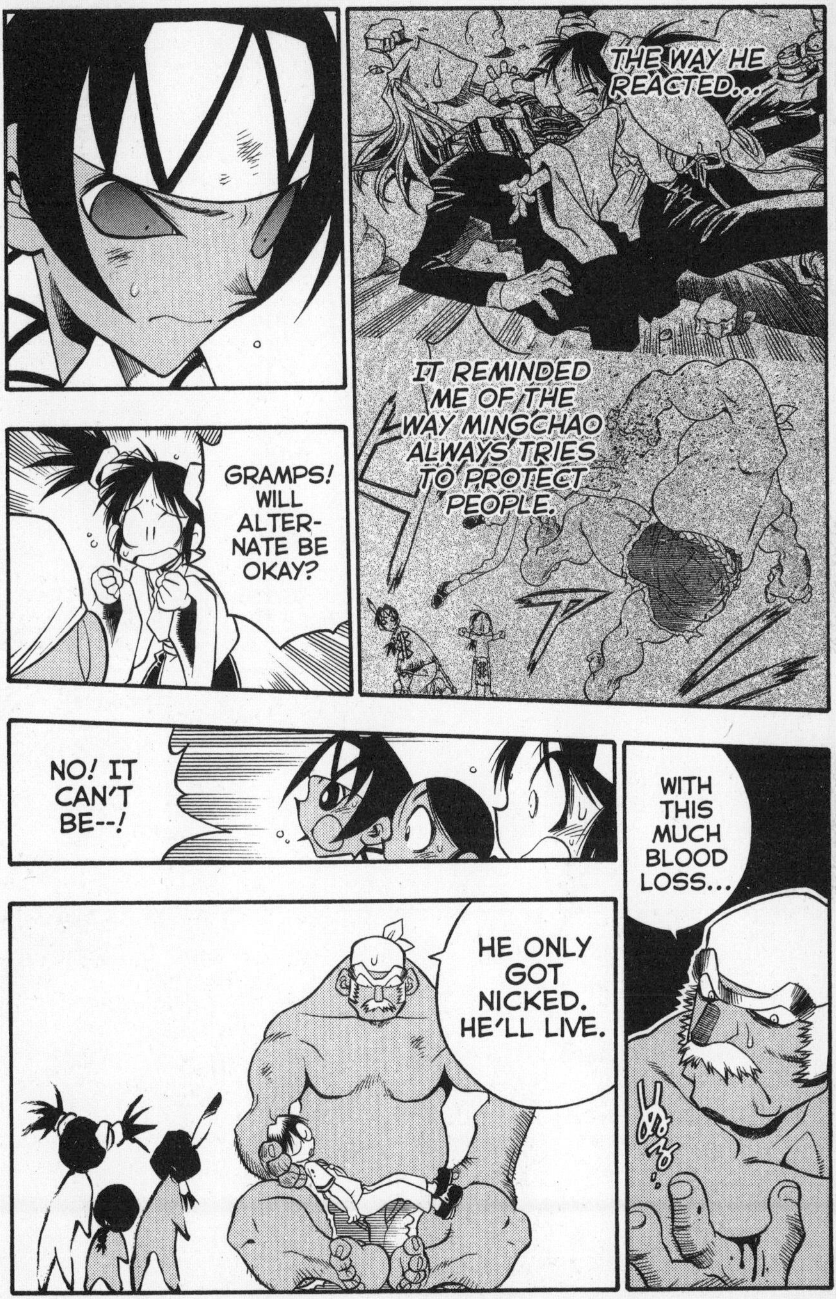
THE WAY HE REACTED...
IT REMINDED ME OF THE WAY MINGCHAO ALWAYS TRIES TO PROTECT PEOPLE.
GRAMPS! WILL ALTER-NATE BE OKAY?
WITH THIS MUCH BLOOD LOSS...
NO! IT CAN'T BE--!
HE ONLY GOT NICKED. HE'LL LIVE.

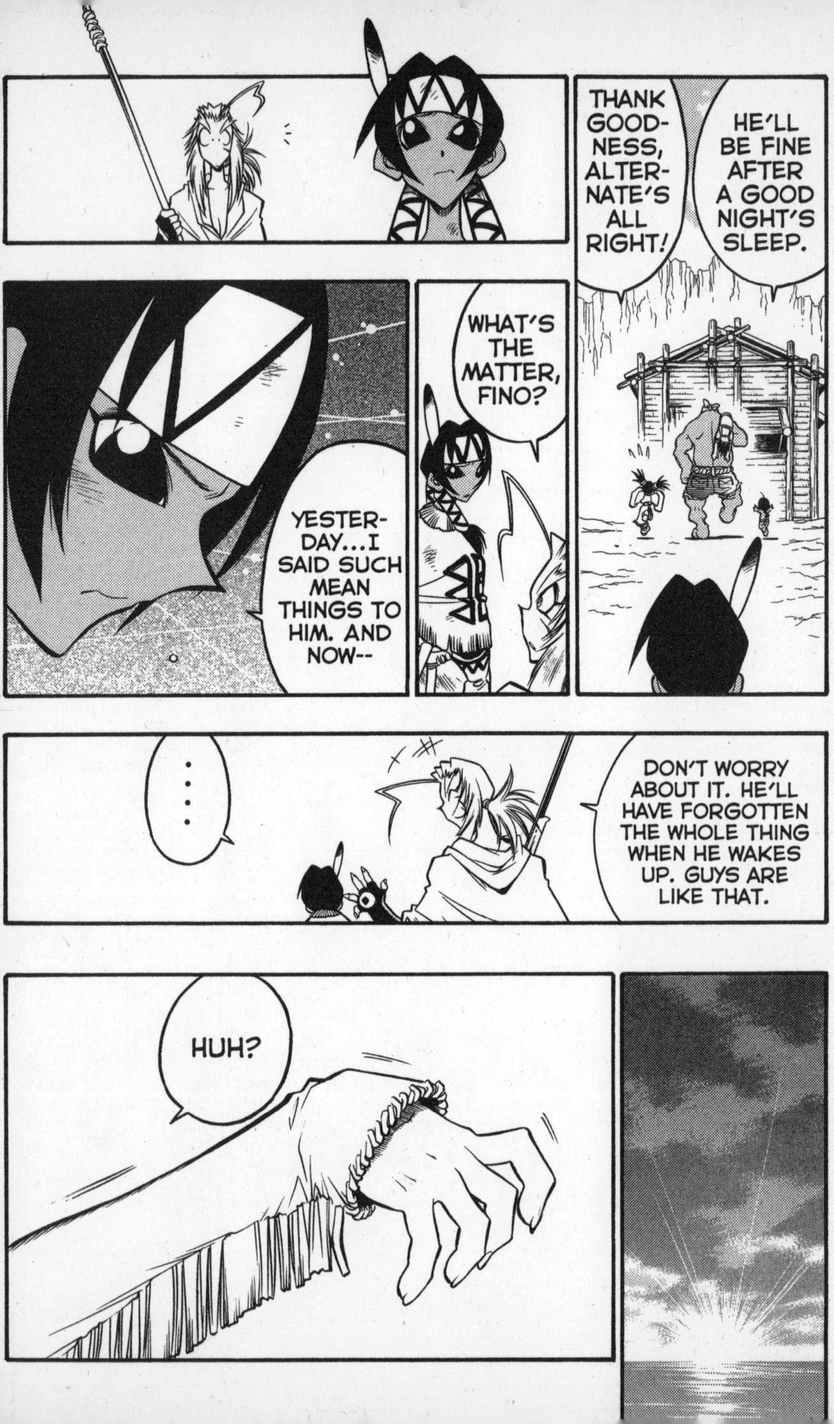
HE'LL BE FINE AFTER A GOOD NIGHT'S SLEEP.
THANK GOODNESS, ALTERNATE'S ALL RIGHT!
WHAT'S THE MATTER, FINO?
YESTERDAY...I SAID SUCH MEAN THINGS TO HIM. AND NOW--
DON'T WORRY ABOUT IT. HE'LL HAVE FORGOTTEN THE WHOLE THING WHEN HE WAKES UP. GUYS ARE LIKE THAT.
....
HUH?

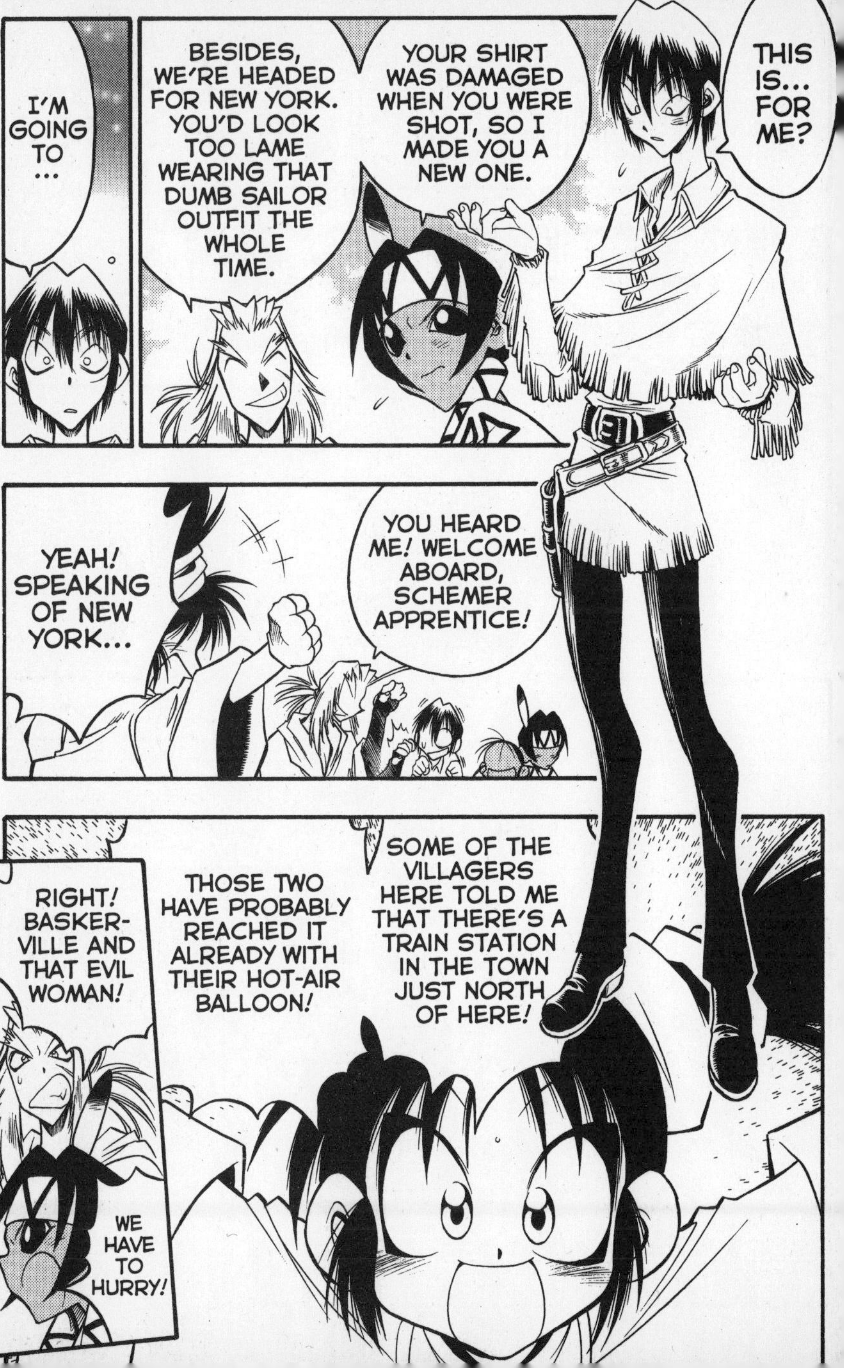
THIS IS... FOR ME?
YOUR SHIRT WAS DAMAGED WHEN YOU WERE SHOT, SO I MADE YOU A NEW ONE.
BESIDES, WE'RE HEADED FOR NEW YORK. YOU'D LOOK TOO LAME WEARING THAT DUMB SAILOR OUTFIT THE WHOLE TIME.
I'M GOING TO ...
YOU HEARD ME! WELCOME ABOARD, SCHEMER APPRENTICE!
YEAH! SPEAKING OF NEW YORK...
SOME OF THE VILLAGERS HERE TOLD ME THAT THERE'S A TRAIN STATION IN THE TOWN JUST NORTH OF HERE!
THOSE TWO HAVE PROBABLY REACHED IT ALREADY WITH THEIR HOT-AIR BALLOON!
RIGHT! BASKER-VILLE AND THAT EVIL WOMAN!
WE HAVE TO HURRY!

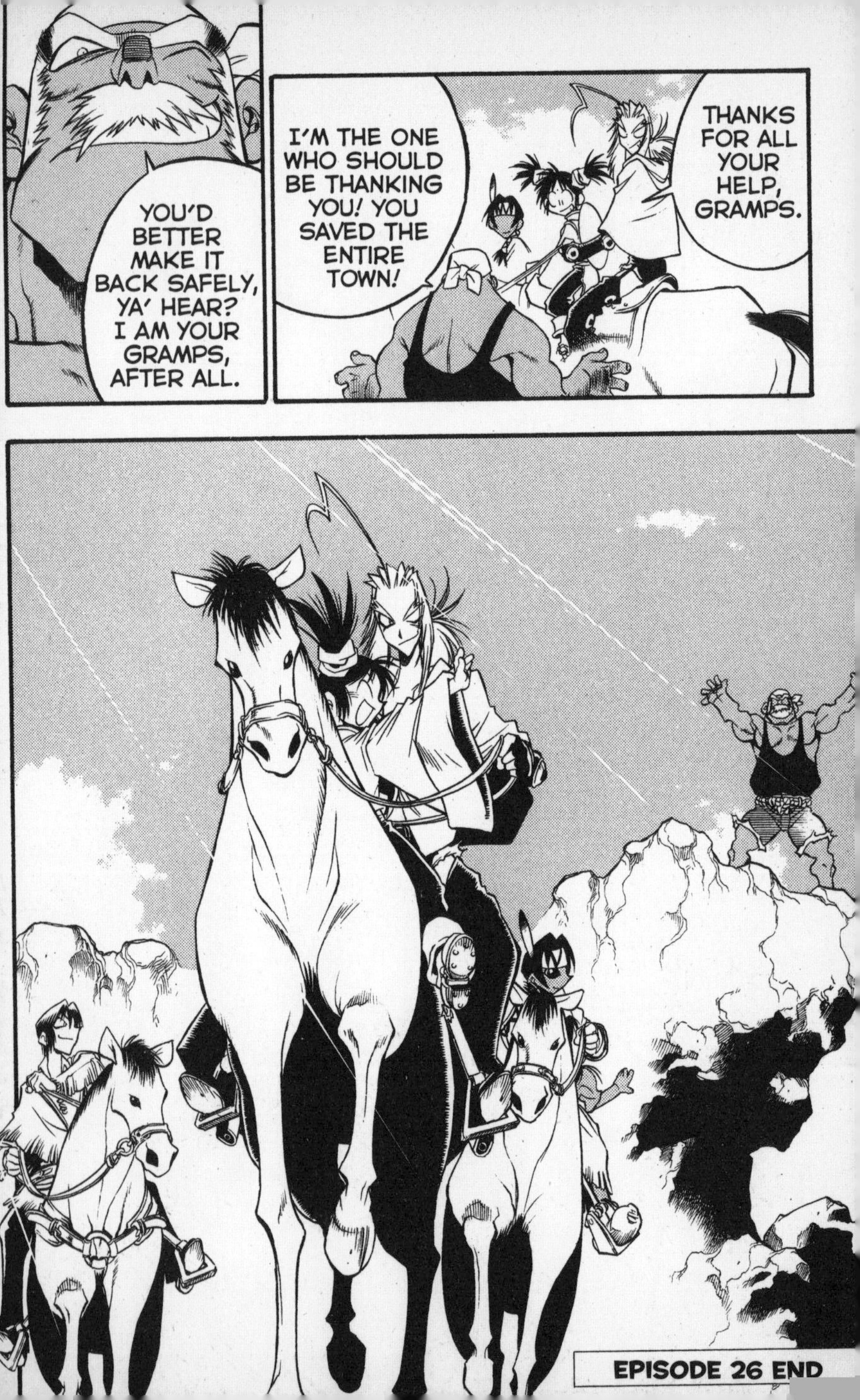
THANKS FOR ALL YOUR HELP, GRAMPS.
I'M THE ONE WHO SHOULD BE THANKING YOU! YOU SAVED THE ENTIRE TOWN!
YOU'D BETTER MAKE IT BACK SAFELY, YA' HEAR? I AM YOUR GRAMPS, AFTER ALL.
EPISODE 26 END

EPISODE 27
STAGECOACH OF DOOM

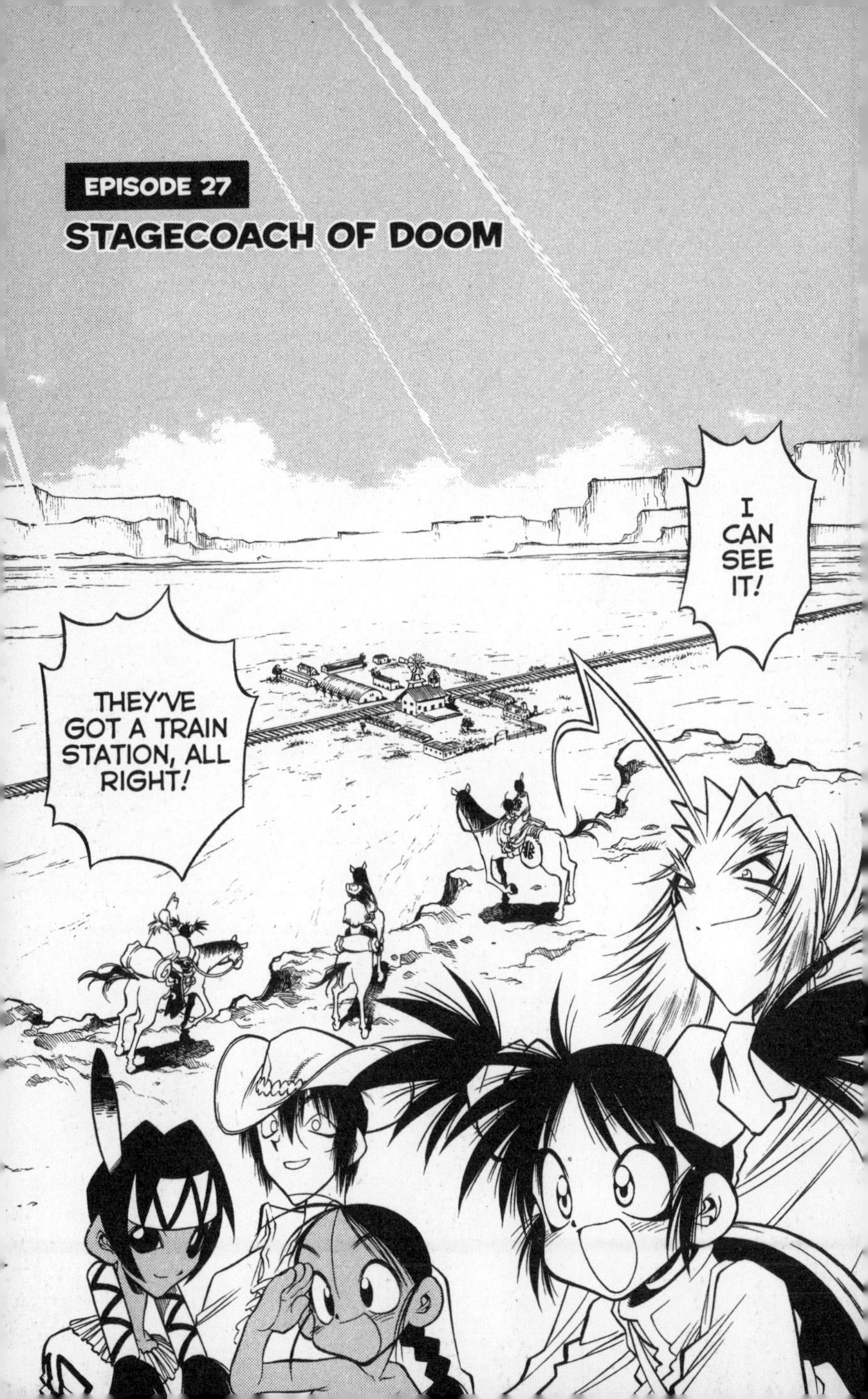
I CAN SEE IT!
THEY'VE GOT A TRAIN STATION, ALL RIGHT!

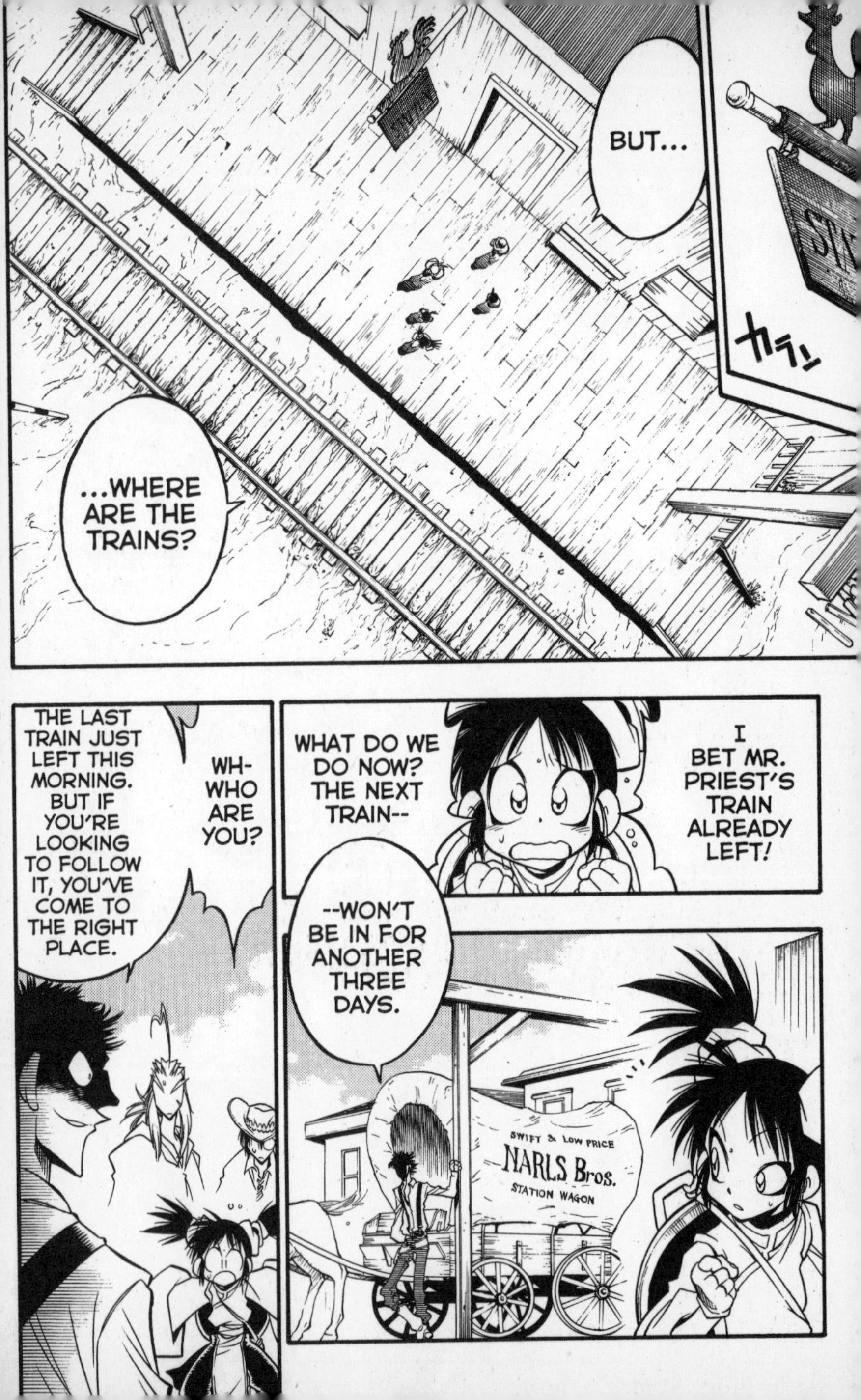
BUT...
カラン
...WHERE ARE THE TRAINS?
I BET MR. PRIEST'S TRAIN ALREADY LEFT!
WHAT DO WE DO NOW? THE NEXT TRAIN--
--WON'T BE IN FOR ANOTHER THREE DAYS.
SWIFT & LOW PRICE
NARLS Bros.
STATION WAGON
THE LAST TRAIN JUST LEFT THIS MORNING. BUT IF YOU'RE LOOKING TO FOLLOW IT, YOU'VE COME TO THE RIGHT PLACE.
WH- WHO ARE YOU?

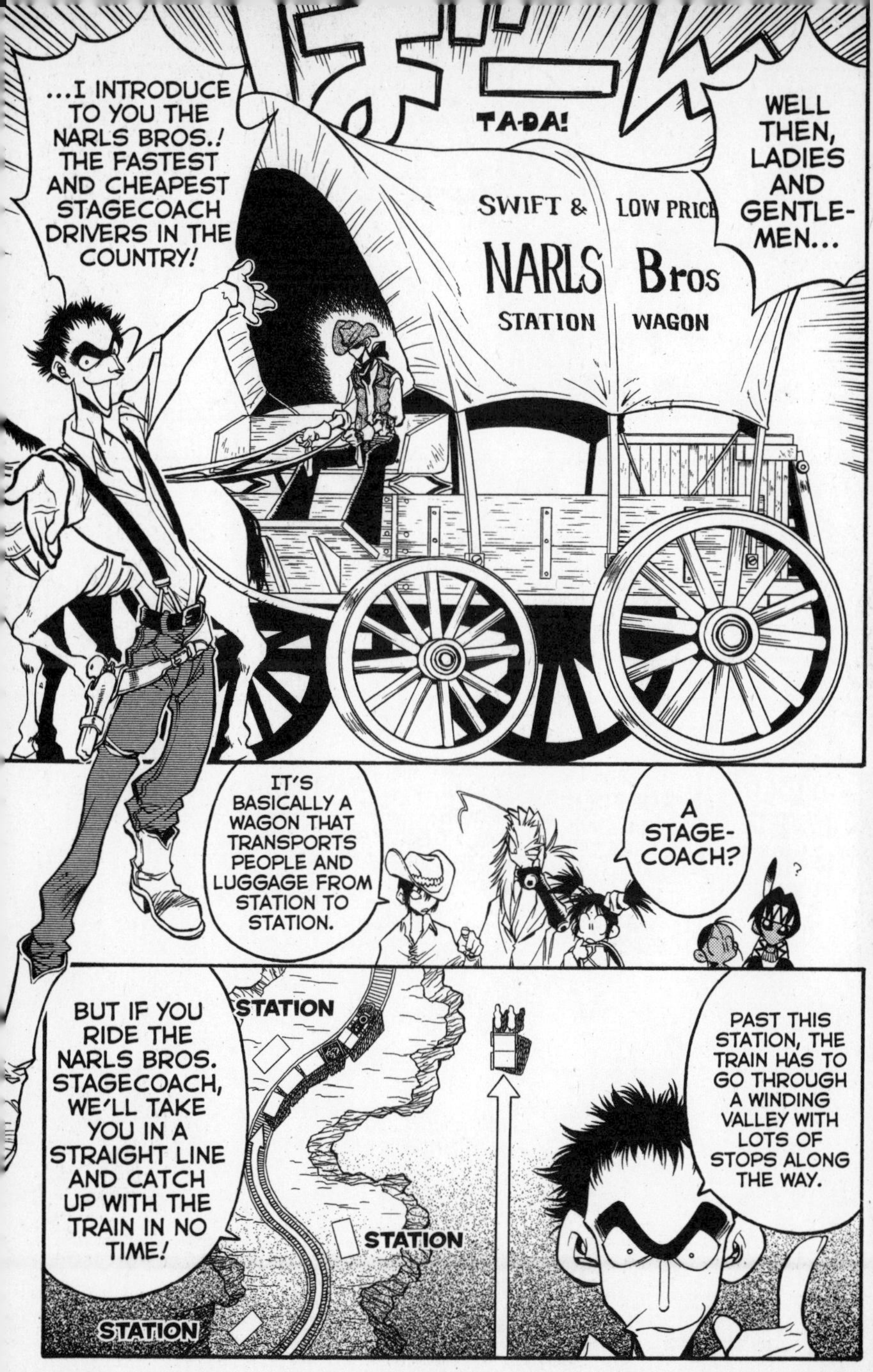
WELL THEN, LADIES AND GENTLE-MEN...
TA-DA!
SWIFT & LOW PRICE
NARLS Bros
STATION WAGON
...I INTRODUCE TO YOU THE NARLS BROS.! THE FASTEST AND CHEAPEST STAGECOACH DRIVERS IN THE COUNTRY!
A STAGE-COACH?
?
IT'S BASICALLY A WAGON THAT TRANSPORTS PEOPLE AND LUGGAGE FROM STATION TO STATION.
PAST THIS STATION, THE TRAIN HAS TO GO THROUGH A WINDING VALLEY WITH LOTS OF STOPS ALONG THE WAY.
STATION
STATION
STATION
BUT IF YOU RIDE THE NARLS BROS. STAGECOACH, WE'LL TAKE YOU IN A STRAIGHT LINE AND CATCH UP WITH THE TRAIN IN NO TIME!

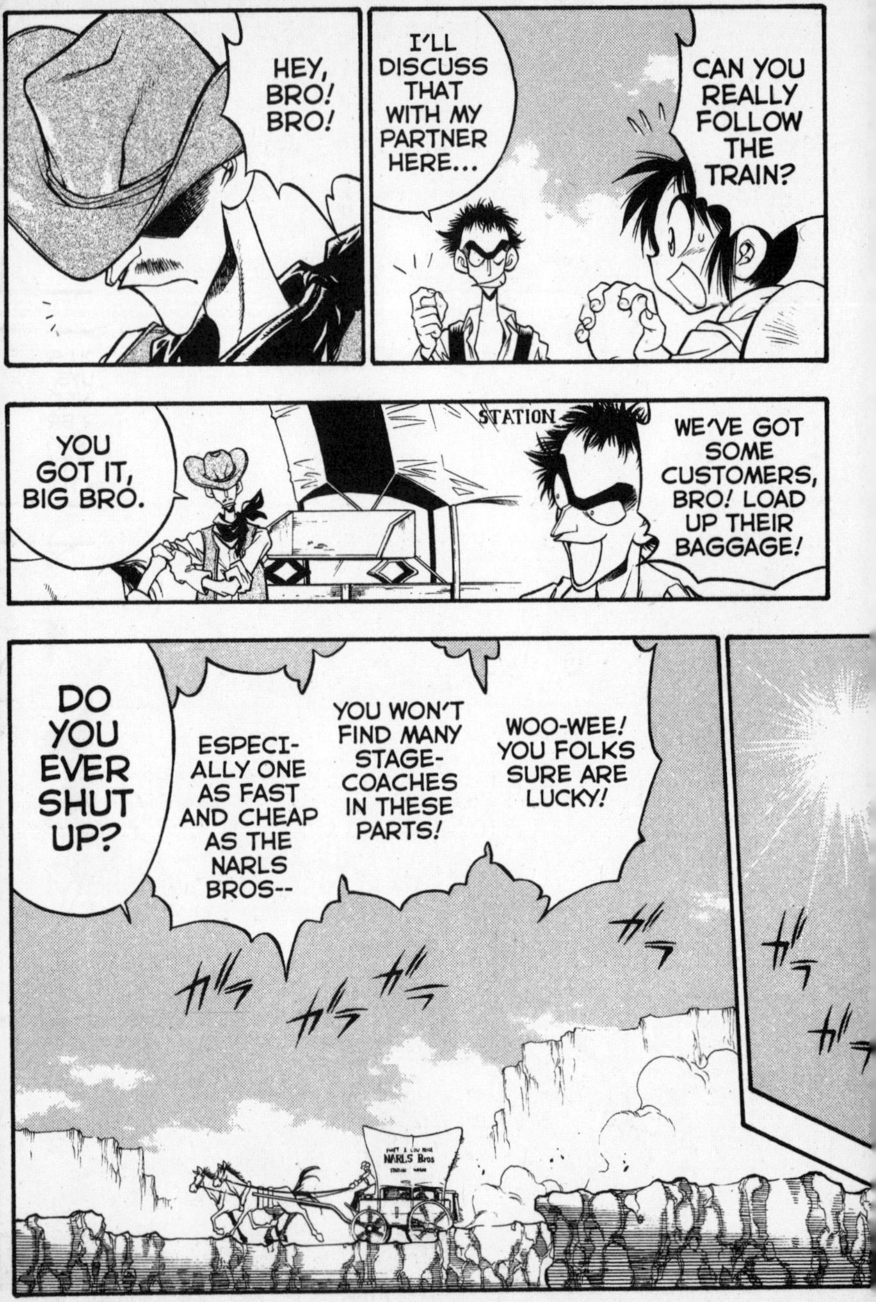
CAN YOU REALLY FOLLOW THE TRAIN?
I'LL DISCUSS THAT WITH MY PARTNER HERE...
HEY, BRO! BRO!
WE'VE GOT SOME CUSTOMERS, BRO! LOAD UP THEIR BAGGAGE!
STATION
YOU GOT IT, BIG BRO.
WOO-WEE! YOU FOLKS SURE ARE LUCKY!
YOU WON'T FIND MANY STAGE-COACHES IN THESE PARTS!
ESPECI-ALLY ONE AS FAST AND CHEAP AS THE NARLS BROS--
DO YOU EVER SHUT UP?
NARLS Bros

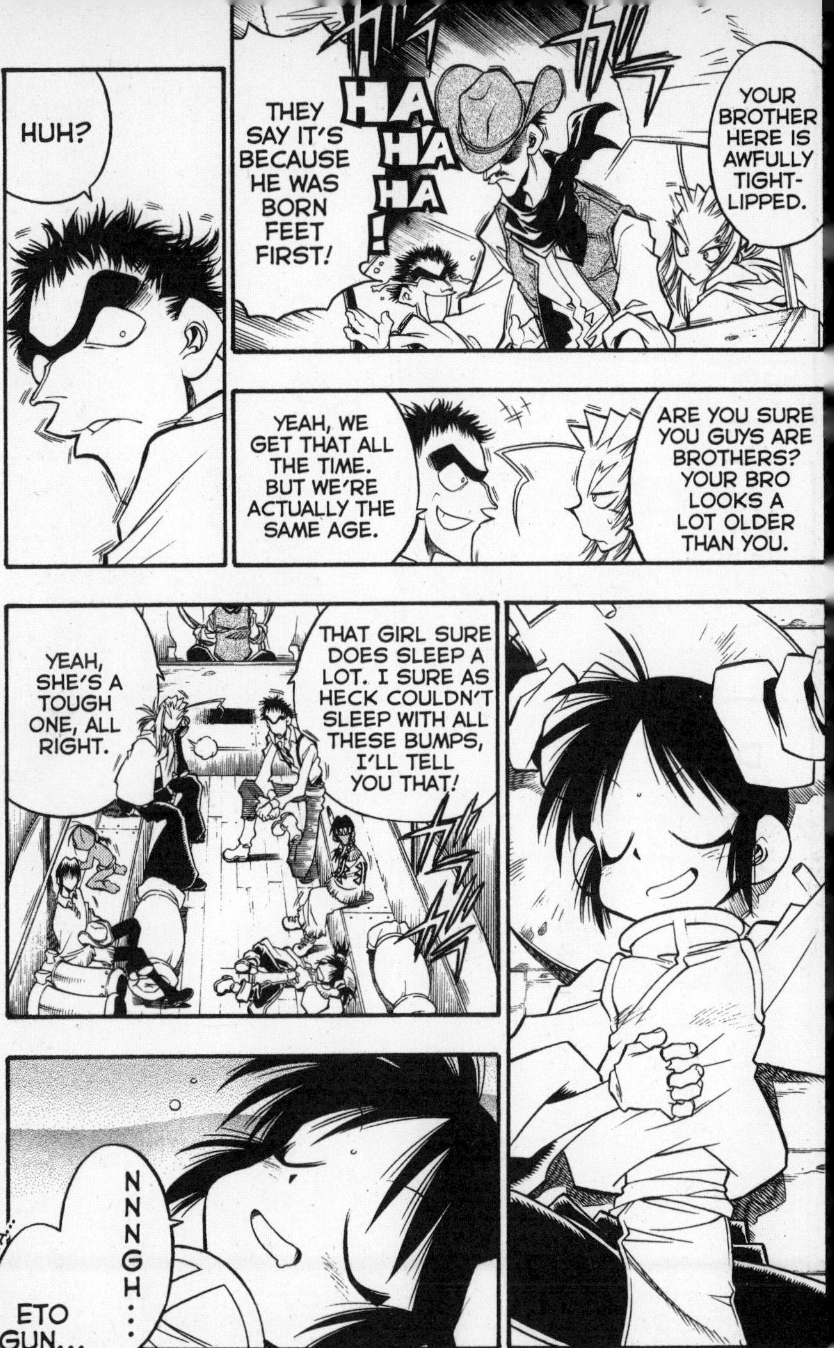
YOUR BROTHER HERE IS AWFULLY TIGHT-LIPPED.
HA HA HA!
THEY SAY IT'S BECAUSE HE WAS BORN FEET FIRST!
ARE YOU SURE YOU GUYS ARE BROTHERS? YOUR BRO LOOKS A LOT OLDER THAN YOU.
YEAH, WE GET THAT ALL THE TIME. BUT WE'RE ACTUALLY THE SAME AGE.
HUH?
THAT GIRL SURE DOES SLEEP A LOT. I SURE AS HECK COULDN'T SLEEP WITH ALL THESE BUMPS, I'LL TELL YOU THAT!
YEAH, SHE'S A TOUGH ONE, ALL RIGHT.
NNNGH...
MNYA...
ETO GUN...

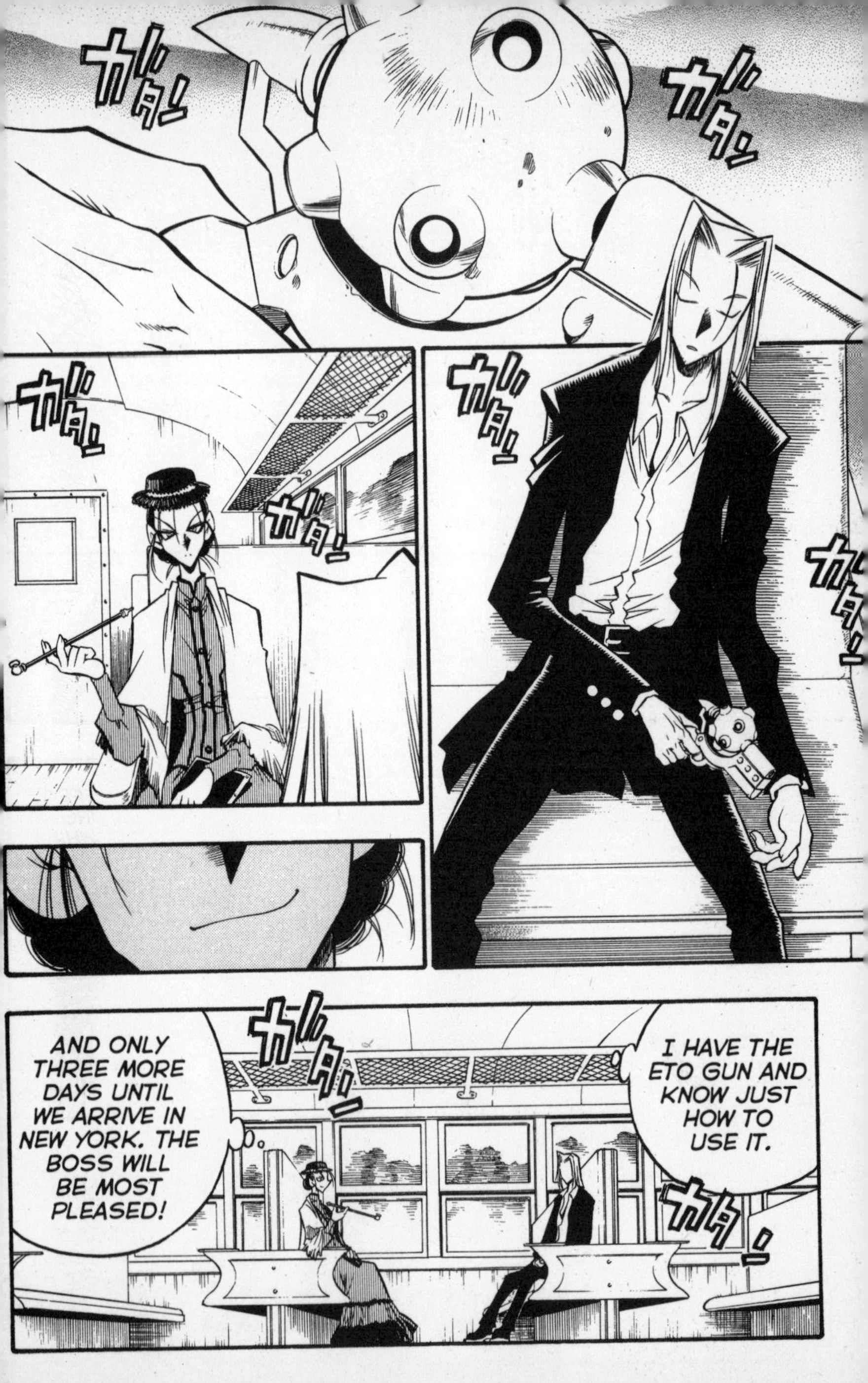

I HAVE THE ETO GUN AND KNOW JUST HOW TO USE IT.
AND ONLY THREE MORE DAYS UNTIL WE ARRIVE IN NEW YORK. THE BOSS WILL BE MOST PLEASED!

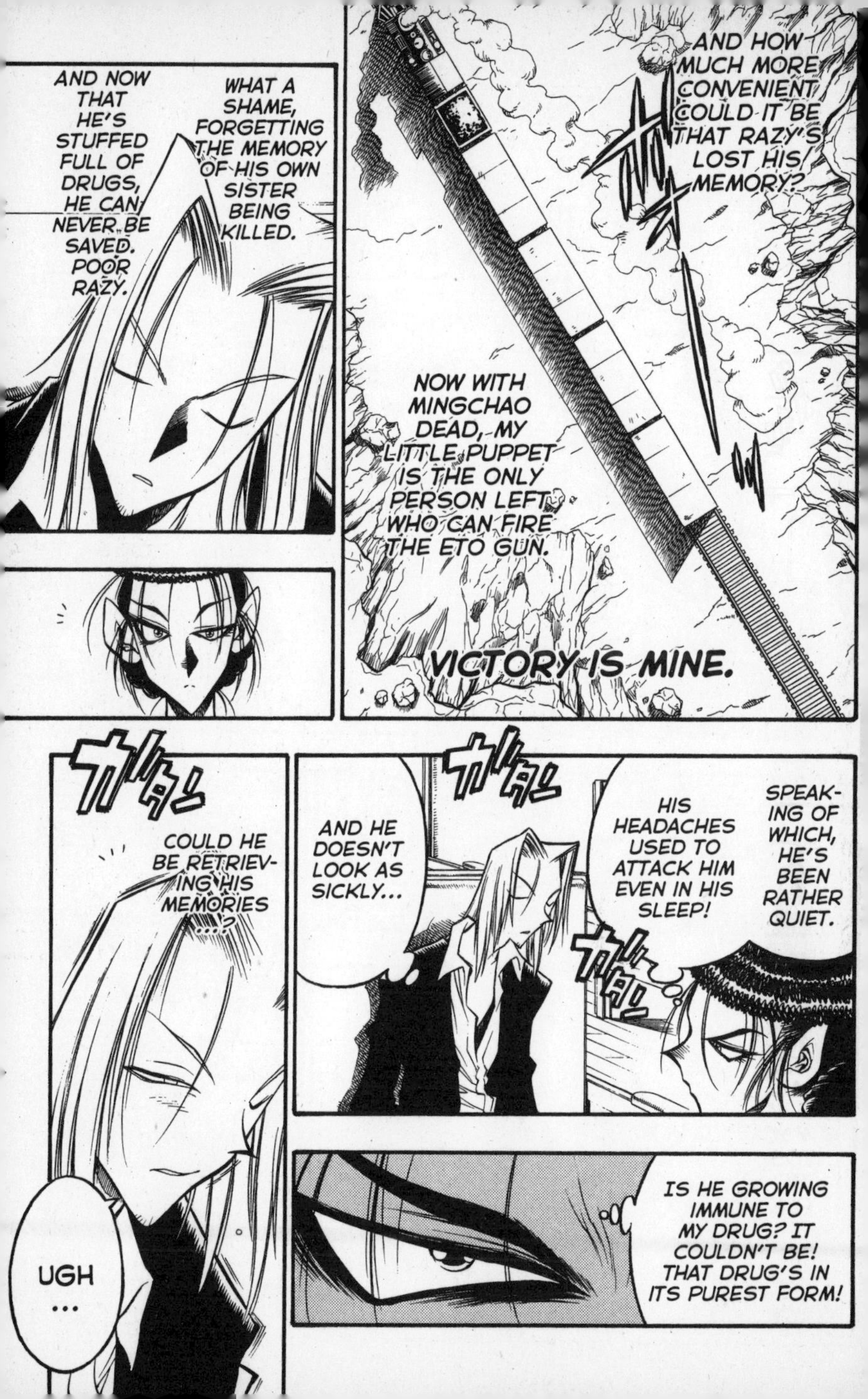
AND HOW MUCH MORE CONVENIENT COULD IT BE THAT RAZY'S LOST HIS MEMORY?
NOW WITH MINGCHAO DEAD, MY LITTLE PUPPET IS THE ONLY PERSON LEFT WHO CAN FIRE THE ETO GUN.
VICTORY IS MINE.
WHAT A SHAME, FORGETTING THE MEMORY OF HIS OWN SISTER BEING KILLED.
AND NOW THAT HE'S STUFFED FULL OF DRUGS, HE CAN NEVER BE SAVED. POOR RAZY.
SPEAKING OF WHICH, HE'S BEEN RATHER QUIET.
HIS HEADACHES USED TO ATTACK HIM EVEN IN HIS SLEEP!
AND HE DOESN'T LOOK AS SICKLY...
IS HE GROWING IMMUNE TO MY DRUG? IT COULDN'T BE! THAT DRUG'S IN ITS PUREST FORM!
COULD HE BE RETRIEVING HIS MEMORIES...?
UGH...

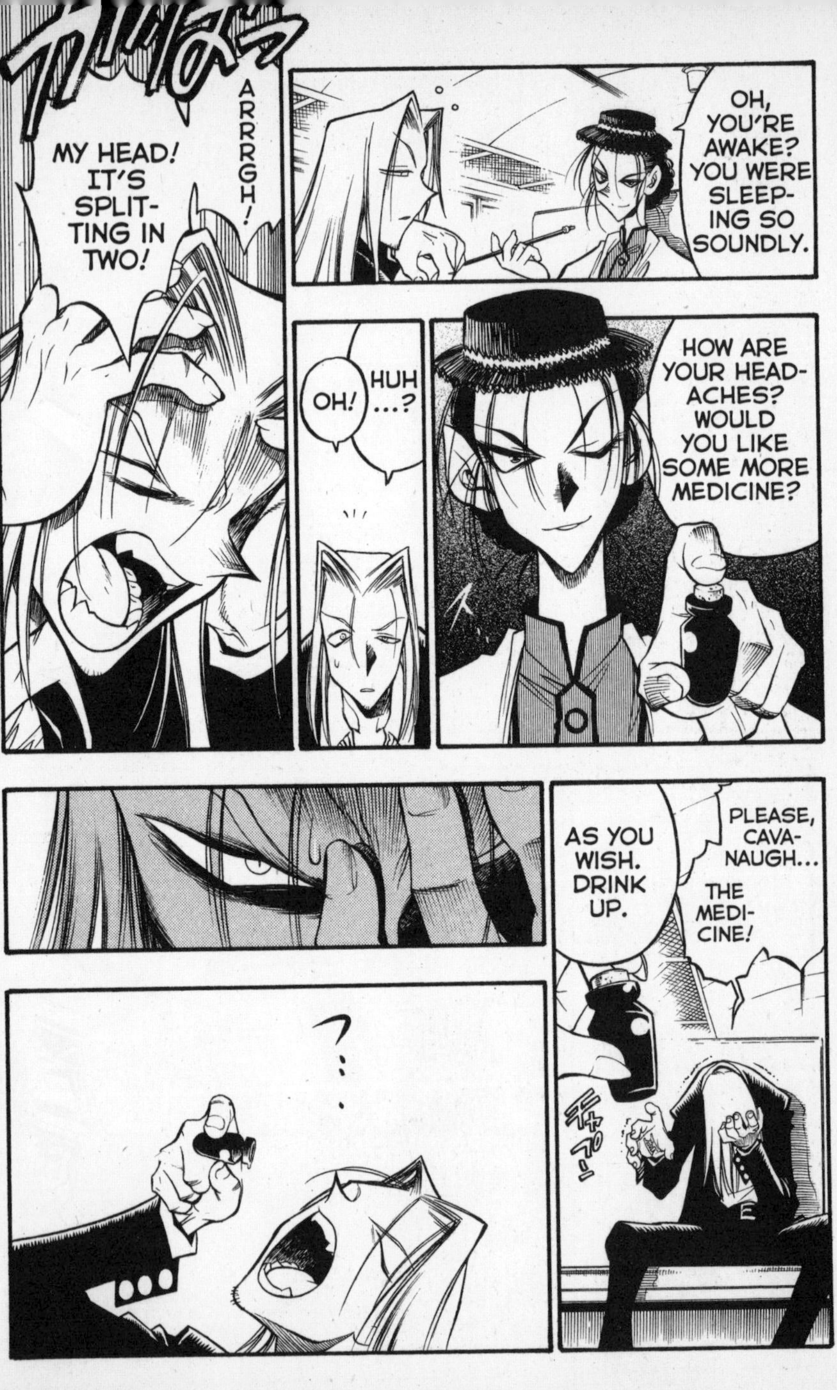
OH, YOU'RE AWAKE? YOU WERE SLEEP-ING SO SOUNDLY.
HOW ARE YOUR HEAD-ACHES? WOULD YOU LIKE SOME MORE MEDICINE?
HUH ...?
OH!
ARRRGH!
MY HEAD! IT'S SPLIT-TING IN TWO!
PLEASE, CAVA-NAUGH...
THE MEDI-CINE!
AS YOU WISH. DRINK UP.

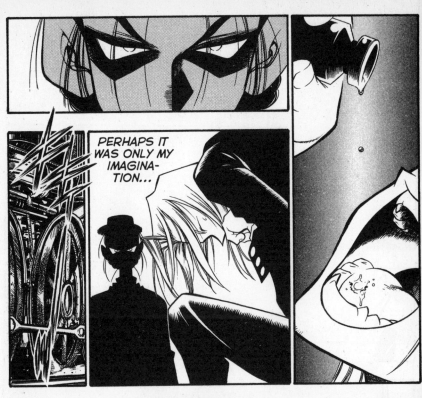

PERHAPS IT WAS ONLY MY IMAGINATION...

ANOTHER STATION?

WHO DESIGNED THIS BLASTED ROUTE?

WE'RE WAY OUT IN THE COUNTRYSIDE. THERE ARE HARDLY ANY PASSENGERS GETTING ON AND OFF AT ALL!

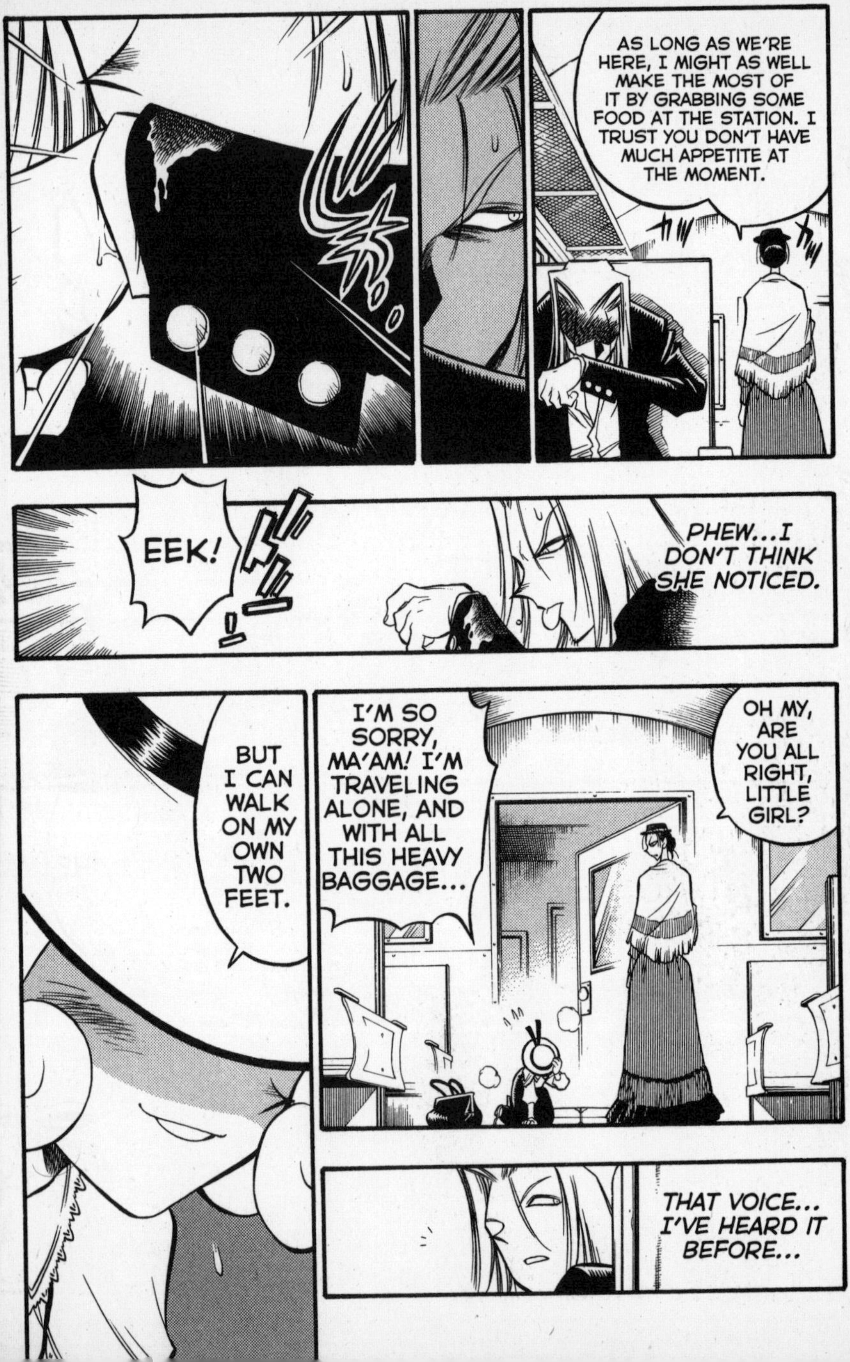
AS LONG AS WE'RE HERE, I MIGHT AS WELL MAKE THE MOST OF IT BY GRABBING SOME FOOD AT THE STATION. I TRUST YOU DON'T HAVE MUCH APPETITE AT THE MOMENT.
PHEW...I DON'T THINK SHE NOTICED.
EEK!
OH MY, ARE YOU ALL RIGHT, LITTLE GIRL?
I'M SO SORRY, MA'AM! I'M TRAVELING ALONE, AND WITH ALL THIS HEAVY BAGGAGE...
THAT VOICE... I'VE HEARD IT BEFORE...
BUT I CAN WALK ON MY OWN TWO FEET.

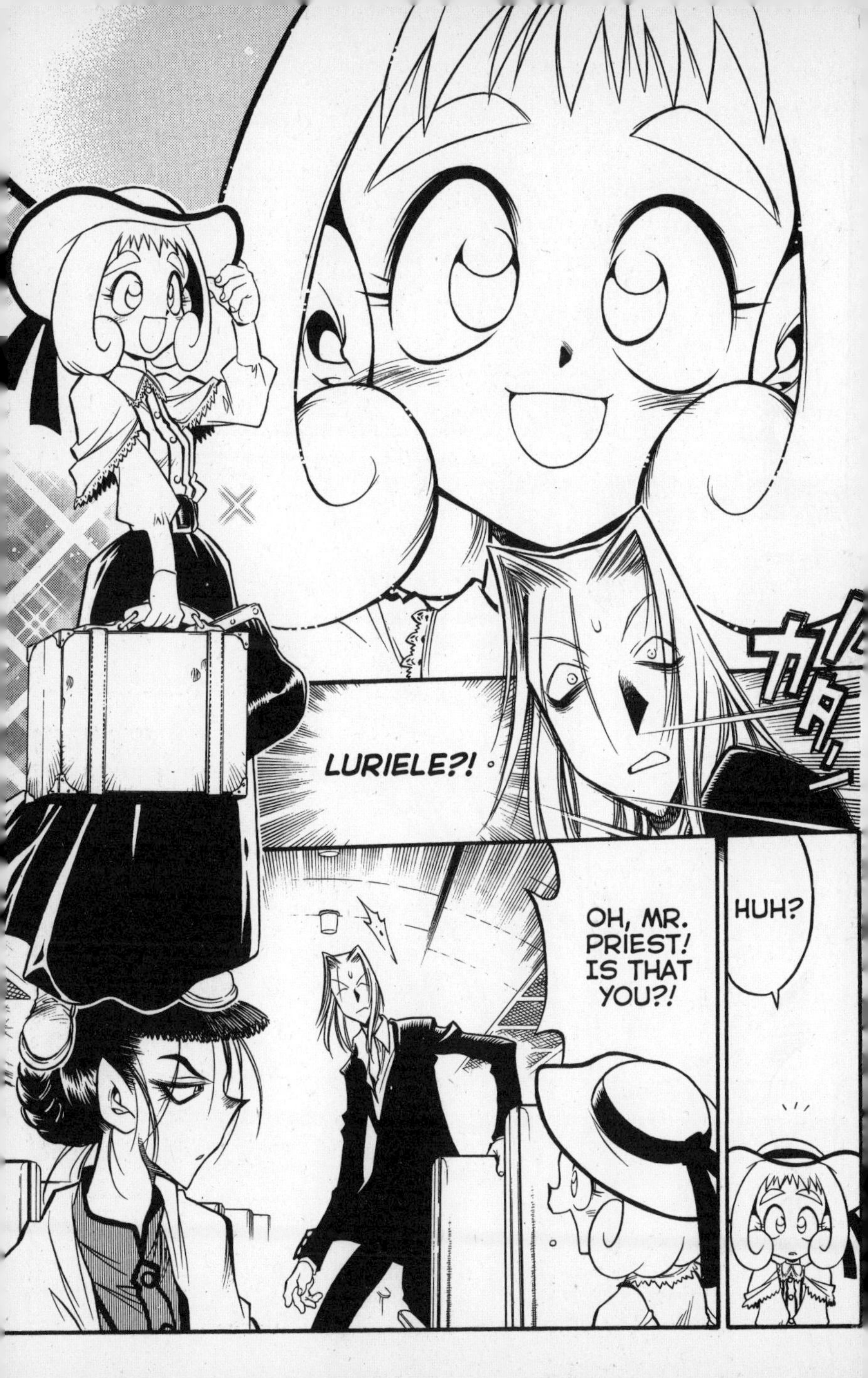
LURIELE?!
HUH?
OH, MR. PRIEST! IS THAT YOU?!

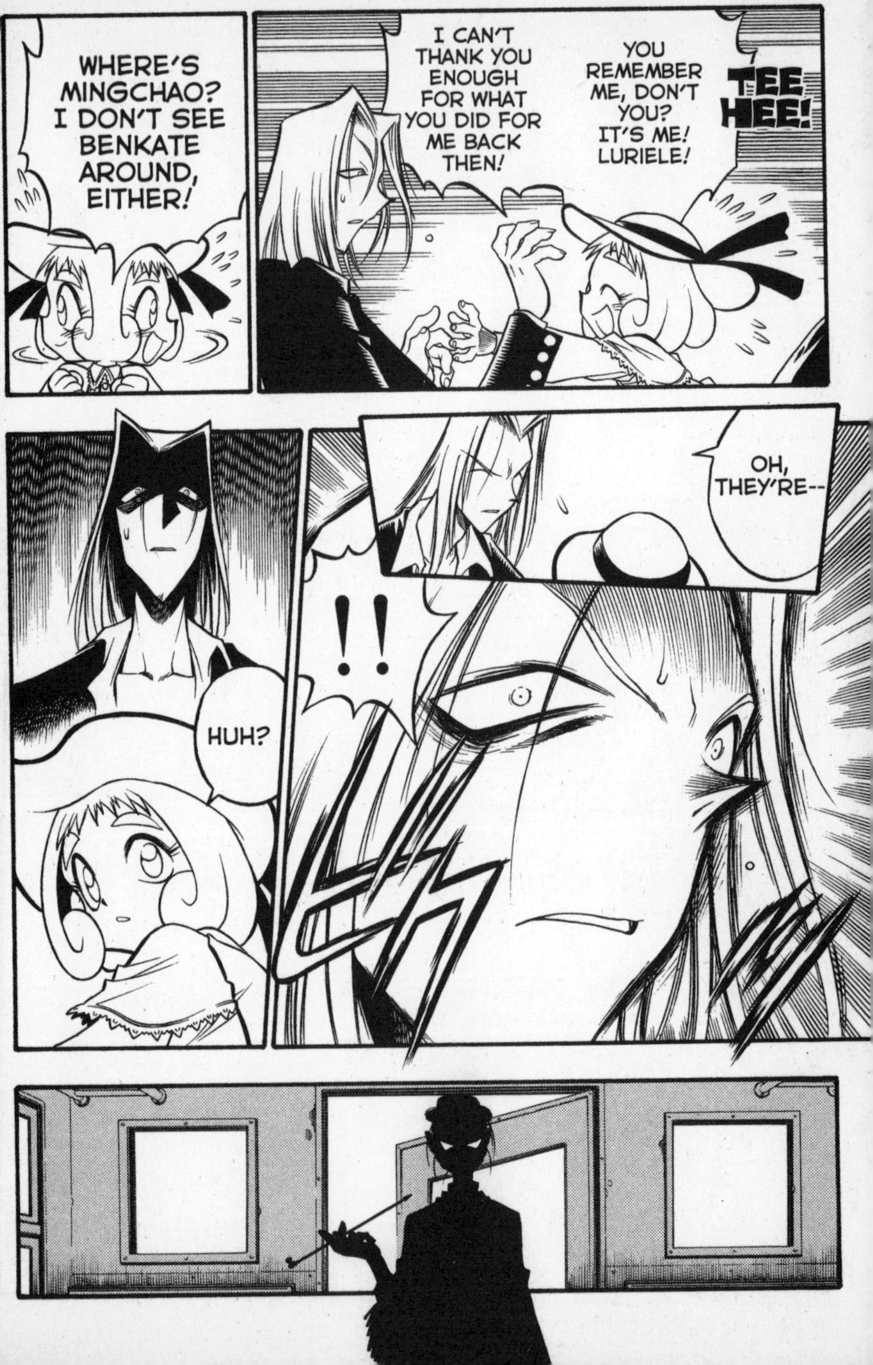
TEE HEE!
YOU REMEMBER ME, DON'T YOU? IT'S ME! LURIELE!
I CAN'T THANK YOU ENOUGH FOR WHAT YOU DID FOR ME BACK THEN!
WHERE'S MINGCHAO? I DON'T SEE BENKATE AROUND, EITHER!
OH, THEY'RE--
!!
HUH?

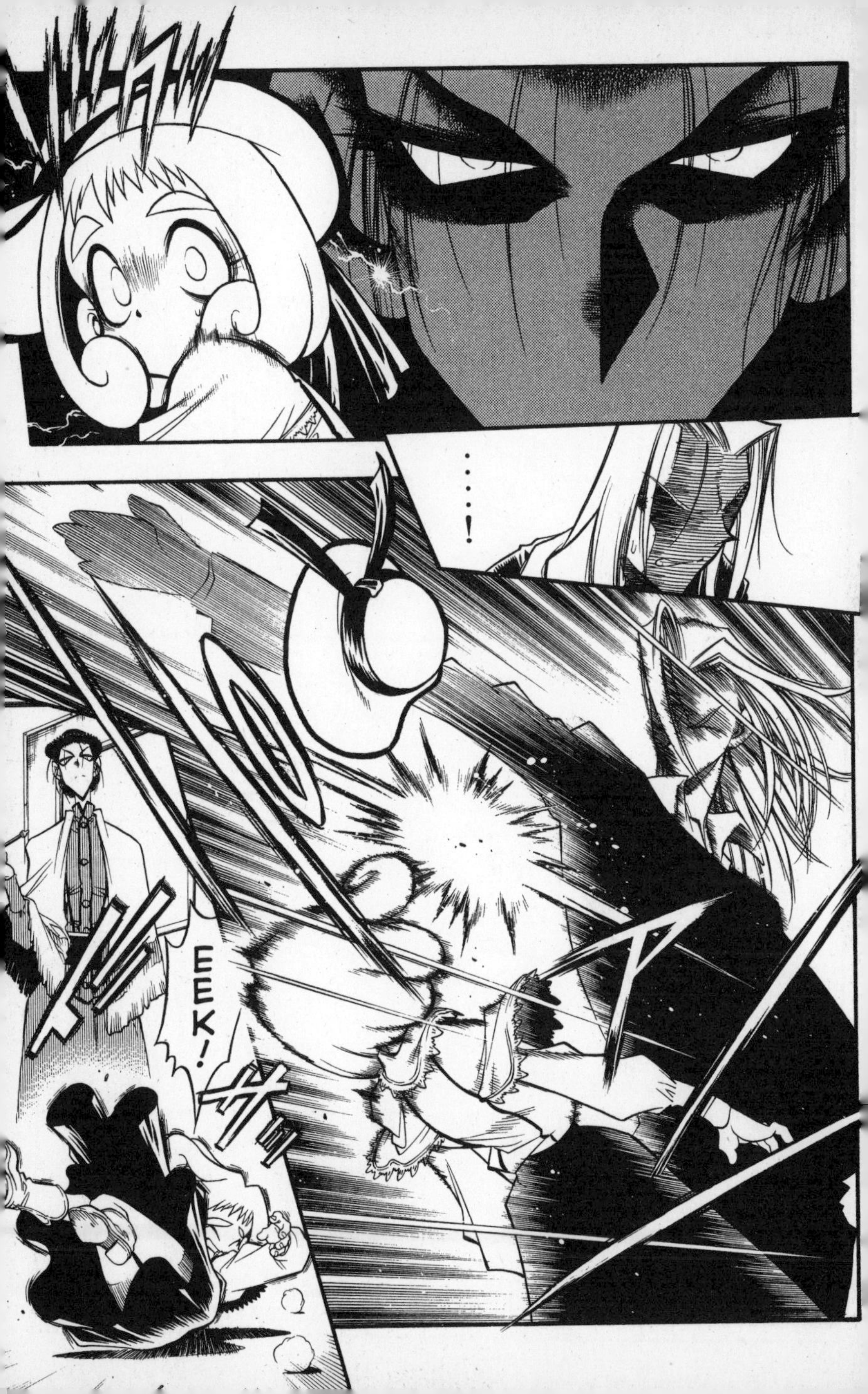

...!
EEK!

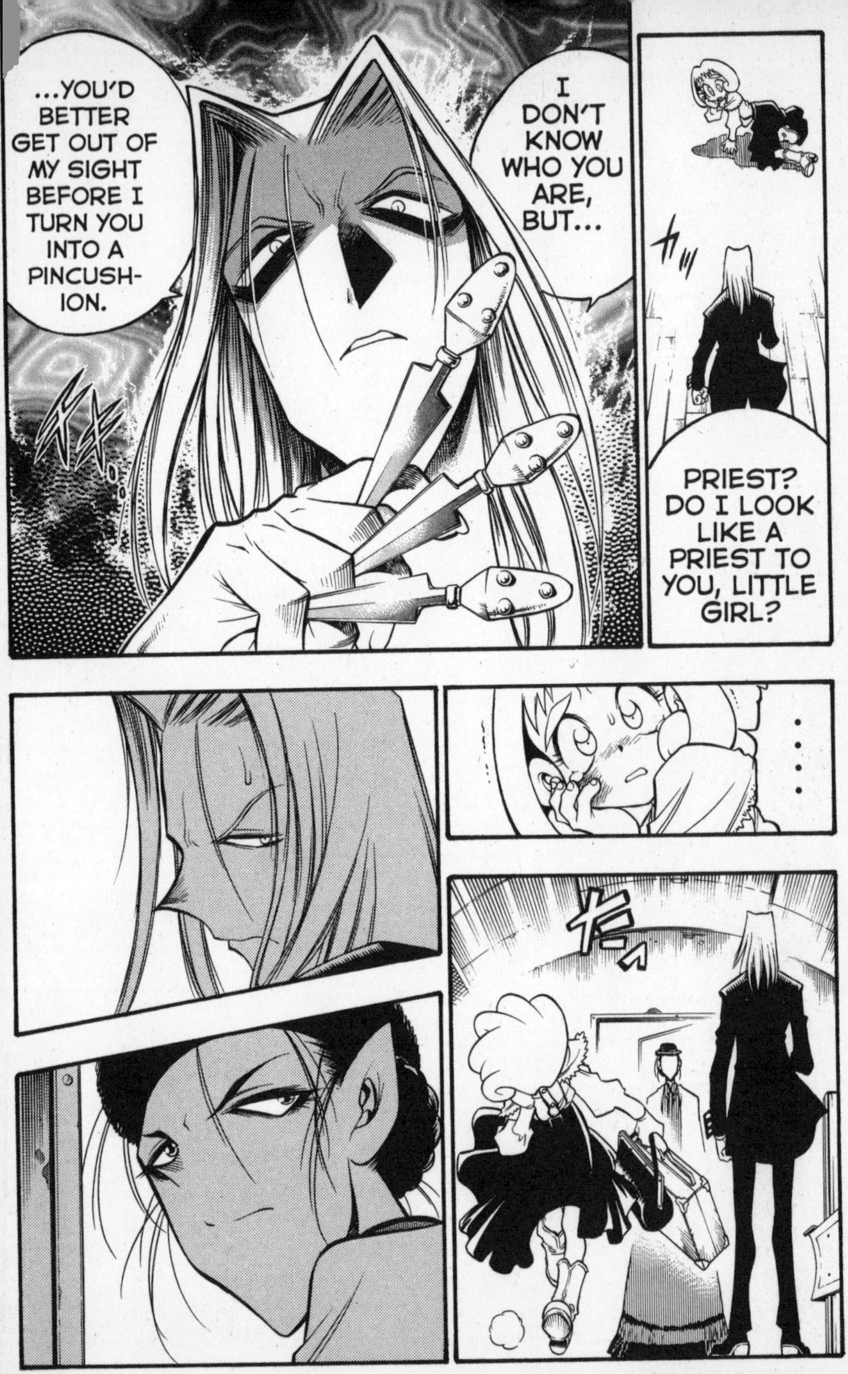
PRIEST? DO I LOOK LIKE A PRIEST TO YOU, LITTLE GIRL?
I DON'T KNOW WHO YOU ARE, BUT...
...YOU'D BETTER GET OUT OF MY SIGHT BEFORE I TURN YOU INTO A PINCUSH-ION.
....

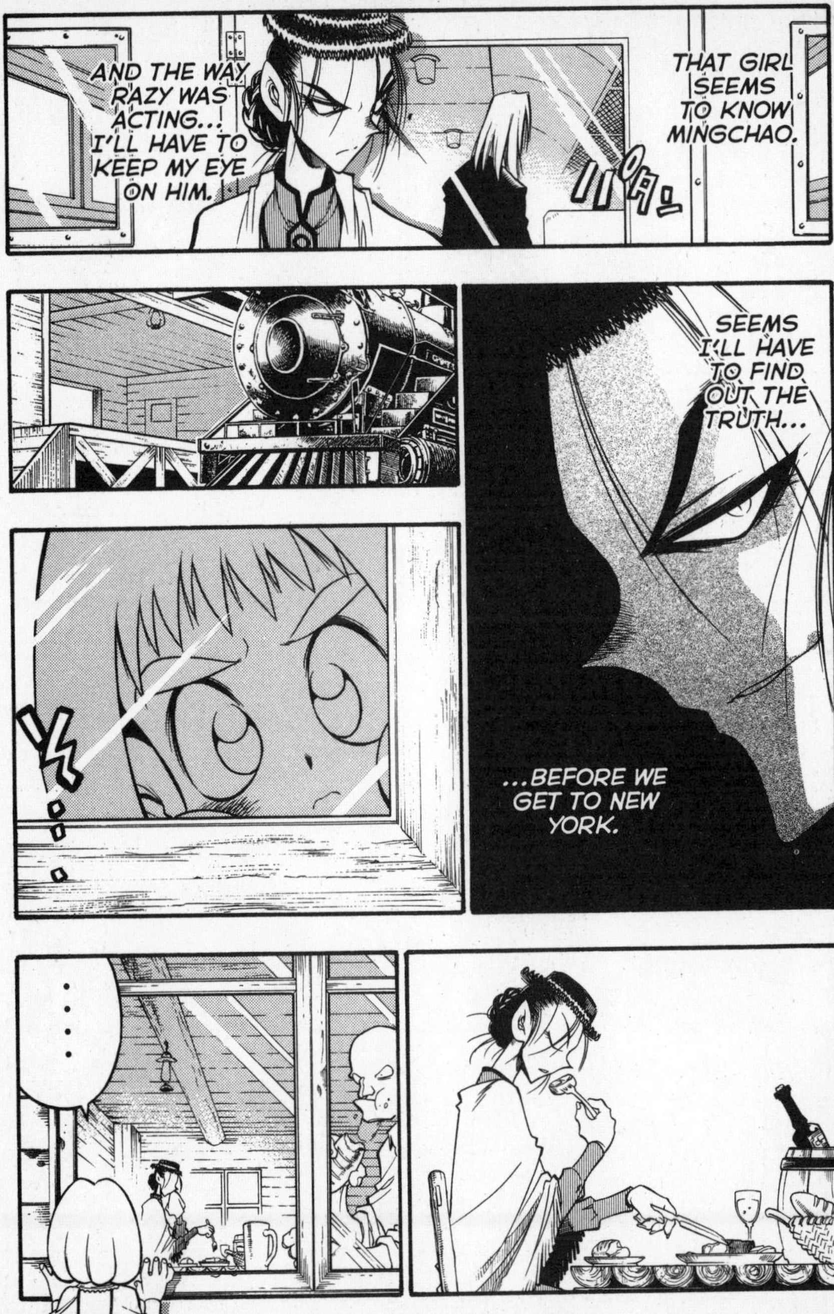
THAT GIRL SEEMS TO KNOW MINGCHAO.
AND THE WAY RAZY WAS ACTING... I'LL HAVE TO KEEP MY EYE ON HIM.
SEEMS I'LL HAVE TO FIND OUT THE TRUTH...
...BEFORE WE GET TO NEW YORK.
....

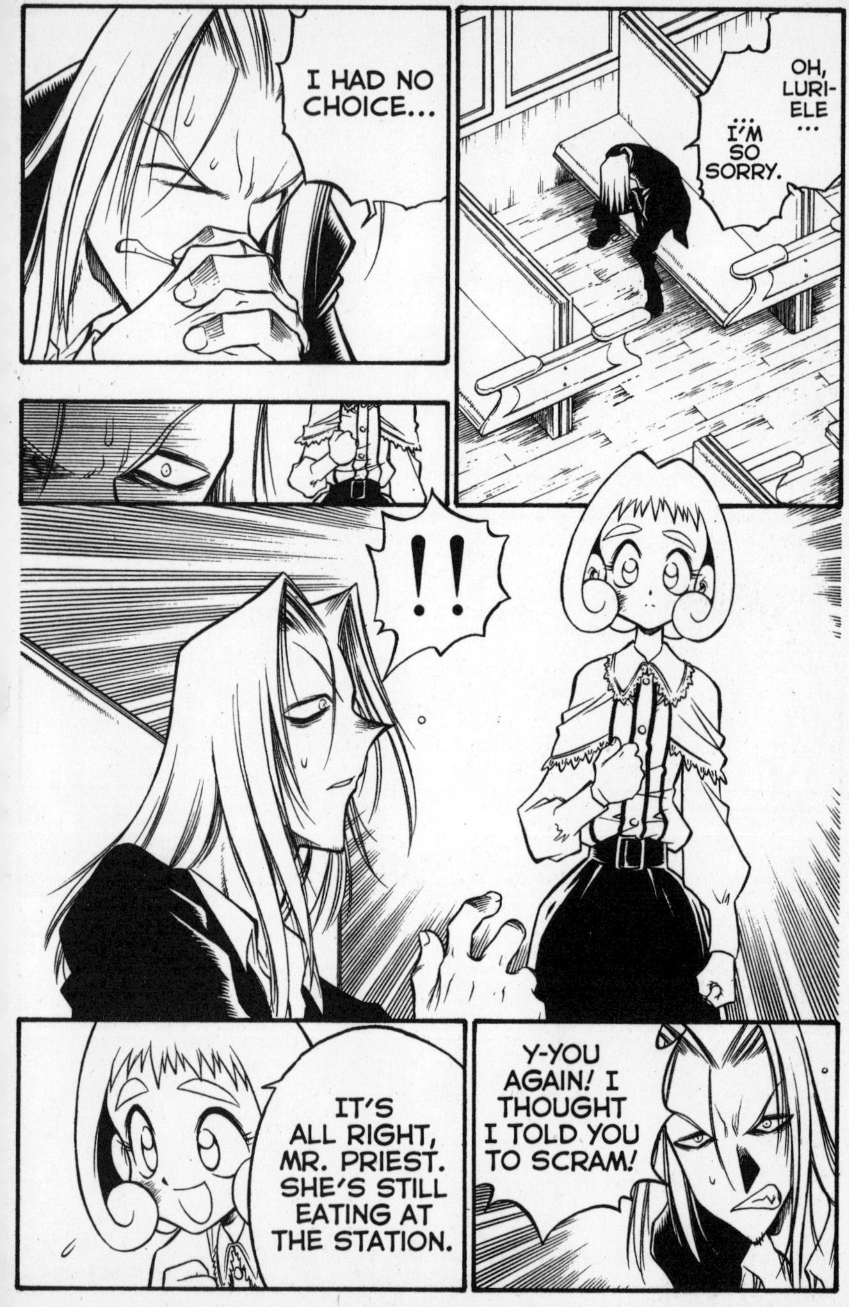
OH, LURI-ELE ...
... I'M SO SORRY.
I HAD NO CHOICE...
!!
Y-YOU AGAIN! I THOUGHT I TOLD YOU TO SCRAM!
IT'S ALL RIGHT, MR. PRIEST. SHE'S STILL EATING AT THE STATION.

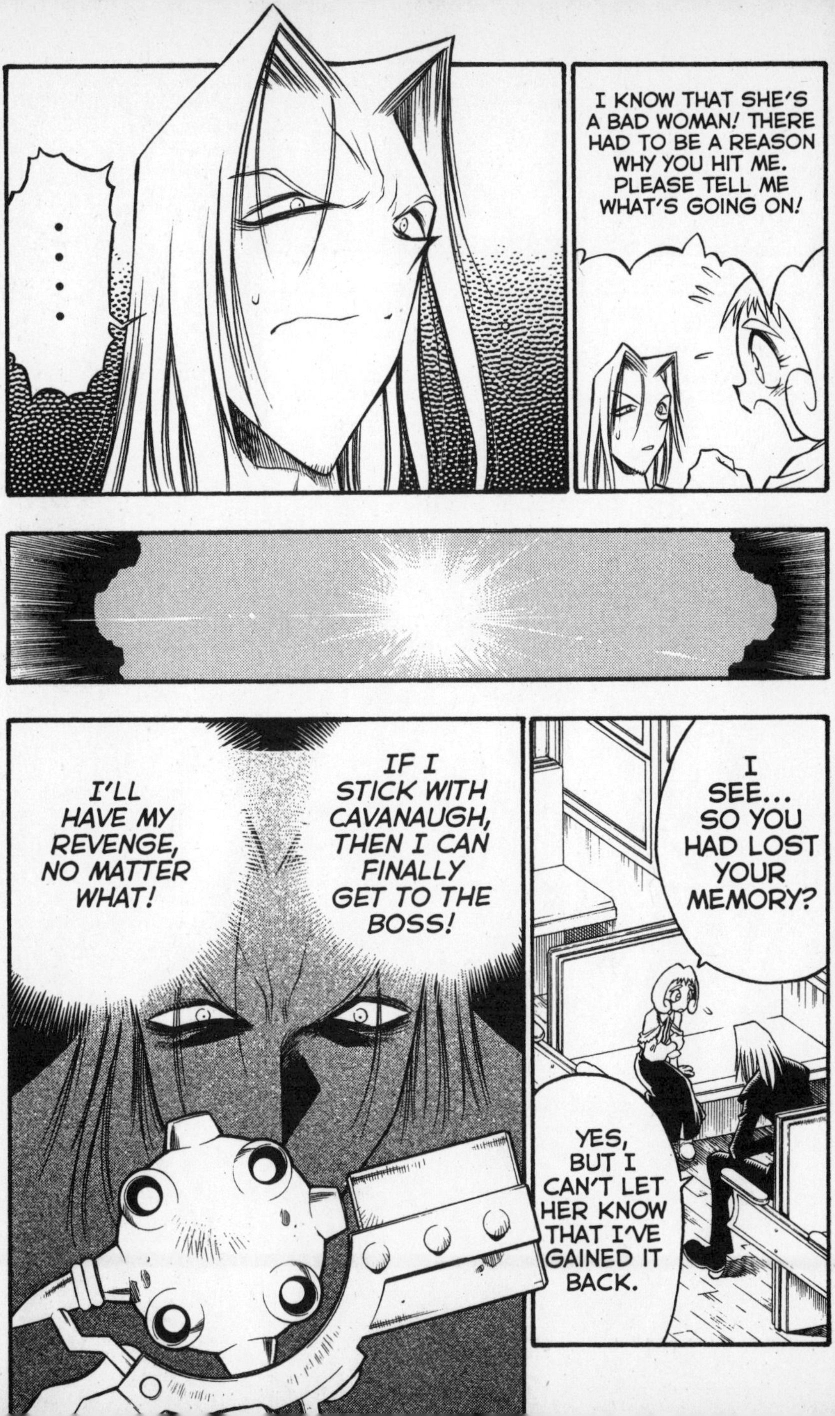
I KNOW THAT SHE'S A BAD WOMAN! THERE HAD TO BE A REASON WHY YOU HIT ME. PLEASE TELL ME WHAT'S GOING ON!
....
I SEE... SO YOU HAD LOST YOUR MEMORY?
YES, BUT I CAN'T LET HER KNOW THAT I'VE GAINED IT BACK.
IF I STICK WITH CAVANAUGH, THEN I CAN FINALLY GET TO THE BOSS!
I'LL HAVE MY REVENGE, NO MATTER WHAT!

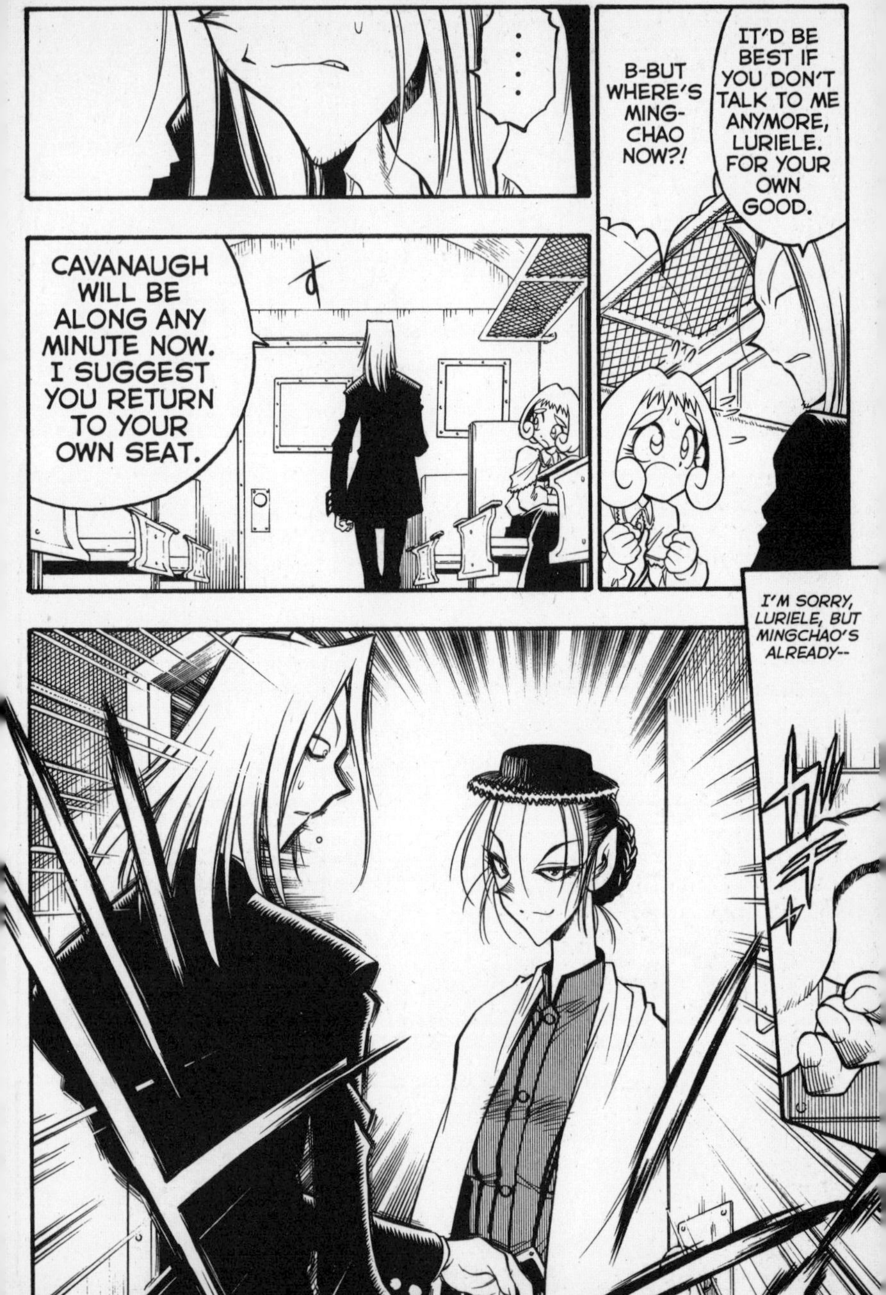
IT'D BE BEST IF YOU DON'T TALK TO ME ANYMORE, LURIELE. FOR YOUR OWN GOOD.
B-BUT WHERE'S MING-CHAO NOW?!
....
CAVANAUGH WILL BE ALONG ANY MINUTE NOW. I SUGGEST YOU RETURN TO YOUR OWN SEAT.
I'M SORRY, LURIELE, BUT MINGCHAO'S ALREADY--

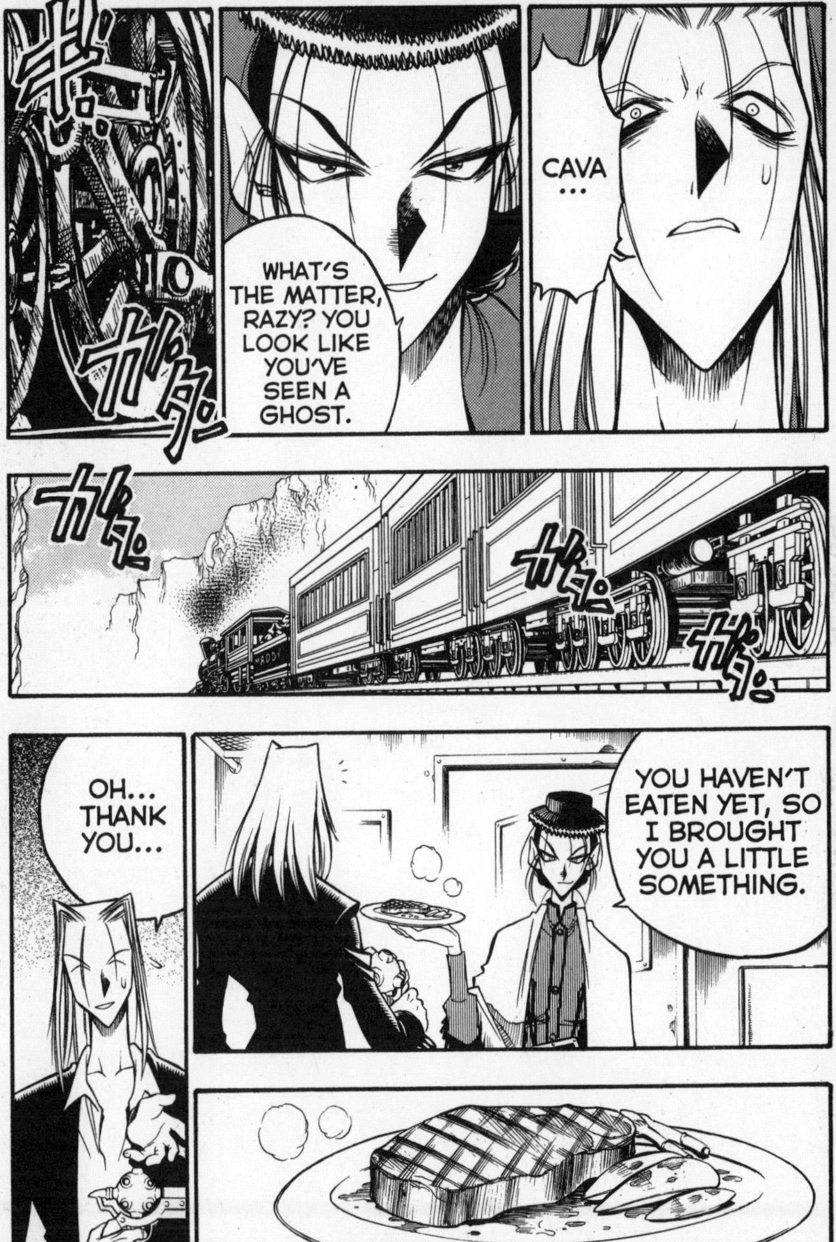
CAVA
...
WHAT'S THE MATTER, RAZY? YOU LOOK LIKE YOU'VE SEEN A GHOST.
YOU HAVEN'T EATEN YET, SO I BROUGHT YOU A LITTLE SOMETHING.
OH... THANK YOU...

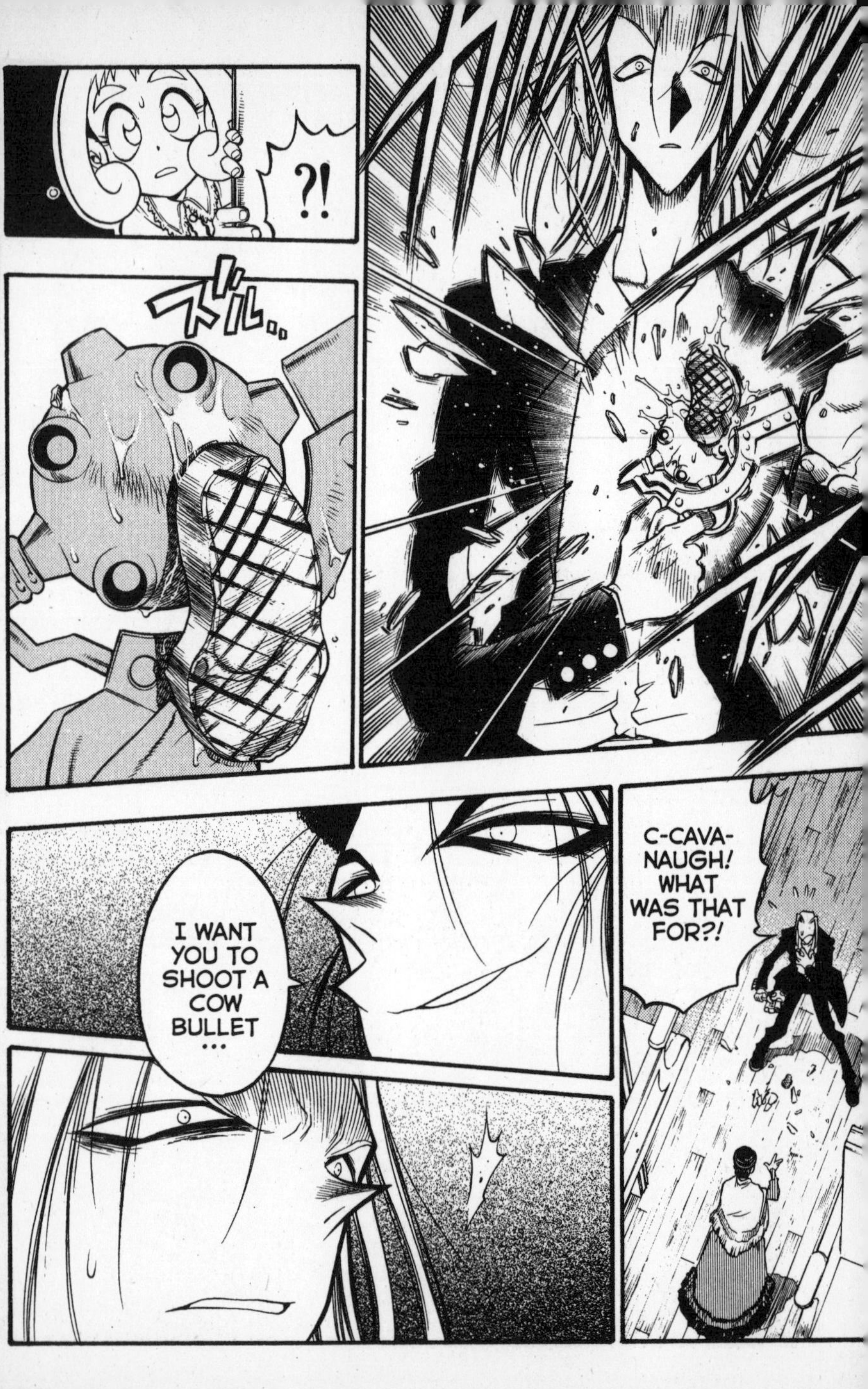
?!
ズル..
C-CAVA-NAUGH! WHAT WAS THAT FOR?!
I WANT YOU TO SHOOT A COW BULLET ...

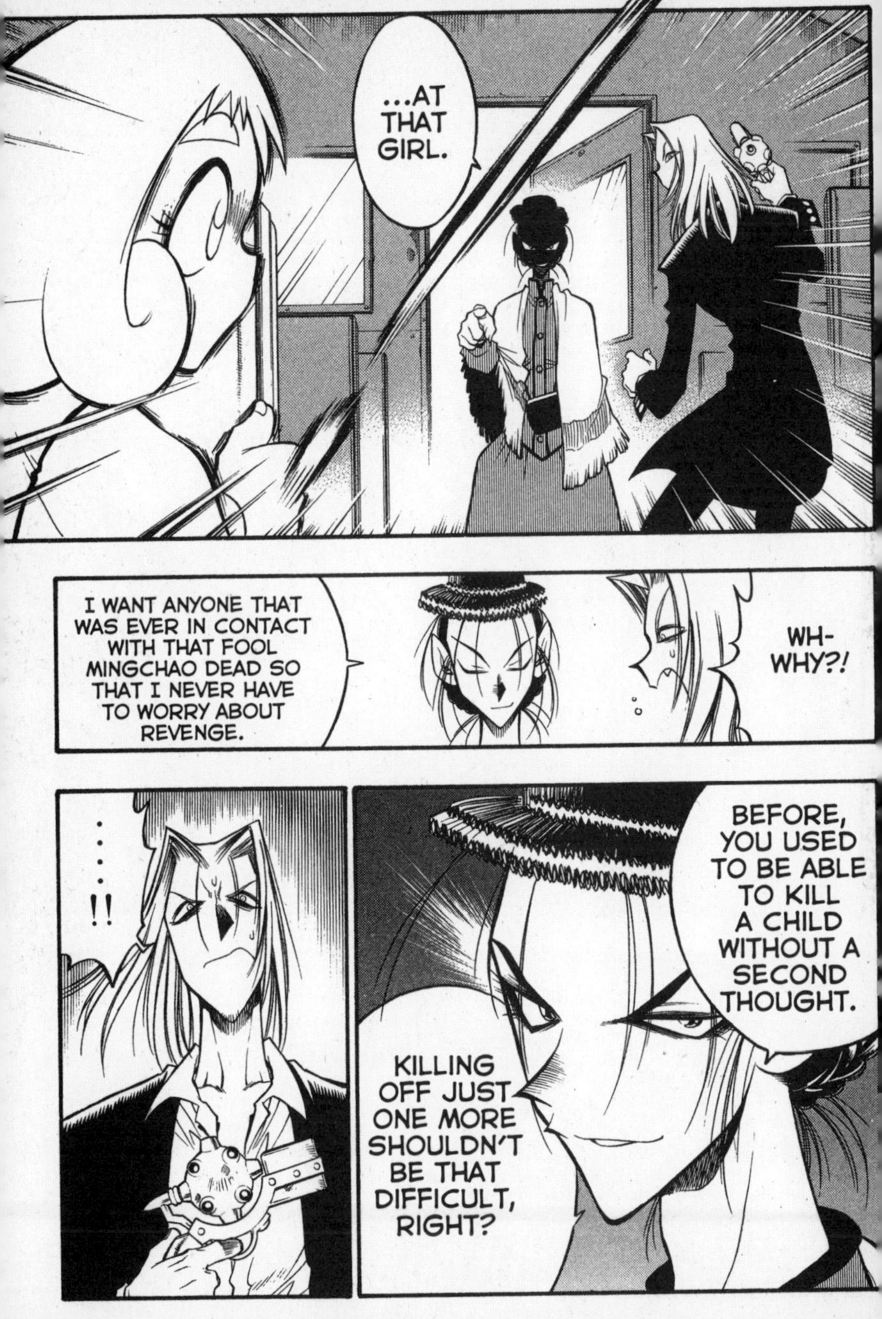
...AT THAT GIRL.
WH- WHY?!
I WANT ANYONE THAT WAS EVER IN CONTACT WITH THAT FOOL MINGCHAO DEAD SO THAT I NEVER HAVE TO WORRY ABOUT REVENGE.
BEFORE, YOU USED TO BE ABLE TO KILL A CHILD WITHOUT A SECOND THOUGHT.
KILLING OFF JUST ONE MORE SHOULDN'T BE THAT DIFFICULT, RIGHT?
......!!

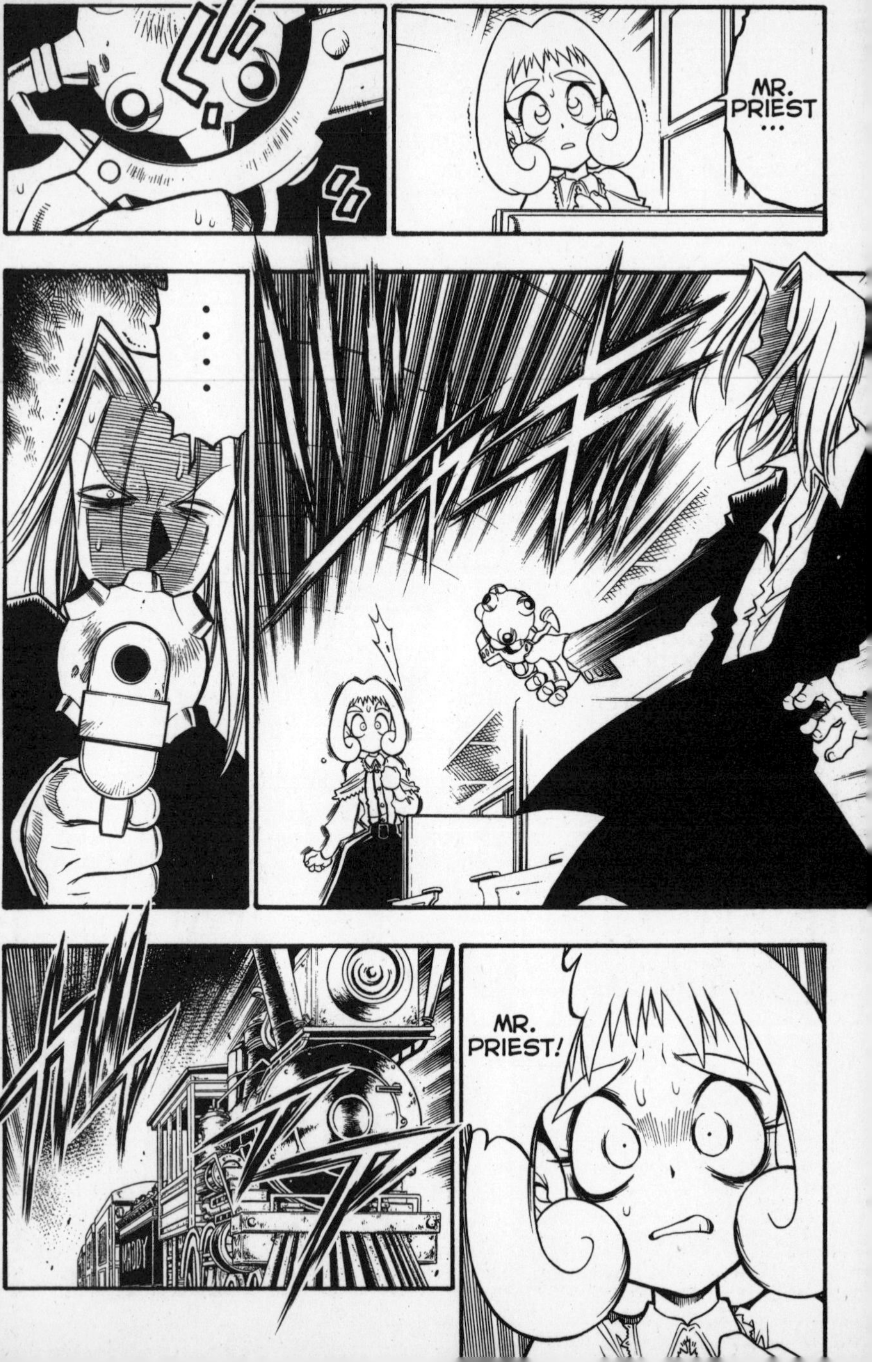
MR. PRIEST ...
....
MR. PRIEST!

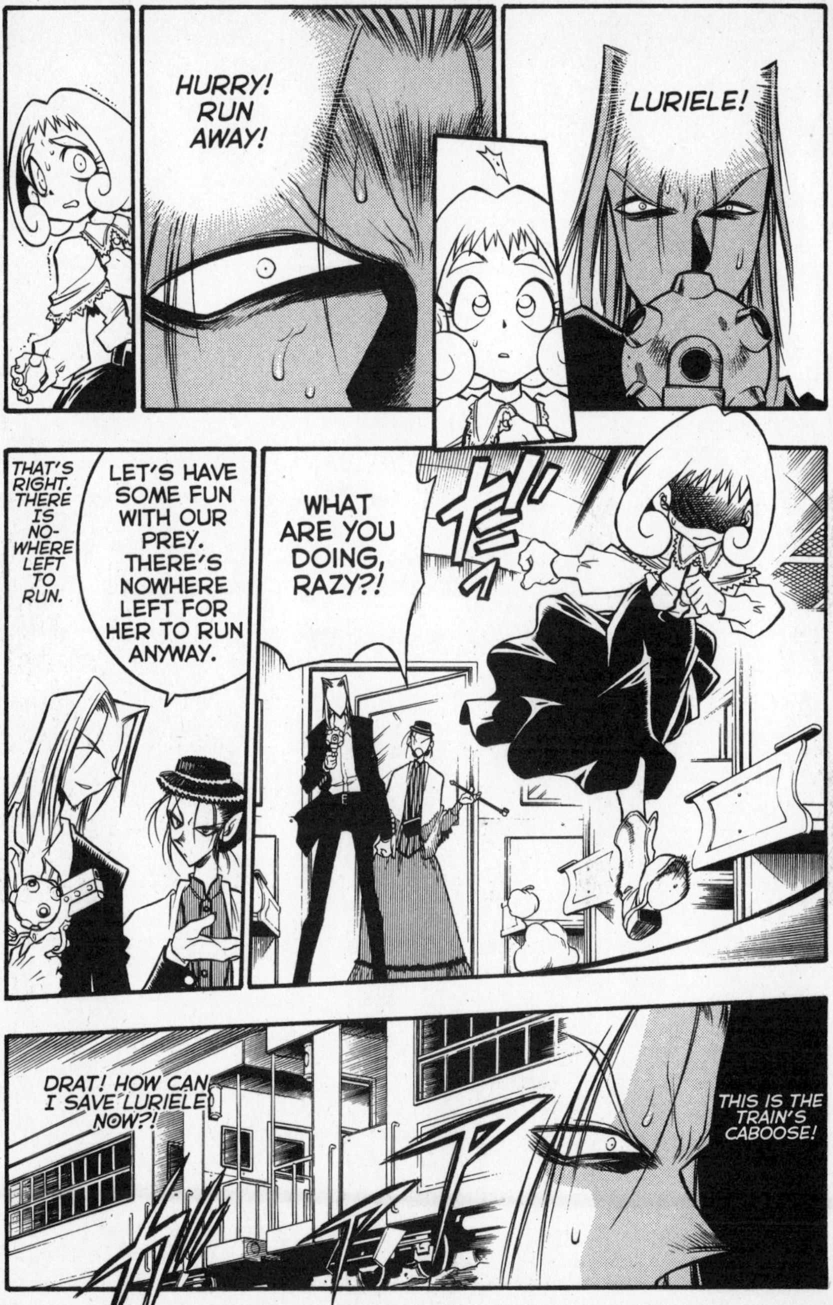
LURIELE!
HURRY! RUN AWAY!
WHAT ARE YOU DOING, RAZY?!
LET'S HAVE SOME FUN WITH OUR PREY. THERE'S NOWHERE LEFT FOR HER TO RUN ANYWAY.
THAT'S RIGHT. THERE IS NO-WHERE LEFT TO RUN.
THIS IS THE TRAIN'S CABOOSE!
DRAT! HOW CAN I SAVE LURIELE NOW?!

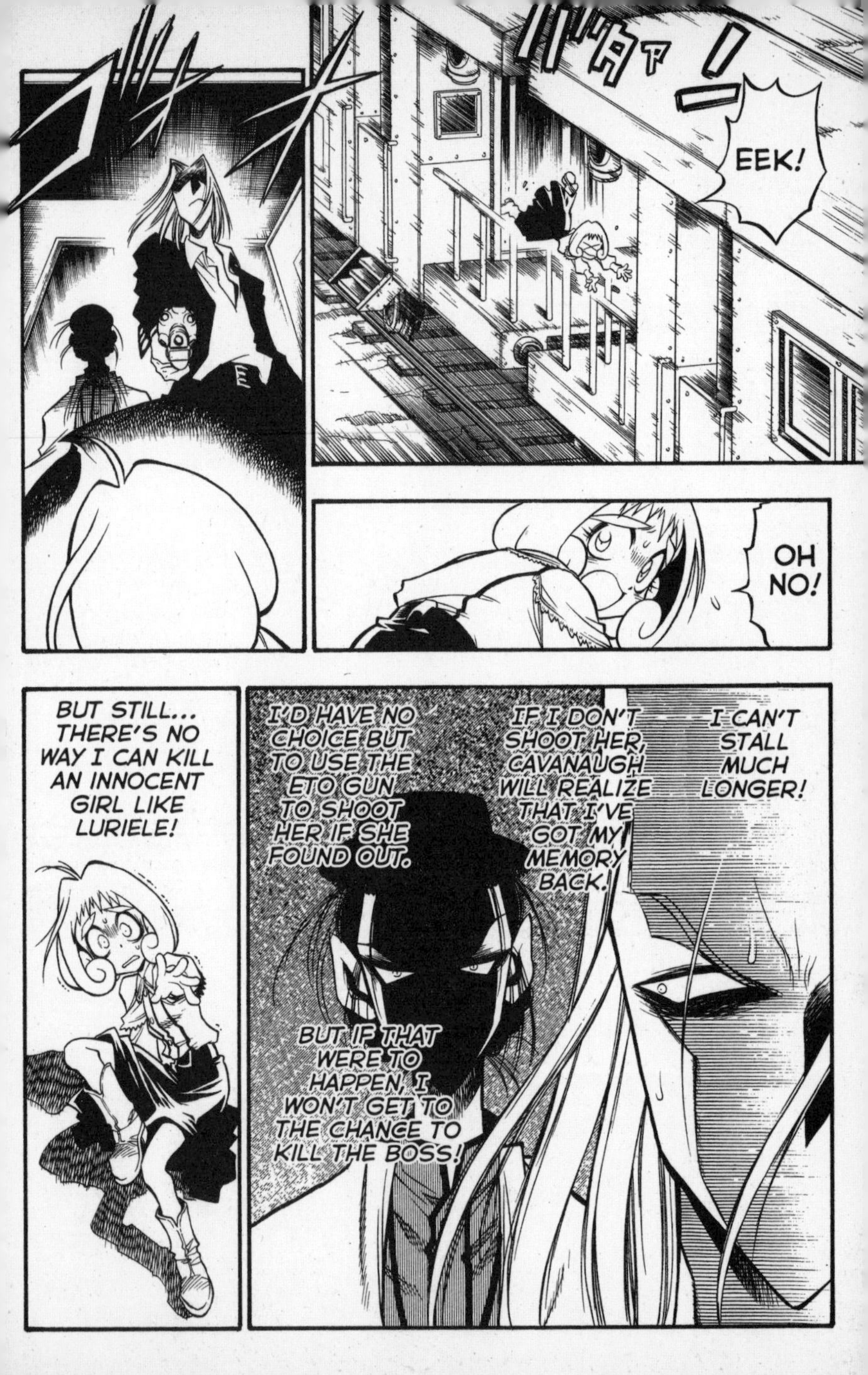
EEK!
OH NO!
I CAN'T STALL MUCH LONGER!
IF I DON'T SHOOT HER, CAVANAUGH WILL REALIZE THAT I'VE GOT MY MEMORY BACK.
I'D HAVE NO CHOICE BUT TO USE THE ETO GUN TO SHOOT HER IF SHE FOUND OUT.
BUT IF THAT WERE TO HAPPEN, I WON'T GET TO THE CHANCE TO KILL THE BOSS!
BUT STILL... THERE'S NO WAY I CAN KILL AN INNOCENT GIRL LIKE LURIELE!

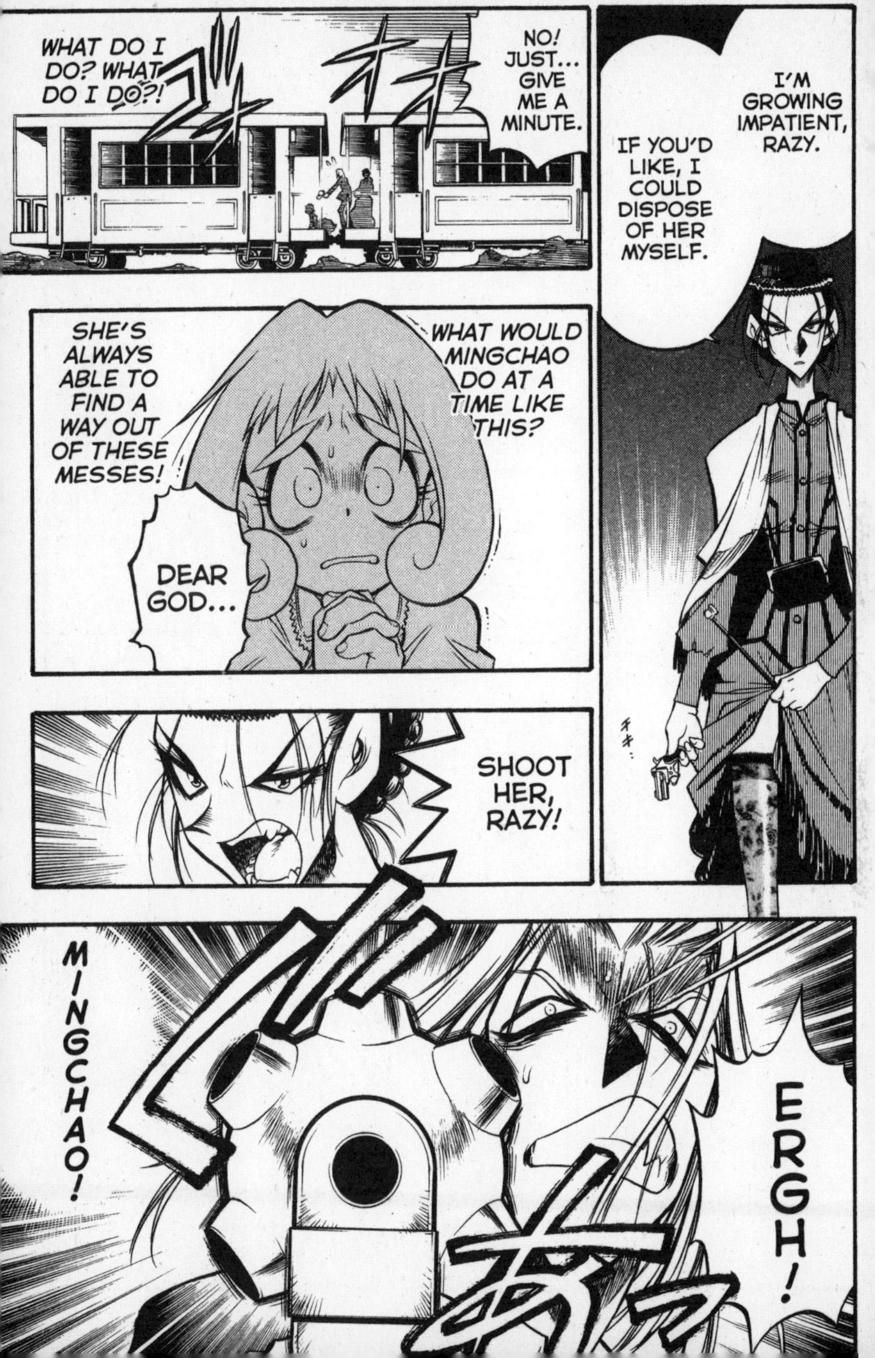
I'M GROWING IMPATIENT, RAZY.
IF YOU'D LIKE, I COULD DISPOSE OF HER MYSELF.
NO! JUST... GIVE ME A MINUTE.
WHAT DO I DO? WHAT DO I DO?!
WHAT WOULD MINGCHAO DO AT A TIME LIKE THIS?
SHE'S ALWAYS ABLE TO FIND A WAY OUT OF THESE MESSES!
DEAR GOD...
SHOOT HER, RAZY!
ERGH!
MINGCHAO!

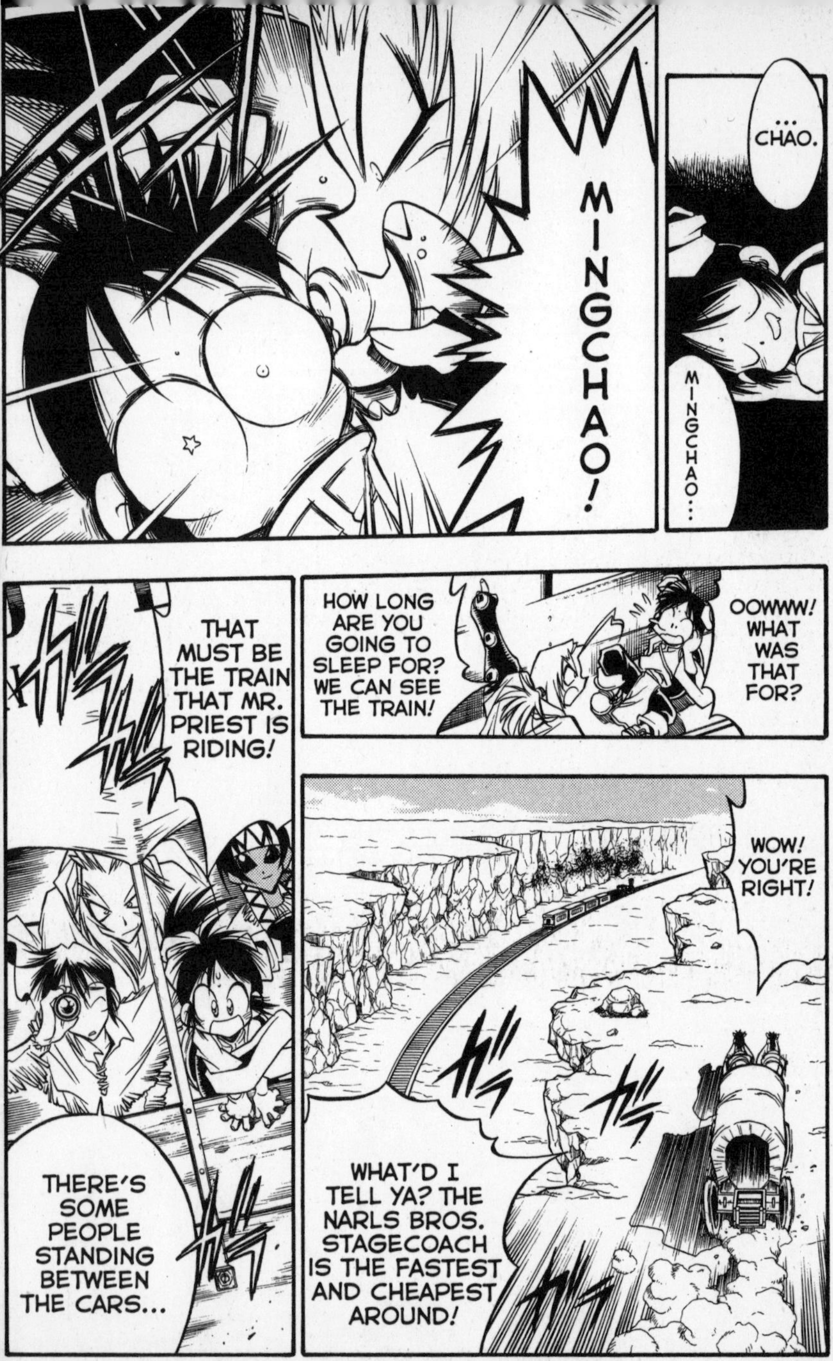
...CHAO.
MINGCHAO...
MINGCHAO!
OOWWW! WHAT WAS THAT FOR?
HOW LONG ARE YOU GOING TO SLEEP FOR? WE CAN SEE THE TRAIN!
WOW! YOU'RE RIGHT!
WHAT'D I TELL YA? THE NARLS BROS. STAGECOACH IS THE FASTEST AND CHEAPEST AROUND!
THAT MUST BE THE TRAIN THAT MR. PRIEST IS RIDING!
THERE'S SOME PEOPLE STANDING BETWEEN THE CARS...

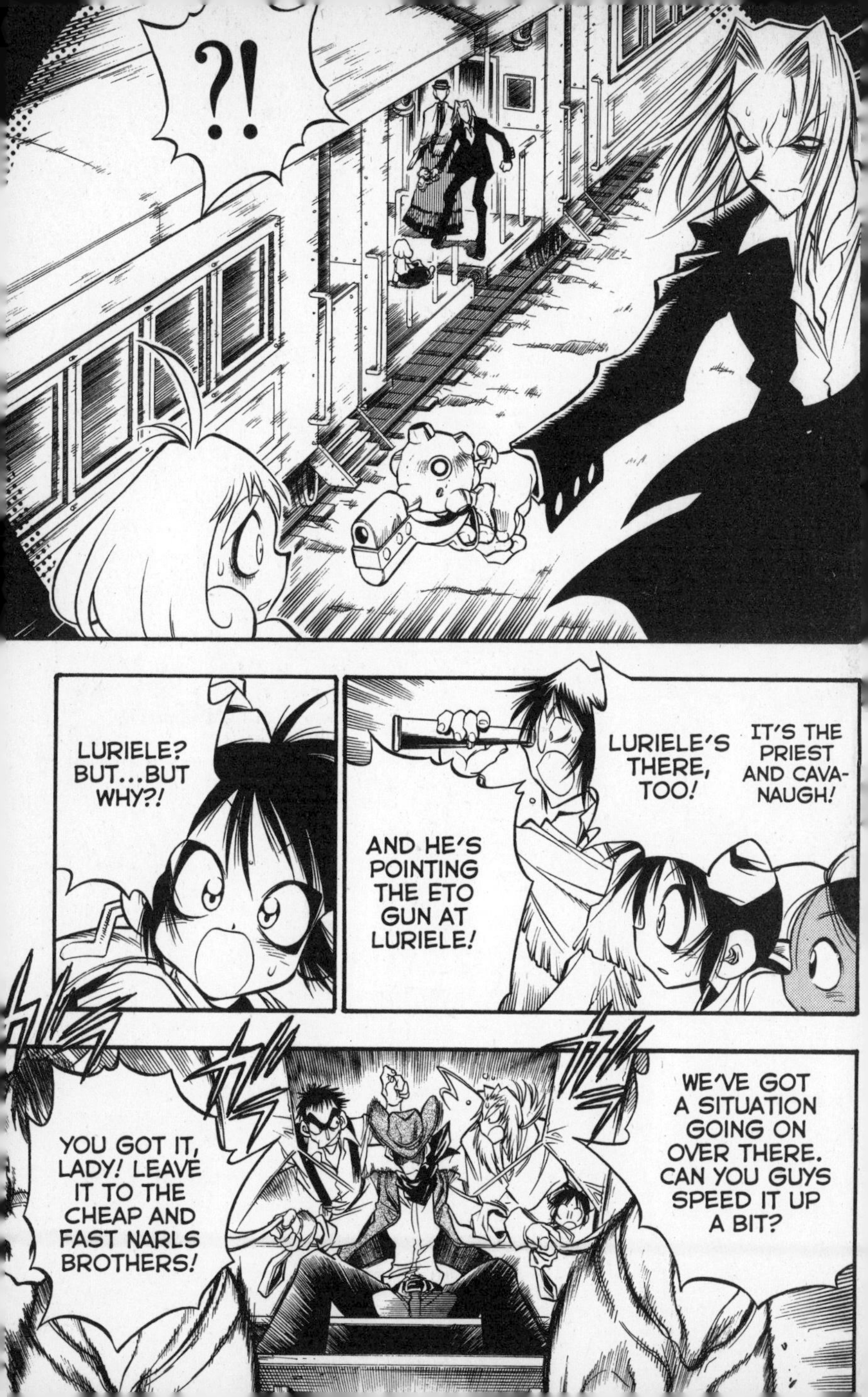
?!
IT'S THE PRIEST AND CAVA-NAUGH!
LURIELE'S THERE, TOO!
AND HE'S POINTING THE ETO GUN AT LURIELE!
LURIELE? BUT...BUT WHY?!
WE'VE GOT A SITUATION GOING ON OVER THERE. CAN YOU GUYS SPEED IT UP A BIT?
YOU GOT IT, LADY! LEAVE IT TO THE CHEAP AND FAST NARLS BROTHERS!

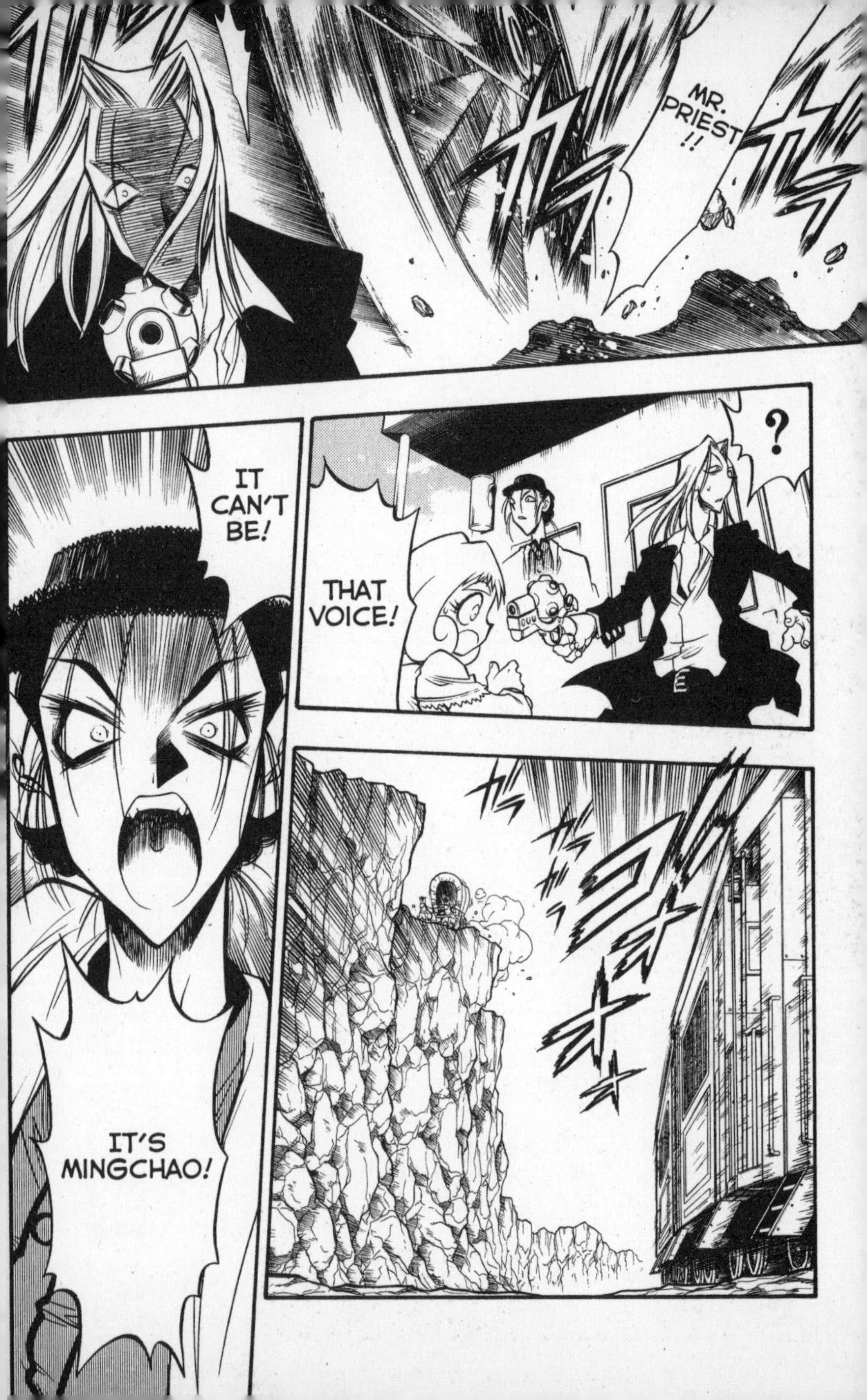
MR. PRIEST!!
?
THAT VOICE!
IT CAN'T BE!
IT'S MINGCHAO!

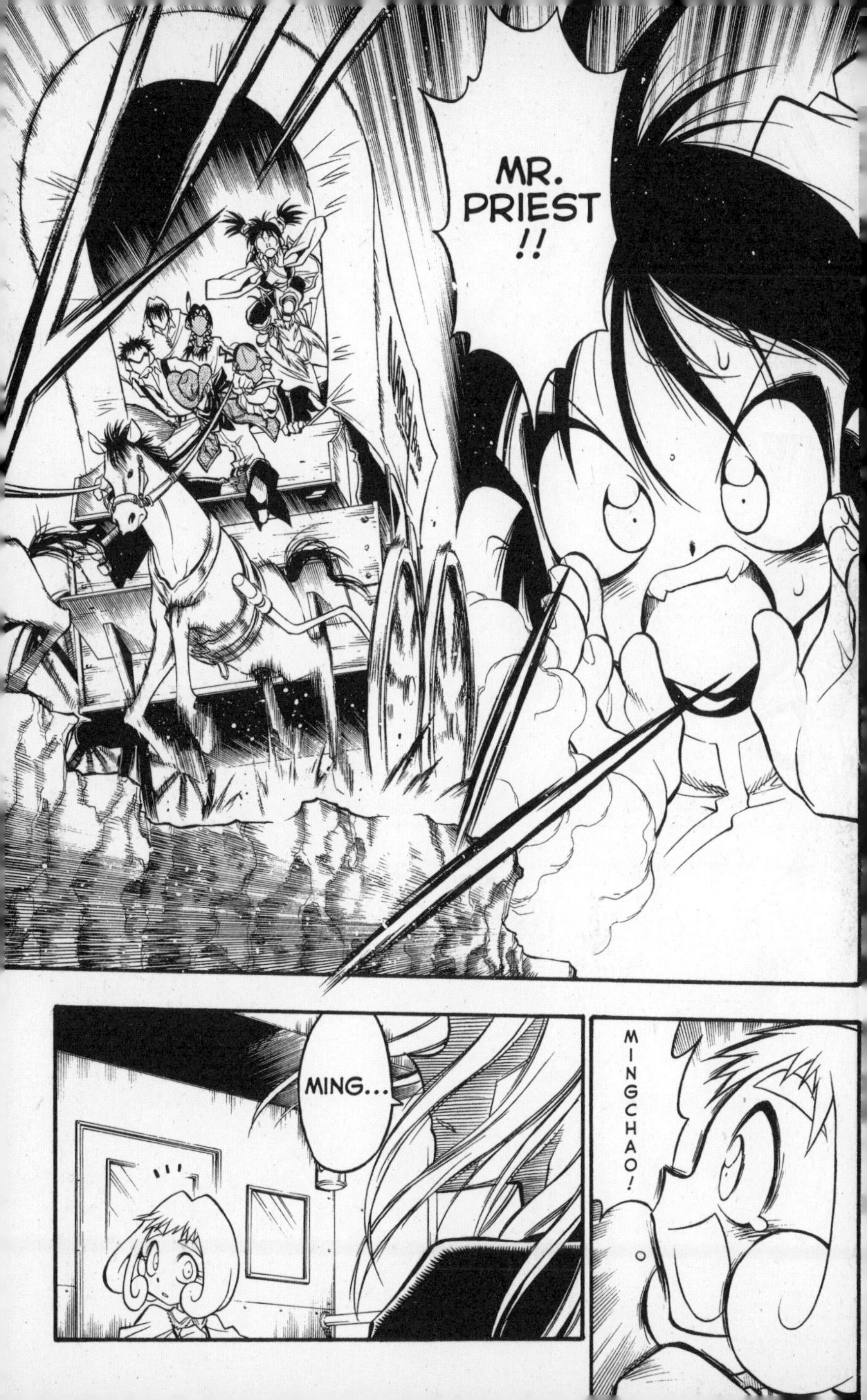
MR. PRIEST !!
MINGCHAO!
MING...

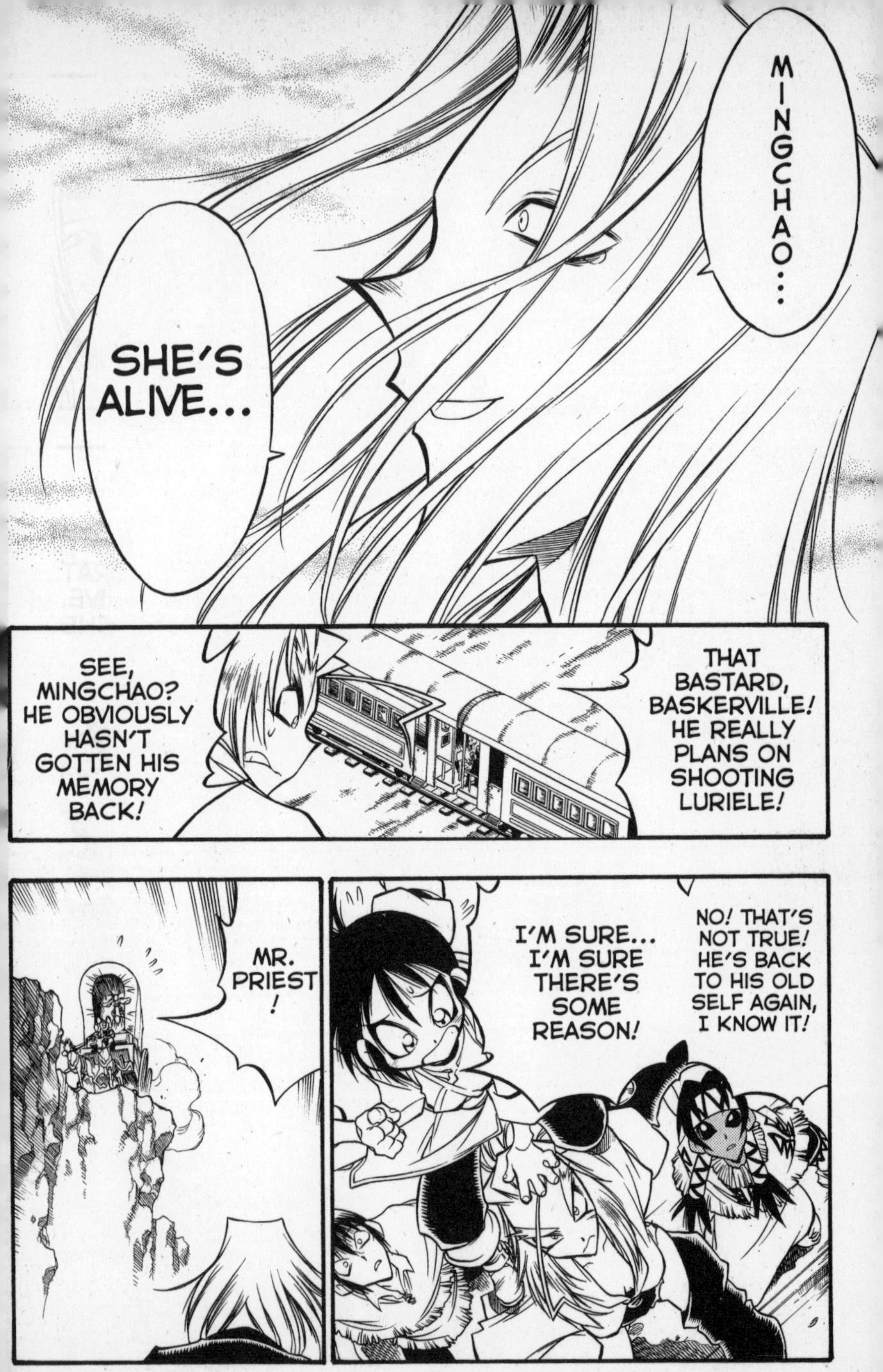
MINGCHAO...
SHE'S ALIVE...
THAT BASTARD, BASKERVILLE! HE REALLY PLANS ON SHOOTING LURIELE!
SEE, MINGCHAO? HE OBVIOUSLY HASN'T GOTTEN HIS MEMORY BACK!
NO! THAT'S NOT TRUE! HE'S BACK TO HIS OLD SELF AGAIN, I KNOW IT!
I'M SURE... I'M SURE THERE'S SOME REASON!
MR. PRIEST!

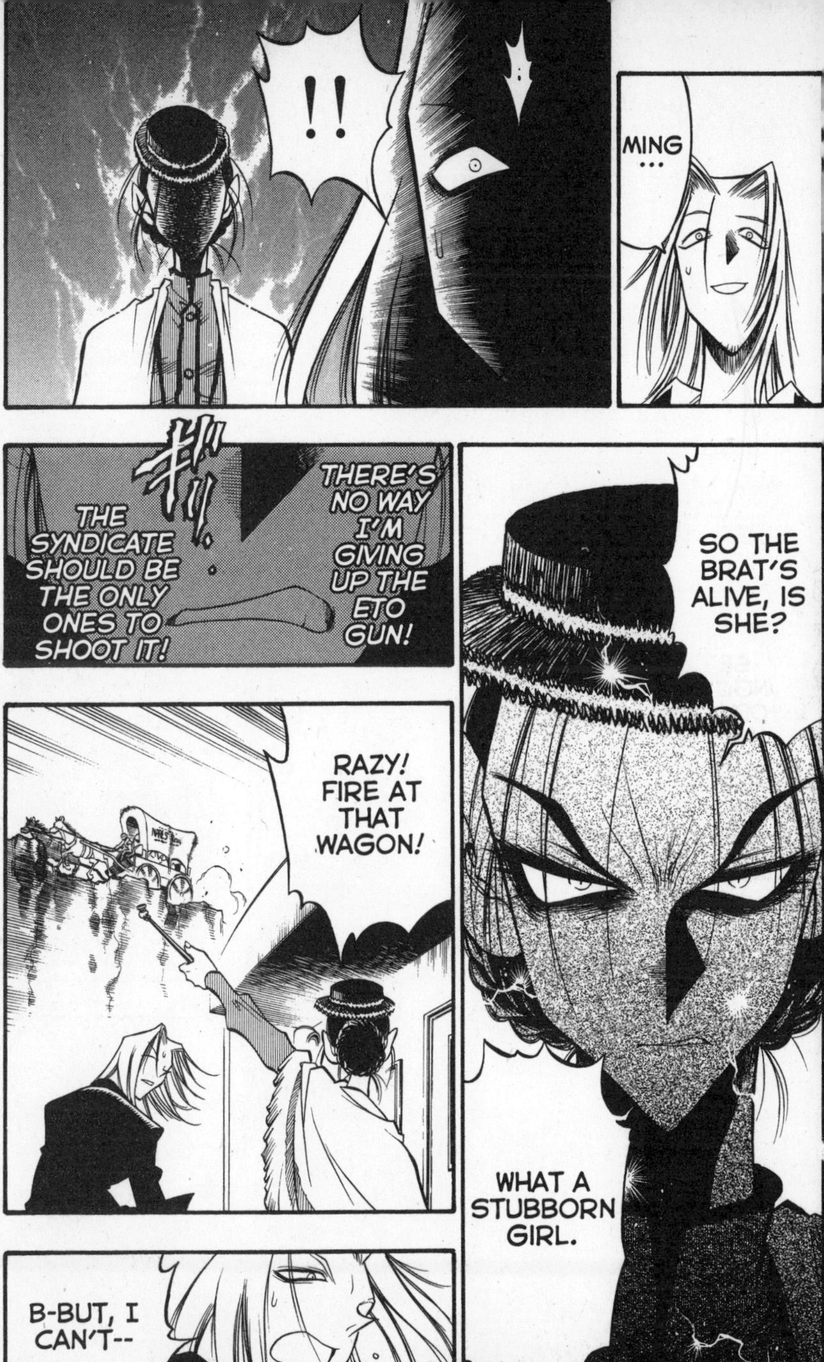
MING ...
!!
SO THE BRAT'S ALIVE, IS SHE?
WHAT A STUBBORN GIRL.
THERE'S NO WAY I'M GIVING UP THE ETO GUN!
THE SYNDICATE SHOULD BE THE ONLY ONES TO SHOOT IT!
RAZY! FIRE AT THAT WAGON!
B-BUT, I CAN'T--

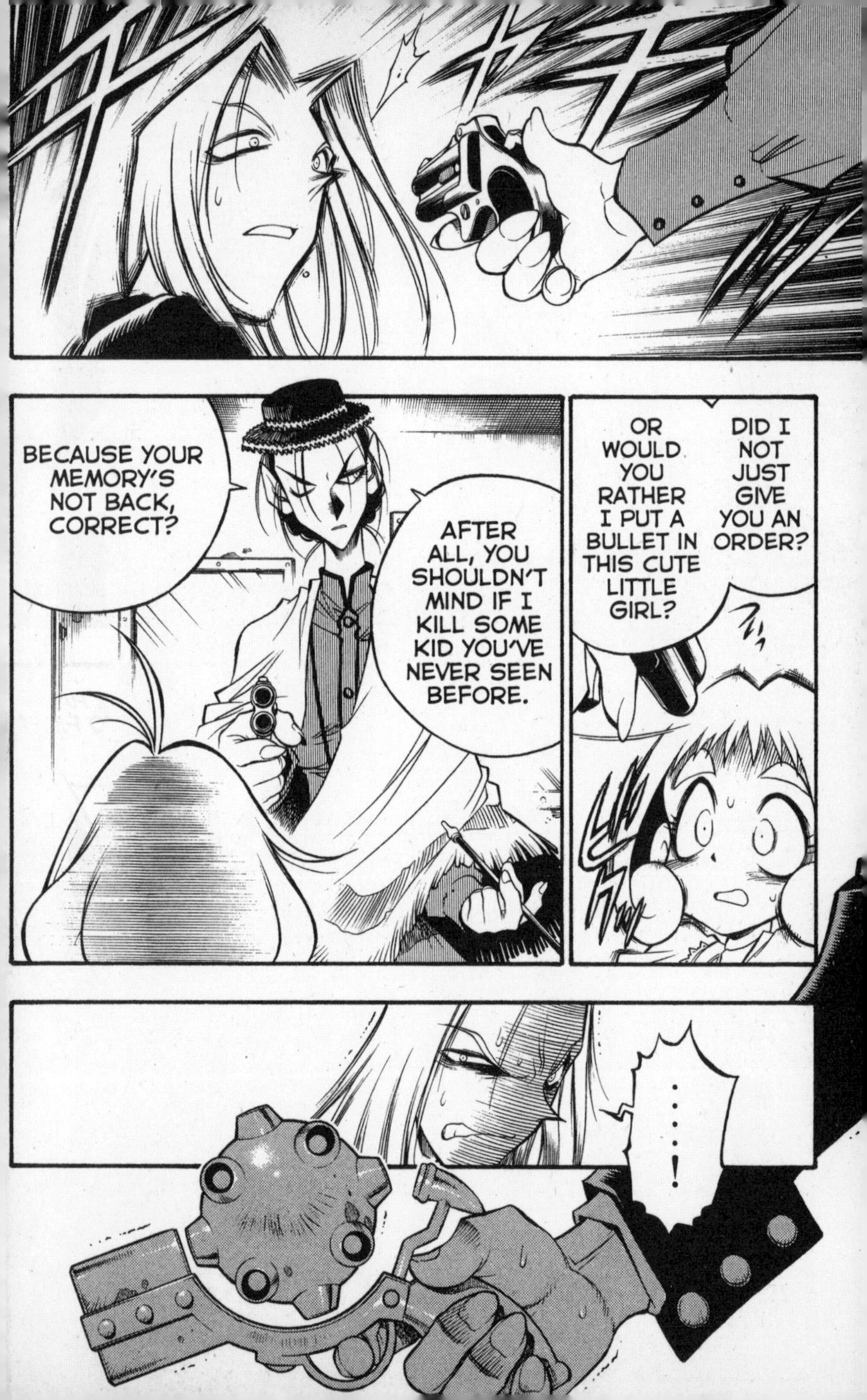
DID I NOT JUST GIVE YOU AN ORDER?
OR WOULD YOU RATHER I PUT A BULLET IN THIS CUTE LITTLE GIRL?
AFTER ALL, YOU SHOULDN'T MIND IF I KILL SOME KID YOU'VE NEVER SEEN BEFORE.
BECAUSE YOUR MEMORY'S NOT BACK, CORRECT?
.....!

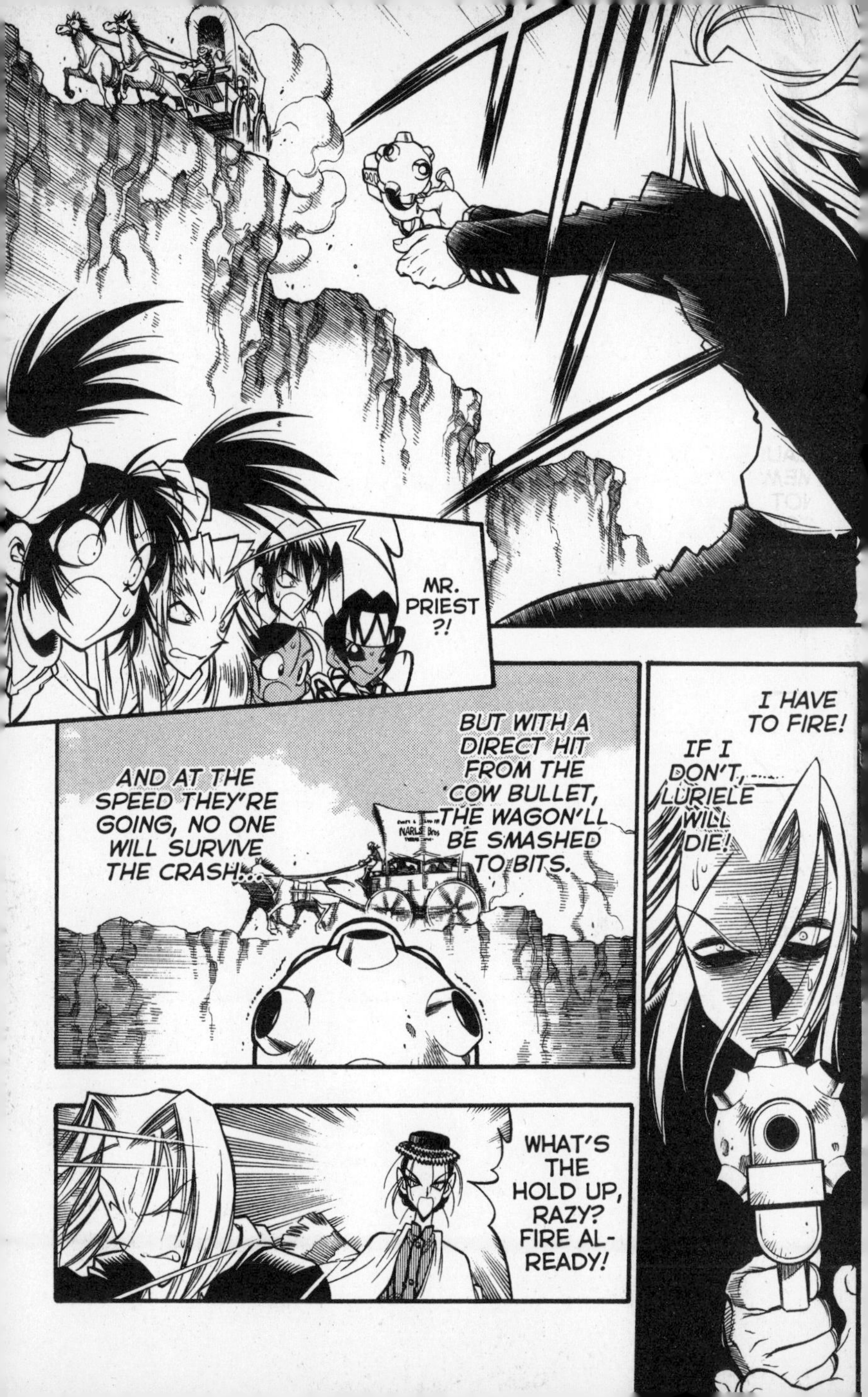
MR. PRIEST ?!
I HAVE TO FIRE!
IF I DON'T, LURIELE WILL DIE!
BUT WITH A DIRECT HIT FROM THE COW BULLET, THE WAGON'LL BE SMASHED TO BITS.
AND AT THE SPEED THEY'RE GOING, NO ONE WILL SURVIVE THE CRASH...
WHAT'S THE HOLD UP, RAZY? FIRE AL-READY!

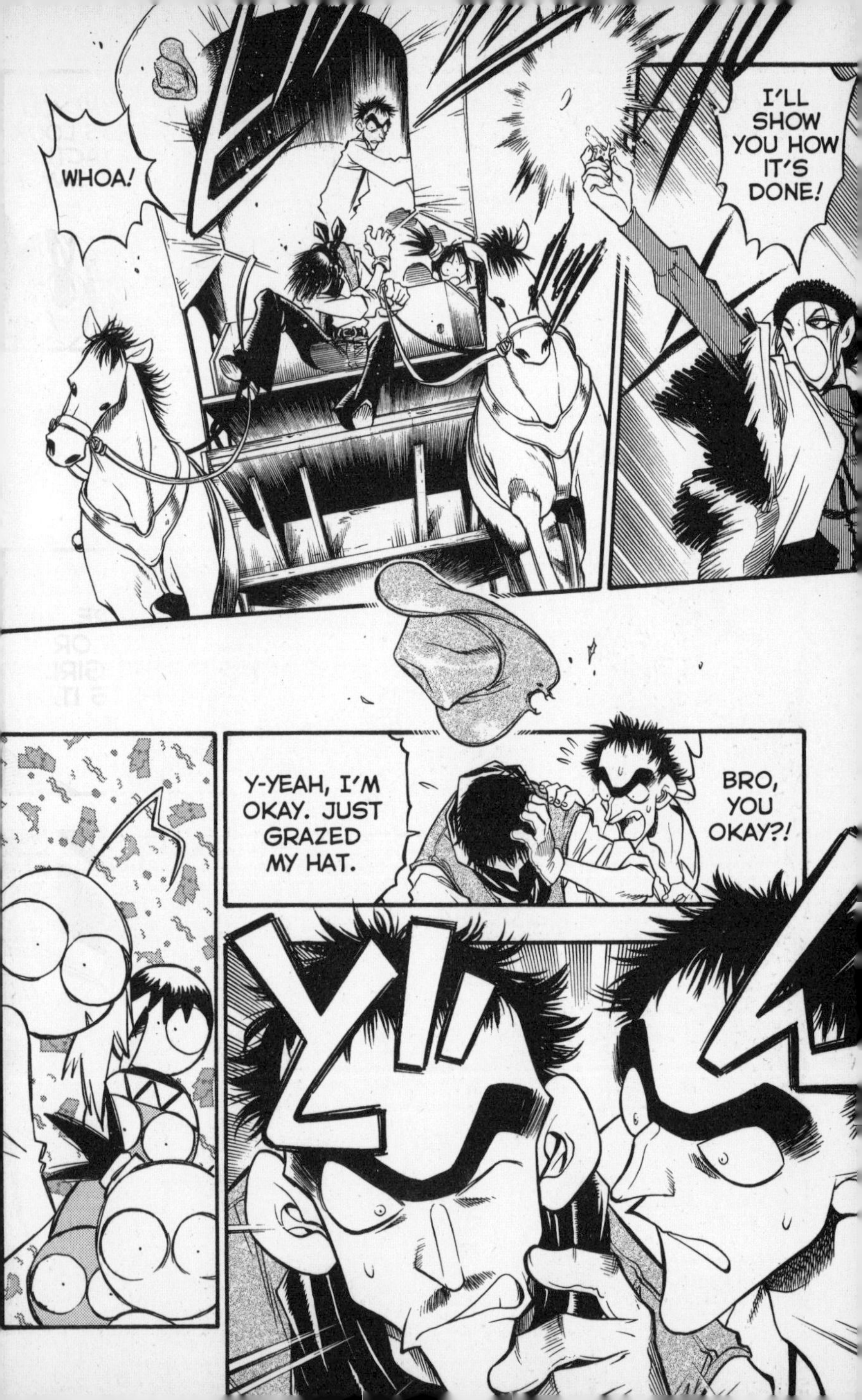
I'LL SHOW YOU HOW IT'S DONE!
WHOA!
BRO, YOU OKAY?!
Y-YEAH, I'M OKAY. JUST GRAZED MY HAT.

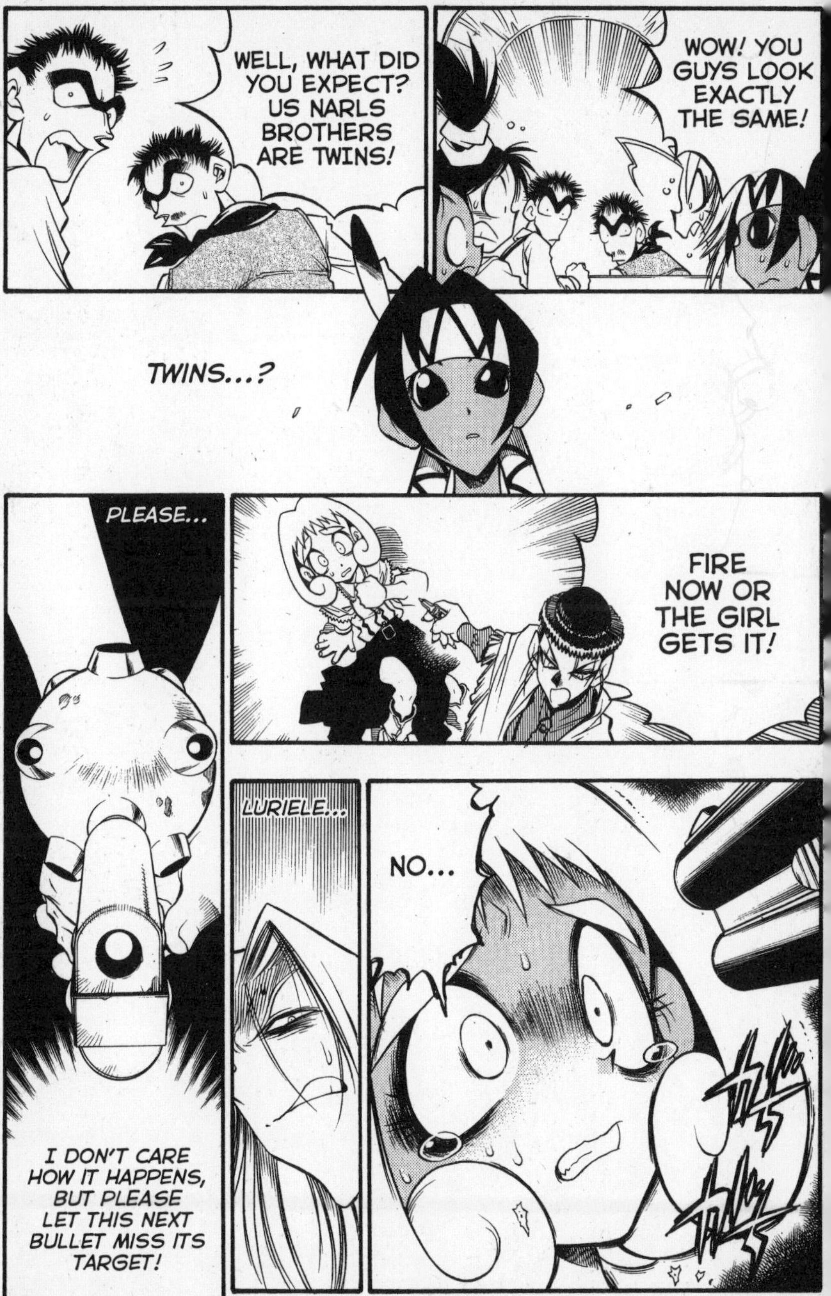
WOW! YOU GUYS LOOK EXACTLY THE SAME!
WELL, WHAT DID YOU EXPECT? US NARLS BROTHERS ARE TWINS!
TWINS...?
FIRE NOW OR THE GIRL GETS IT!
NO...
LURIELE...
PLEASE...
I DON'T CARE HOW IT HAPPENS, BUT PLEASE LET THIS NEXT BULLET MISS ITS TARGET!

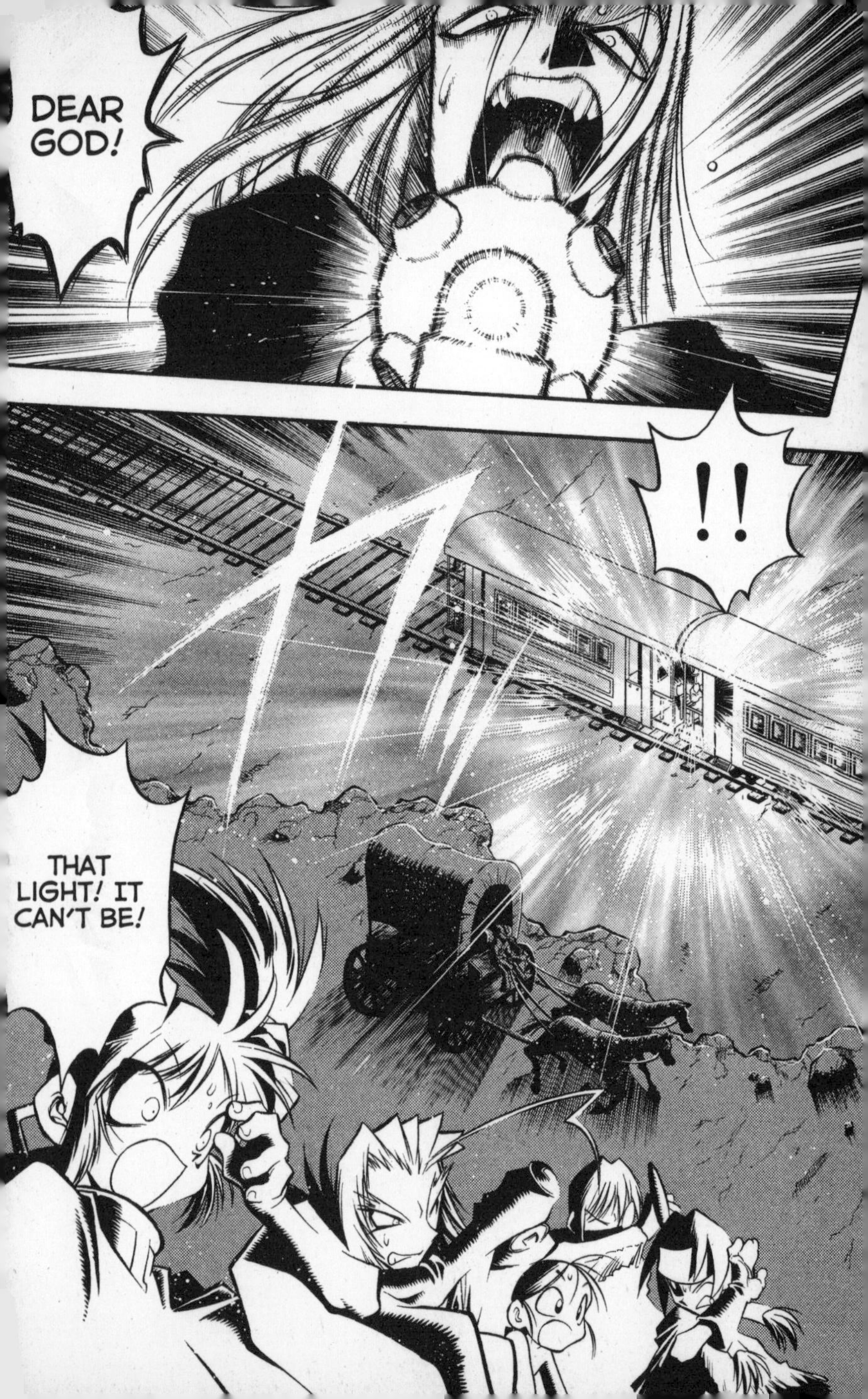
DEAR GOD!
!!
THAT LIGHT! IT CAN'T BE!

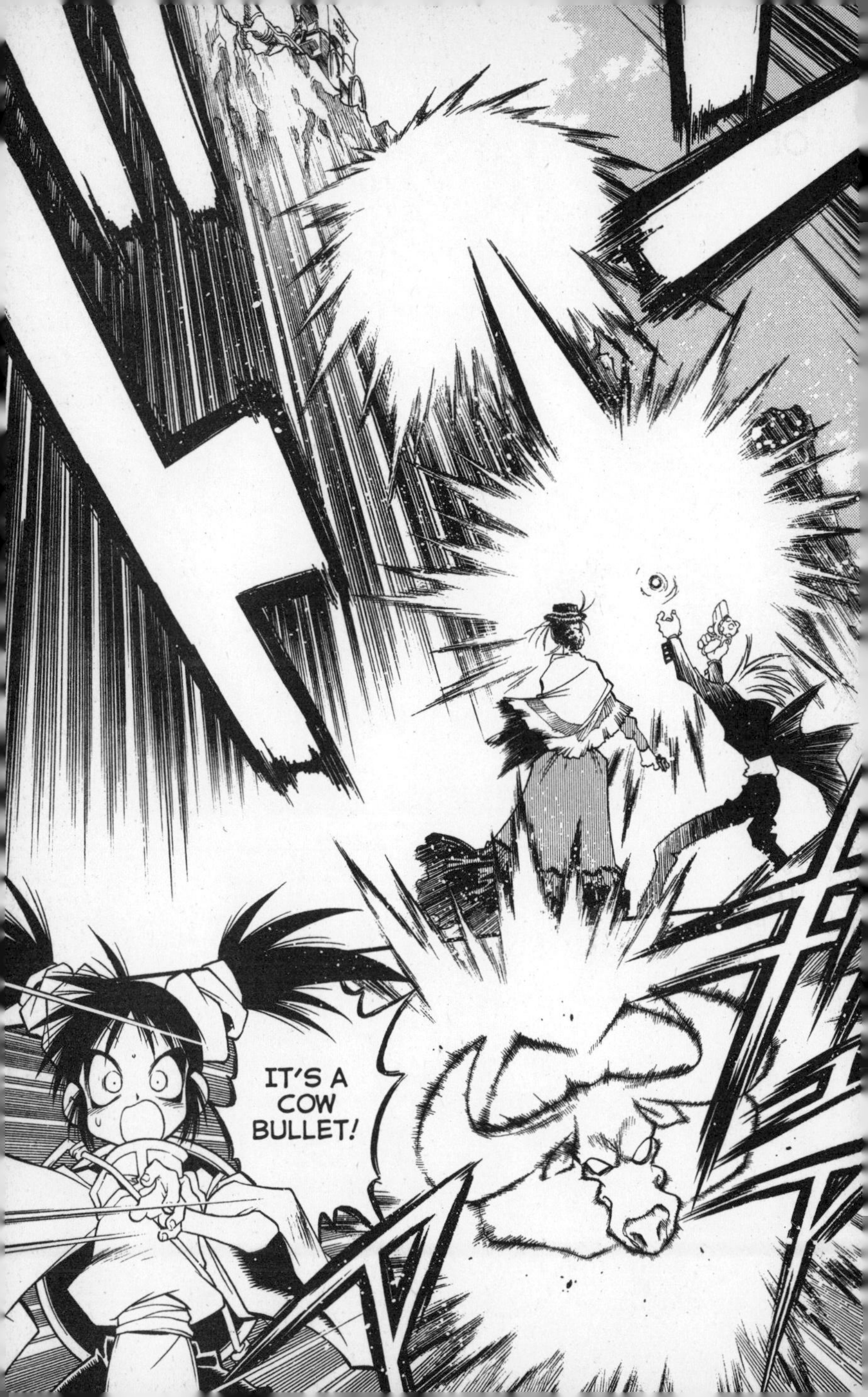
IT'S A COW BULLET!

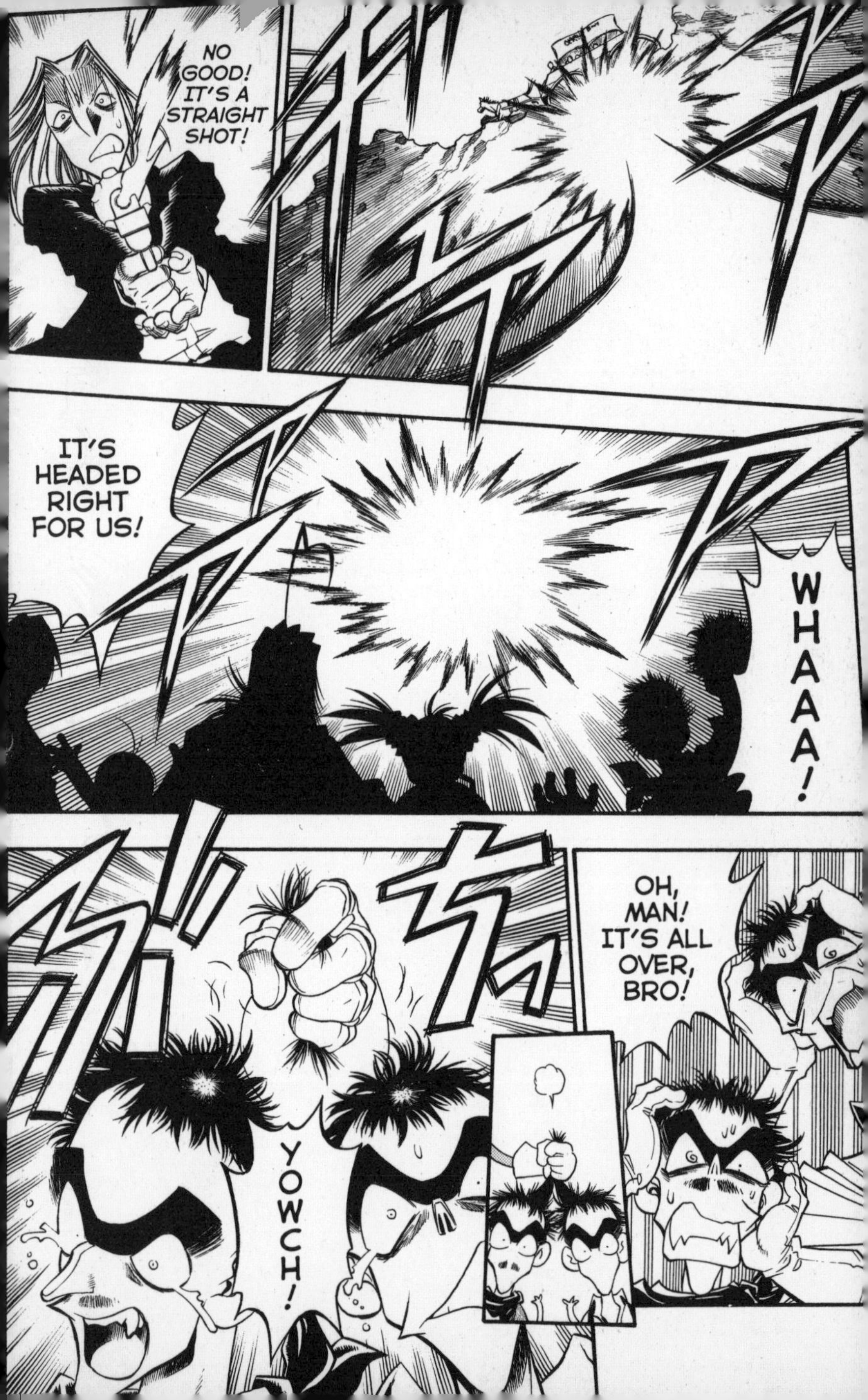
NO GOOD! IT'S A STRAIGHT SHOT!
IT'S HEADED RIGHT FOR US!
WHAAAA!
OH, MAN! IT'S ALL OVER, BRO!
YOWCH!

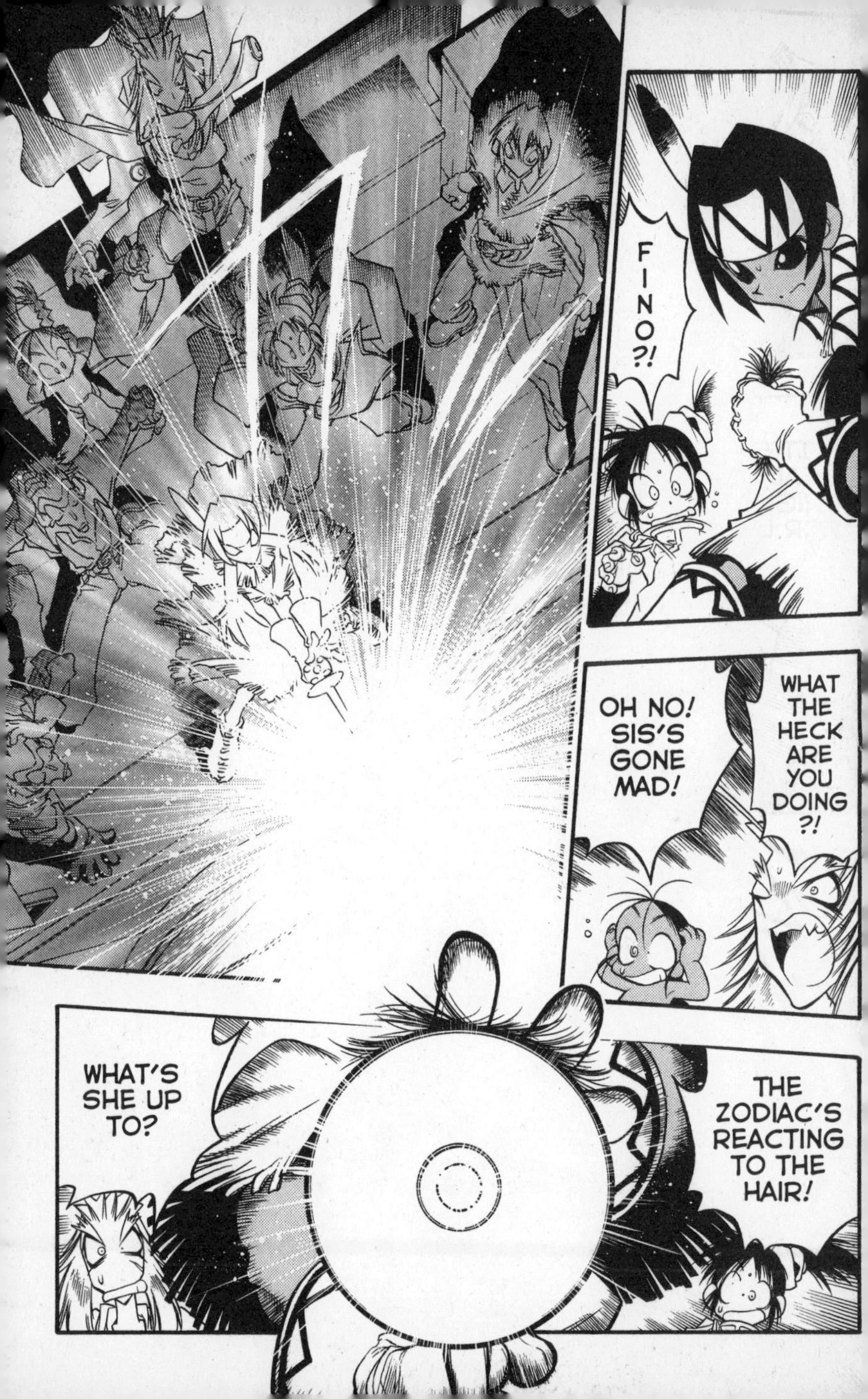
FINO?!
WHAT THE HECK ARE YOU DOING?!
OH NO! SIS'S GONE MAD!
THE ZODIAC'S REACTING TO THE HAIR!
WHAT'S SHE UP TO?

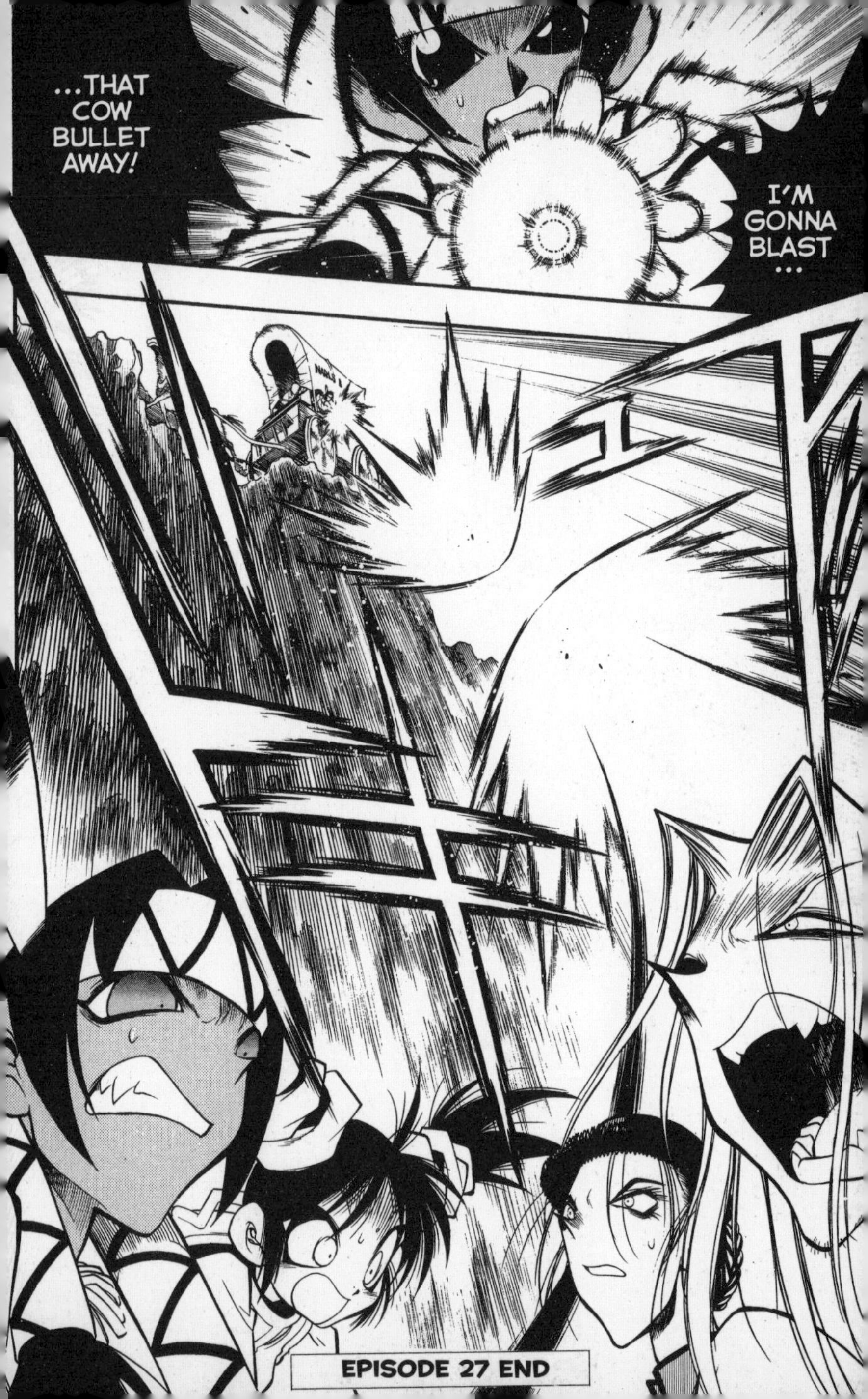
I'M GONNA BLAST ...
...THAT COW BULLET AWAY!

EPISODE 27 END

EPISODE 28

A NEW PROMISE

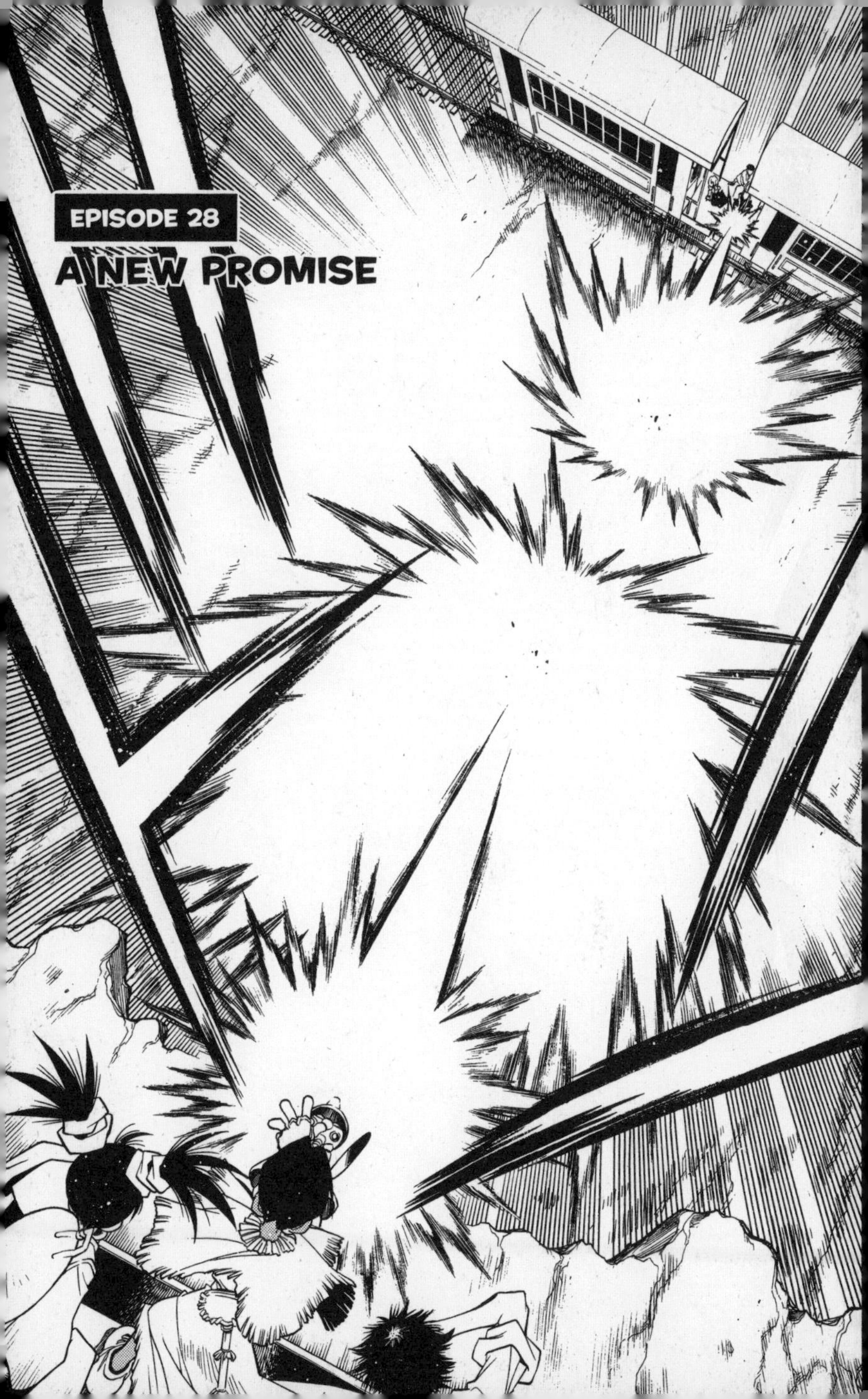

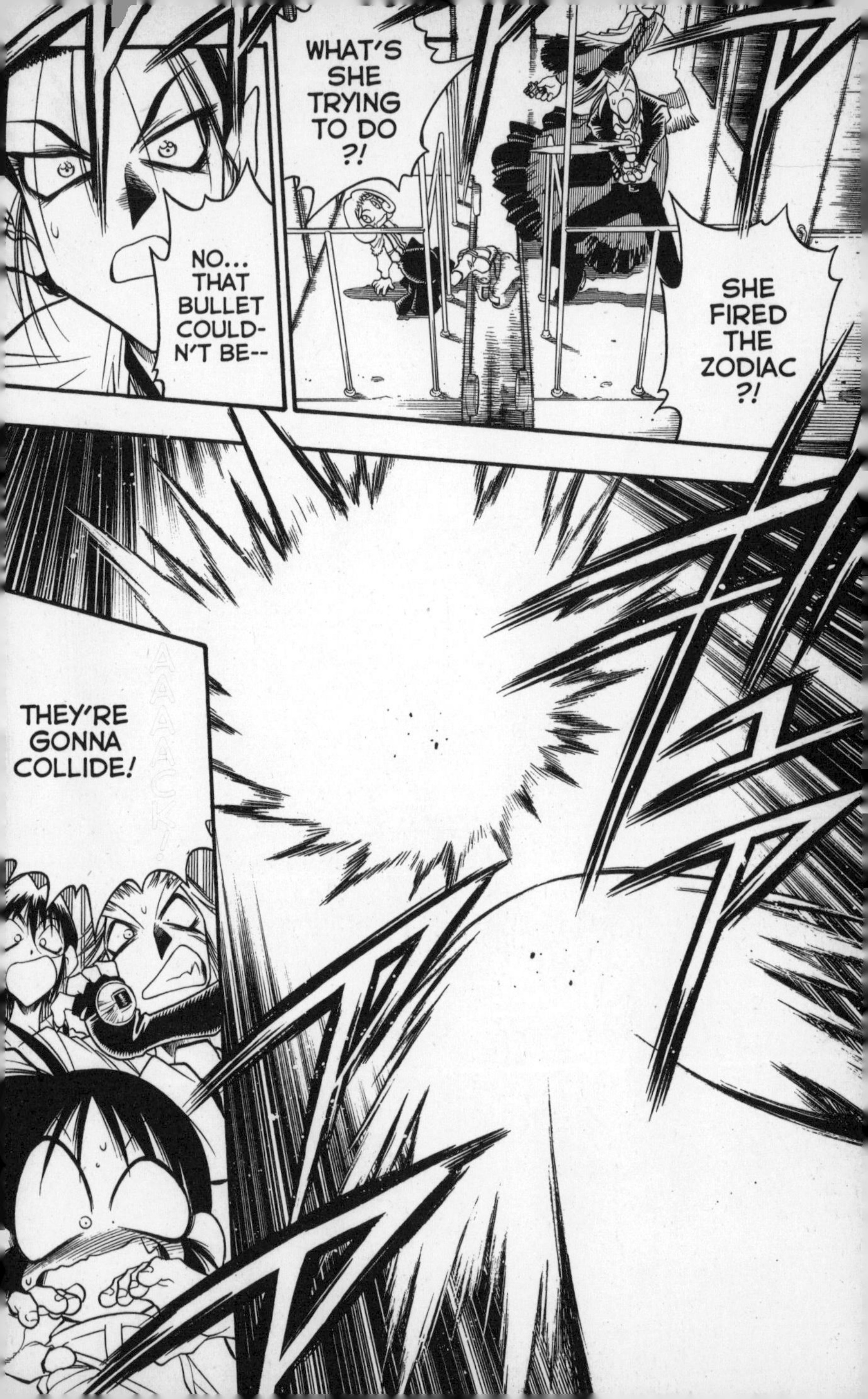
SHE FIRED THE ZODIAC ?!
WHAT'S SHE TRYING TO DO ?!
NO... THAT BULLET COULDN'T BE--
THEY'RE GONNA COLLIDE!
AAAACK!

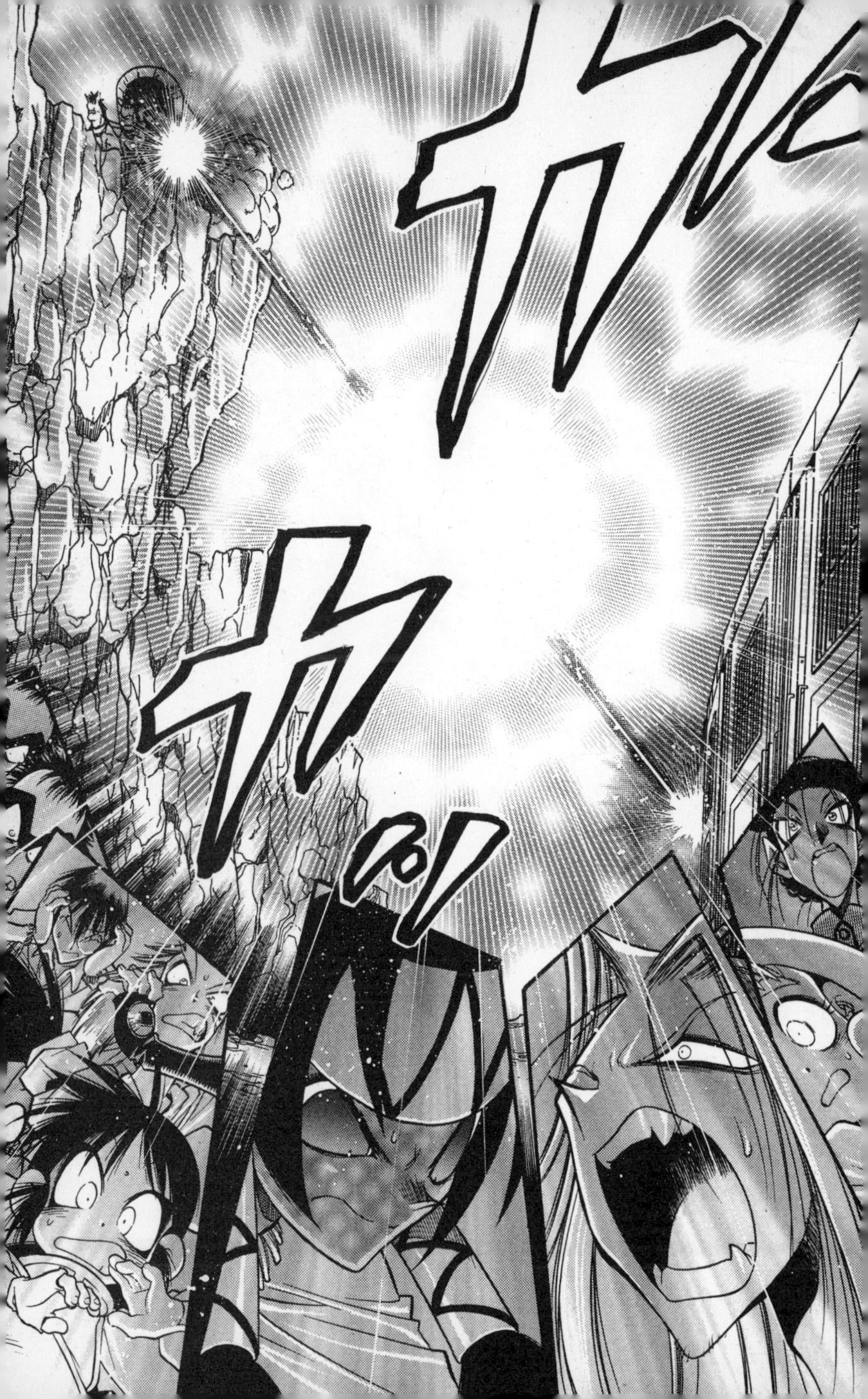

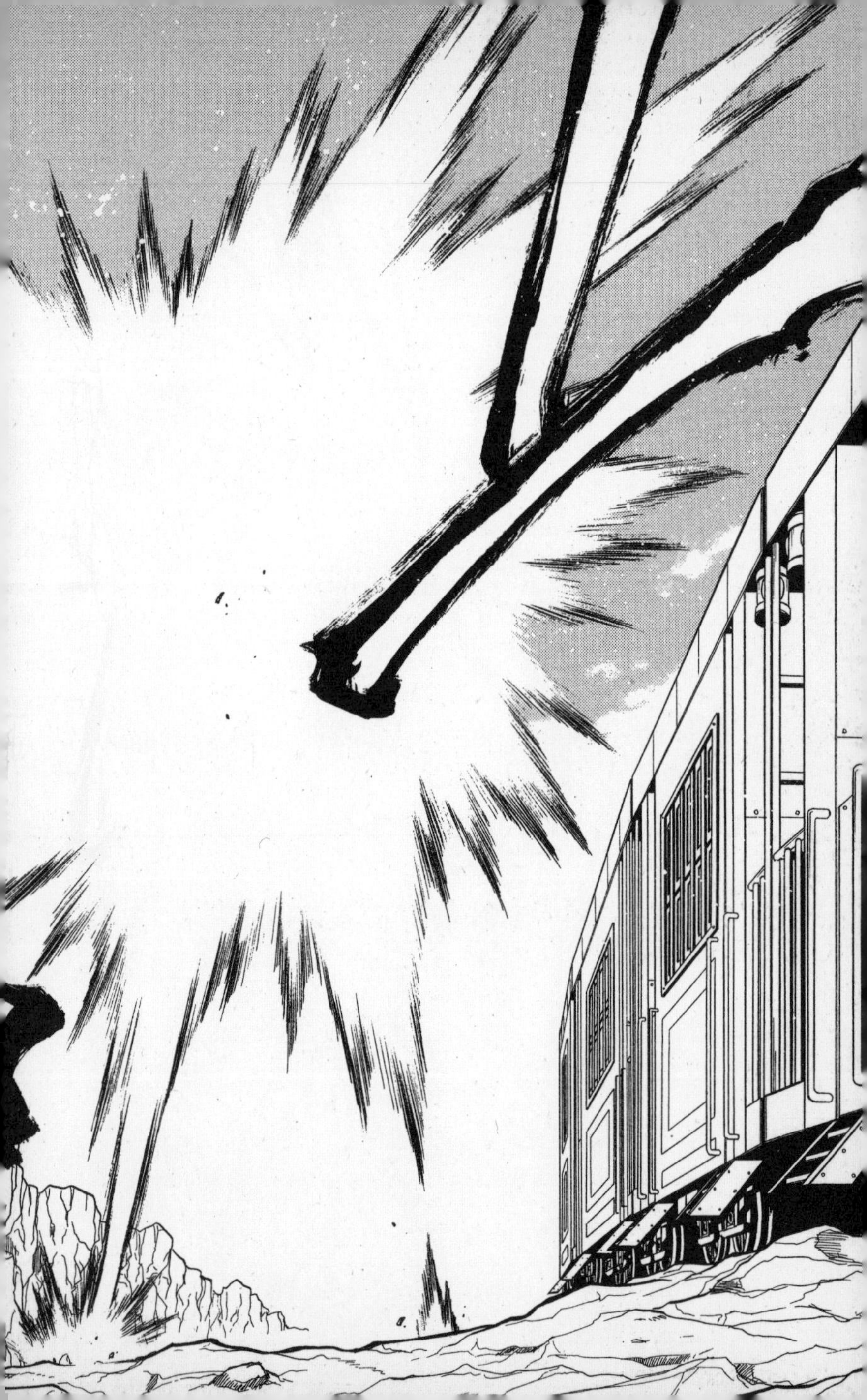

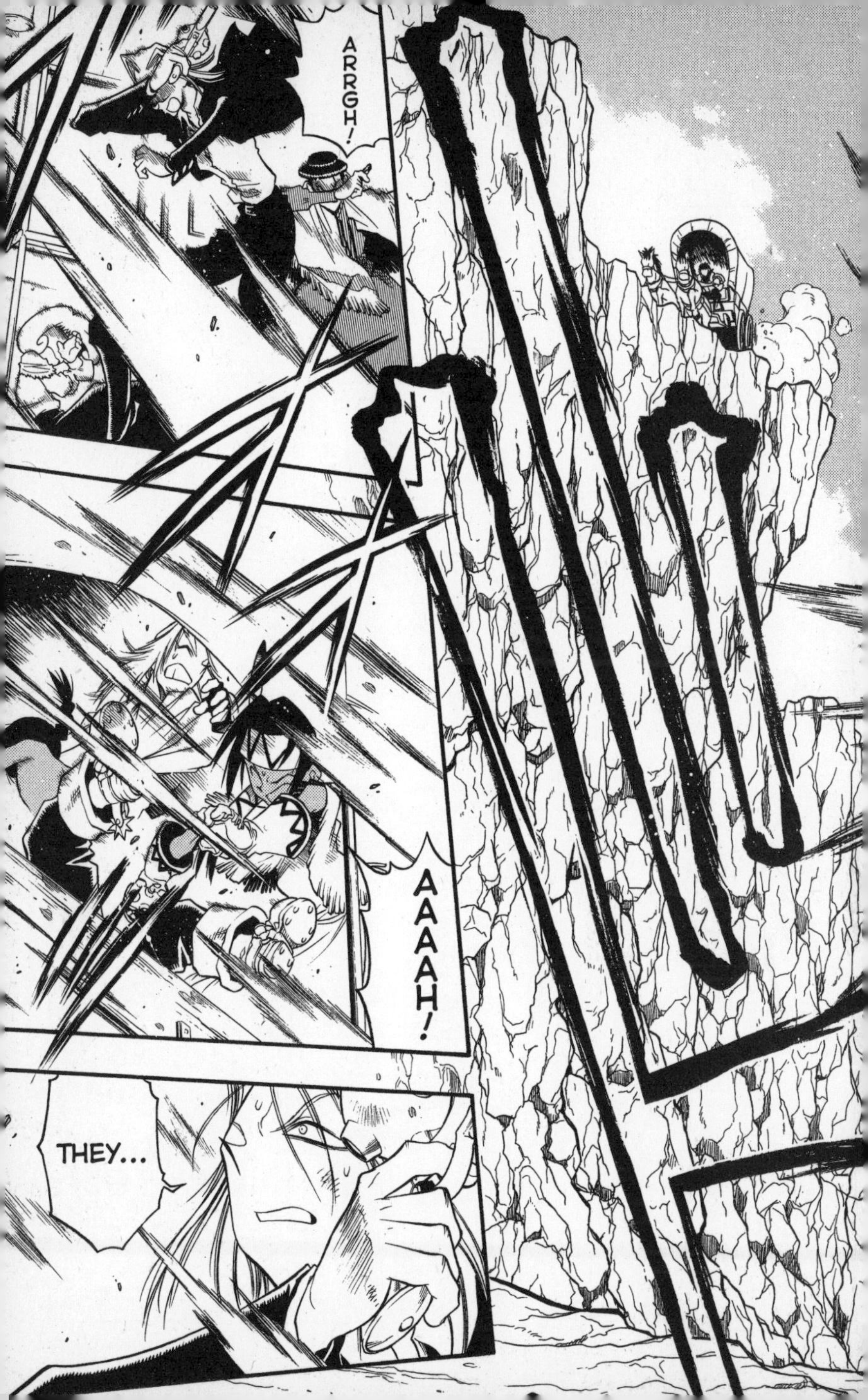
ARRGH!
AAAAH!
THEY...

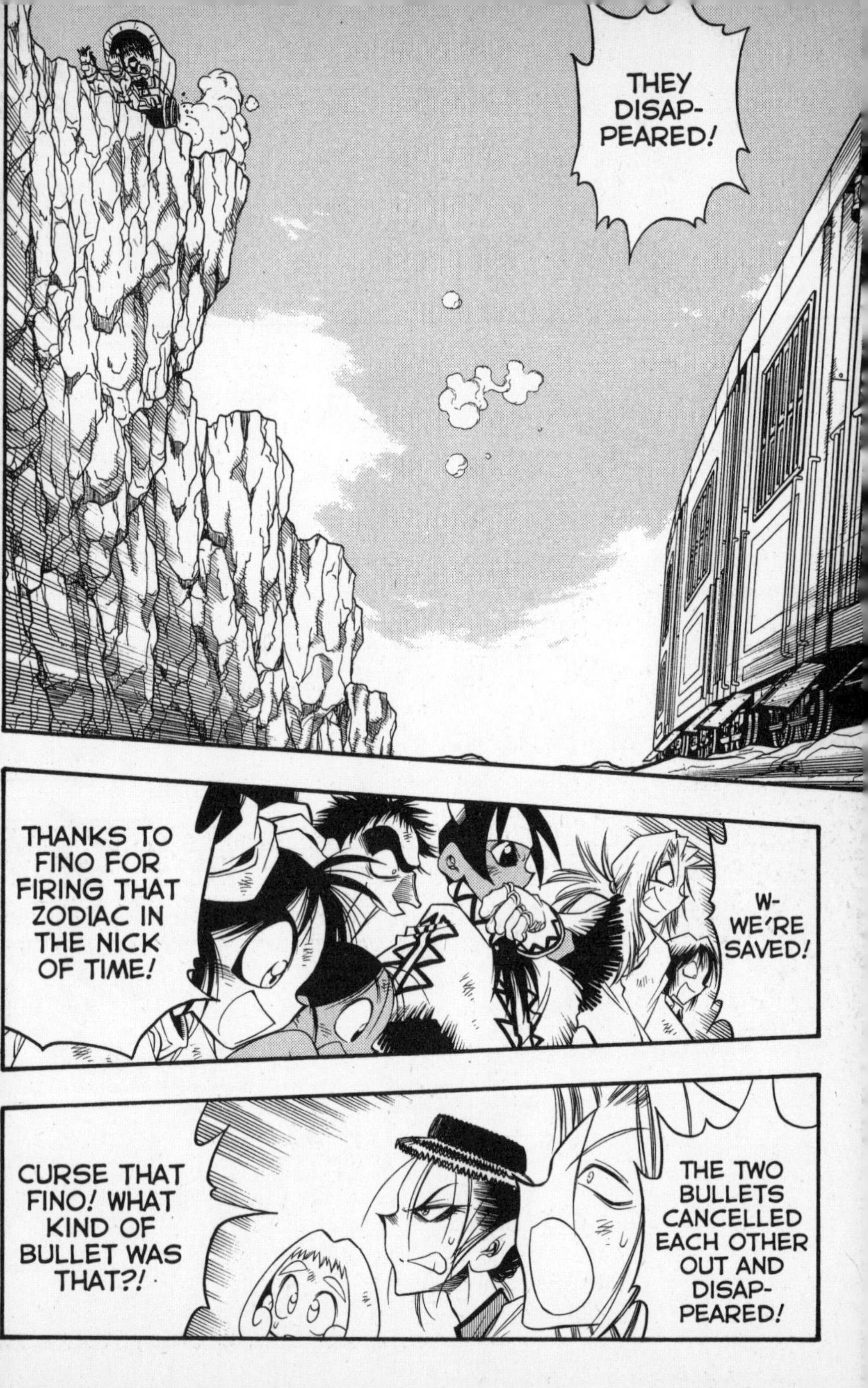
THEY DISAP-PEARED!
W- WE'RE SAVED!
THANKS TO FINO FOR FIRING THAT ZODIAC IN THE NICK OF TIME!
THE TWO BULLETS CANCELLED EACH OTHER OUT AND DISAP-PEARED!
CURSE THAT FINO! WHAT KIND OF BULLET WAS THAT?!

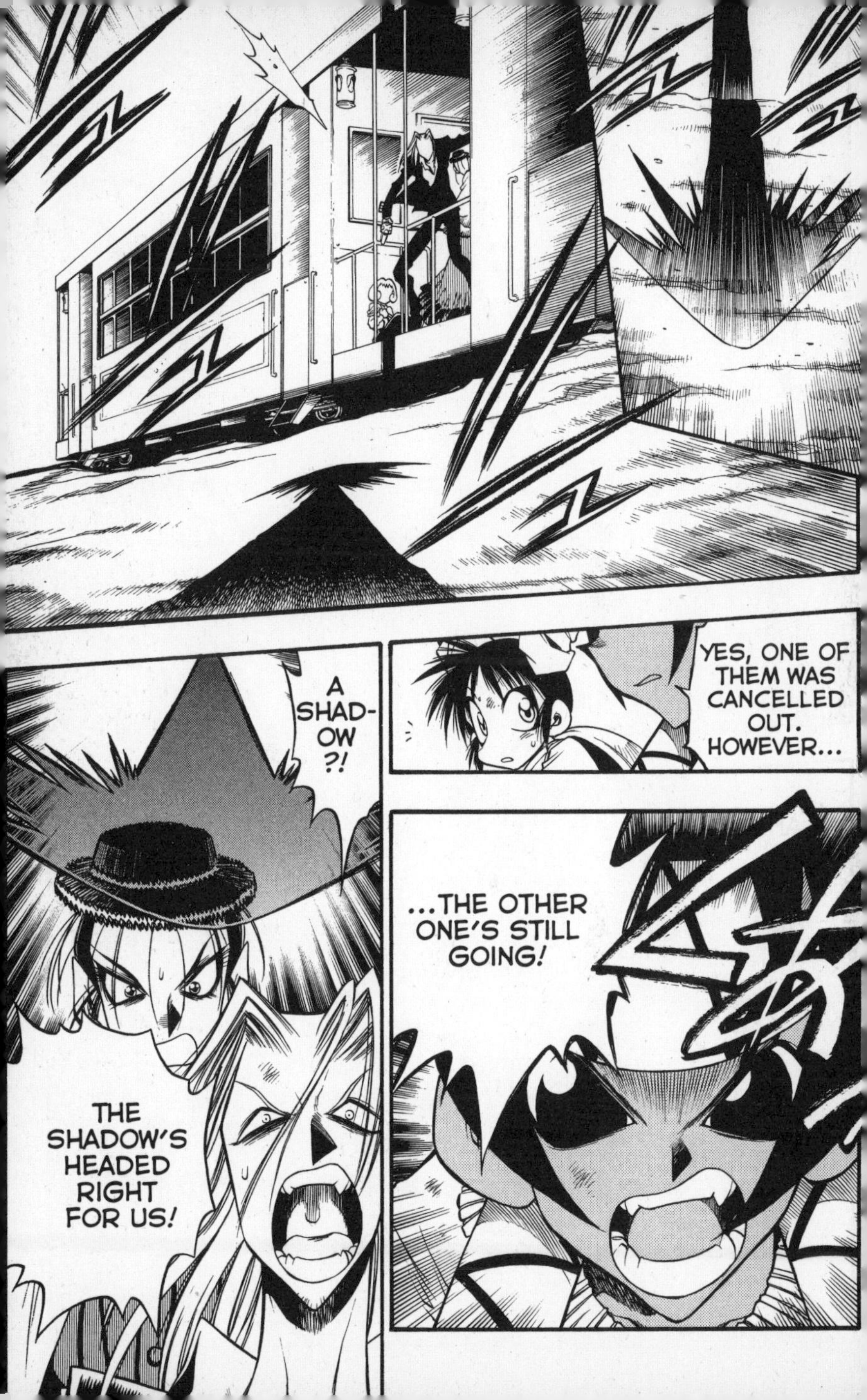

YES, ONE OF THEM WAS CANCELLED OUT. HOWEVER...
...THE OTHER ONE'S STILL GOING!
A SHAD-OW?!
THE SHADOW'S HEADED RIGHT FOR US!

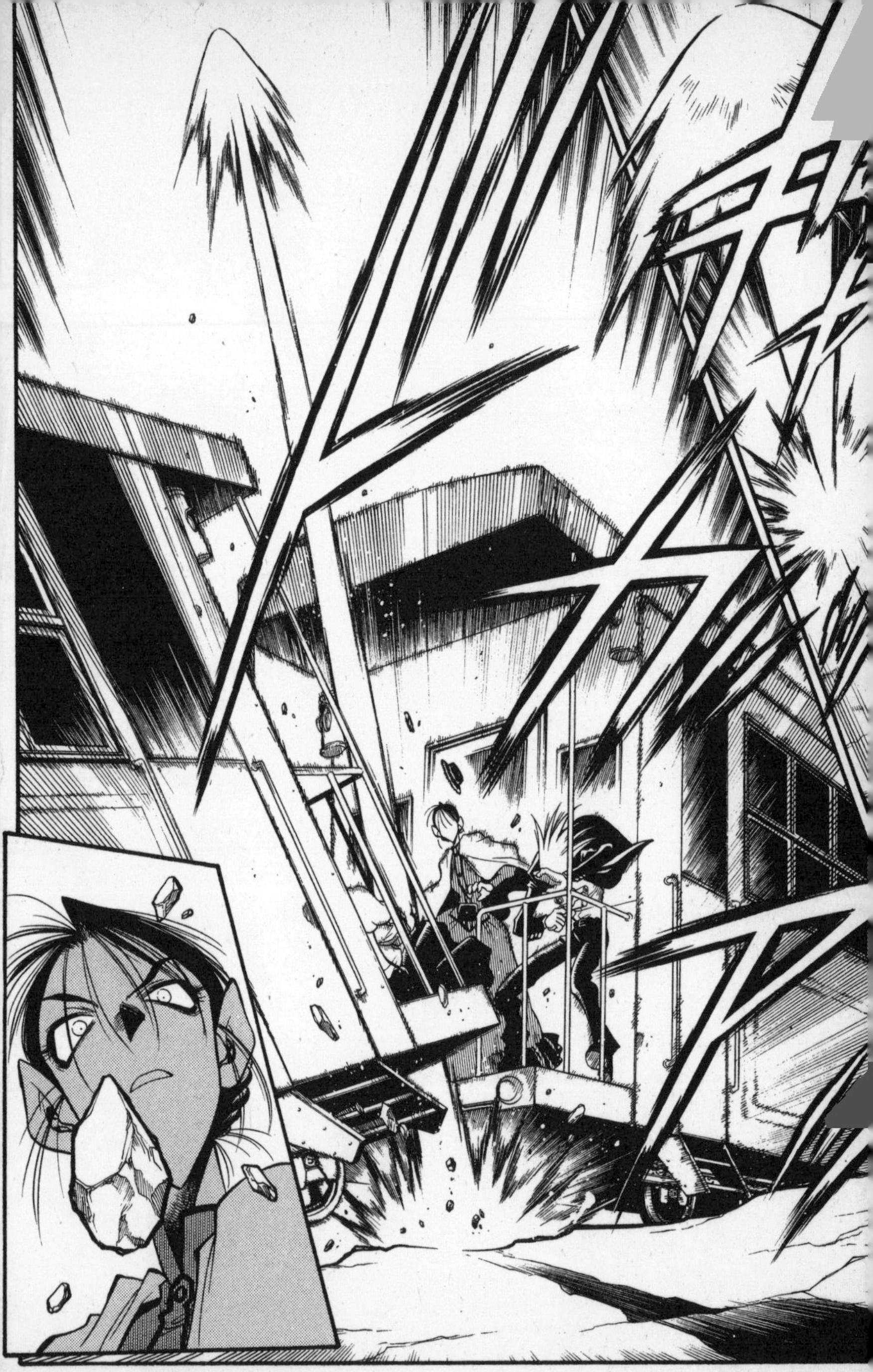

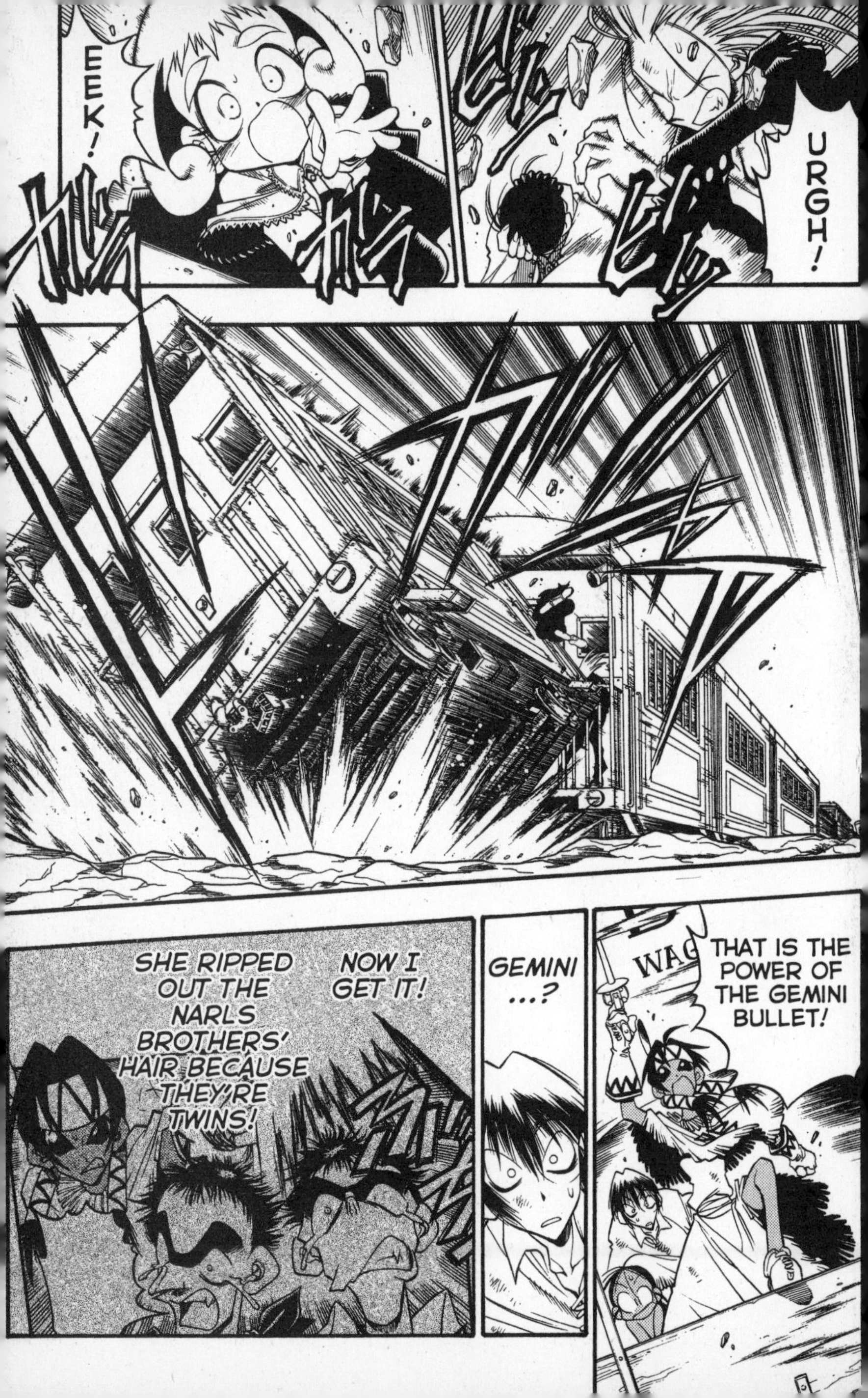
URGH!
EEK!
THAT IS THE POWER OF THE GEMINI BULLET!
GEMINI ...?
NOW I GET IT!
SHE RIPPED OUT THE NARLS BROTHERS' HAIR BECAUSE THEY'RE TWINS!

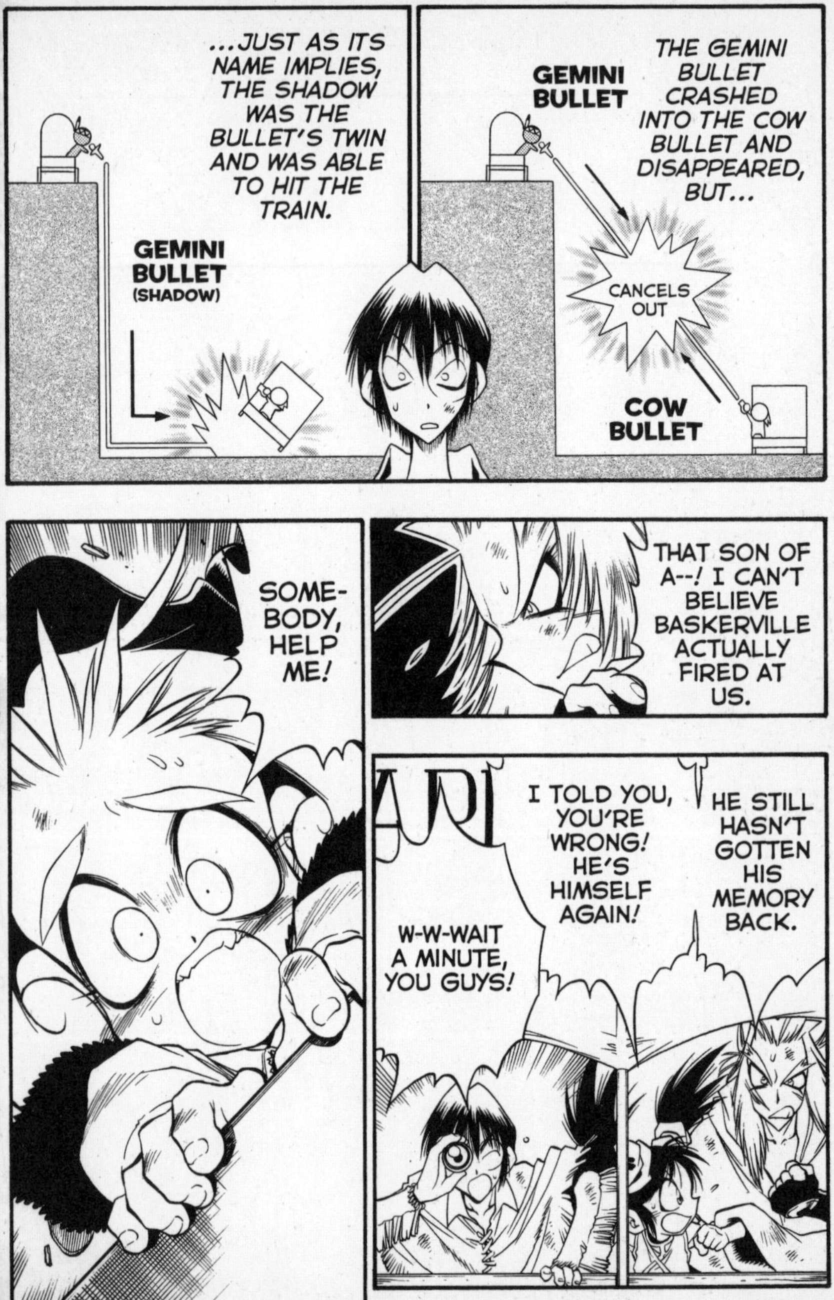
THE GEMINI BULLET CRASHED INTO THE COW BULLET AND DISAPPEARED, BUT...
GEMINI BULLET
CANCELS OUT
COW BULLET
...JUST AS ITS NAME IMPLIES, THE SHADOW WAS THE BULLET'S TWIN AND WAS ABLE TO HIT THE TRAIN.
GEMINI BULLET (SHADOW)
THAT SON OF A--! I CAN'T BELIEVE BASKERVILLE ACTUALLY FIRED AT US.
HE STILL HASN'T GOTTEN HIS MEMORY BACK.
I TOLD YOU, YOU'RE WRONG! HE'S HIMSELF AGAIN!
W-W-WAIT A MINUTE, YOU GUYS!
SOME-BODY, HELP ME!

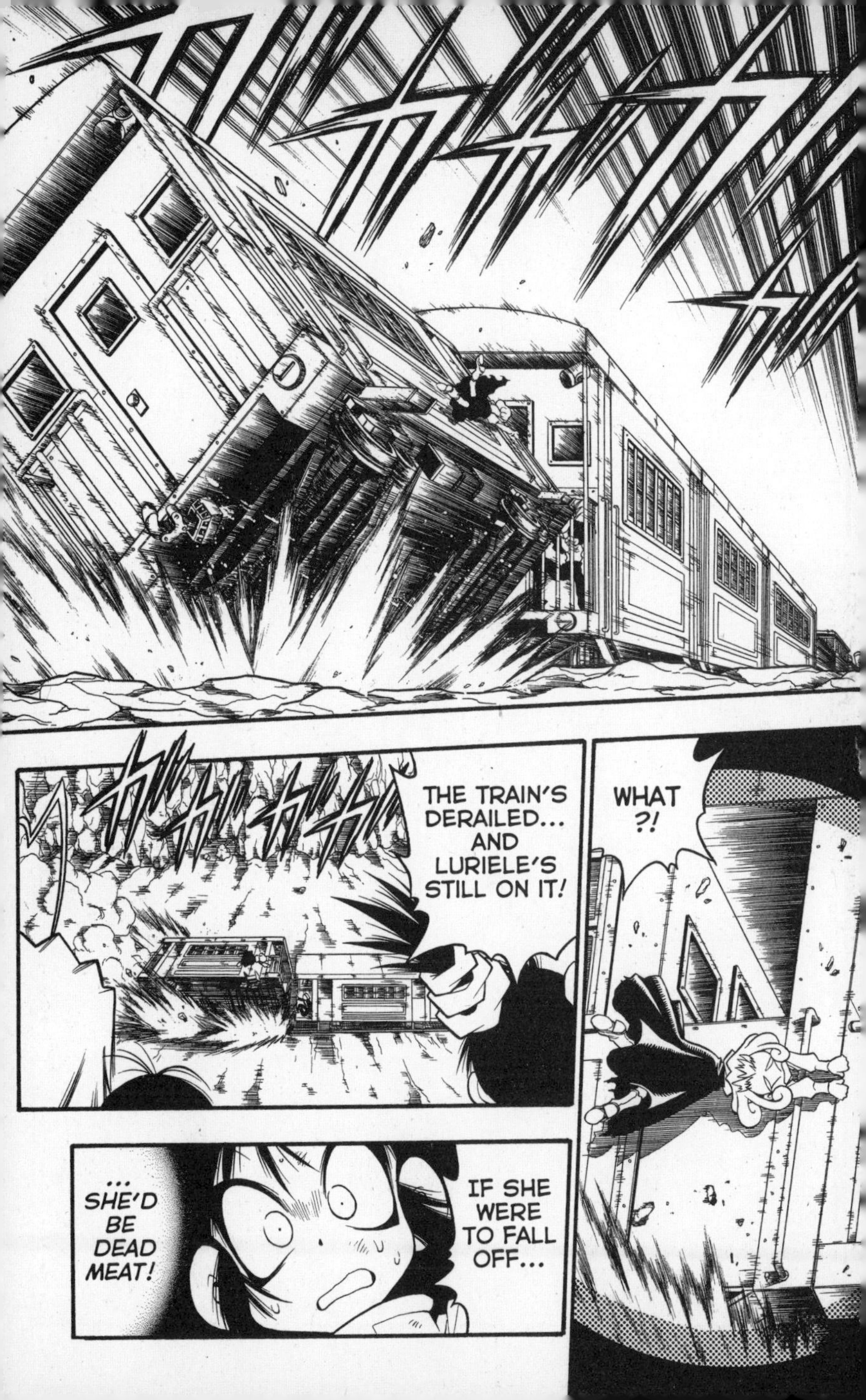
WHAT ?!
THE TRAIN'S DERAILED... AND LURIELE'S STILL ON IT!
IF SHE WERE TO FALL OFF...
... SHE'D BE DEAD MEAT!

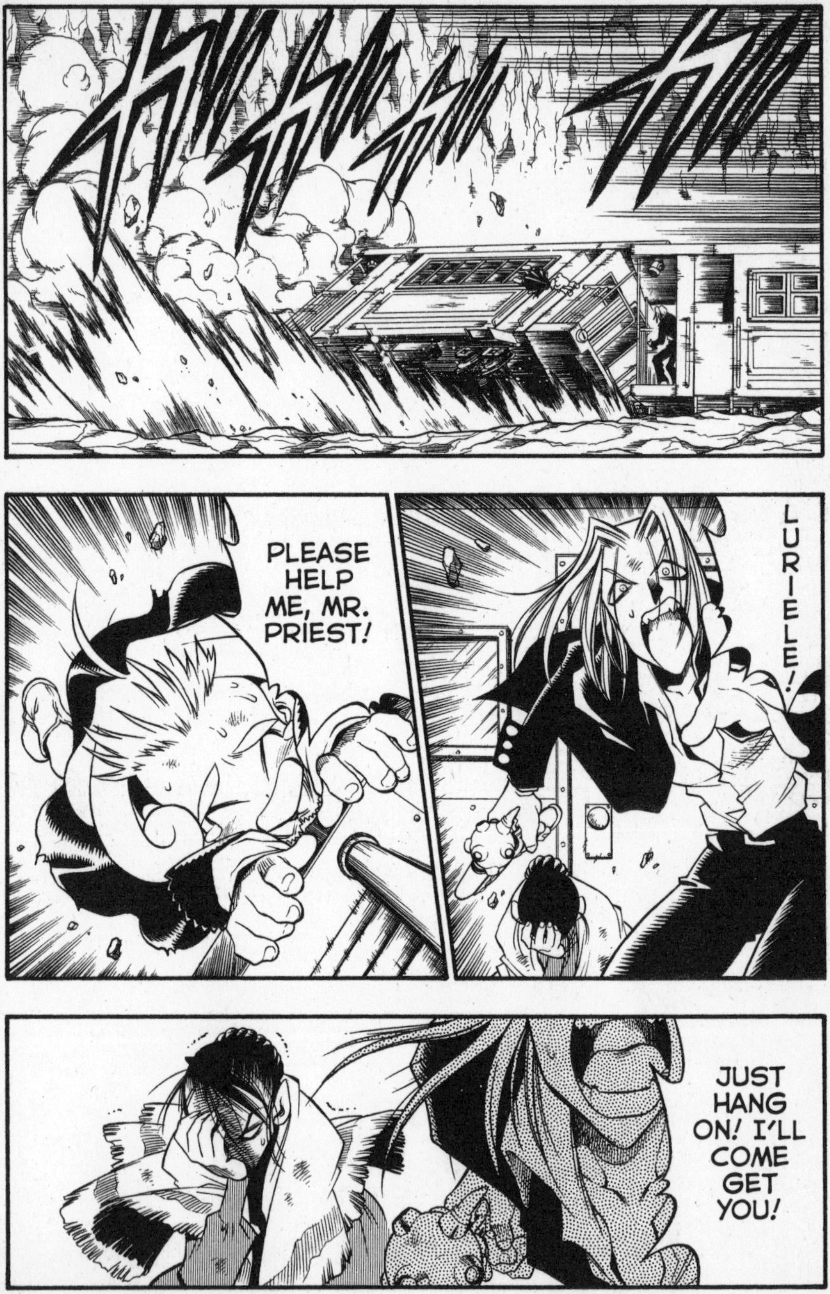
LURIELE!
PLEASE HELP ME, MR. PRIEST!
JUST HANG ON! I'LL COME GET YOU!

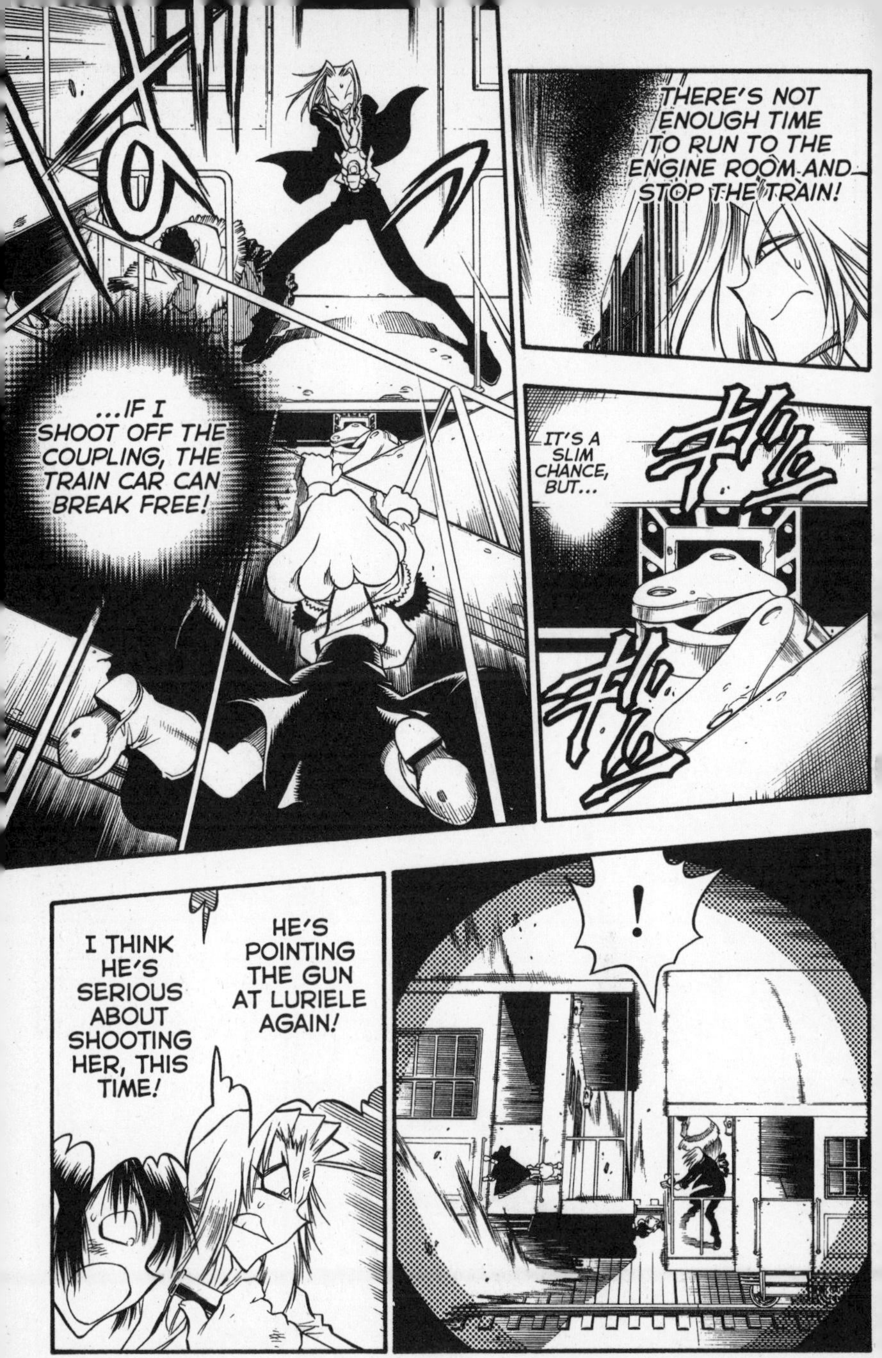
THERE'S NOT ENOUGH TIME TO RUN TO THE ENGINE ROOM AND STOP THE TRAIN!
IT'S A SLIM CHANCE, BUT...
...IF I SHOOT OFF THE COUPLING, THE TRAIN CAR CAN BREAK FREE!
!
HE'S POINTING THE GUN AT LURIELE AGAIN!
I THINK HE'S SERIOUS ABOUT SHOOTING HER, THIS TIME!

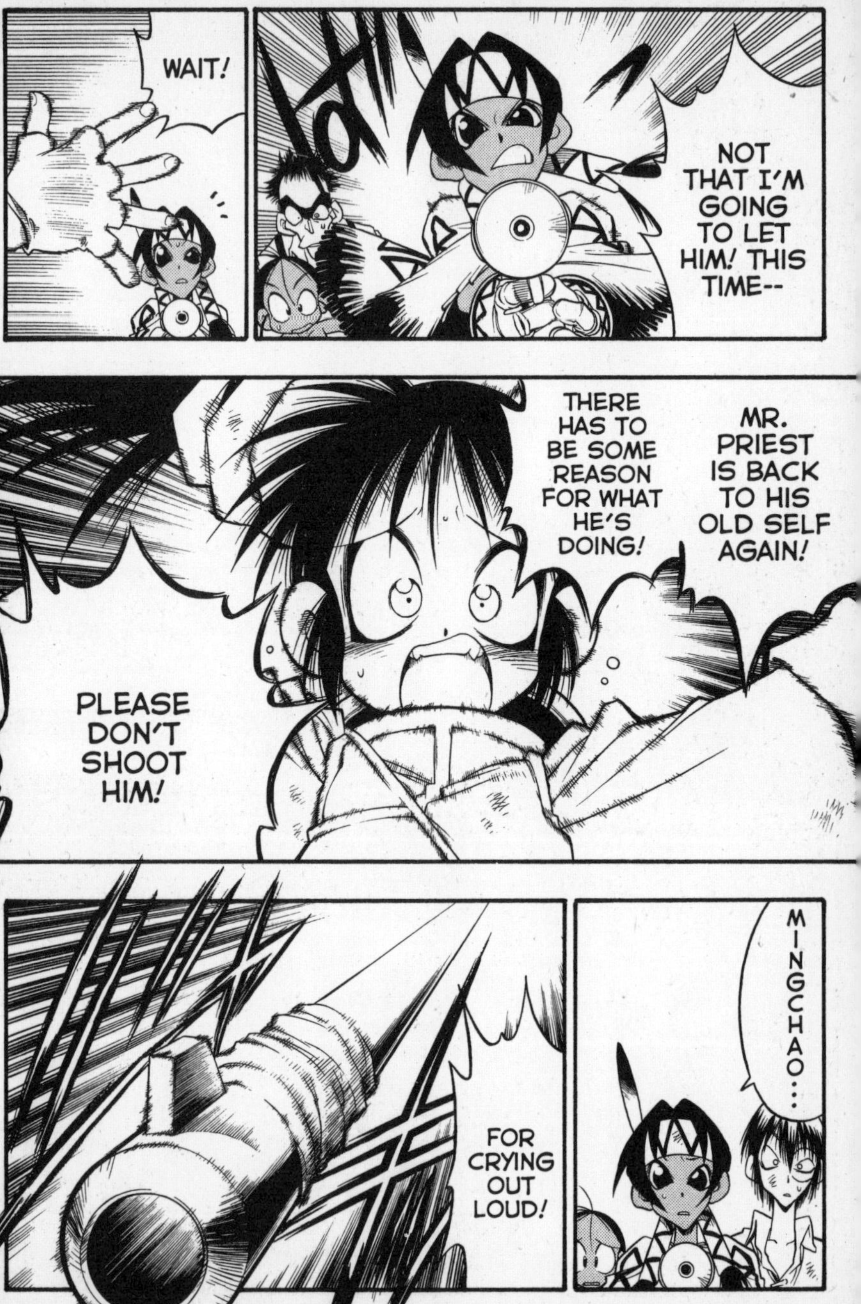
NOT THAT I'M GOING TO LET HIM! THIS TIME--
WAIT!
MR. PRIEST IS BACK TO HIS OLD SELF AGAIN!
THERE HAS TO BE SOME REASON FOR WHAT HE'S DOING!
PLEASE DON'T SHOOT HIM!
MINGCHAO...
FOR CRYING OUT LOUD!

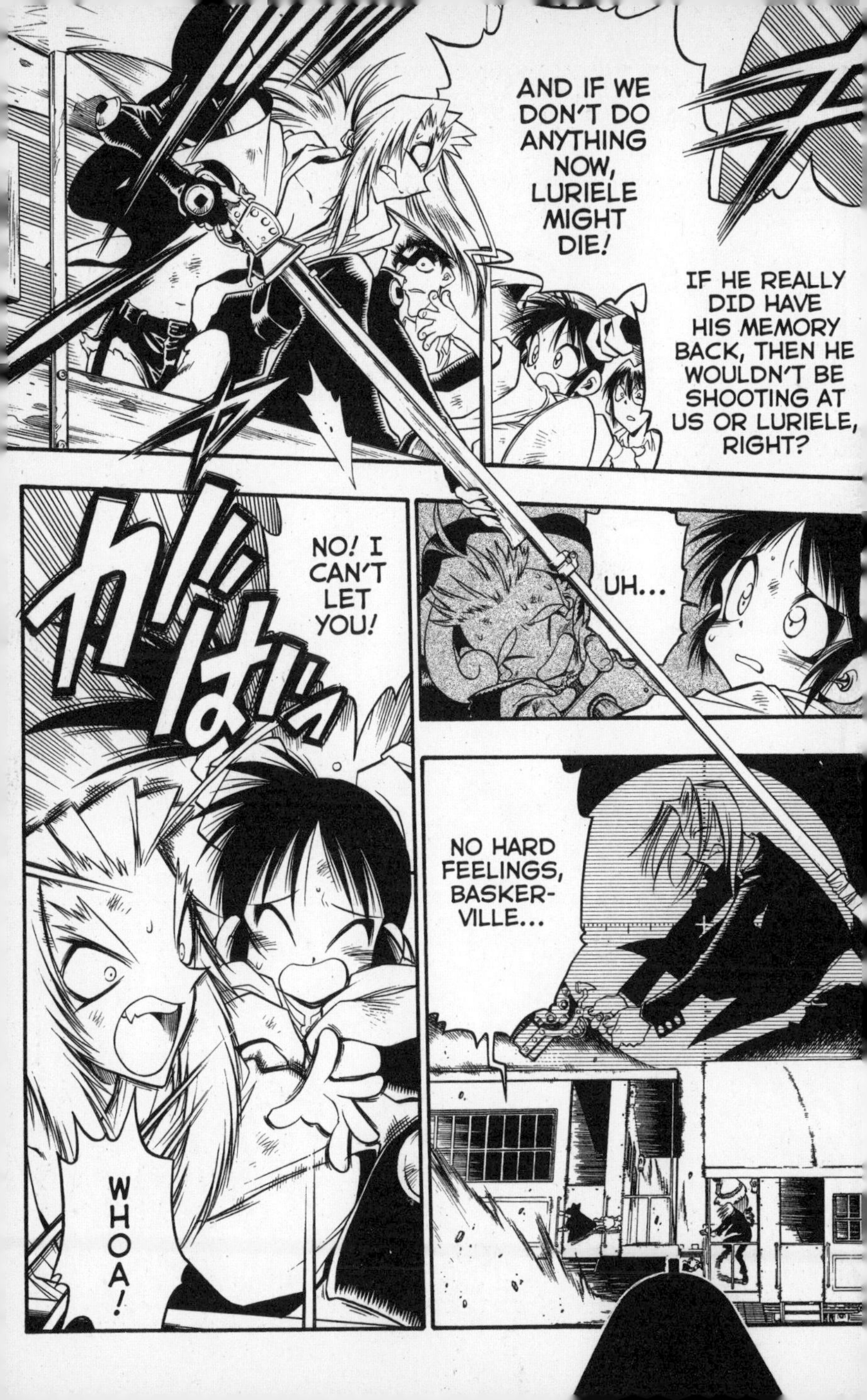
IF HE REALLY DID HAVE HIS MEMORY BACK, THEN HE WOULDN'T BE SHOOTING AT US OR LURIELE, RIGHT?
AND IF WE DON'T DO ANYTHING NOW, LURIELE MIGHT DIE!
UH...
NO HARD FEELINGS, BASKER-VILLE...
NO! I CAN'T LET YOU!
WHOA!

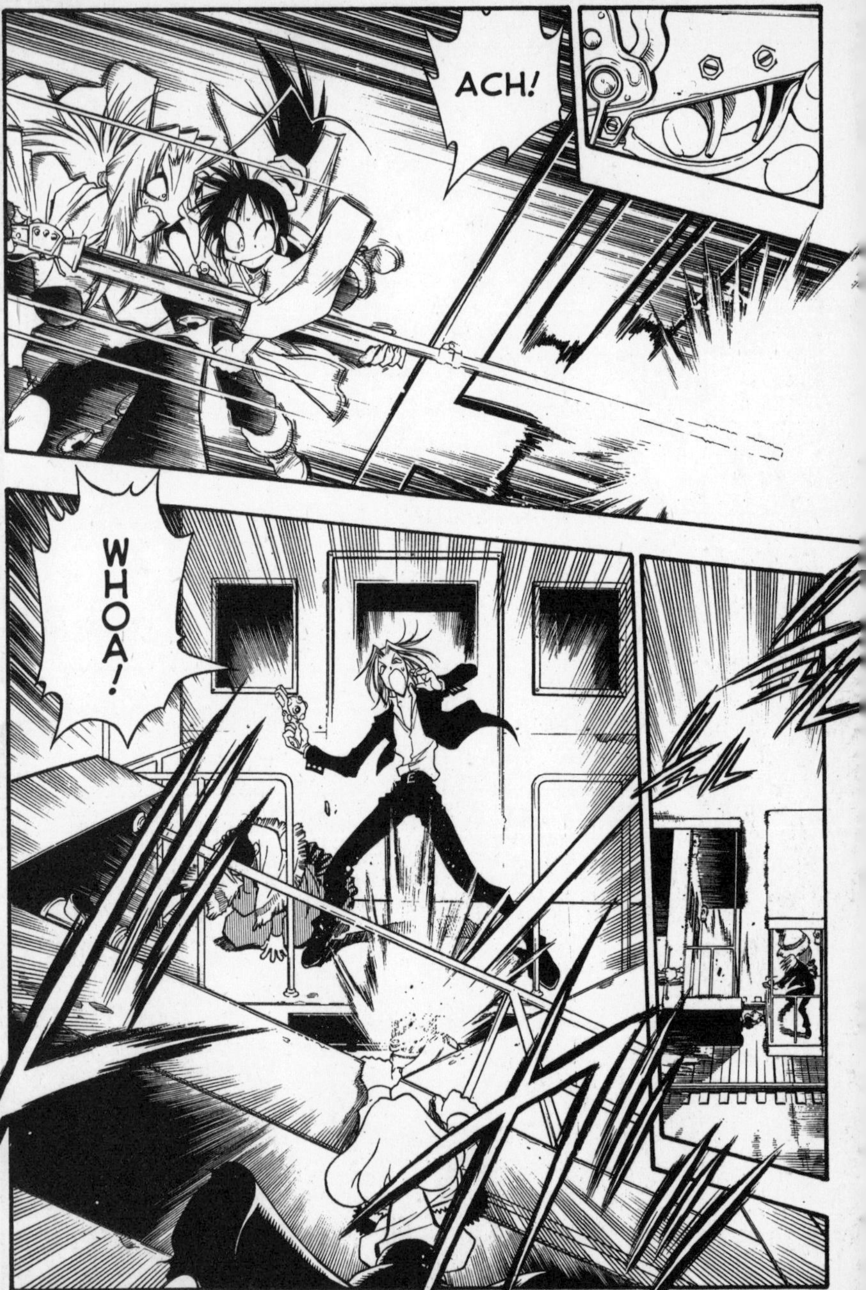
ACH!
WHOA!

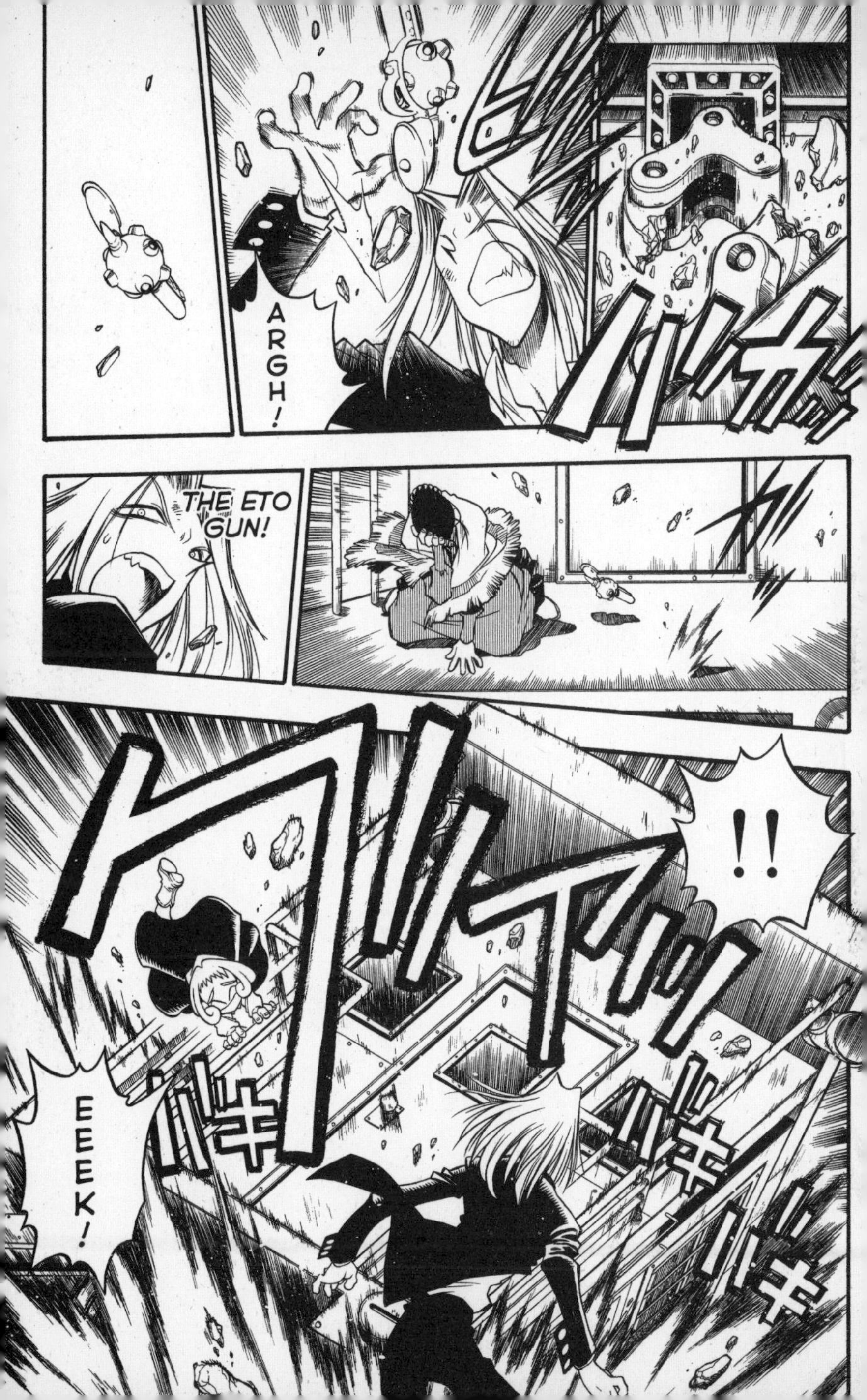

ARGH!
THE ETO GUN!
!!
EEEK!

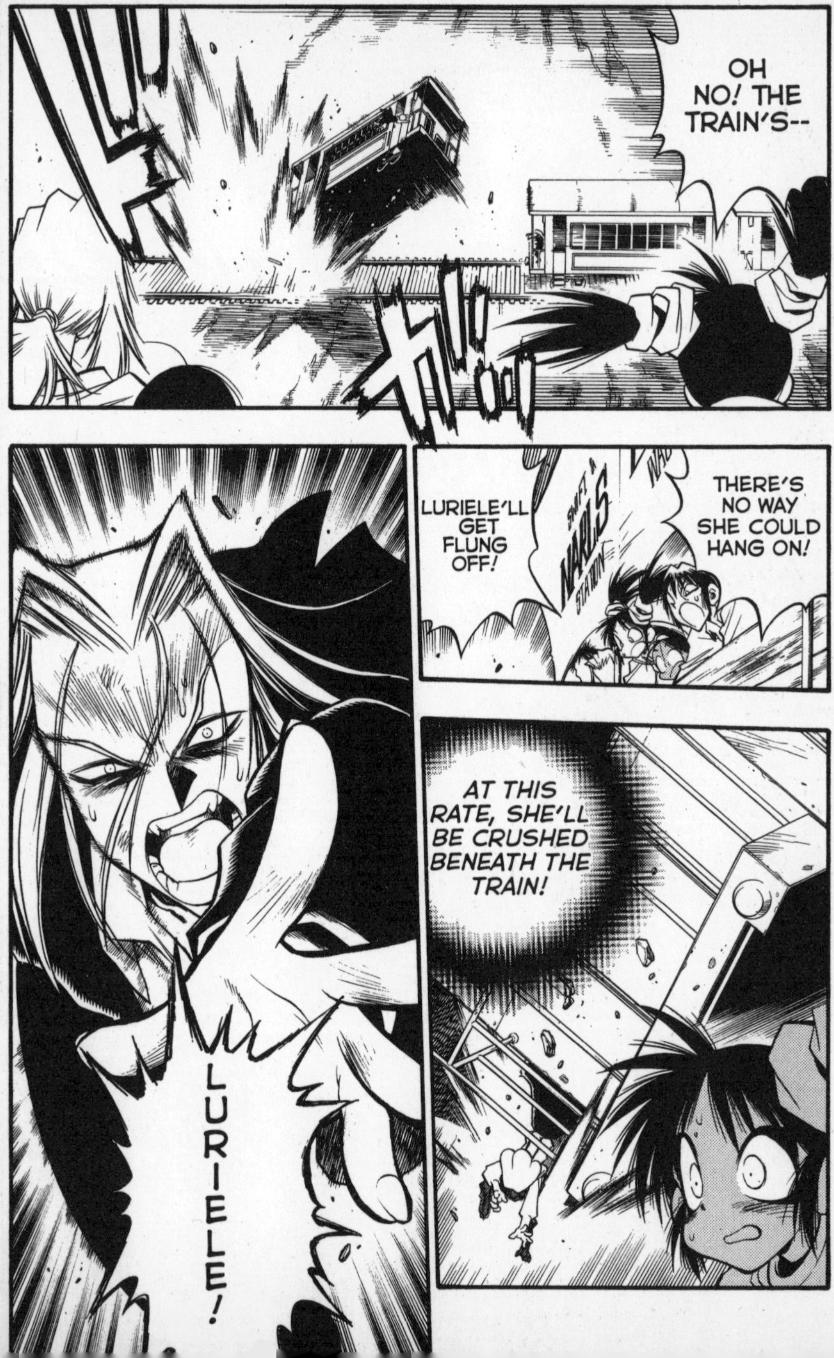
OH NO! THE TRAIN'S--
THERE'S NO WAY SHE COULD HANG ON!
LURIELE'LL GET FLUNG OFF!
AT THIS RATE, SHE'LL BE CRUSHED BENEATH THE TRAIN!
LURIELE!

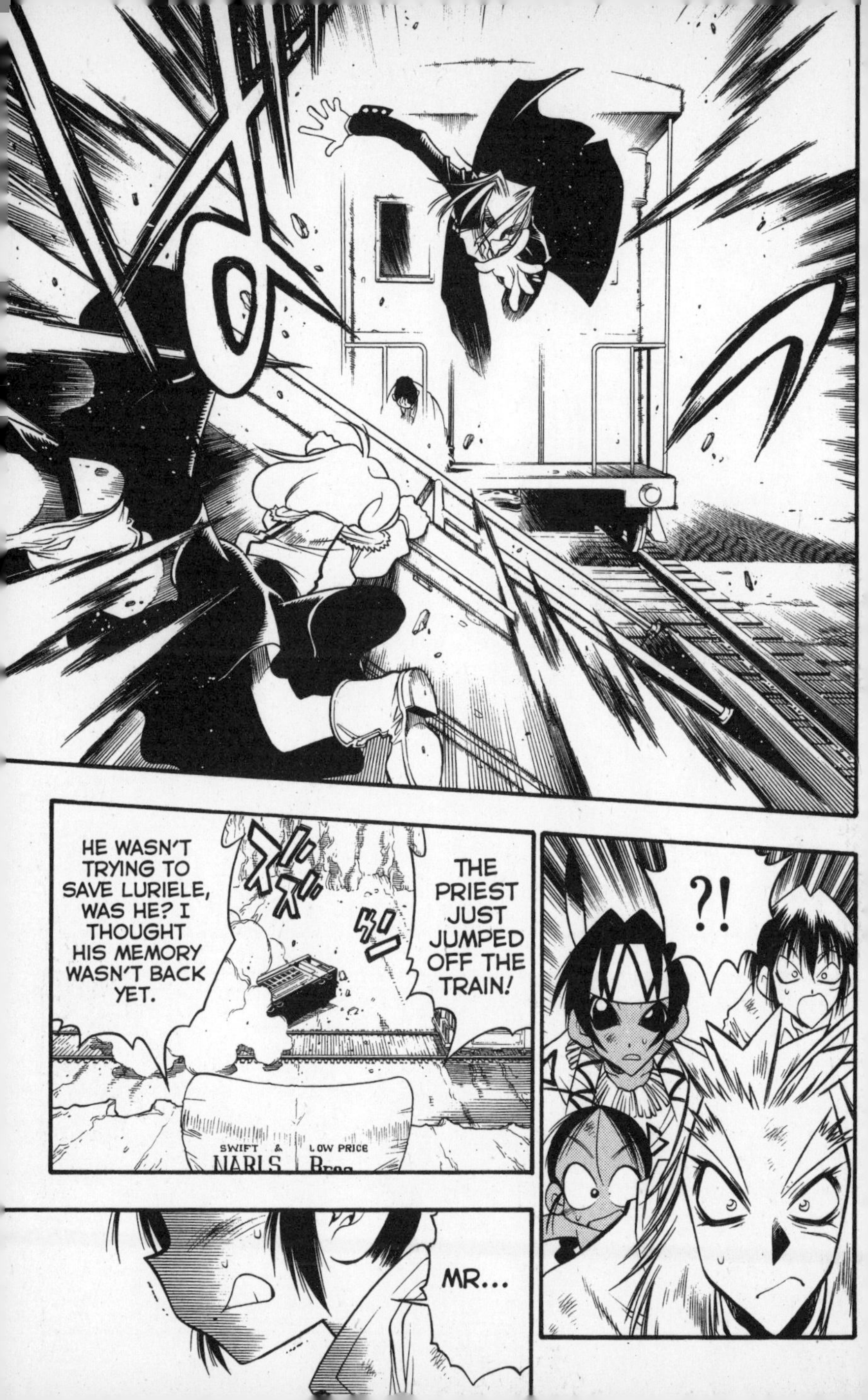
?!
THE PRIEST JUST JUMPED OFF THE TRAIN!
HE WASN'T TRYING TO SAVE LURIELE, WAS HE? I THOUGHT HIS MEMORY WASN'T BACK YET.
SWIFT & LOW PRICE
MR...

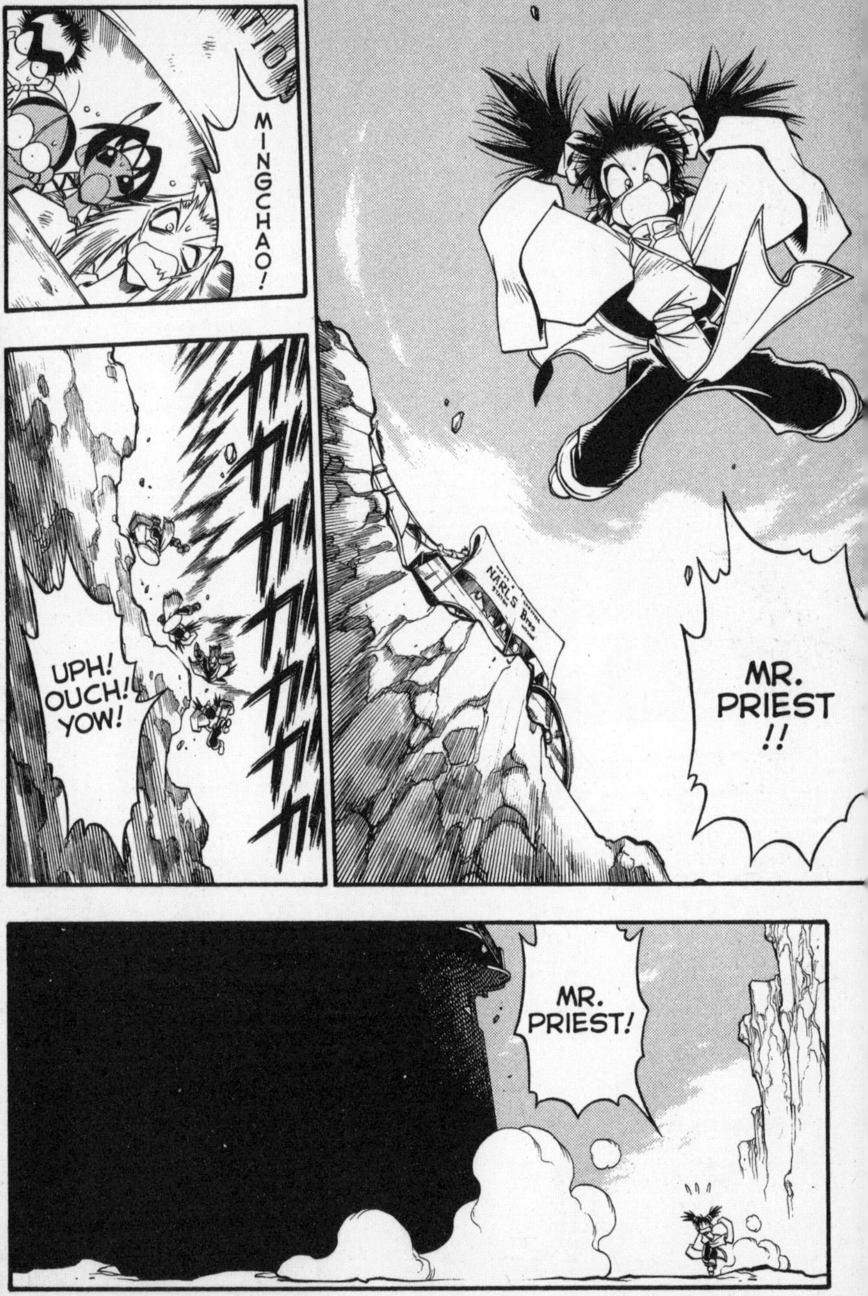
NARLS Bros
MR. PRIEST!!
MINGCHAO!
UPH! OUCH! YOW!
MR. PRIEST!

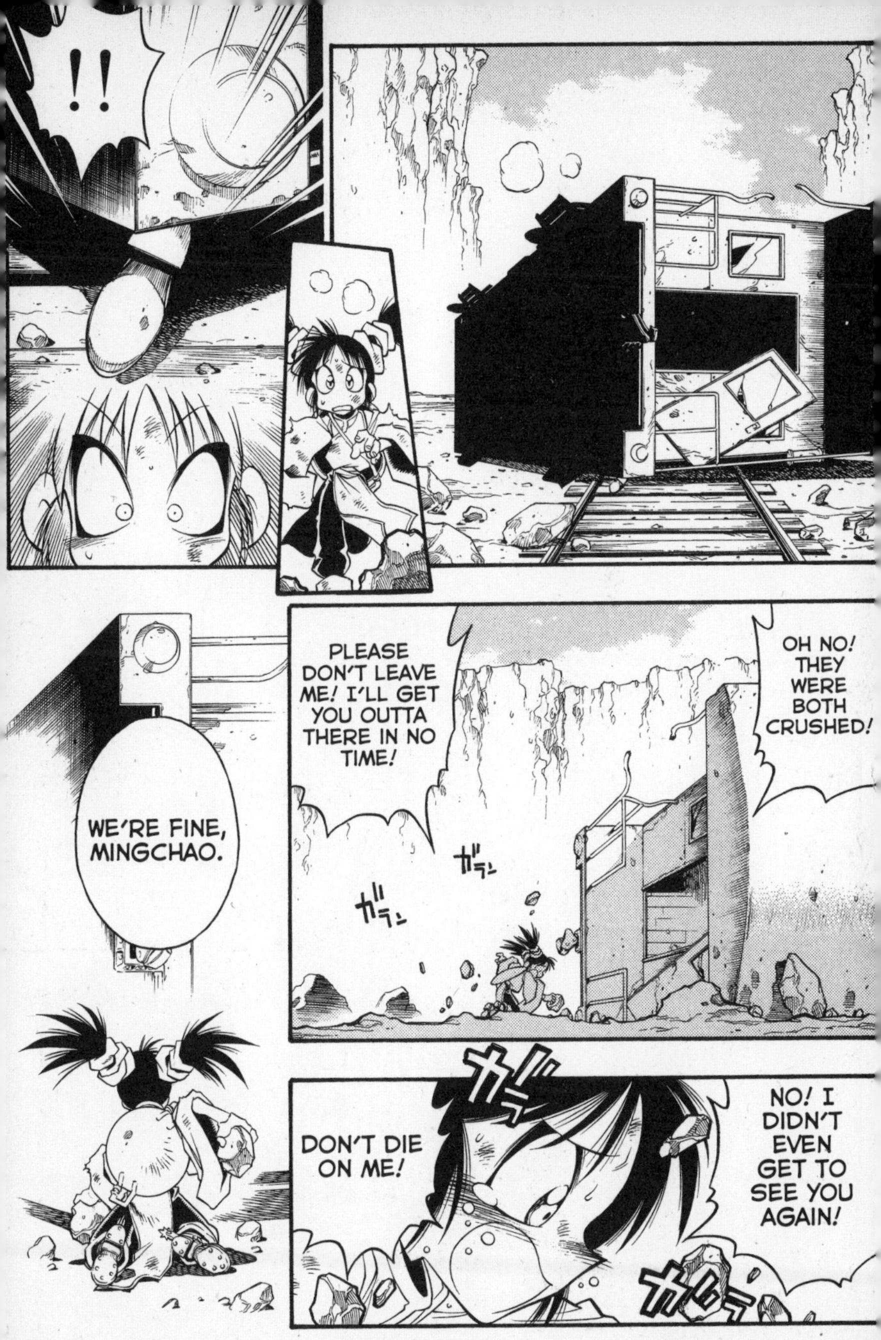
!!
OH NO! THEY WERE BOTH CRUSHED!
PLEASE DON'T LEAVE ME! I'LL GET YOU OUTTA THERE IN NO TIME!
ガラン
ガラン
NO! I DIDN'T EVEN GET TO SEE YOU AGAIN!
DON'T DIE ON ME!
WE'RE FINE, MINGCHAO.

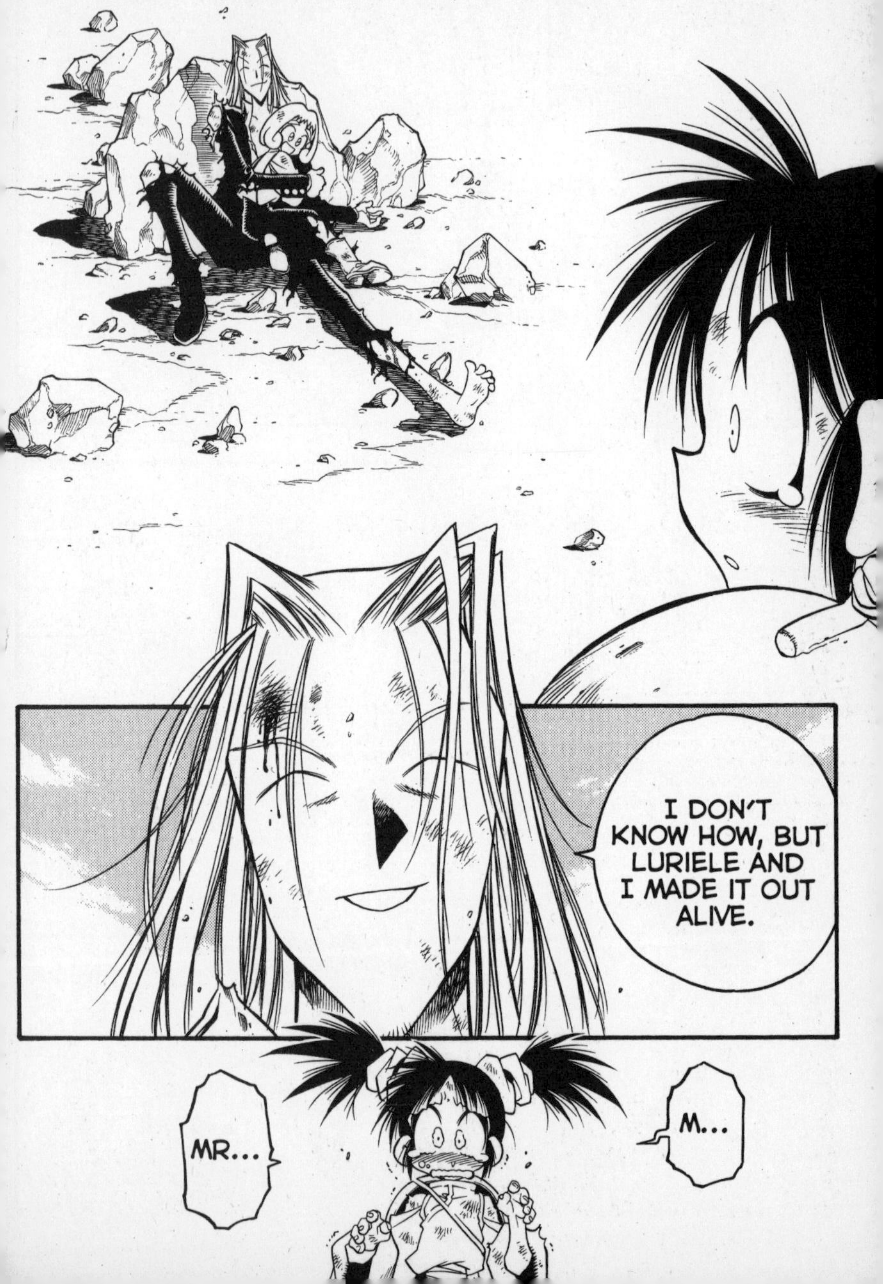
I DON'T KNOW HOW, BUT LURIELE AND I MADE IT OUT ALIVE.
M...
MR...

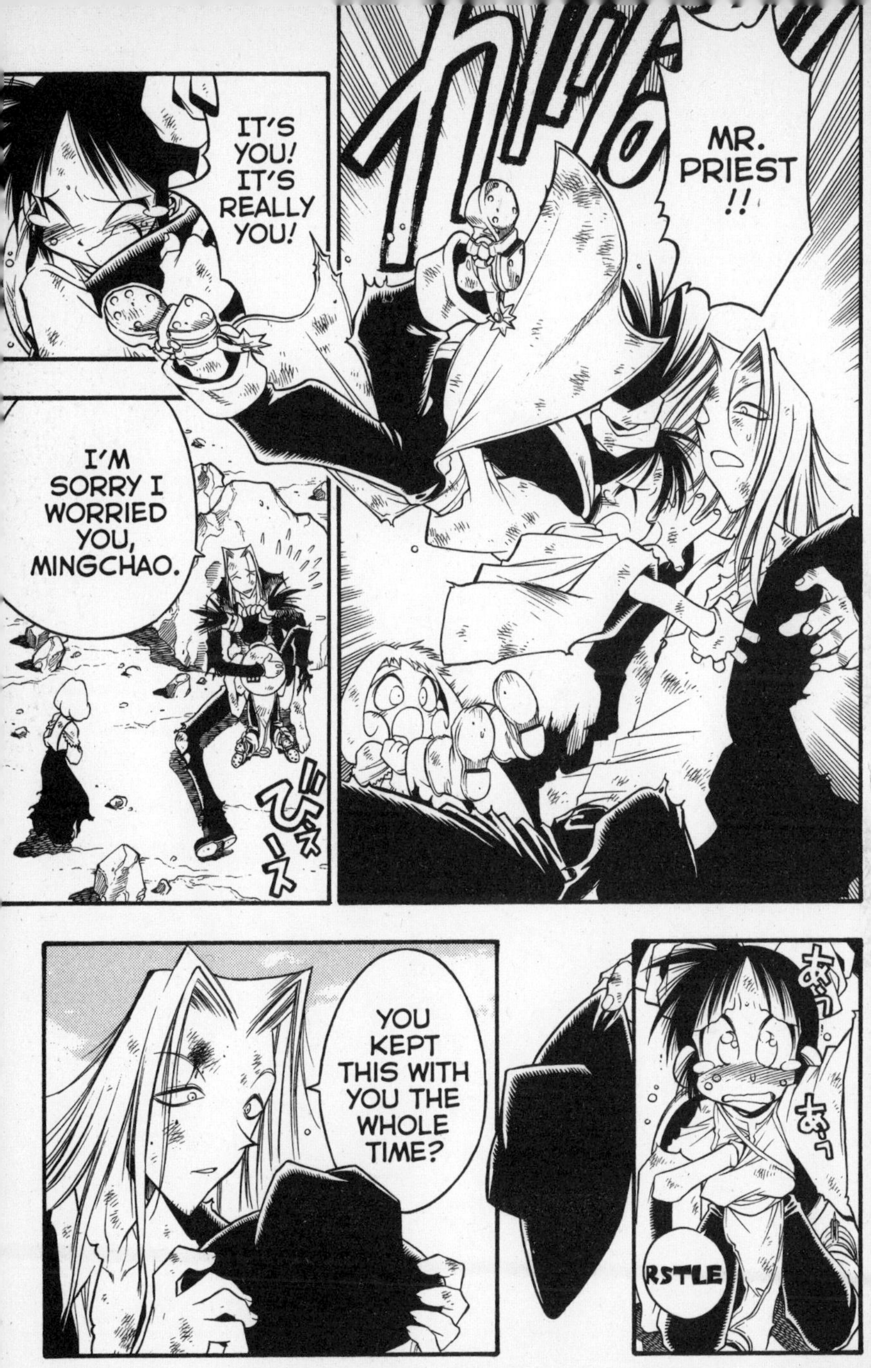
MR. PRIEST !!
IT'S YOU! IT'S REALLY YOU!
I'M SORRY I WORRIED YOU, MINGCHAO.
RSTLE
YOU KEPT THIS WITH YOU THE WHOLE TIME?

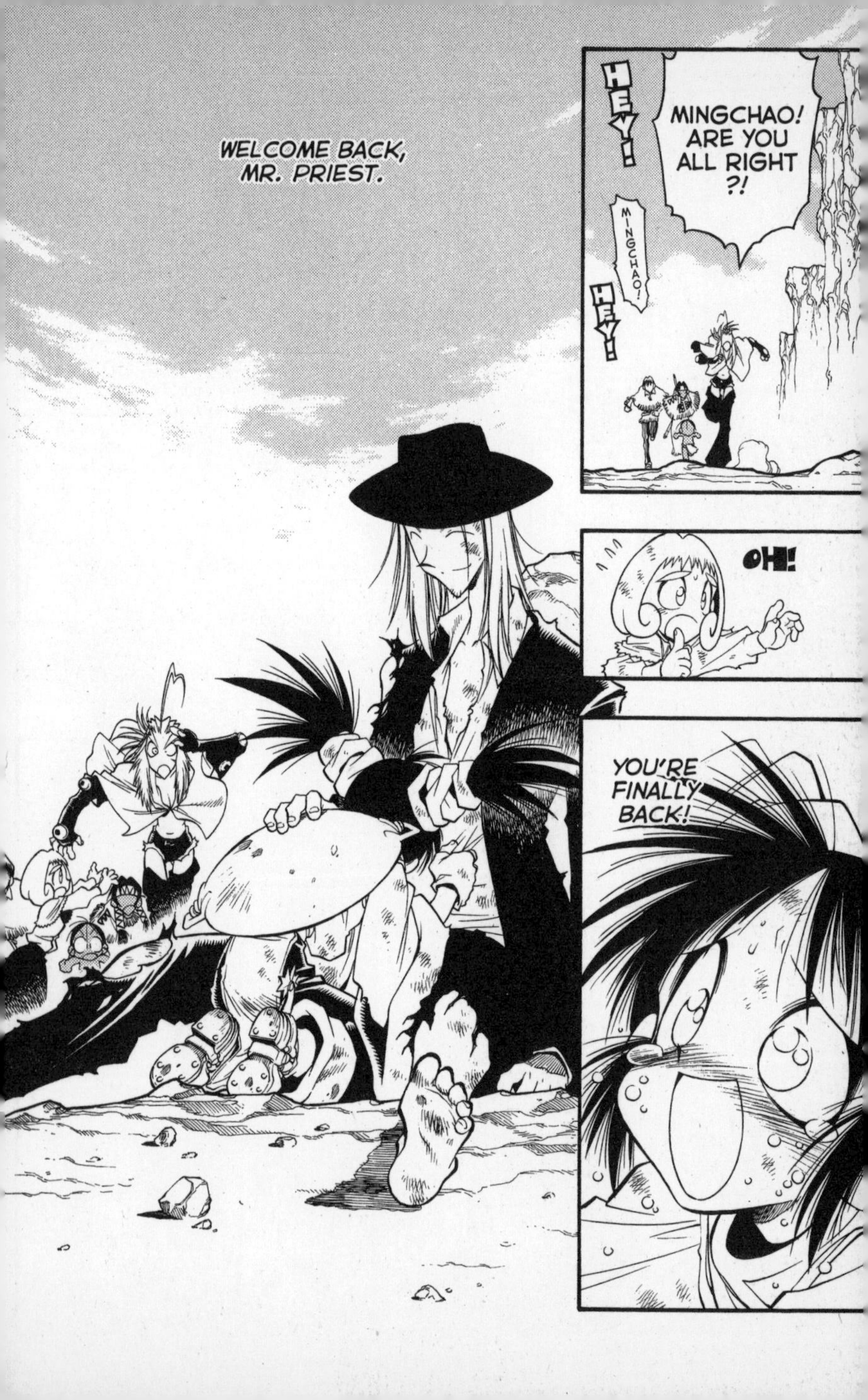
MINGCHAO! ARE YOU ALL RIGHT ?!
HEY!
MINGCHAO!
HEY!
OH!
YOU'RE FINALLY BACK!
WELCOME BACK, MR. PRIEST.

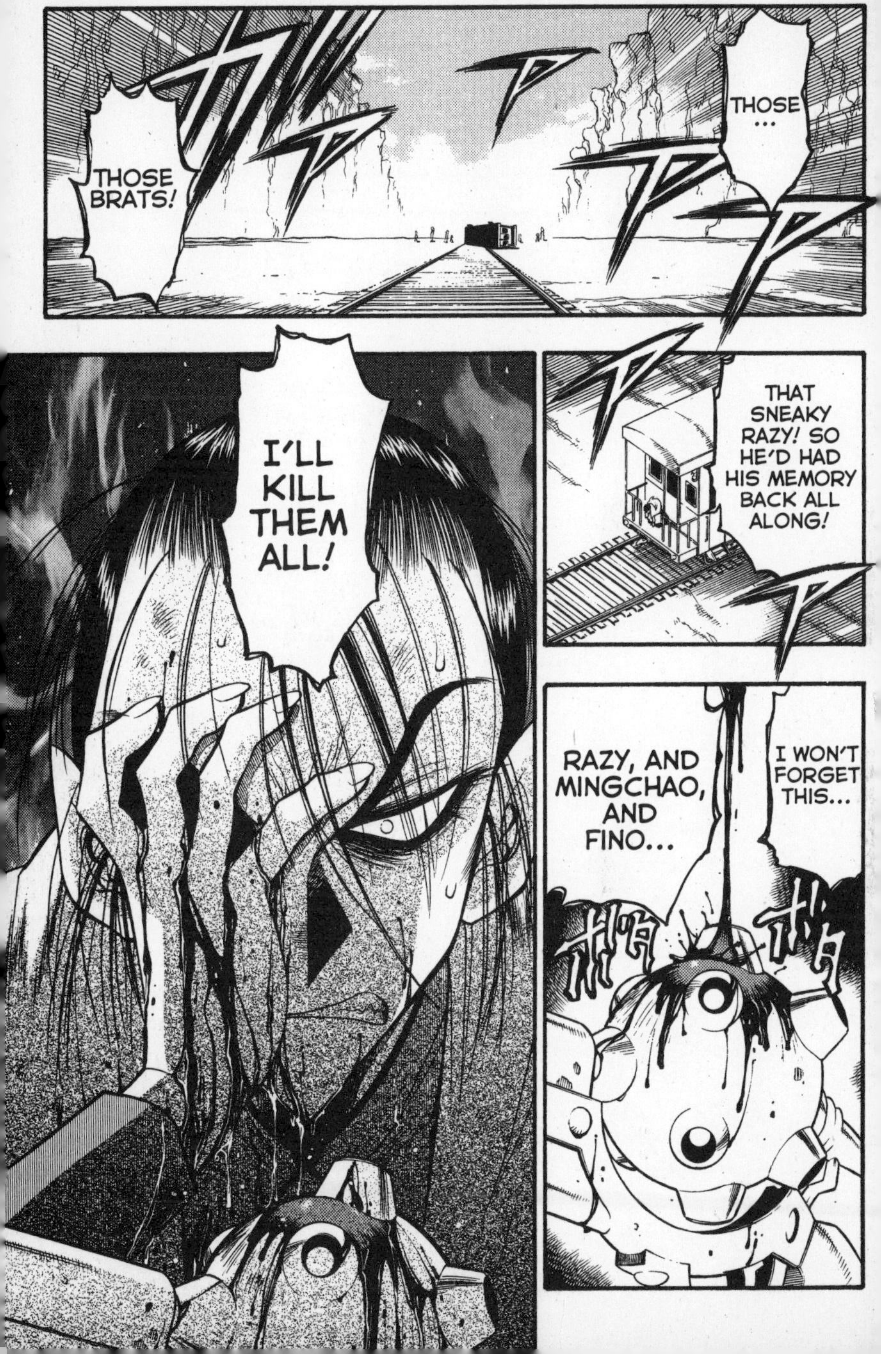
THOSE ...
THOSE BRATS!
THAT SNEAKY RAZY! SO HE'D HAD HIS MEMORY BACK ALL ALONG!
I WON'T FORGET THIS...
RAZY, AND MINGCHAO, AND FINO...
I'LL KILL THEM ALL!

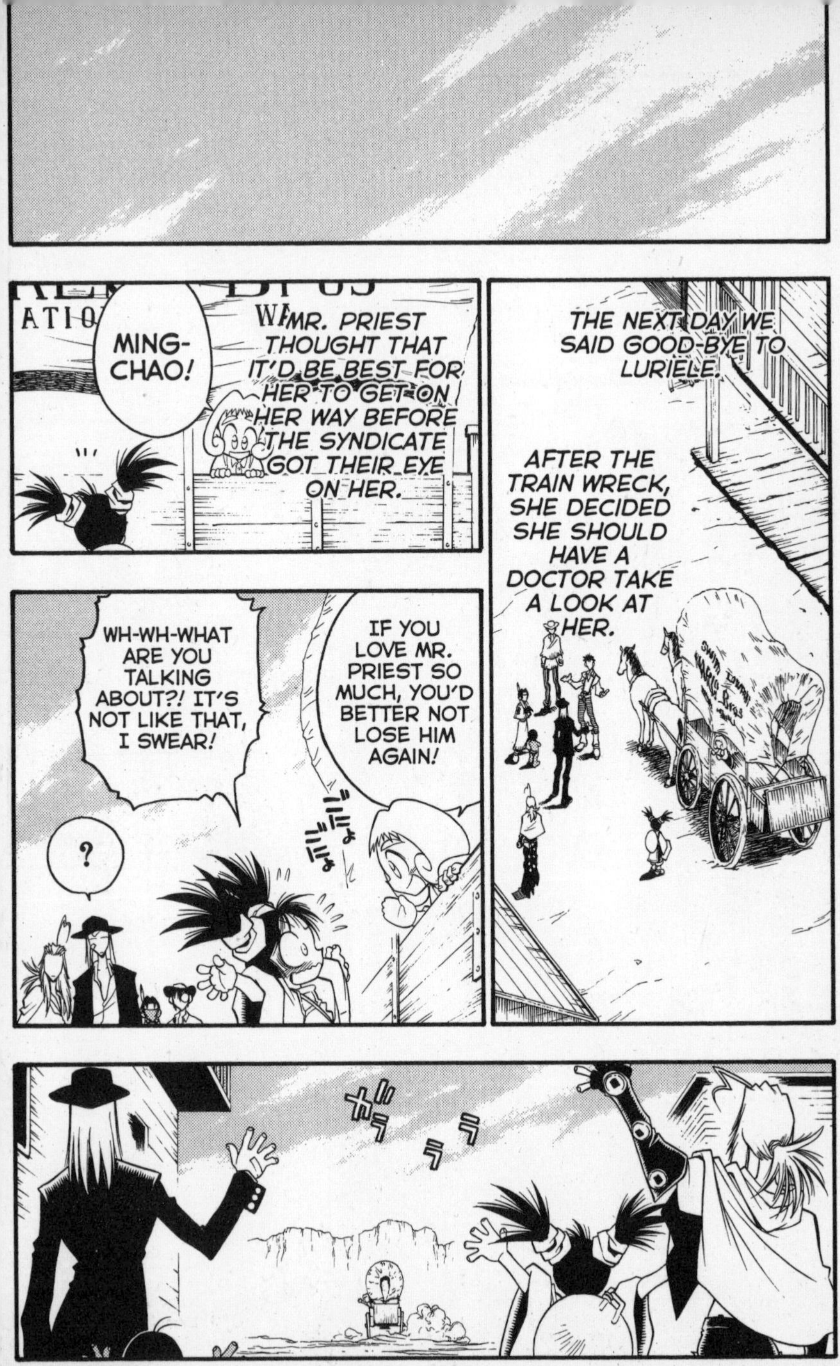
THE NEXT DAY WE SAID GOOD-BYE TO LURIELE.
AFTER THE TRAIN WRECK, SHE DECIDED SHE SHOULD HAVE A DOCTOR TAKE A LOOK AT HER.
MING-CHAO!
MR. PRIEST THOUGHT THAT IT'D BE BEST FOR HER TO GET ON HER WAY BEFORE THE SYNDICATE GOT THEIR EYE ON HER.
IF YOU LOVE MR. PRIEST SO MUCH, YOU'D BETTER NOT LOSE HIM AGAIN!
ごにょごにょ
WH-WH-WHAT ARE YOU TALKING ABOUT?! IT'S NOT LIKE THAT, I SWEAR!
?
ガラ
ラ
ラ

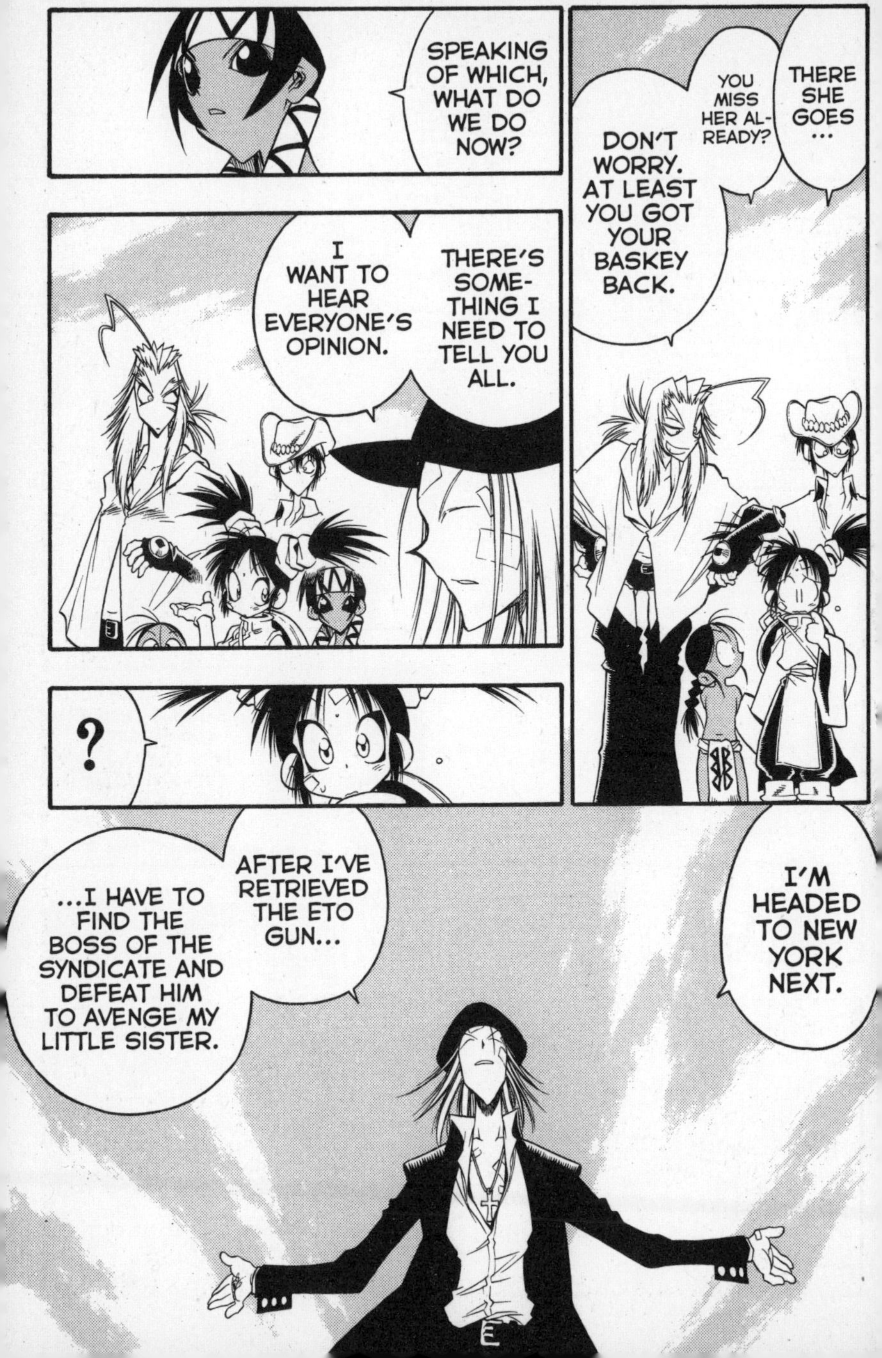
THERE SHE GOES...
YOU MISS HER AL-READY?
DON'T WORRY. AT LEAST YOU GOT YOUR BASKEY BACK.
SPEAKING OF WHICH, WHAT DO WE DO NOW?
THERE'S SOME-THING I NEED TO TELL YOU ALL.
I WANT TO HEAR EVERYONE'S OPINION.
?
I'M HEADED TO NEW YORK NEXT.
AFTER I'VE RETRIEVED THE ETO GUN...
...I HAVE TO FIND THE BOSS OF THE SYNDICATE AND DEFEAT HIM TO AVENGE MY LITTLE SISTER.

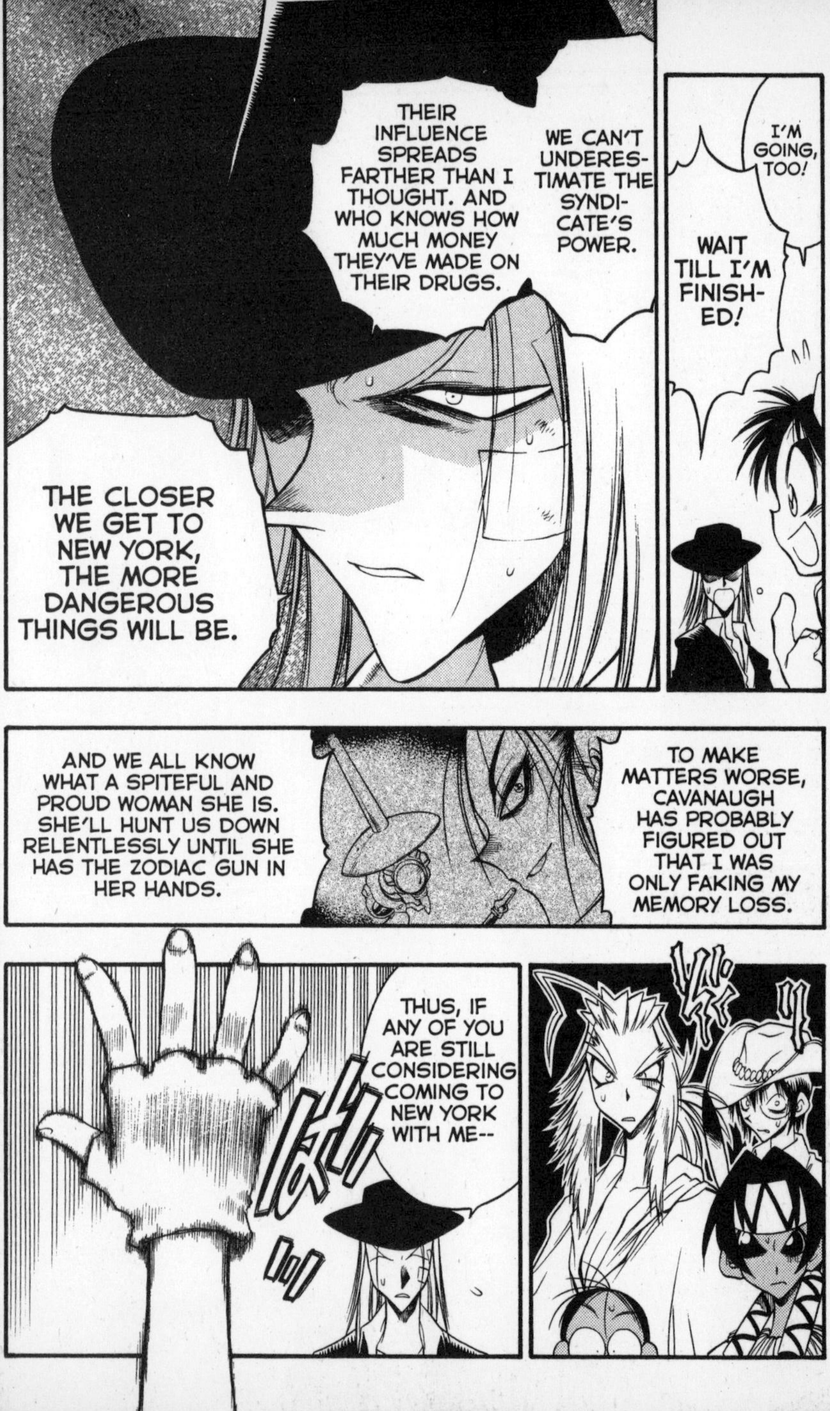
I'M GOING, TOO!
WAIT TILL I'M FINISH-ED!
WE CAN'T UNDERES-TIMATE THE SYNDI-CATE'S POWER.
THEIR INFLUENCE SPREADS FARTHER THAN I THOUGHT. AND WHO KNOWS HOW MUCH MONEY THEY'VE MADE ON THEIR DRUGS.
THE CLOSER WE GET TO NEW YORK, THE MORE DANGEROUS THINGS WILL BE.
TO MAKE MATTERS WORSE, CAVANAUGH HAS PROBABLY FIGURED OUT THAT I WAS ONLY FAKING MY MEMORY LOSS.
AND WE ALL KNOW WHAT A SPITEFUL AND PROUD WOMAN SHE IS. SHE'LL HUNT US DOWN RELENTLESSLY UNTIL SHE HAS THE ZODIAC GUN IN HER HANDS.
THUS, IF ANY OF YOU ARE STILL CONSIDERING COMING TO NEW YORK WITH ME--

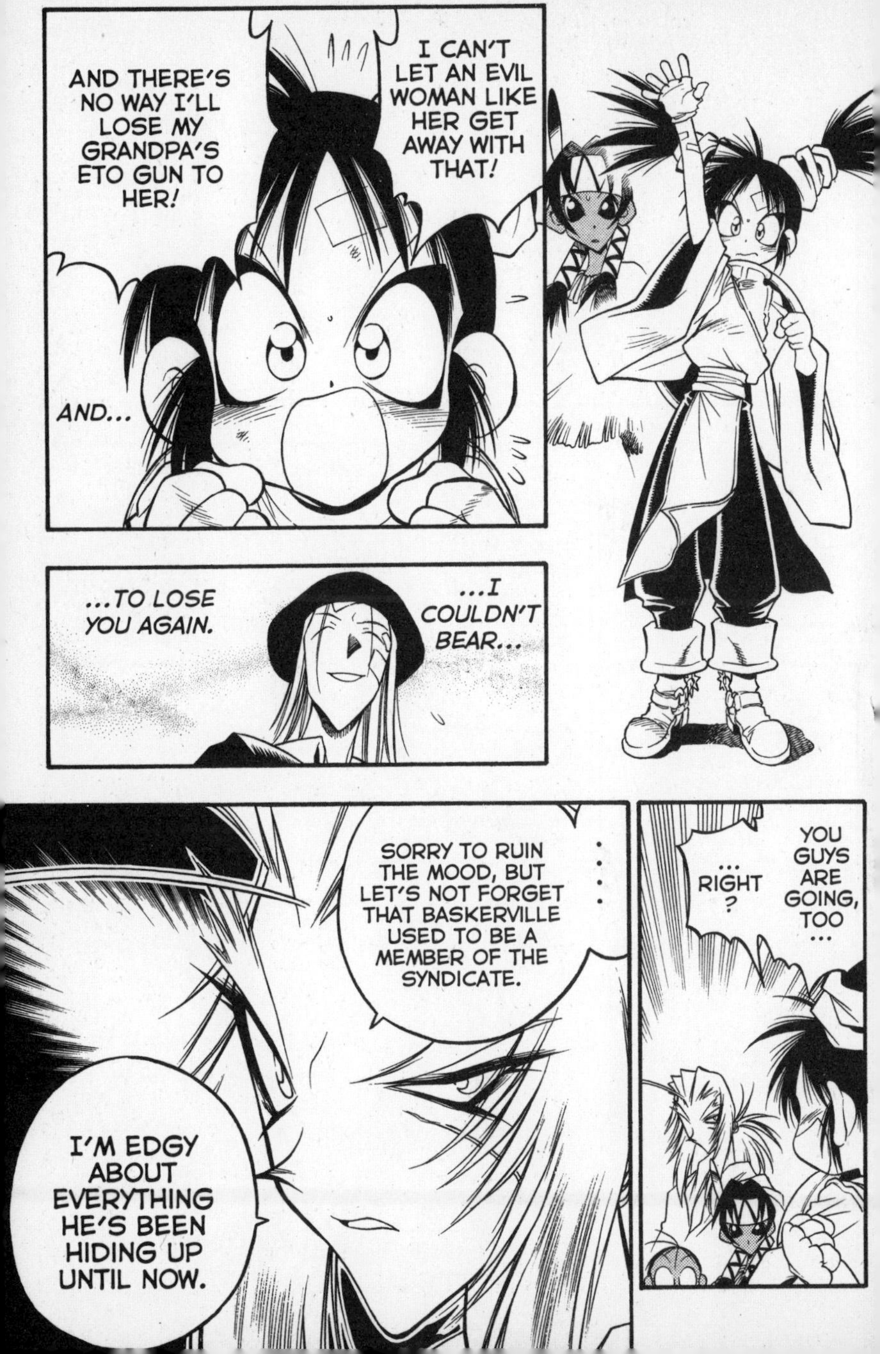
I CAN'T LET AN EVIL WOMAN LIKE HER GET AWAY WITH THAT!
AND THERE'S NO WAY I'LL LOSE MY GRANDPA'S ETO GUN TO HER!
AND...
...I COULDN'T BEAR...
...TO LOSE YOU AGAIN.
YOU GUYS ARE GOING, TOO...
...RIGHT?
....
SORRY TO RUIN THE MOOD, BUT LET'S NOT FORGET THAT BASKERVILLE USED TO BE A MEMBER OF THE SYNDICATE.
I'M EDGY ABOUT EVERYTHING HE'S BEEN HIDING UP UNTIL NOW.

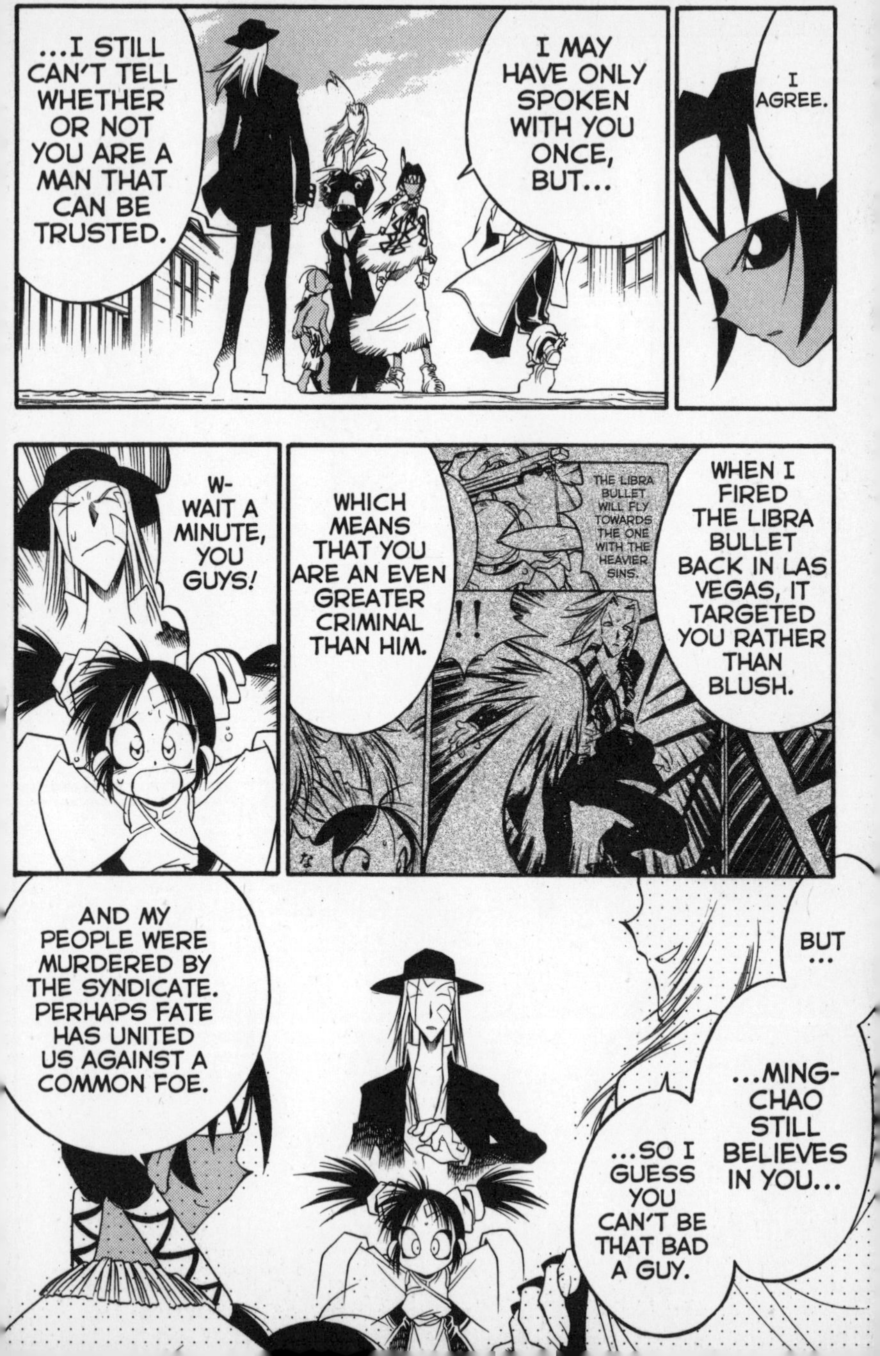
I AGREE.
I MAY HAVE ONLY SPOKEN WITH YOU ONCE, BUT...
...I STILL CAN'T TELL WHETHER OR NOT YOU ARE A MAN THAT CAN BE TRUSTED.
WHEN I FIRED THE LIBRA BULLET BACK IN LAS VEGAS, IT TARGETED YOU RATHER THAN BLUSH.
THE LIBRA BULLET WILL FLY TOWARDS THE ONE WITH THE HEAVIER SINS.
!!
WHICH MEANS THAT YOU ARE AN EVEN GREATER CRIMINAL THAN HIM.
W-WAIT A MINUTE, YOU GUYS!
BUT...
...MING-CHAO STILL BELIEVES IN YOU...
...SO I GUESS YOU CAN'T BE THAT BAD A GUY.
AND MY PEOPLE WERE MURDERED BY THE SYNDICATE. PERHAPS FATE HAS UNITED US AGAINST A COMMON FOE.

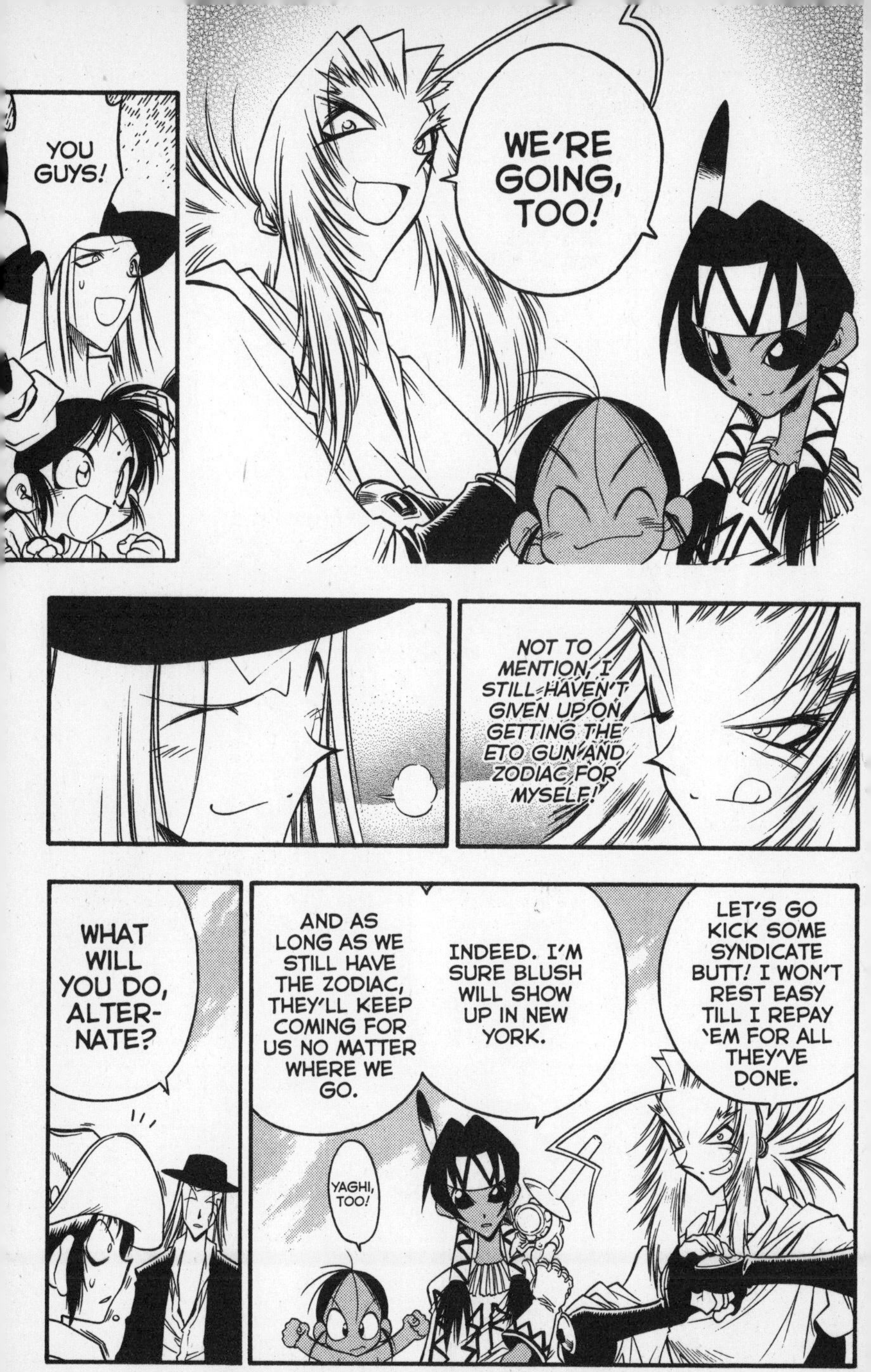
WE'RE GOING, TOO!
YOU GUYS!
NOT TO MENTION, I STILL HAVEN'T GIVEN UP ON GETTING THE ETO GUN AND ZODIAC FOR MYSELF!
LET'S GO KICK SOME SYNDICATE BUTT! I WON'T REST EASY TILL I REPAY 'EM FOR ALL THEY'VE DONE.
INDEED. I'M SURE BLUSH WILL SHOW UP IN NEW YORK.
AND AS LONG AS WE STILL HAVE THE ZODIAC, THEY'LL KEEP COMING FOR US NO MATTER WHERE WE GO.
YAGHI, TOO!
WHAT WILL YOU DO, ALTERNATE?

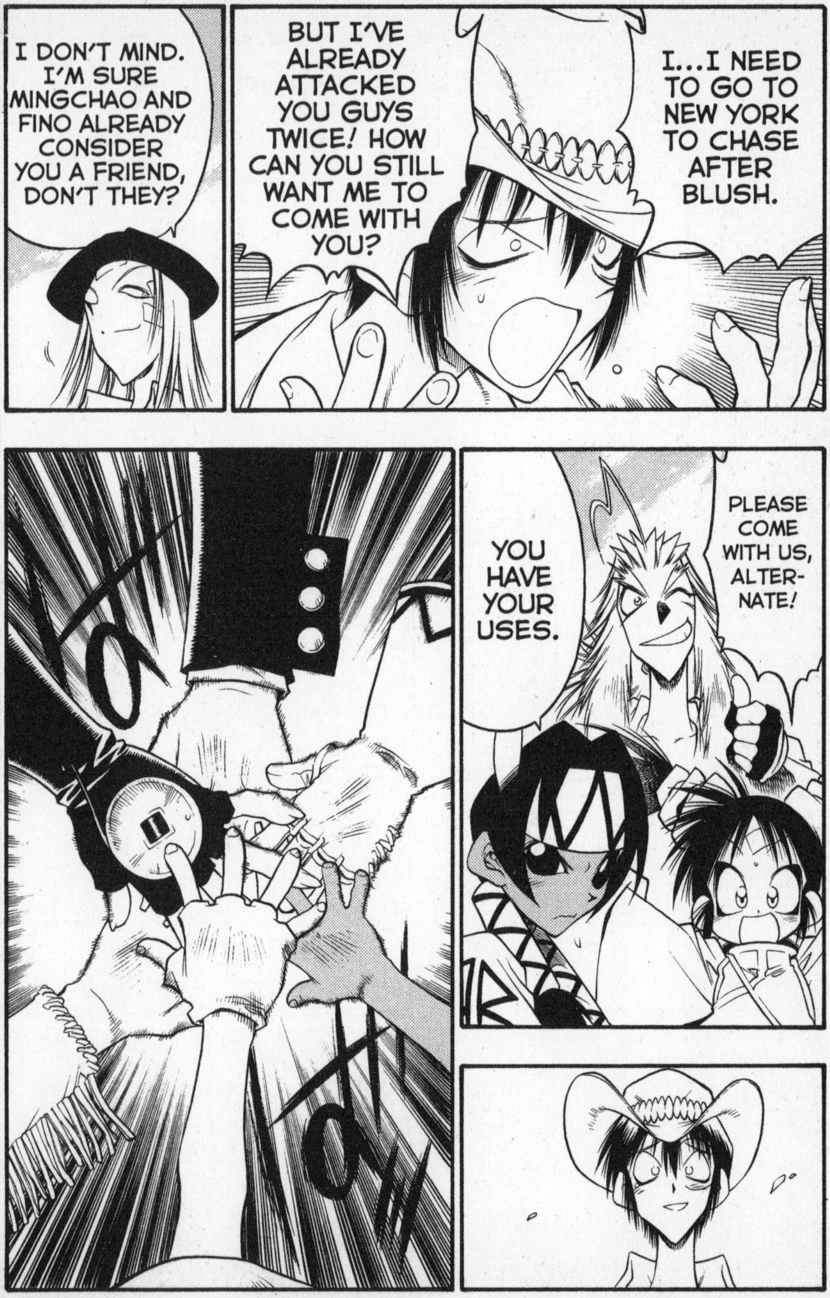
I...I NEED TO GO TO NEW YORK TO CHASE AFTER BLUSH.
BUT I'VE ALREADY ATTACKED YOU GUYS TWICE! HOW CAN YOU STILL WANT ME TO COME WITH YOU?
I DON'T MIND. I'M SURE MINGCHAO AND FINO ALREADY CONSIDER YOU A FRIEND, DON'T THEY?
PLEASE COME WITH US, ALTER-NATE!
YOU HAVE YOUR USES.

LET'S GO TO NEW YORK!

. . .

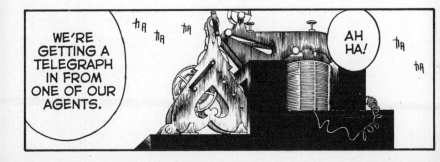

WE'RE GETTING A TELEGRAPH IN FROM ONE OF OUR AGENTS.

AH HA!

IT'S JUST AS YOU PREDICTED! THEY'RE HEADED FOR TOWN!

MS. CAVA-NAUGH!

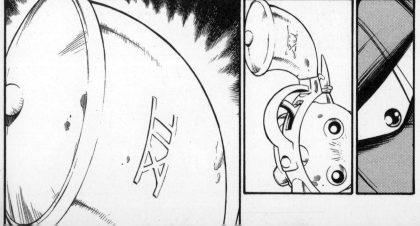

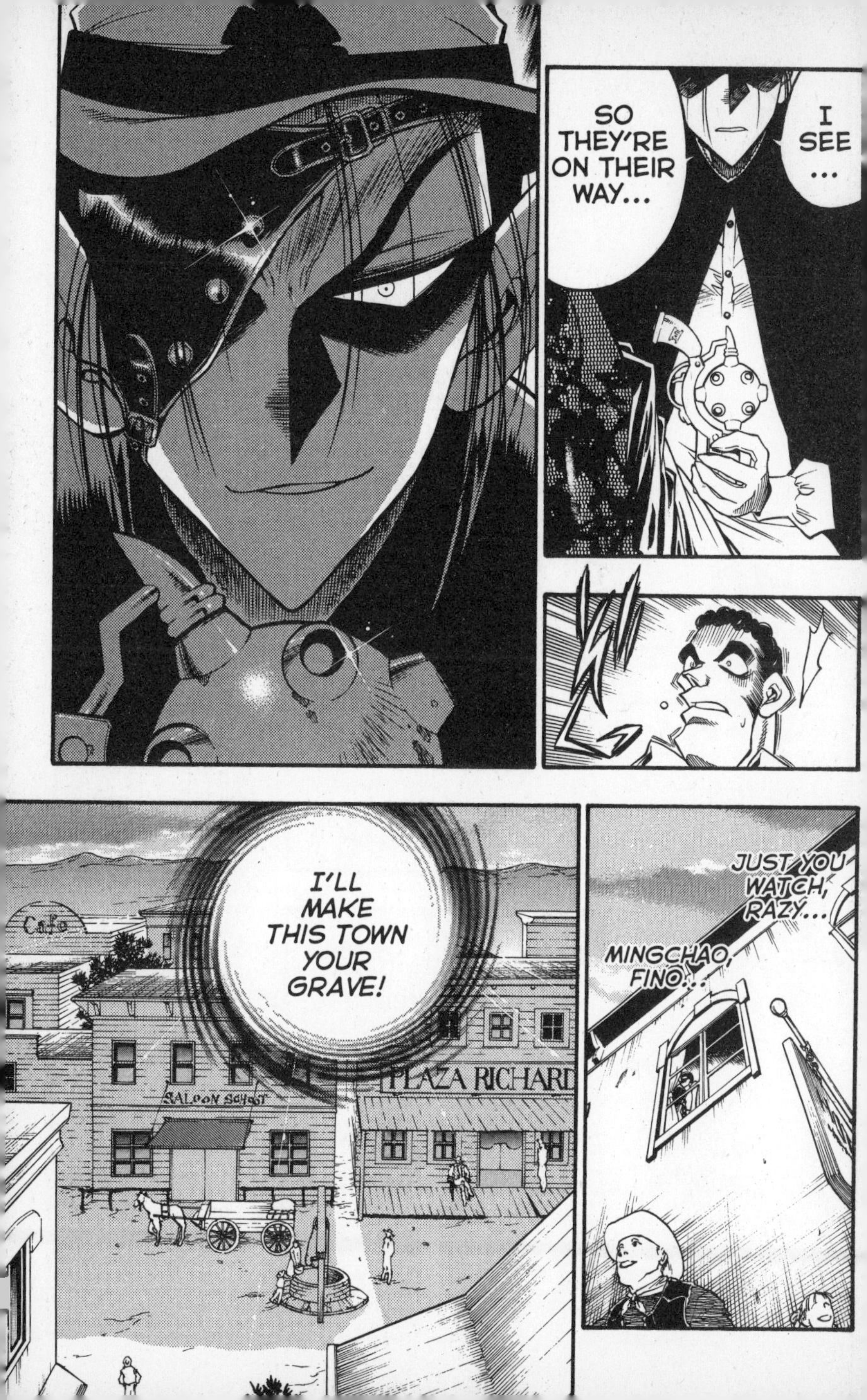
I SEE ...
SO THEY'RE ON THEIR WAY...
JUST YOU WATCH, RAZY...
MINGCHAO, FINO...
I'LL MAKE THIS TOWN YOUR GRAVE!
Cafe
PLAZA RICHARD

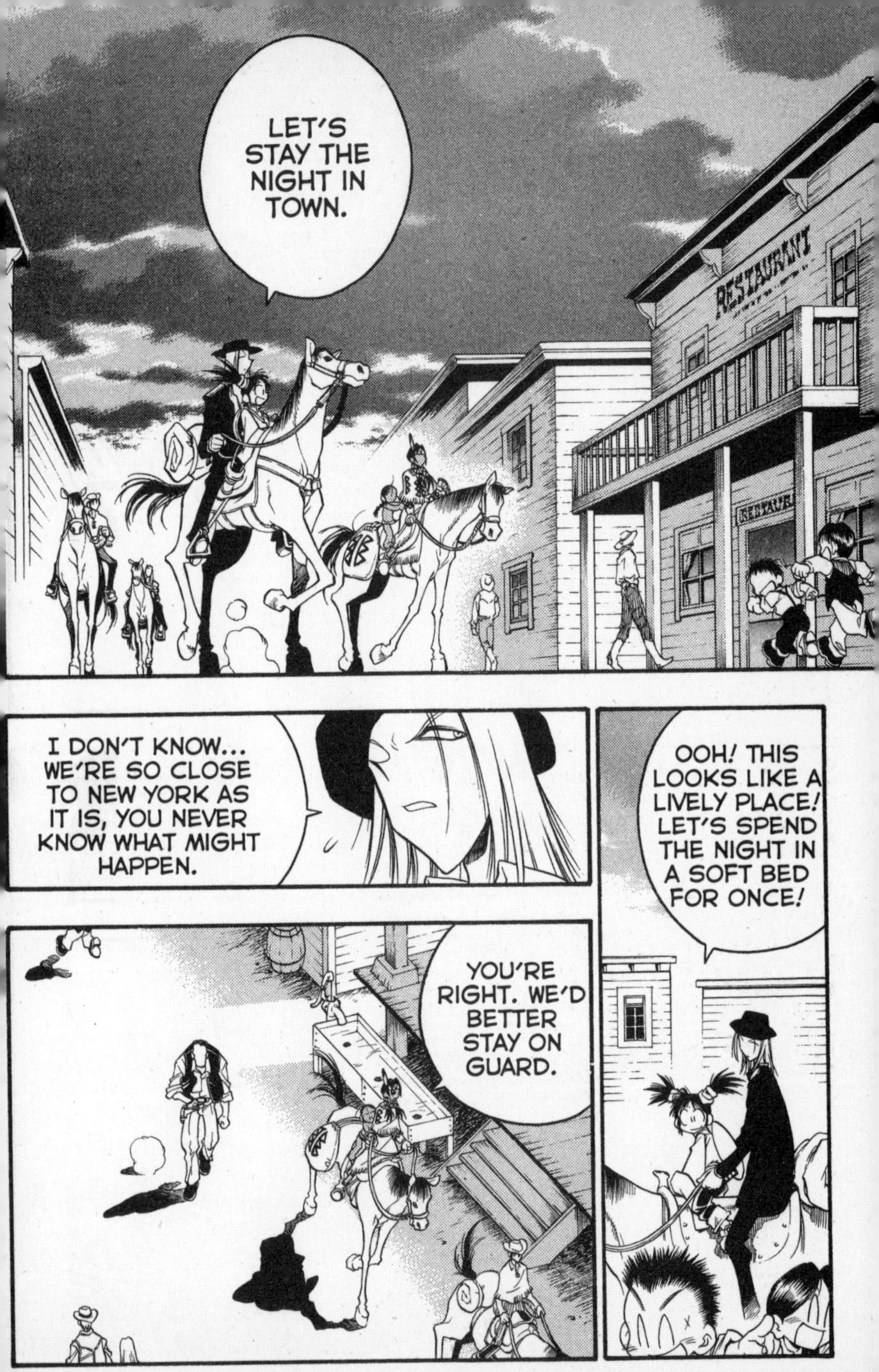
LET'S STAY THE NIGHT IN TOWN.
RESTAURANT
OOH! THIS LOOKS LIKE A LIVELY PLACE! LET'S SPEND THE NIGHT IN A SOFT BED FOR ONCE!
I DON'T KNOW... WE'RE SO CLOSE TO NEW YORK AS IT IS, YOU NEVER KNOW WHAT MIGHT HAPPEN.
YOU'RE RIGHT. WE'D BETTER STAY ON GUARD.

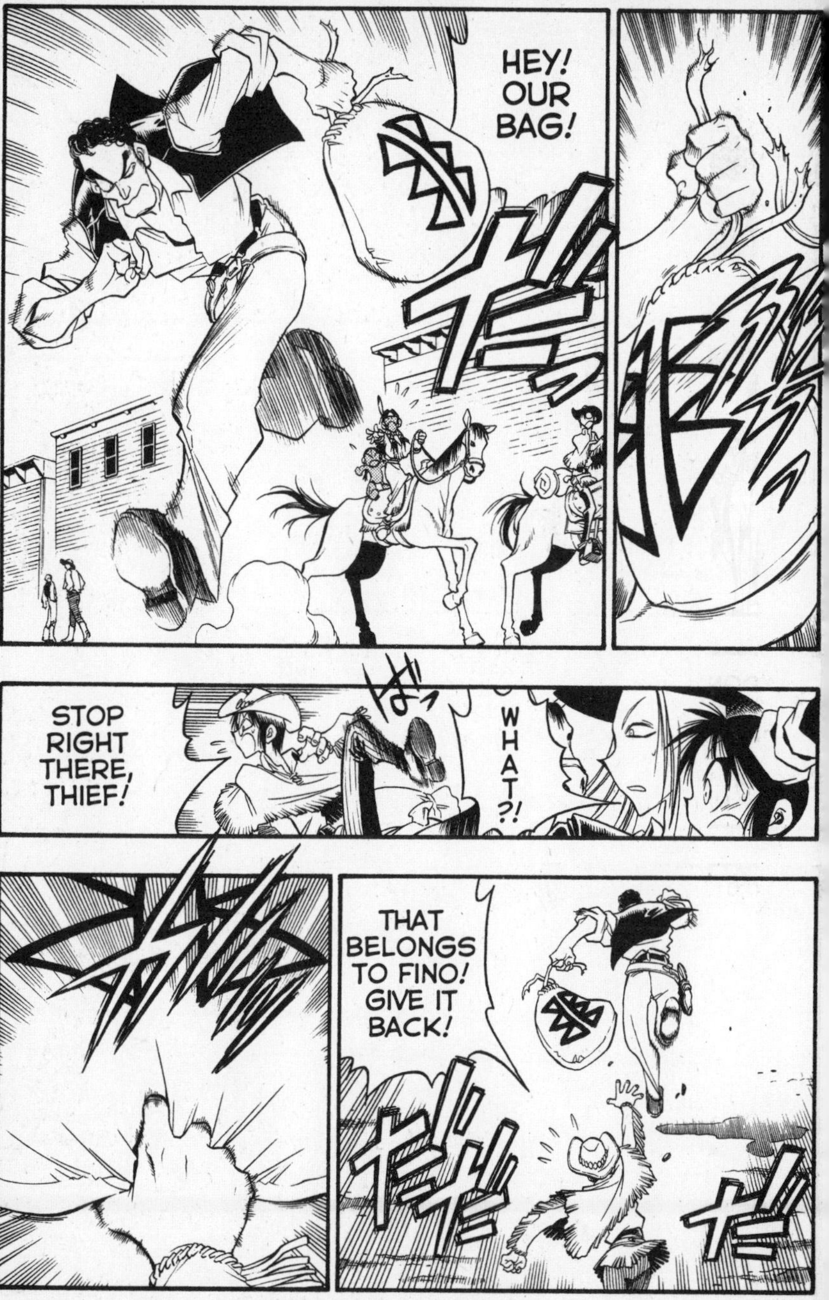
HEY! OUR BAG!
WHAT?!
STOP RIGHT THERE, THIEF!
THAT BELONGS TO FINO! GIVE IT BACK!

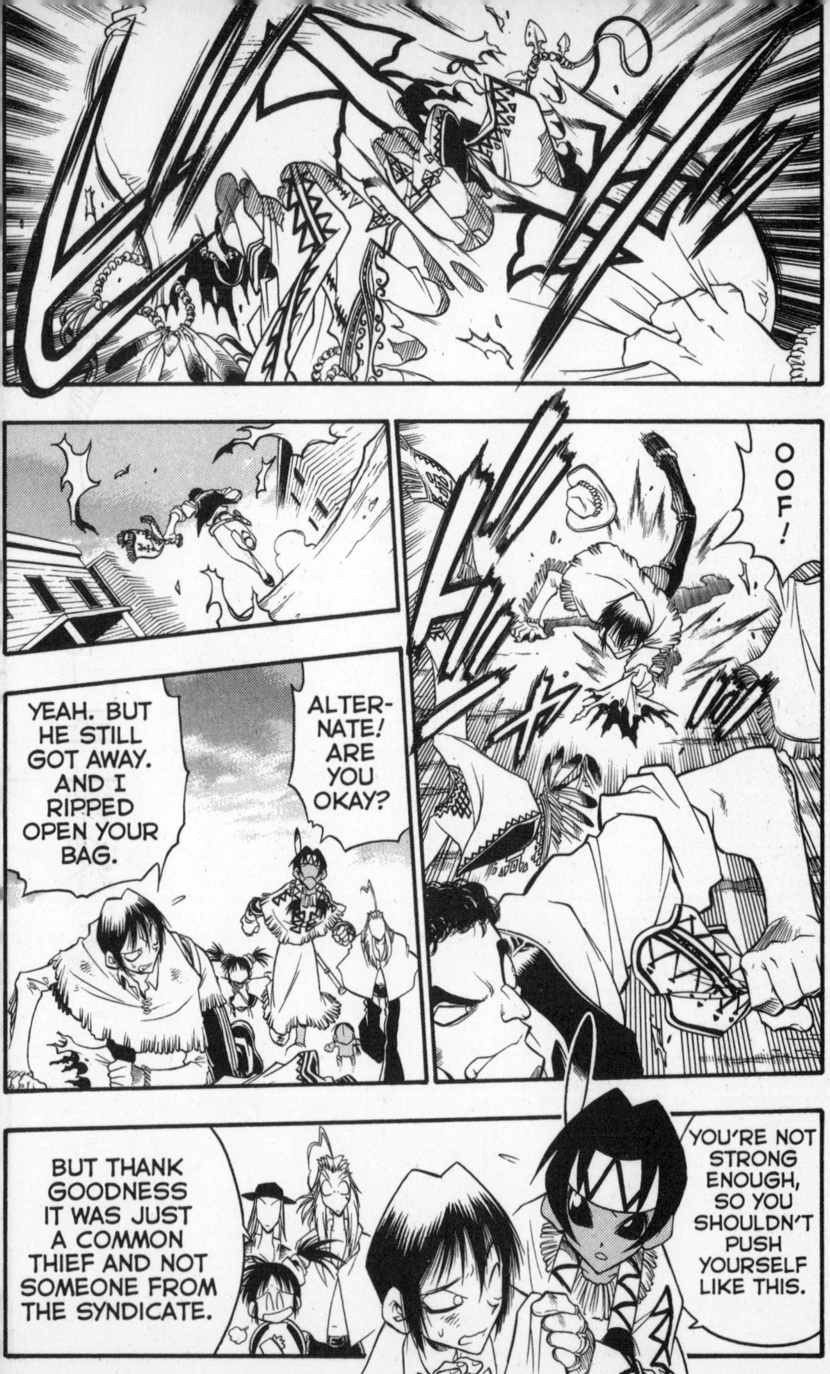
OOF!
ALTER-NATE! ARE YOU OKAY?
YEAH. BUT HE STILL GOT AWAY. AND I RIPPED OPEN YOUR BAG.
YOU'RE NOT STRONG ENOUGH, SO YOU SHOULDN'T PUSH YOURSELF LIKE THIS.
BUT THANK GOODNESS IT WAS JUST A COMMON THIEF AND NOT SOMEONE FROM THE SYNDICATE.

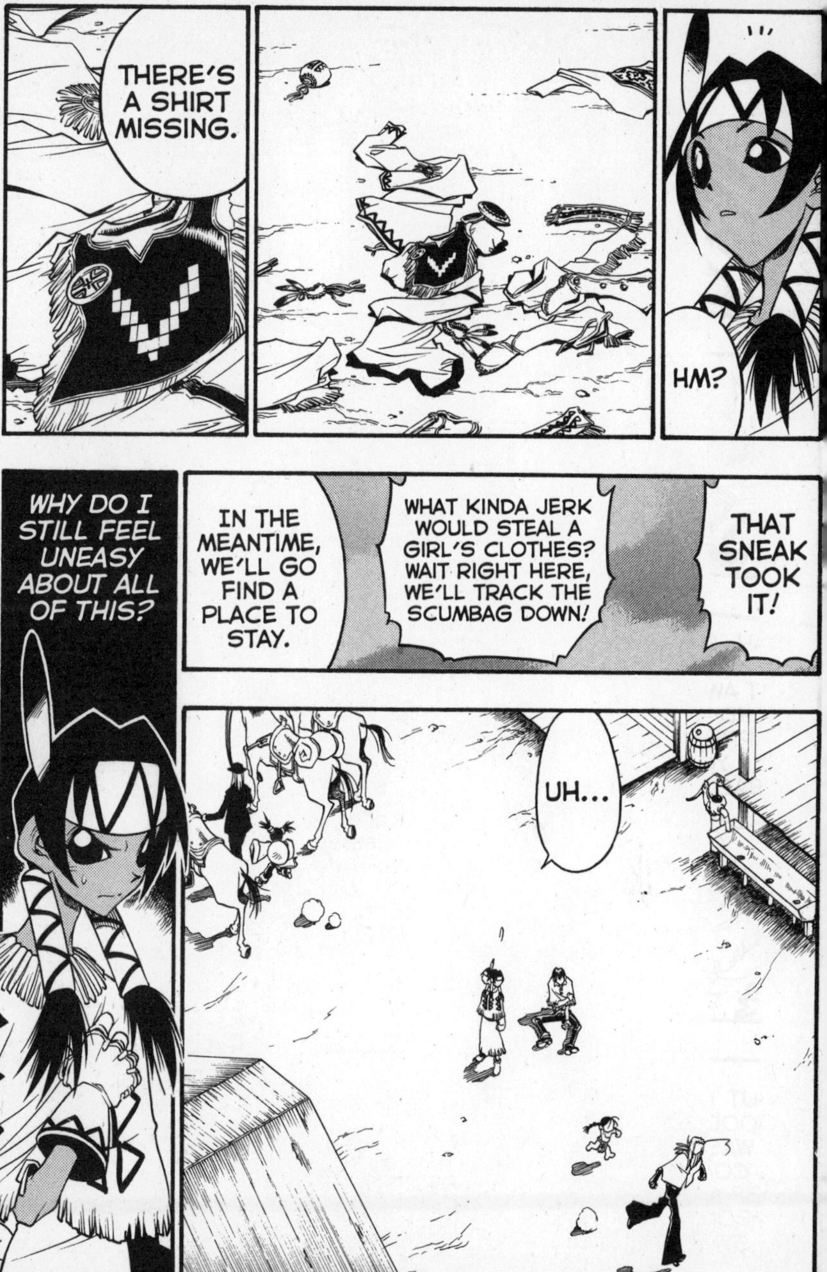
HM?
THERE'S A SHIRT MISSING.
THAT SNEAK TOOK IT!
WHAT KINDA JERK WOULD STEAL A GIRL'S CLOTHES? WAIT RIGHT HERE, WE'LL TRACK THE SCUMBAG DOWN!
IN THE MEANTIME, WE'LL GO FIND A PLACE TO STAY.
UH...
WHY DO I STILL FEEL UNEASY ABOUT ALL OF THIS?

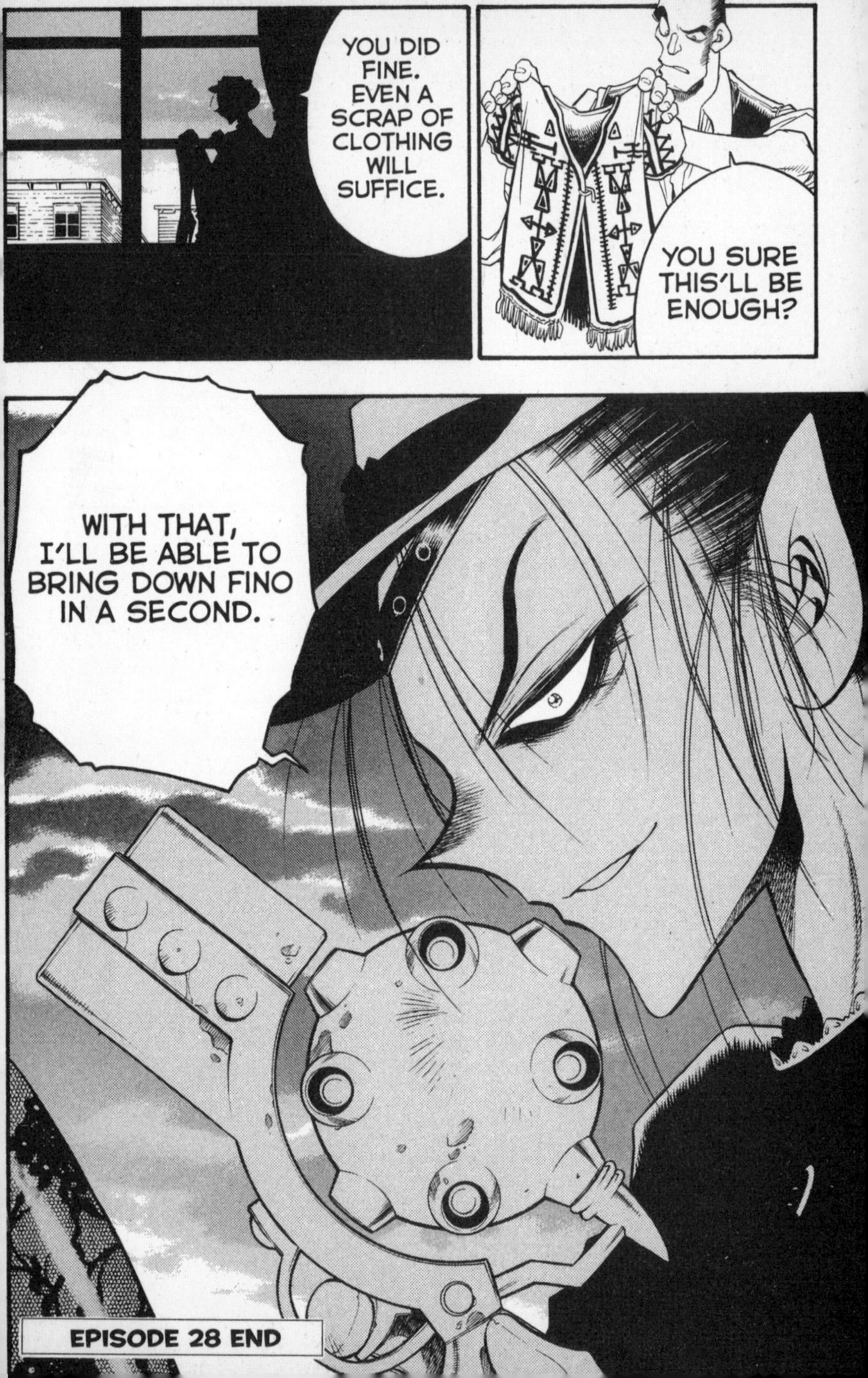
YOU SURE THIS'LL BE ENOUGH?
YOU DID FINE. EVEN A SCRAP OF CLOTHING WILL SUFFICE.
WITH THAT, I'LL BE ABLE TO BRING DOWN FINO IN A SECOND.
EPISODE 28 END

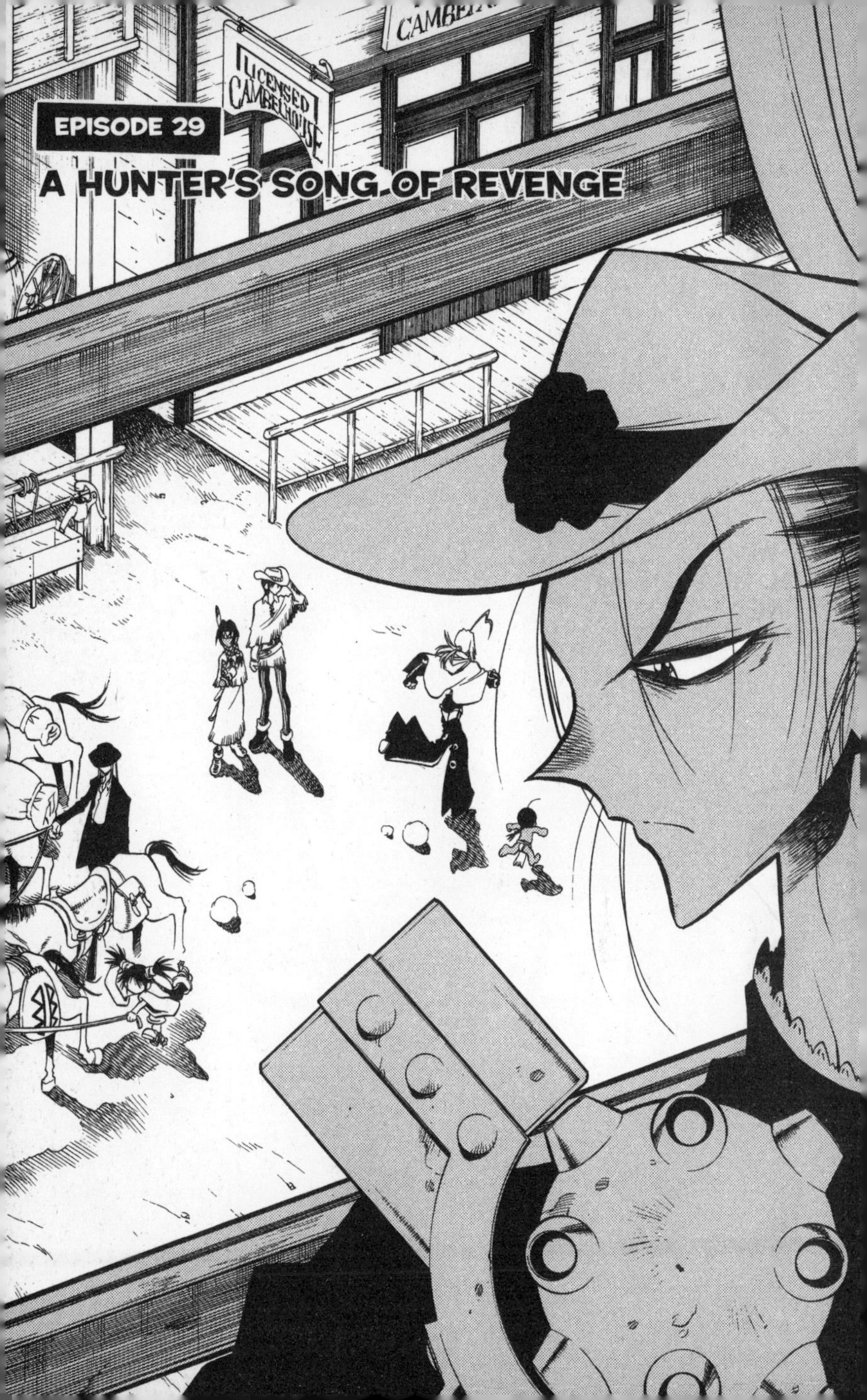
EPISODE 29
A HUNTER'S SONG OF REVENGE
LICENSED CAMBLEHOUSE
CAMBE

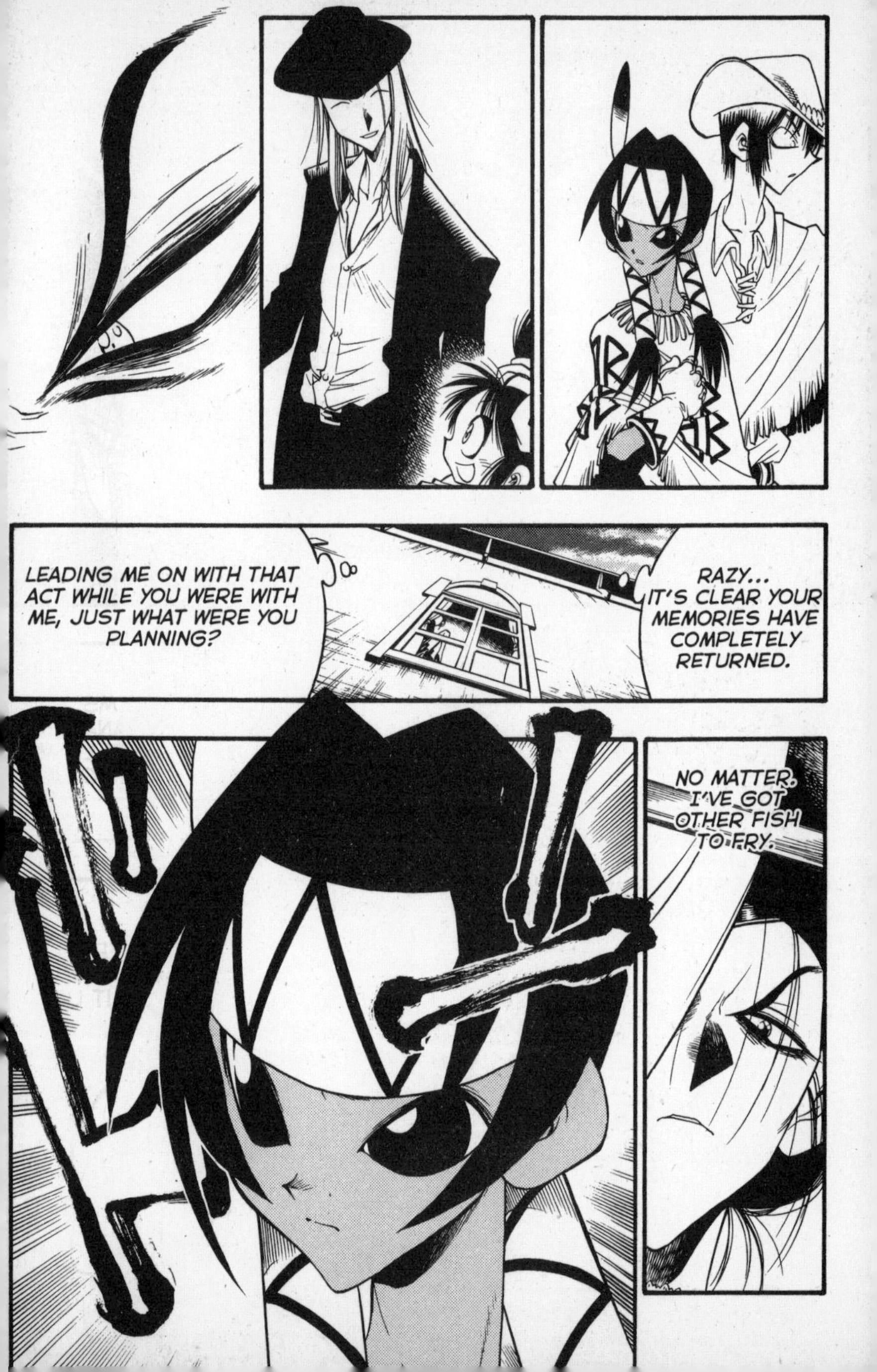
RAZY... IT'S CLEAR YOUR MEMORIES HAVE COMPLETELY RETURNED.
LEADING ME ON WITH THAT ACT WHILE YOU WERE WITH ME, JUST WHAT WERE YOU PLANNING?
NO MATTER. I'VE GOT OTHER FISH TO FRY.

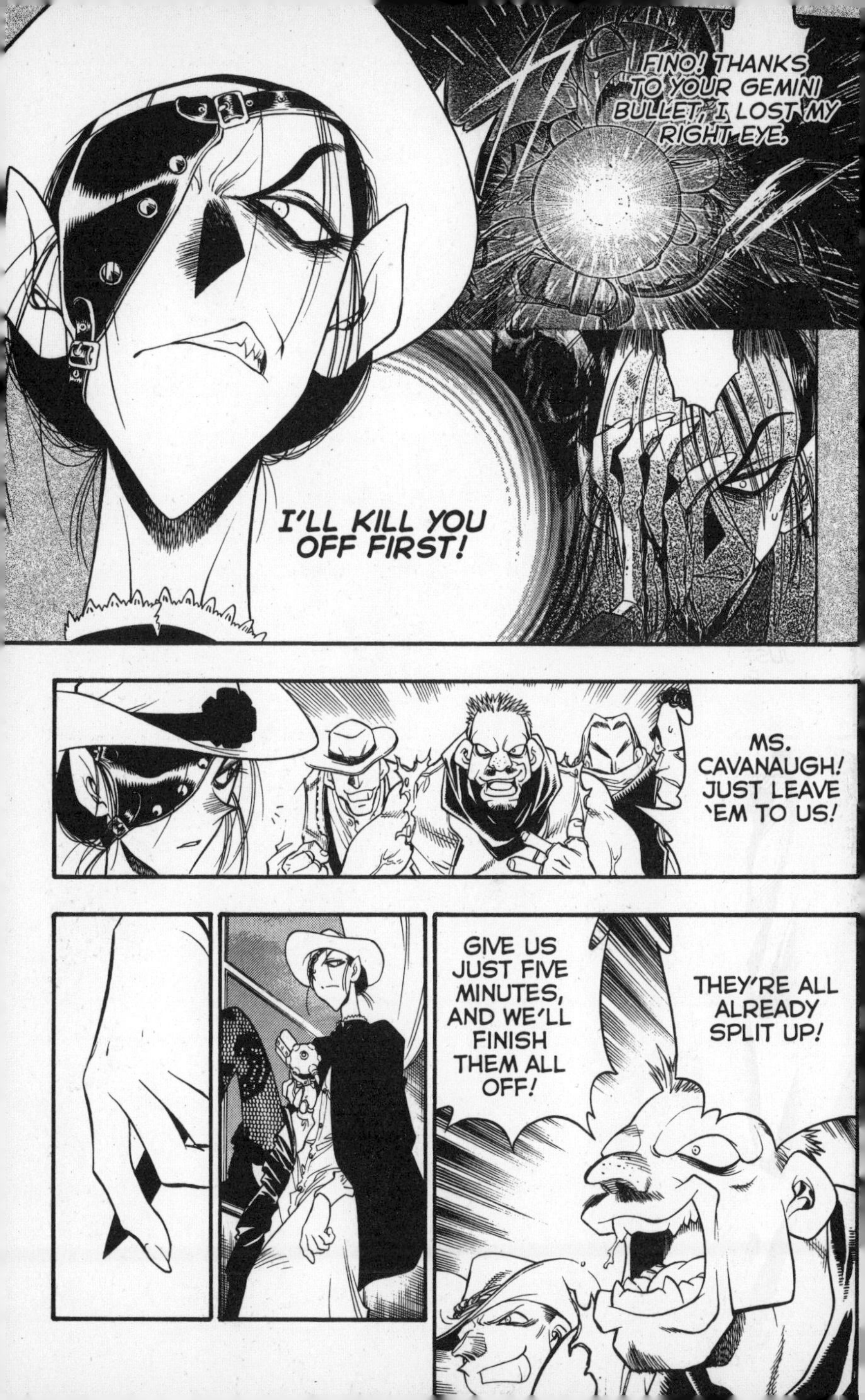
FINO! THANKS TO YOUR GEMINI BULLET, I LOST MY RIGHT EYE.
I'LL KILL YOU OFF FIRST!
MS. CAVANAUGH! JUST LEAVE 'EM TO US!
THEY'RE ALL ALREADY SPLIT UP!
GIVE US JUST FIVE MINUTES, AND WE'LL FINISH THEM ALL OFF!

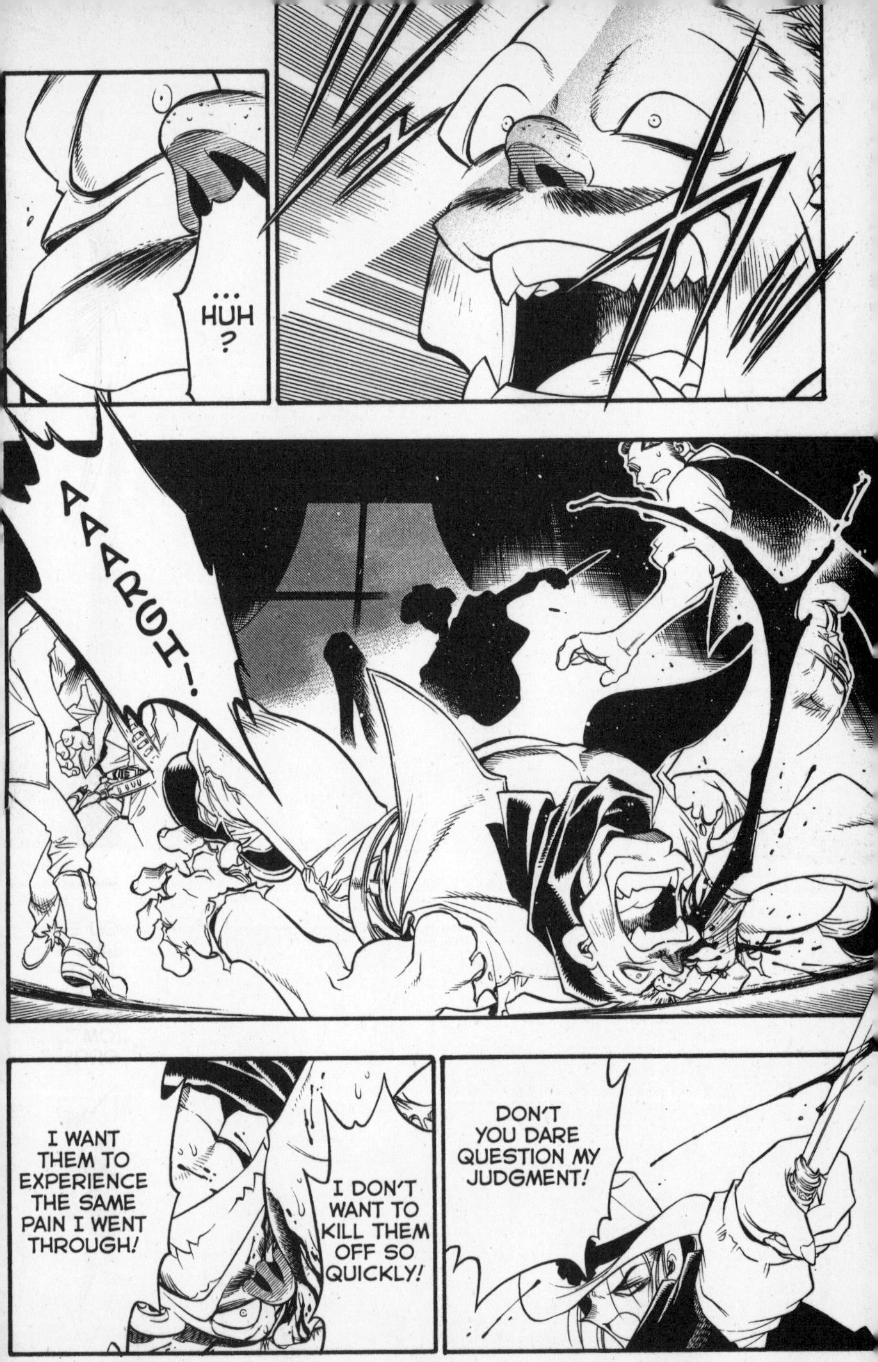
...HUH?
AAARGH!
DON'T YOU DARE QUESTION MY JUDGMENT!
I DON'T WANT TO KILL THEM OFF SO QUICKLY!
I WANT THEM TO EXPERIENCE THE SAME PAIN I WENT THROUGH!

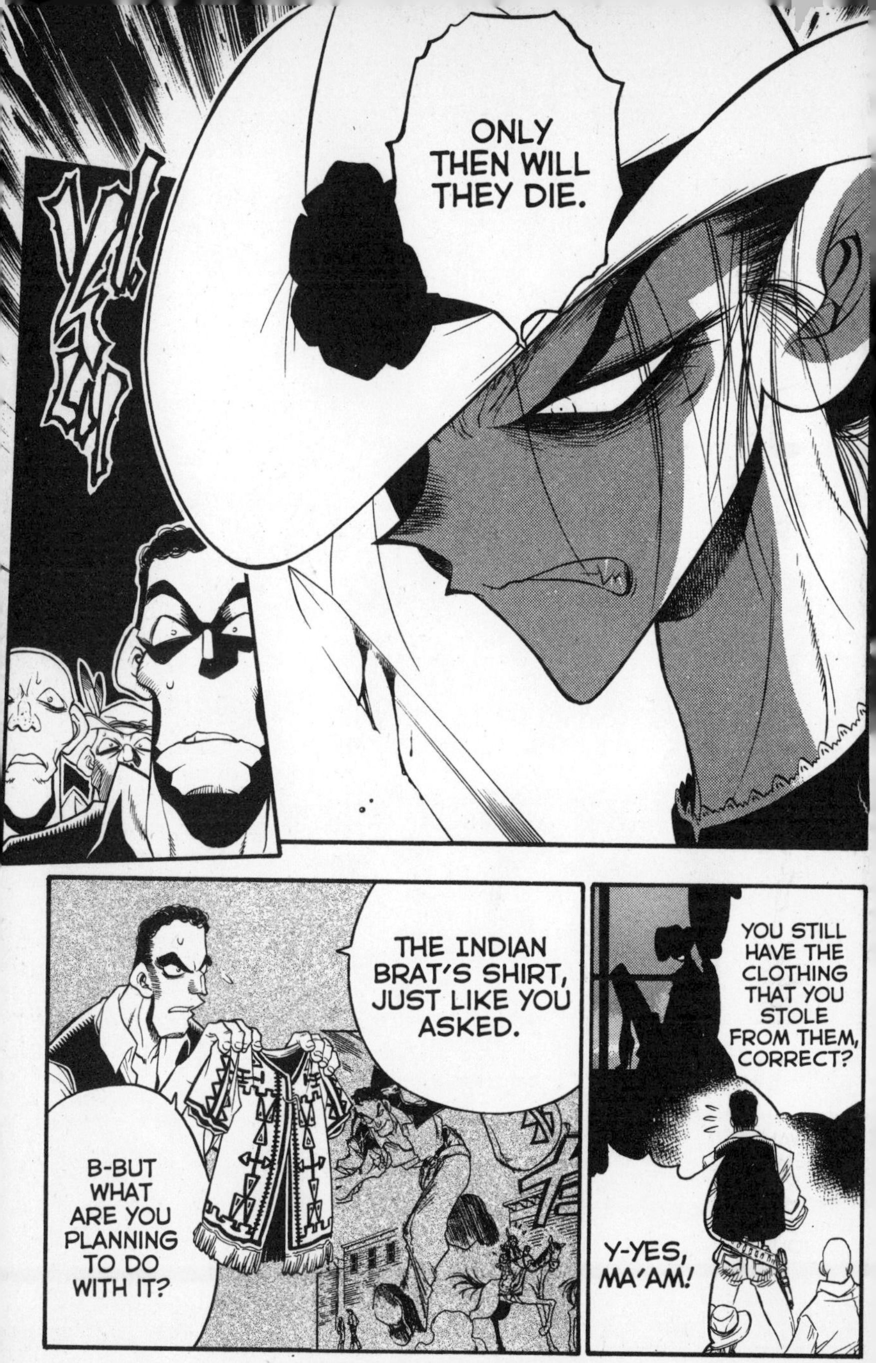
ONLY THEN WILL THEY DIE.
YOU STILL HAVE THE CLOTHING THAT YOU STOLE FROM THEM, CORRECT?
Y-YES, MA'AM!
THE INDIAN BRAT'S SHIRT, JUST LIKE YOU ASKED.
B-BUT WHAT ARE YOU PLANNING TO DO WITH IT?

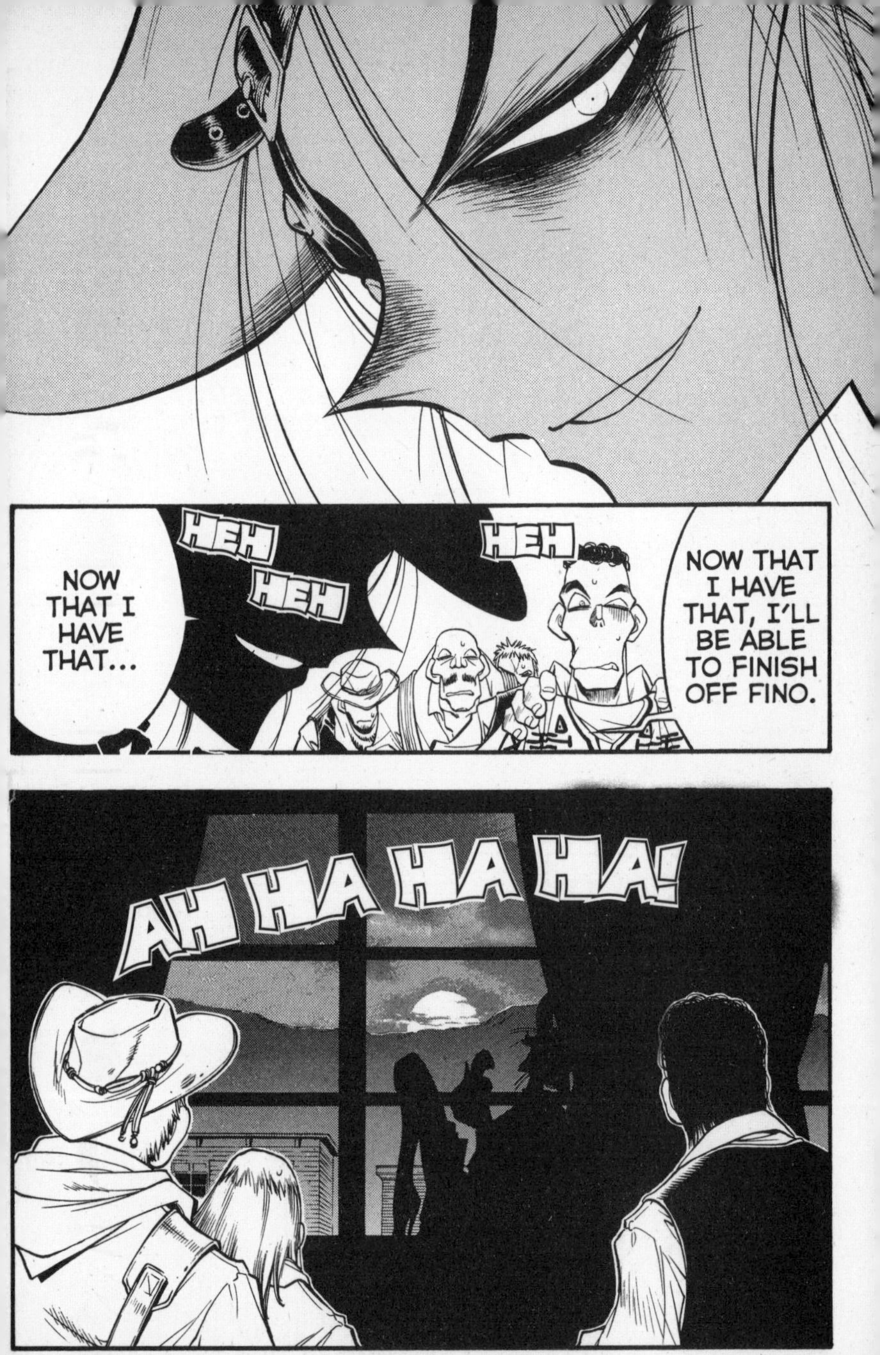
NOW THAT I HAVE THAT, I'LL BE ABLE TO FINISH OFF FINO.
HEH
HEH
HEH
NOW THAT I HAVE THAT...
AH HA HA HA HA!

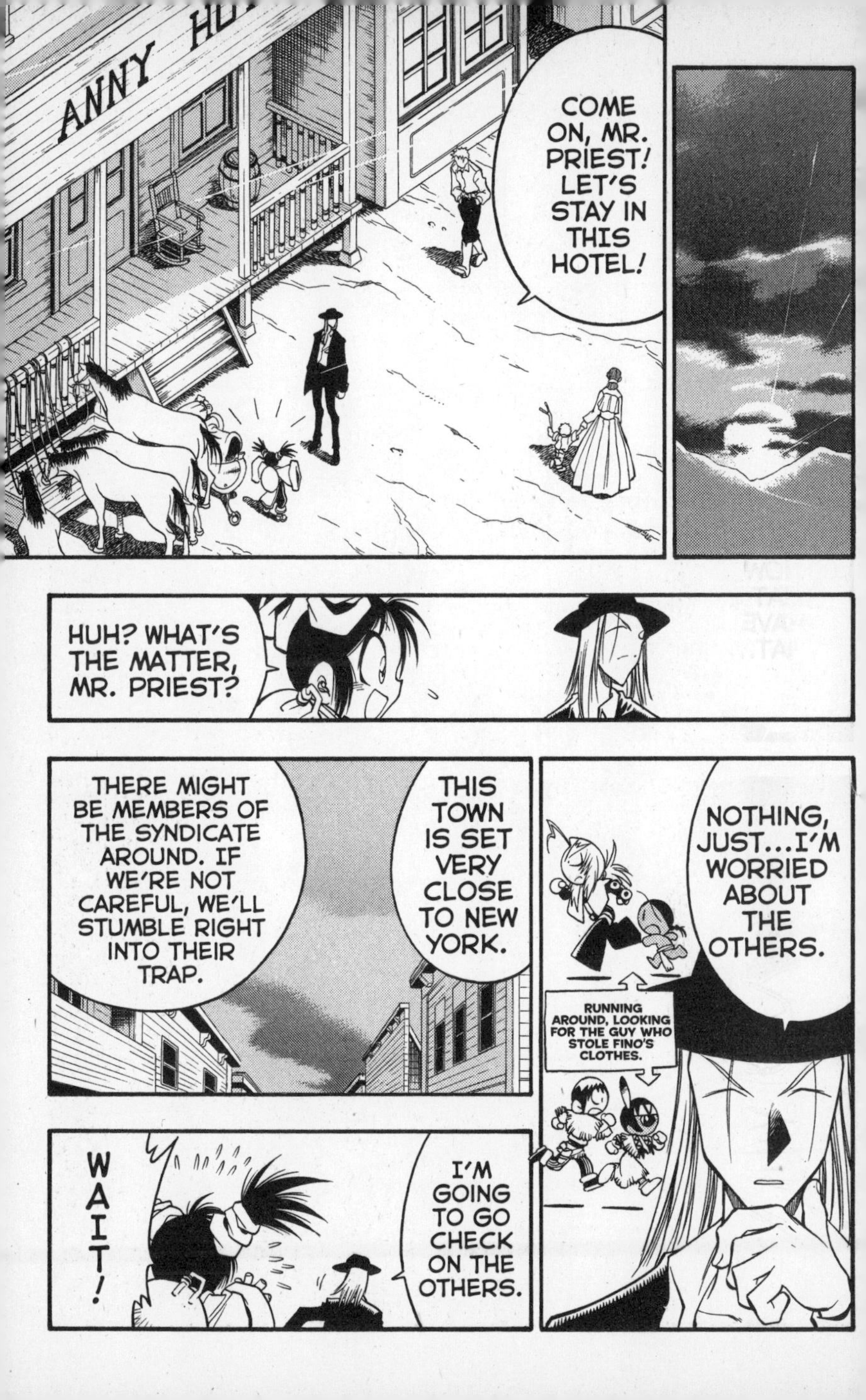
COME ON, MR. PRIEST! LET'S STAY IN THIS HOTEL!
HUH? WHAT'S THE MATTER, MR. PRIEST?
NOTHING, JUST...I'M WORRIED ABOUT THE OTHERS.
RUNNING AROUND, LOOKING FOR THE GUY WHO STOLE FINO'S CLOTHES.
THIS TOWN IS SET VERY CLOSE TO NEW YORK.
THERE MIGHT BE MEMBERS OF THE SYNDICATE AROUND. IF WE'RE NOT CAREFUL, WE'LL STUMBLE RIGHT INTO THEIR TRAP.
I'M GOING TO GO CHECK ON THE OTHERS.
WAIT!

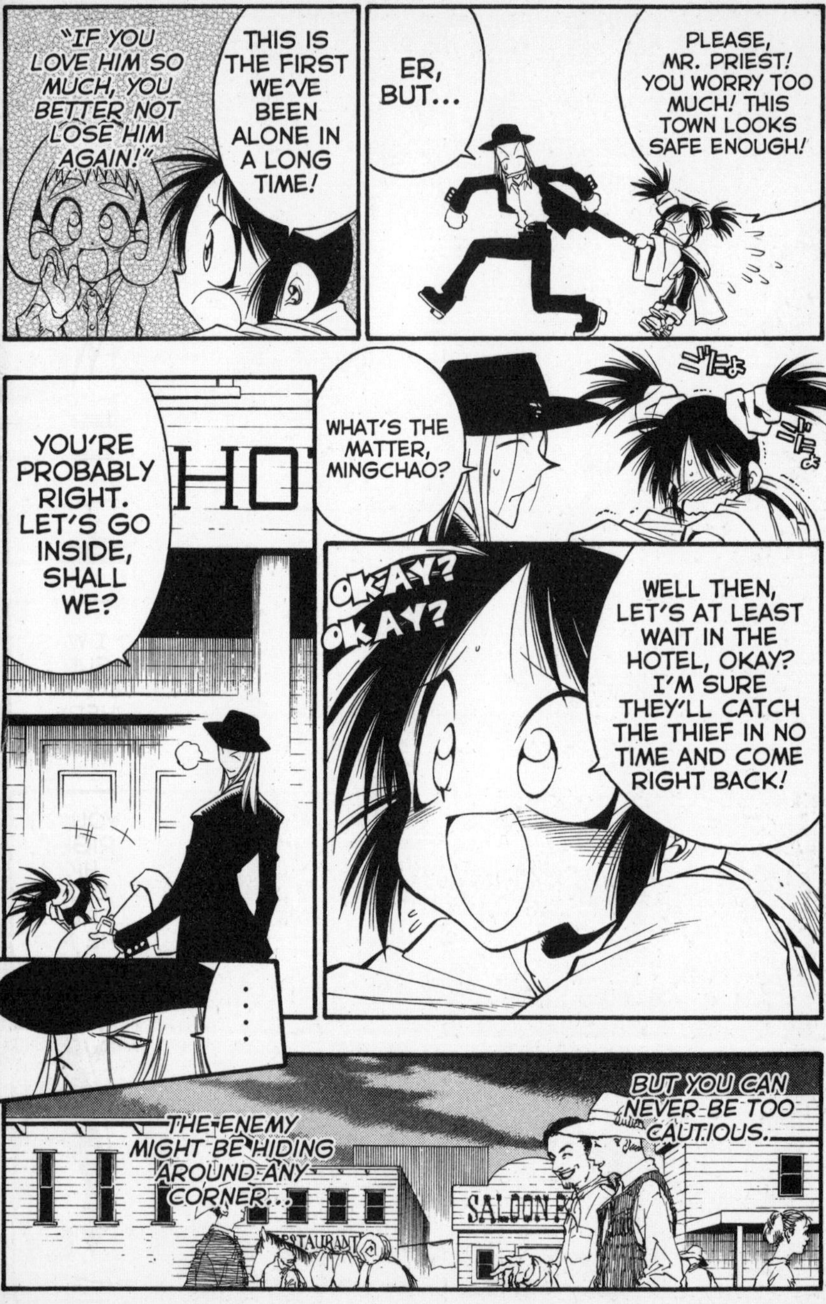
PLEASE, MR. PRIEST! YOU WORRY TOO MUCH! THIS TOWN LOOKS SAFE ENOUGH!
ER, BUT...
THIS IS THE FIRST WE'VE BEEN ALONE IN A LONG TIME!
"IF YOU LOVE HIM SO MUCH, YOU BETTER NOT LOSE HIM AGAIN!"
ごにょ
ごにょ
WHAT'S THE MATTER, MINGCHAO?
WELL THEN, LET'S AT LEAST WAIT IN THE HOTEL, OKAY? I'M SURE THEY'LL CATCH THE THIEF IN NO TIME AND COME RIGHT BACK!
OKAY? OKAY?
HO
YOU'RE PROBABLY RIGHT. LET'S GO INSIDE, SHALL WE?
....
BUT YOU CAN NEVER BE TOO CAUTIOUS.
THE ENEMY MIGHT BE HIDING AROUND ANY CORNER...
SALOON
RESTAURANT

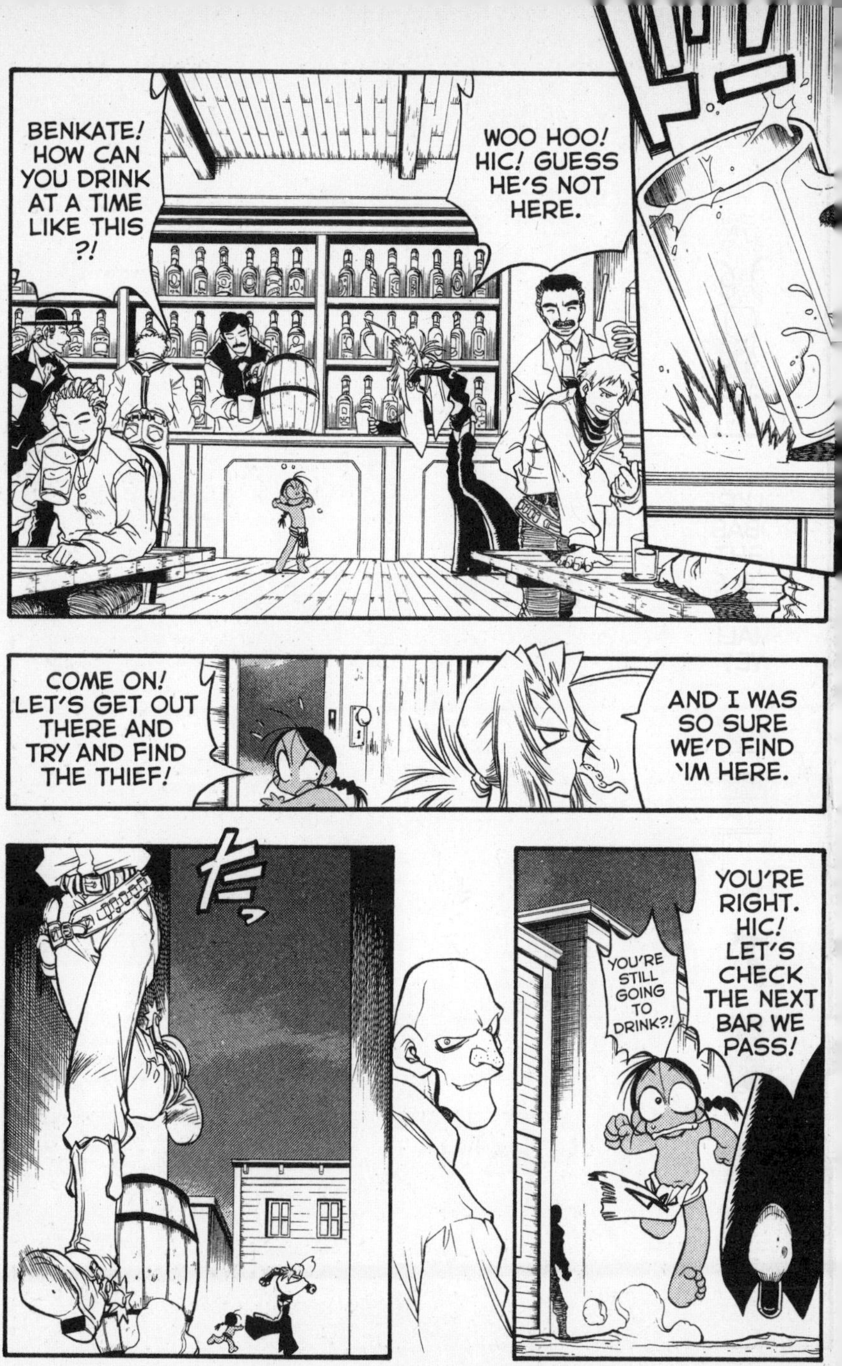
WOO HOO! HIC! GUESS HE'S NOT HERE.
BENKATE! HOW CAN YOU DRINK AT A TIME LIKE THIS?!
AND I WAS SO SURE WE'D FIND 'IM HERE.
COME ON! LET'S GET OUT THERE AND TRY AND FIND THE THIEF!
YOU'RE RIGHT. HIC! LET'S CHECK THE NEXT BAR WE PASS!
YOU'RE STILL GOING TO DRINK?!

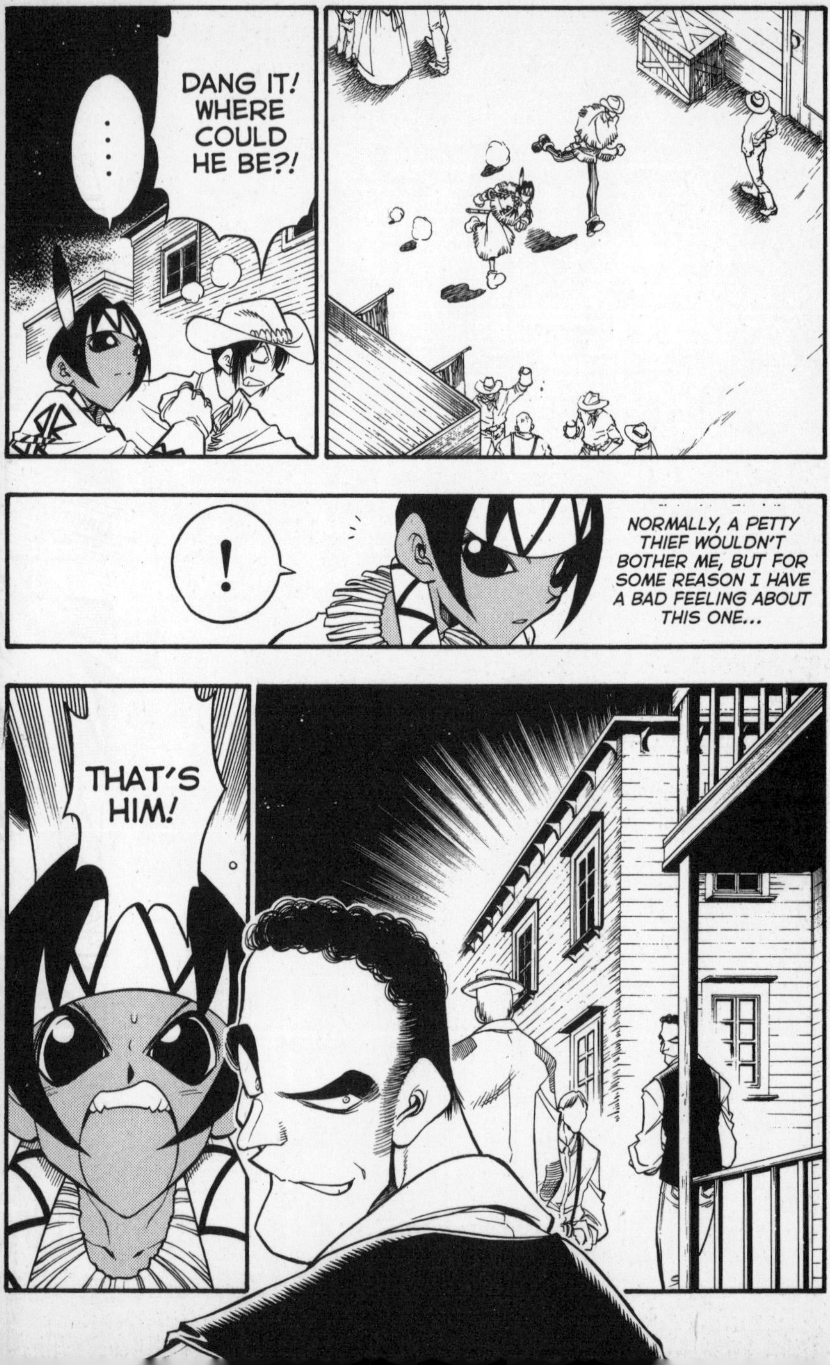
DANG IT! WHERE COULD HE BE?!
....
NORMALLY, A PETTY THIEF WOULDN'T BOTHER ME, BUT FOR SOME REASON I HAVE A BAD FEELING ABOUT THIS ONE...
!
THAT'S HIM!

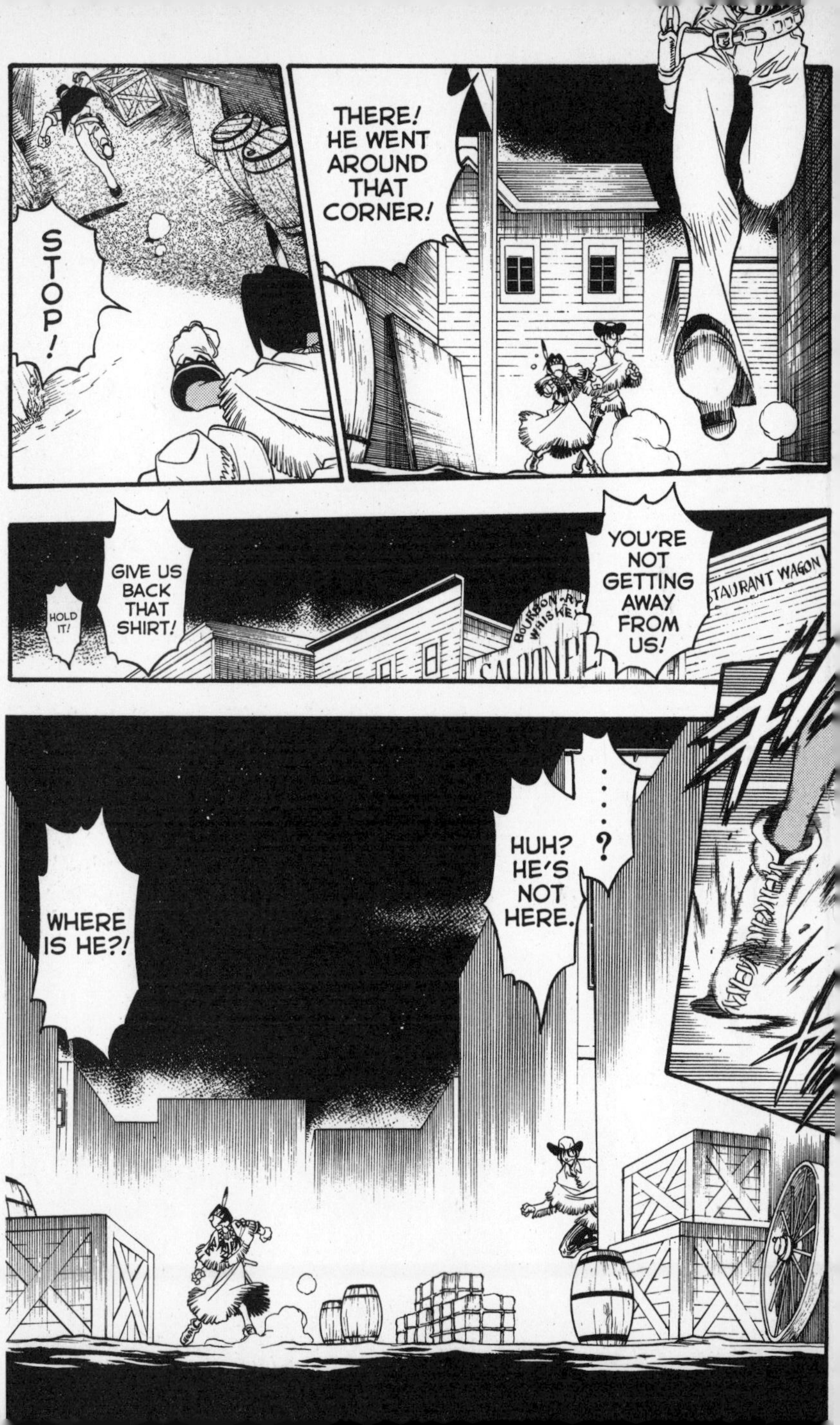
THERE! HE WENT AROUND THAT CORNER!
STOP!
YOU'RE NOT GETTING AWAY FROM US!
GIVE US BACK THAT SHIRT!
HOLD IT!
....?
HUH? HE'S NOT HERE.
WHERE IS HE?!

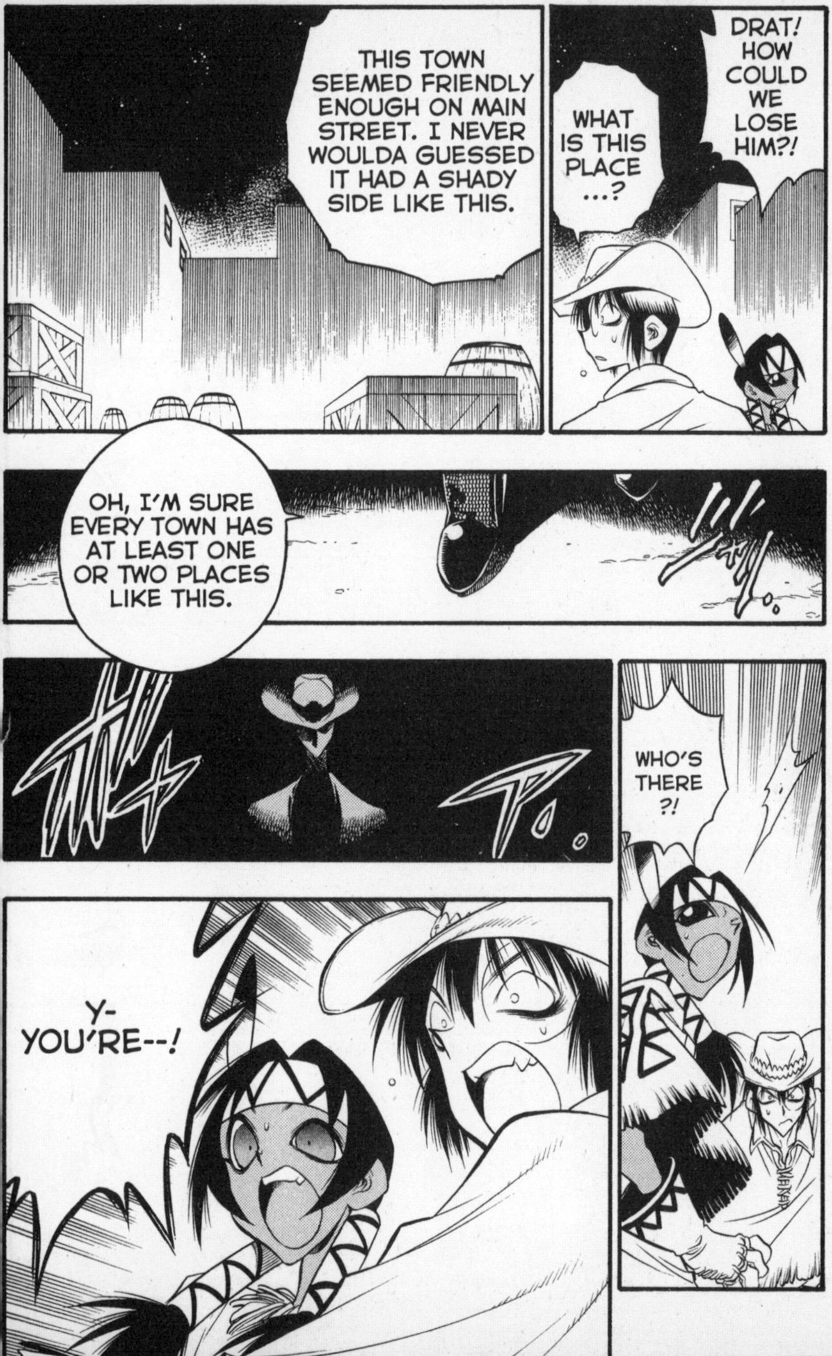
DRAT! HOW COULD WE LOSE HIM?!
WHAT IS THIS PLACE ...?
THIS TOWN SEEMED FRIENDLY ENOUGH ON MAIN STREET. I NEVER WOULDA GUESSED IT HAD A SHADY SIDE LIKE THIS.
OH, I'M SURE EVERY TOWN HAS AT LEAST ONE OR TWO PLACES LIKE THIS.
WHO'S THERE ?!
Y- YOU'RE--!

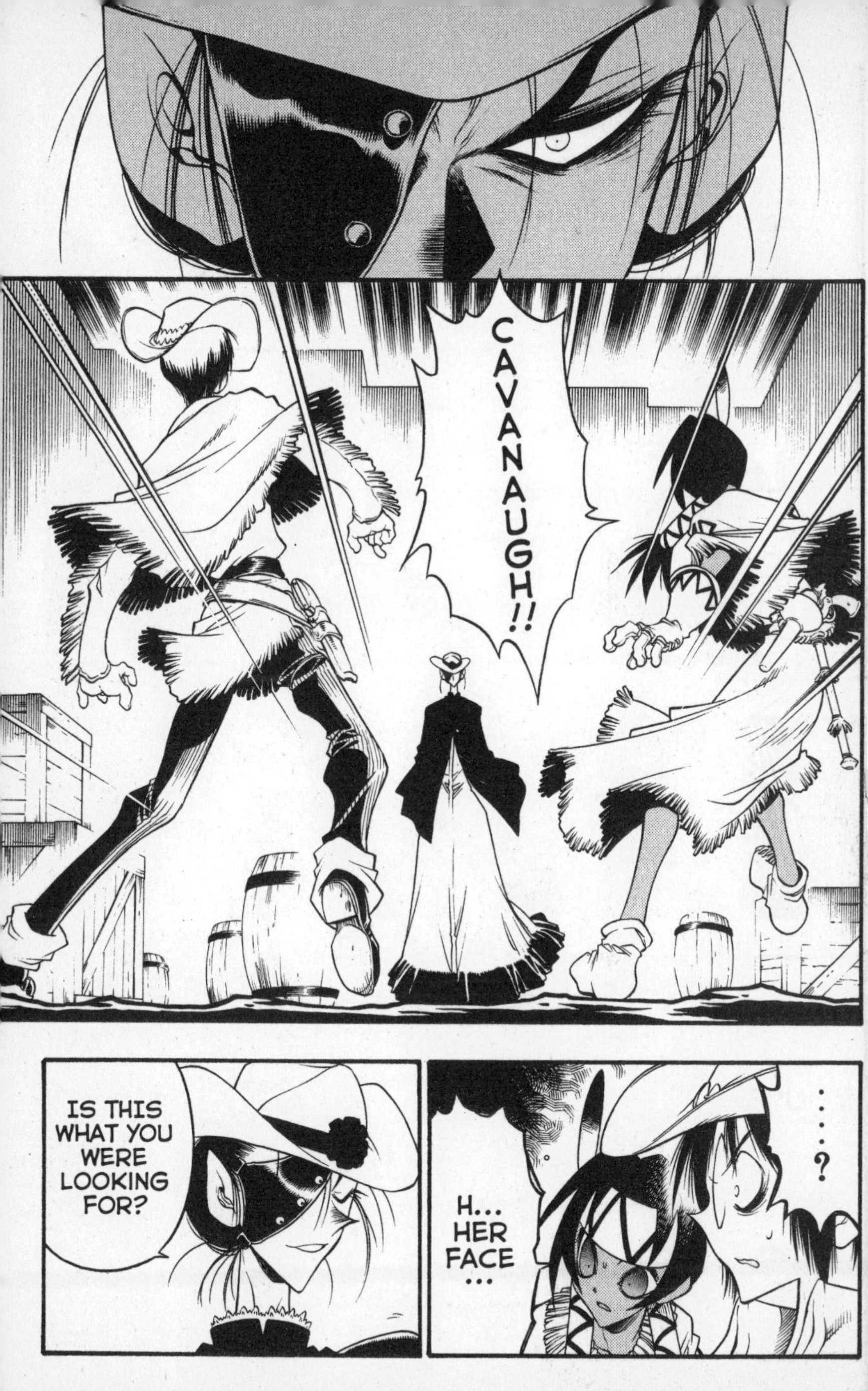
CAVANAUGH!!
....?
H... HER FACE...
IS THIS WHAT YOU WERE LOOKING FOR?

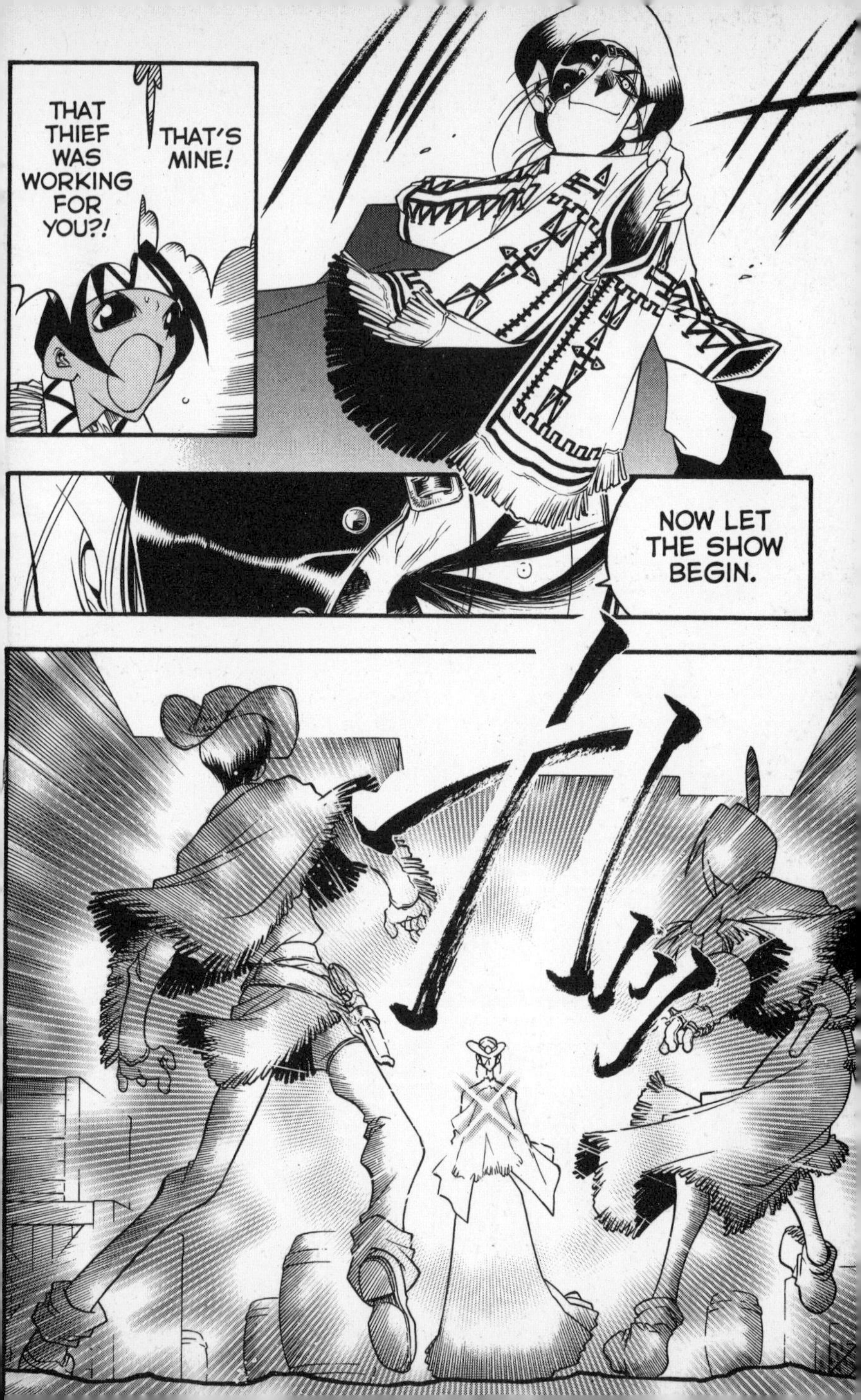
THAT'S MINE!
THAT THIEF WAS WORKING FOR YOU?!
NOW LET THE SHOW BEGIN.

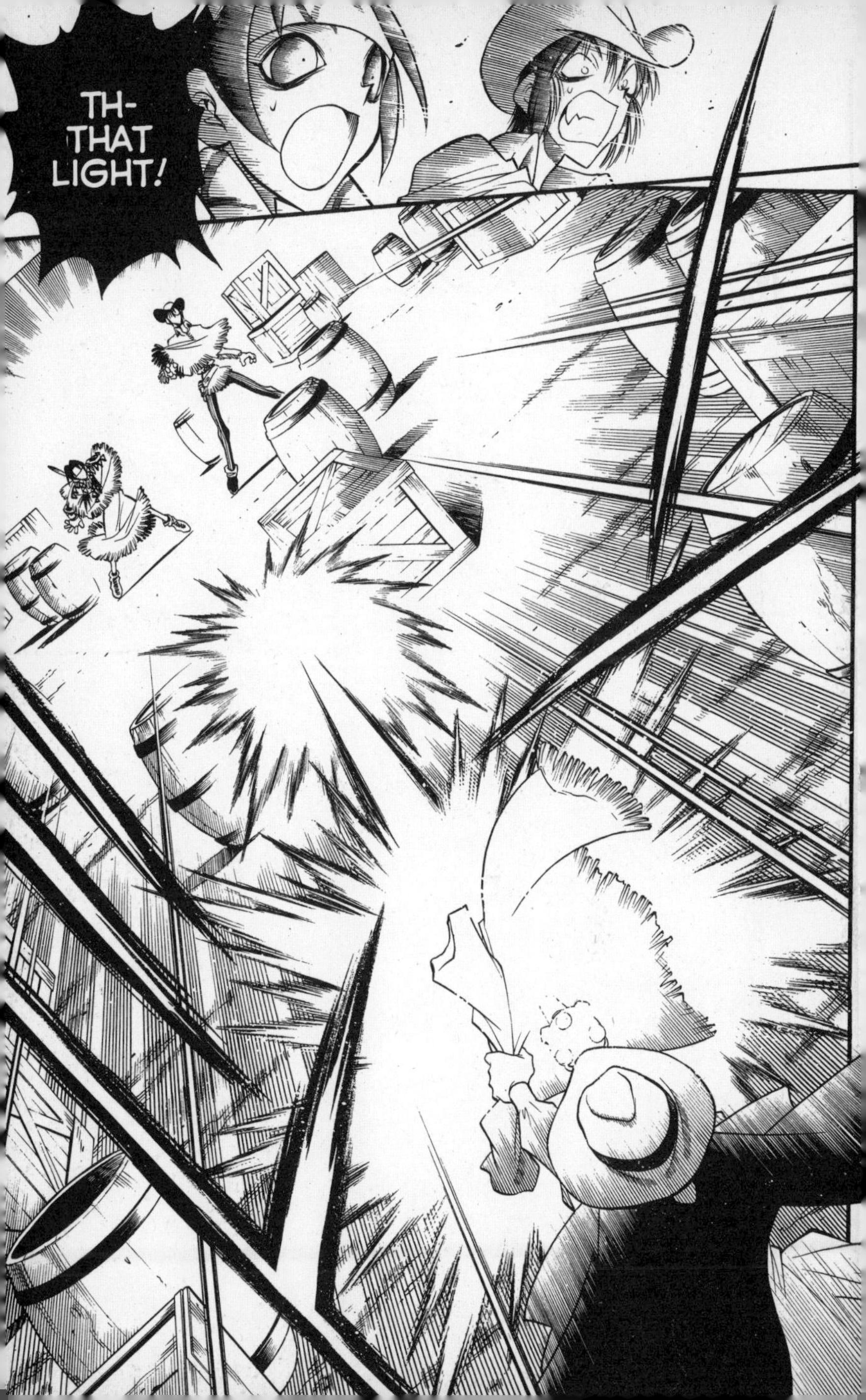
TH-THAT LIGHT!

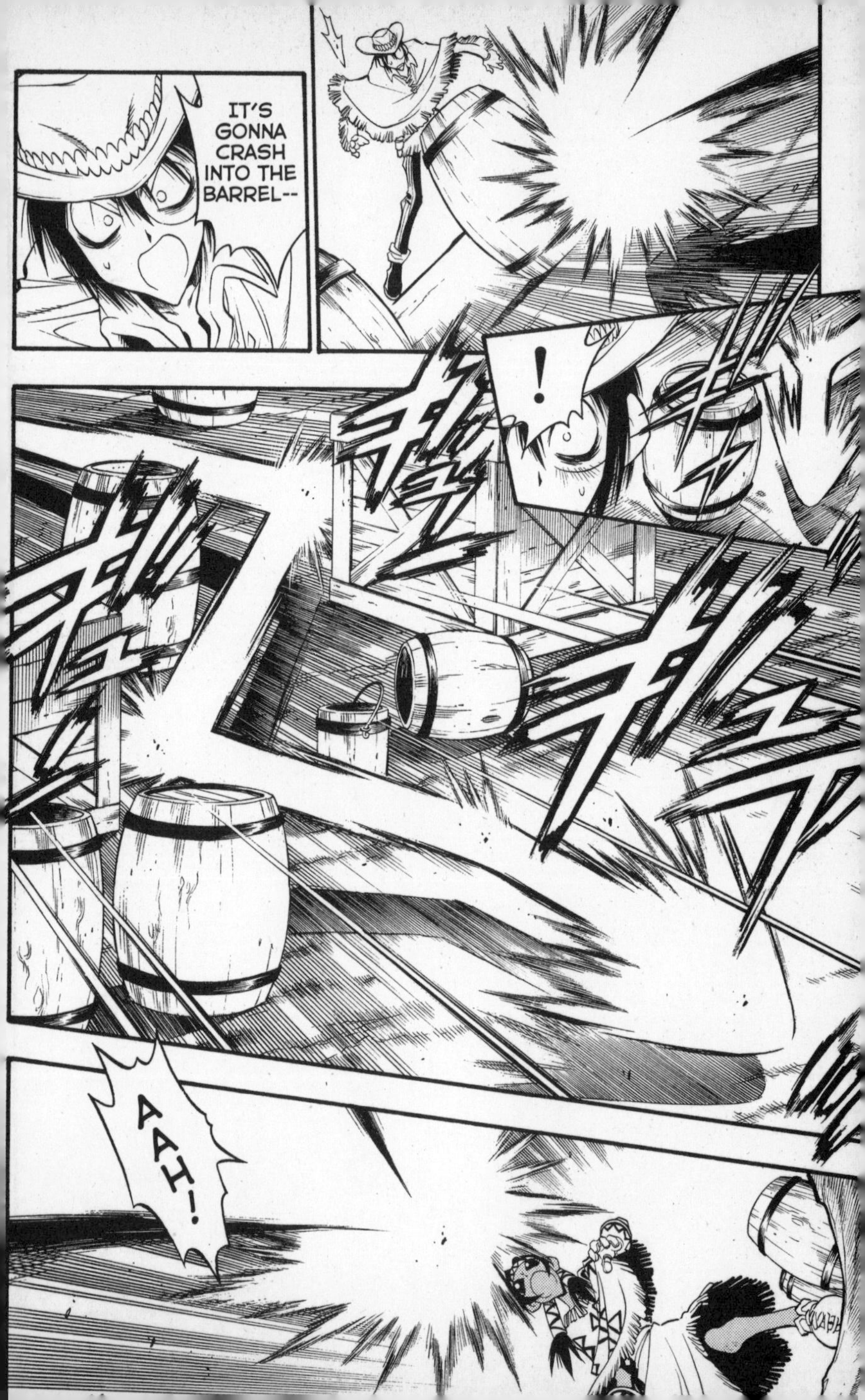
IT'S GONNA CRASH INTO THE BARREL--
!
AAH!

WATCH OUT!

I KNEW IT...

Y-YOU SAVED ME, ALTER- NATE.

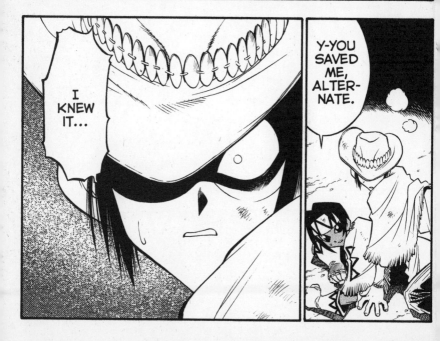

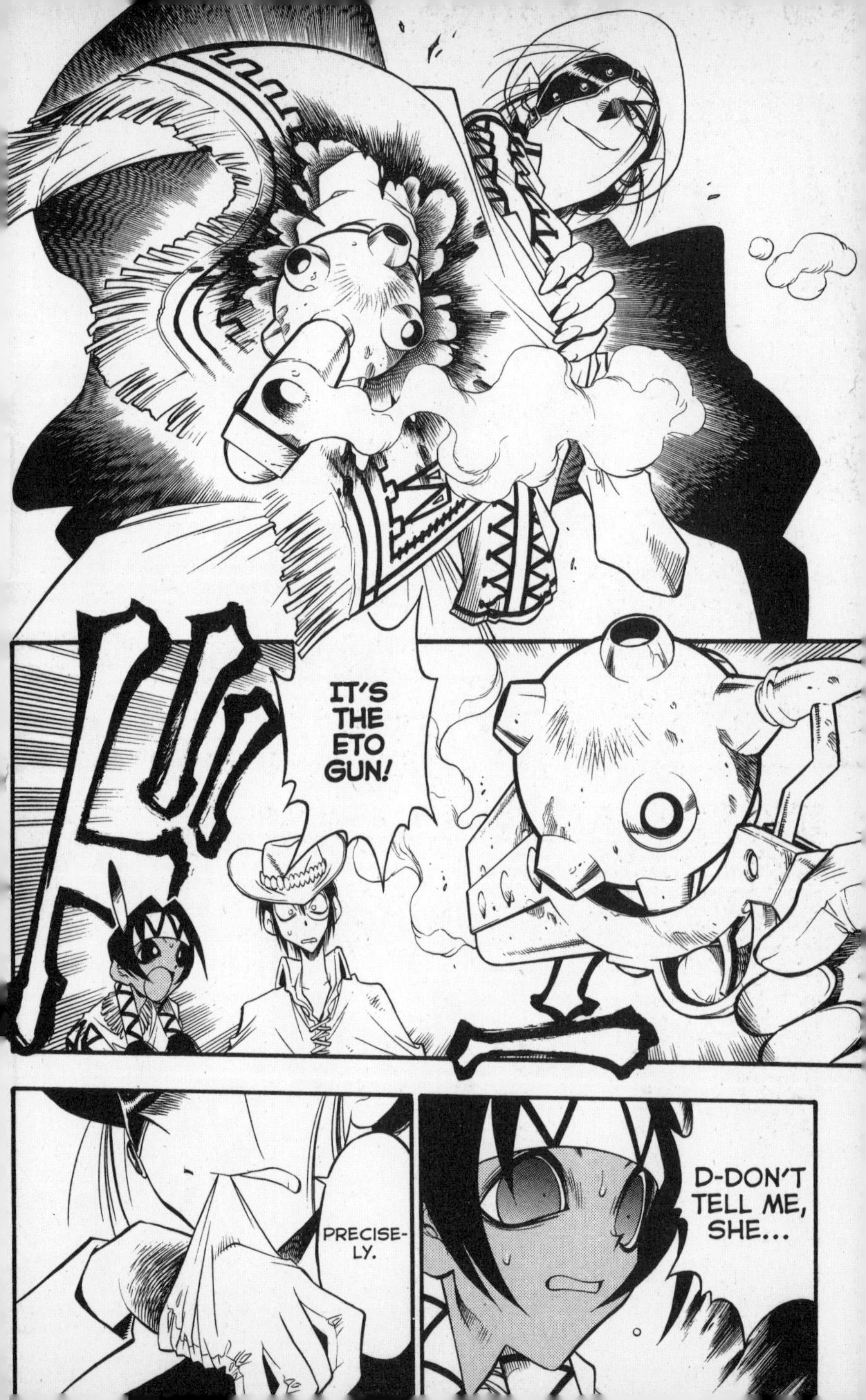
IT'S THE ETO GUN!
D-DON'T TELL ME, SHE...
PRECISE-LY.

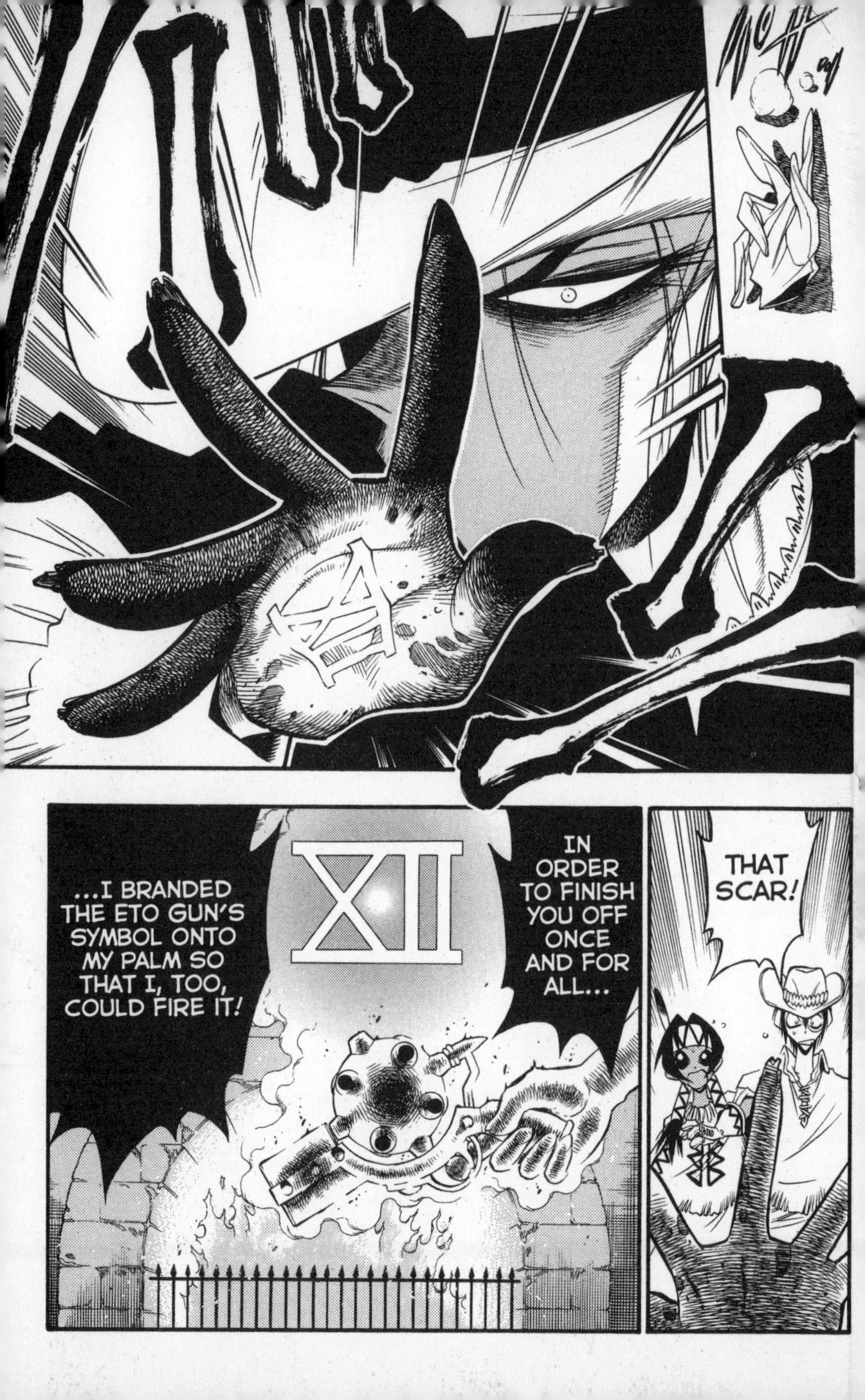
THAT SCAR!
IN ORDER TO FINISH YOU OFF ONCE AND FOR ALL...
XII
...I BRANDED THE ETO GUN'S SYMBOL ONTO MY PALM SO THAT I, TOO, COULD FIRE IT!

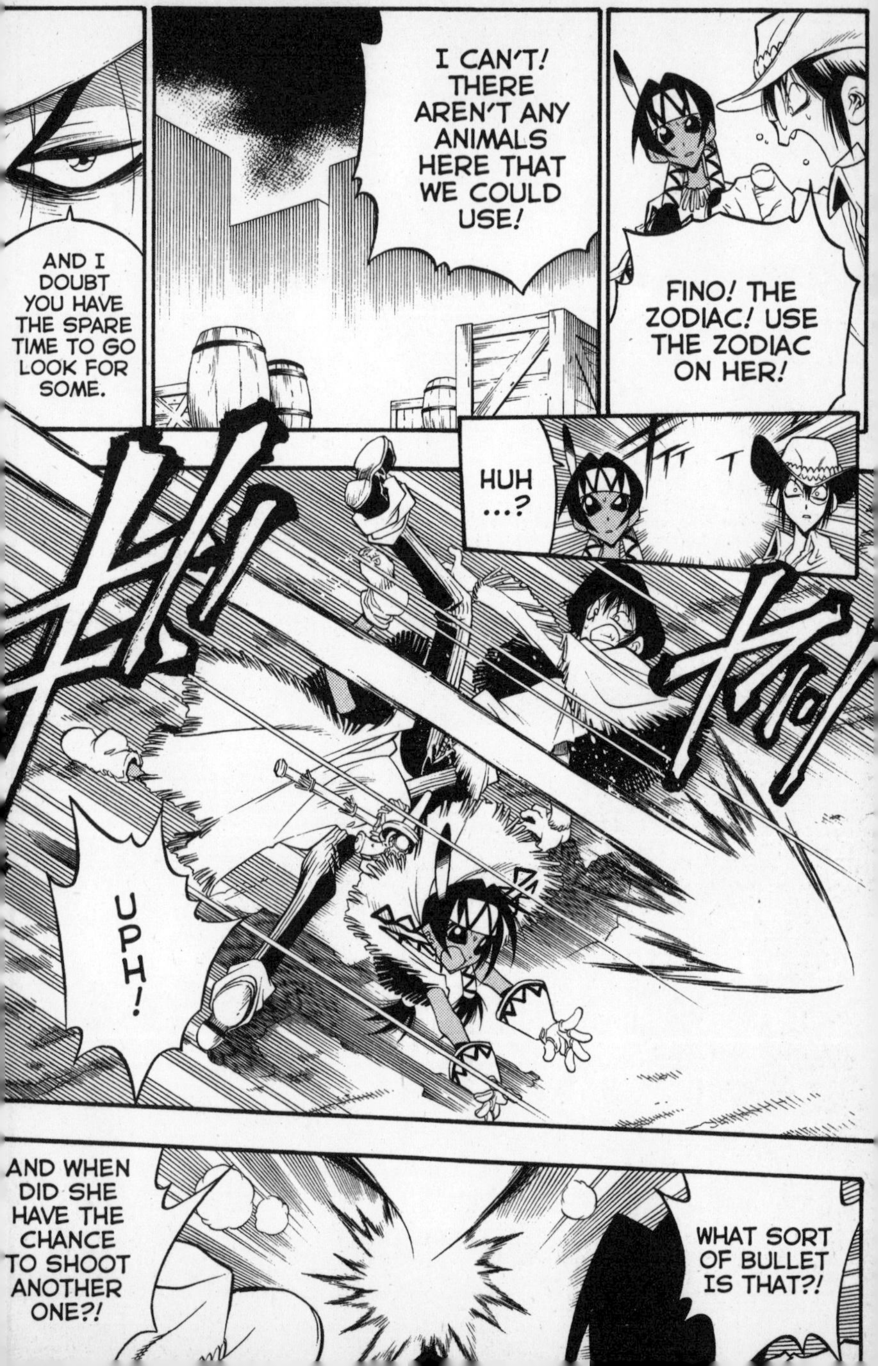
FINO! THE ZODIAC! USE THE ZODIAC ON HER!
I CAN'T! THERE AREN'T ANY ANIMALS HERE THAT WE COULD USE!
AND I DOUBT YOU HAVE THE SPARE TIME TO GO LOOK FOR SOME.
HUH ...?
UPH!
WHAT SORT OF BULLET IS THAT?!
AND WHEN DID SHE HAVE THE CHANCE TO SHOOT ANOTHER ONE?!

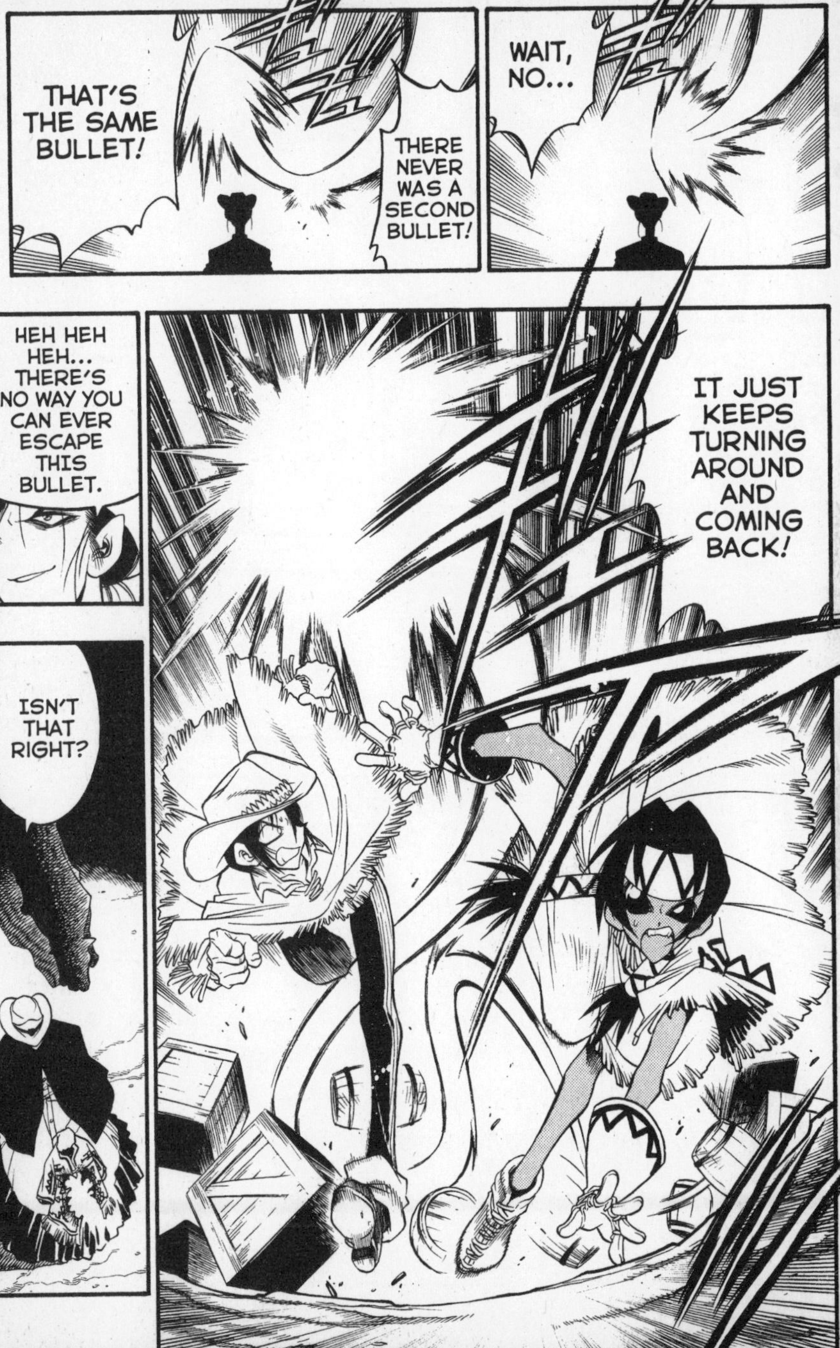
WAIT, NO...
THAT'S THE SAME BULLET!
THERE NEVER WAS A SECOND BULLET!
IT JUST KEEPS TURNING AROUND AND COMING BACK!
HEH HEH HEH... THERE'S NO WAY YOU CAN EVER ESCAPE THIS BULLET.
ISN'T THAT RIGHT?

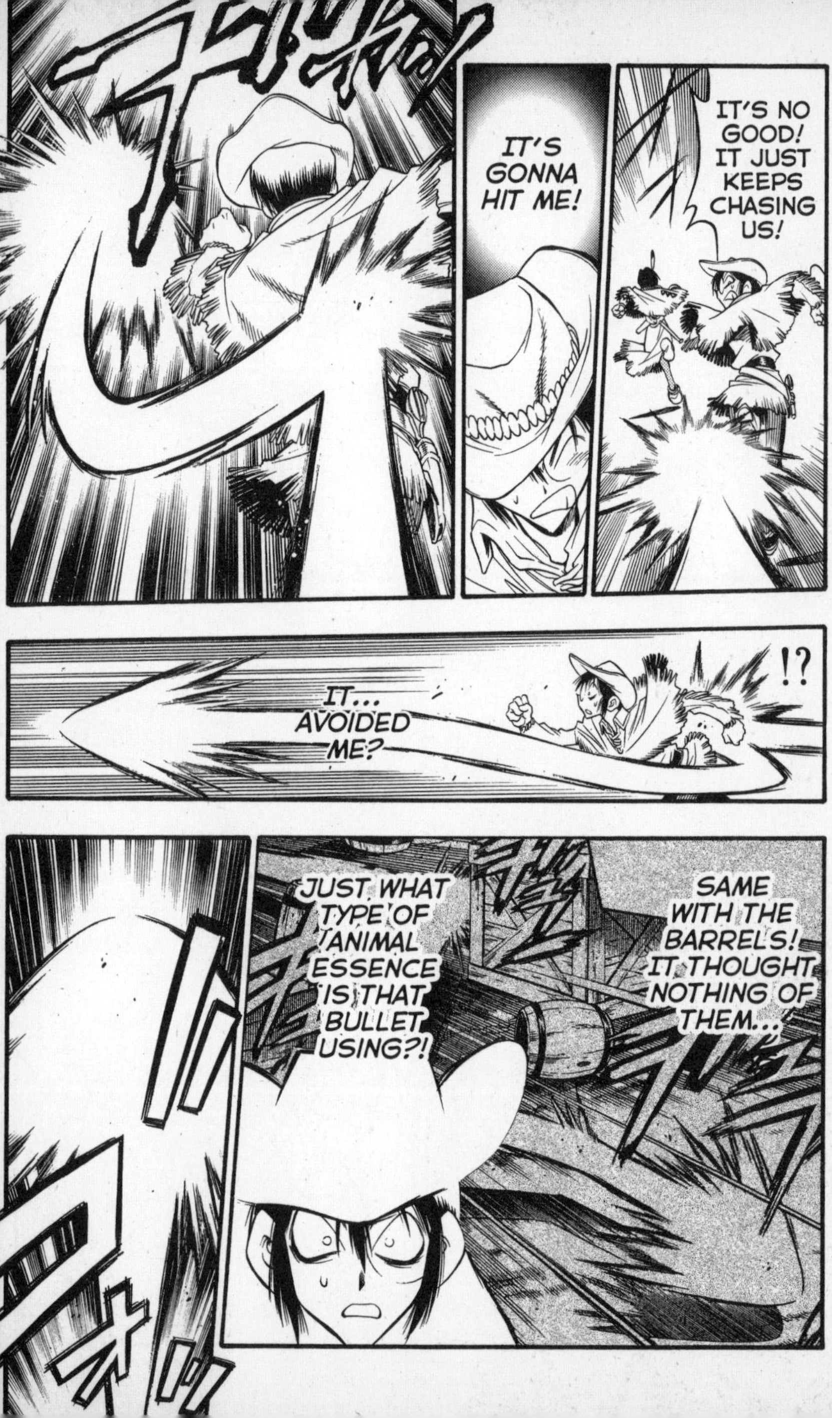
IT'S NO GOOD! IT JUST KEEPS CHASING US!
IT'S GONNA HIT ME!
!?
IT... AVOIDED ME?
SAME WITH THE BARRELS! IT THOUGHT NOTHING OF THEM...
JUST WHAT TYPE OF ANIMAL ESSENCE IS THAT BULLET USING?!

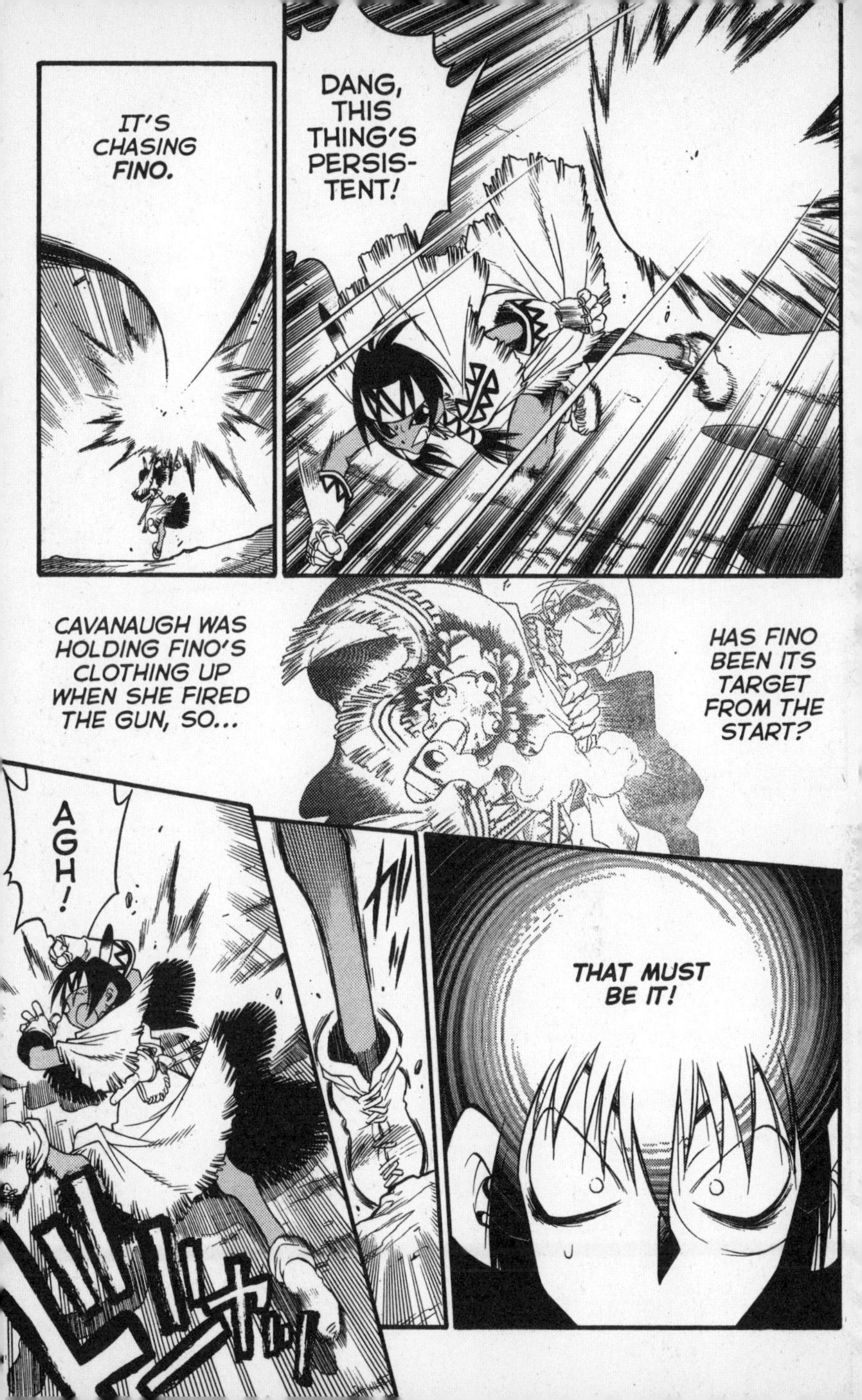
DANG, THIS THING'S PERSIS- TENT!
IT'S CHASING FINO.
HAS FINO BEEN ITS TARGET FROM THE START?
CAVANAUGH WAS HOLDING FINO'S CLOTHING UP WHEN SHE FIRED THE GUN, SO...
THAT MUST BE IT!
AGH!

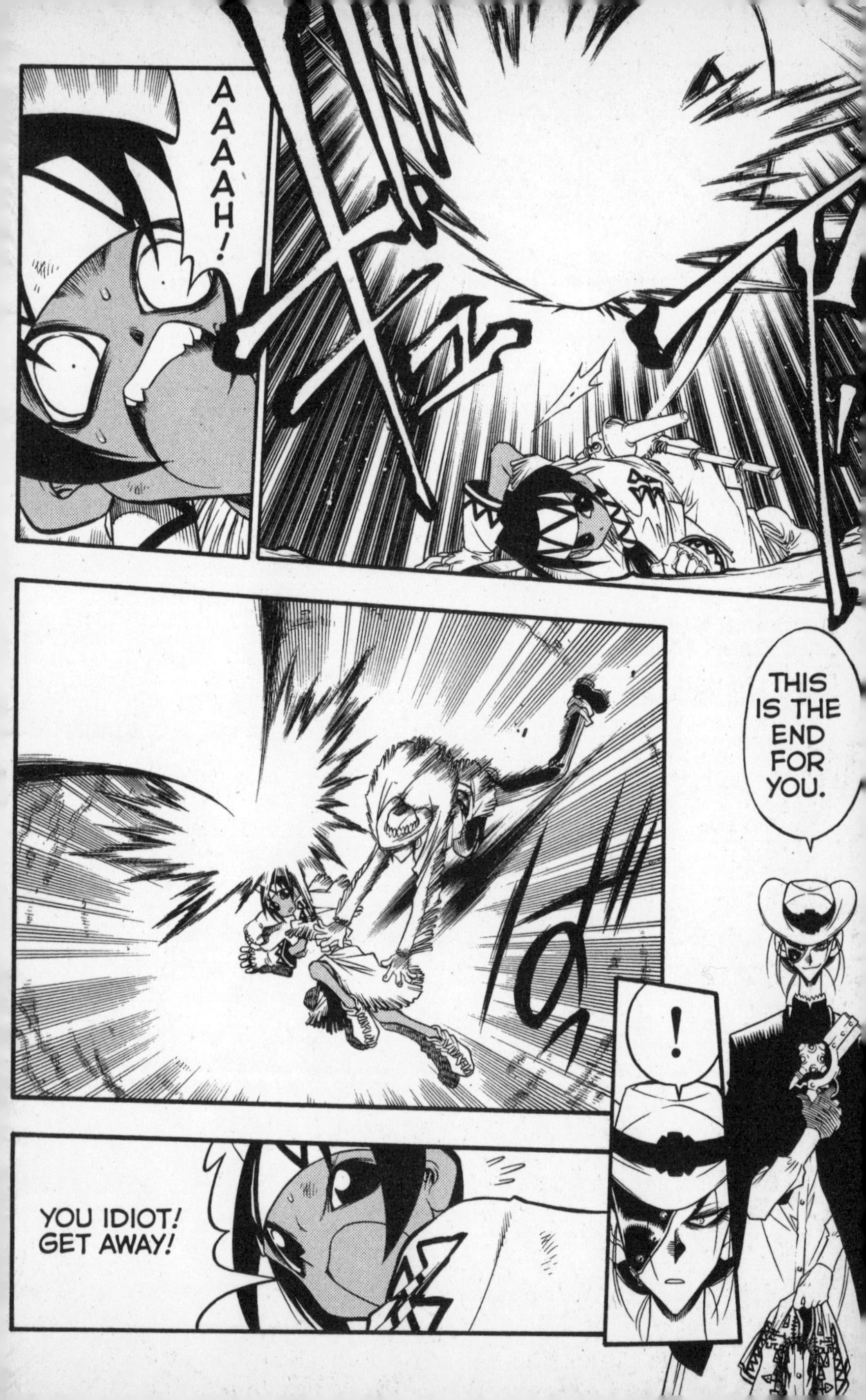
AAAAAH!
THIS IS THE END FOR YOU.
!
YOU IDIOT! GET AWAY!

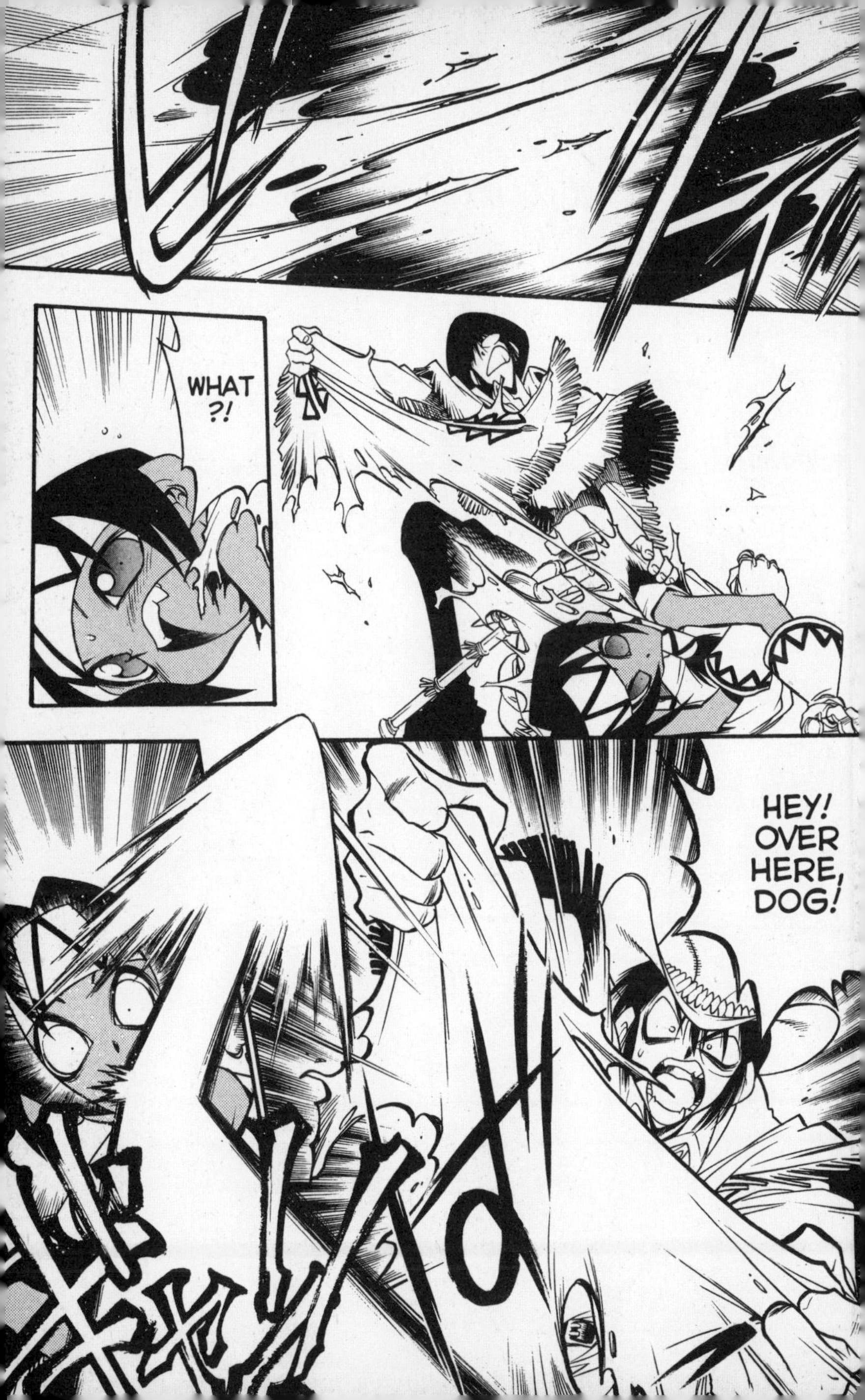
WHAT ?!
HEY! OVER HERE, DOG!

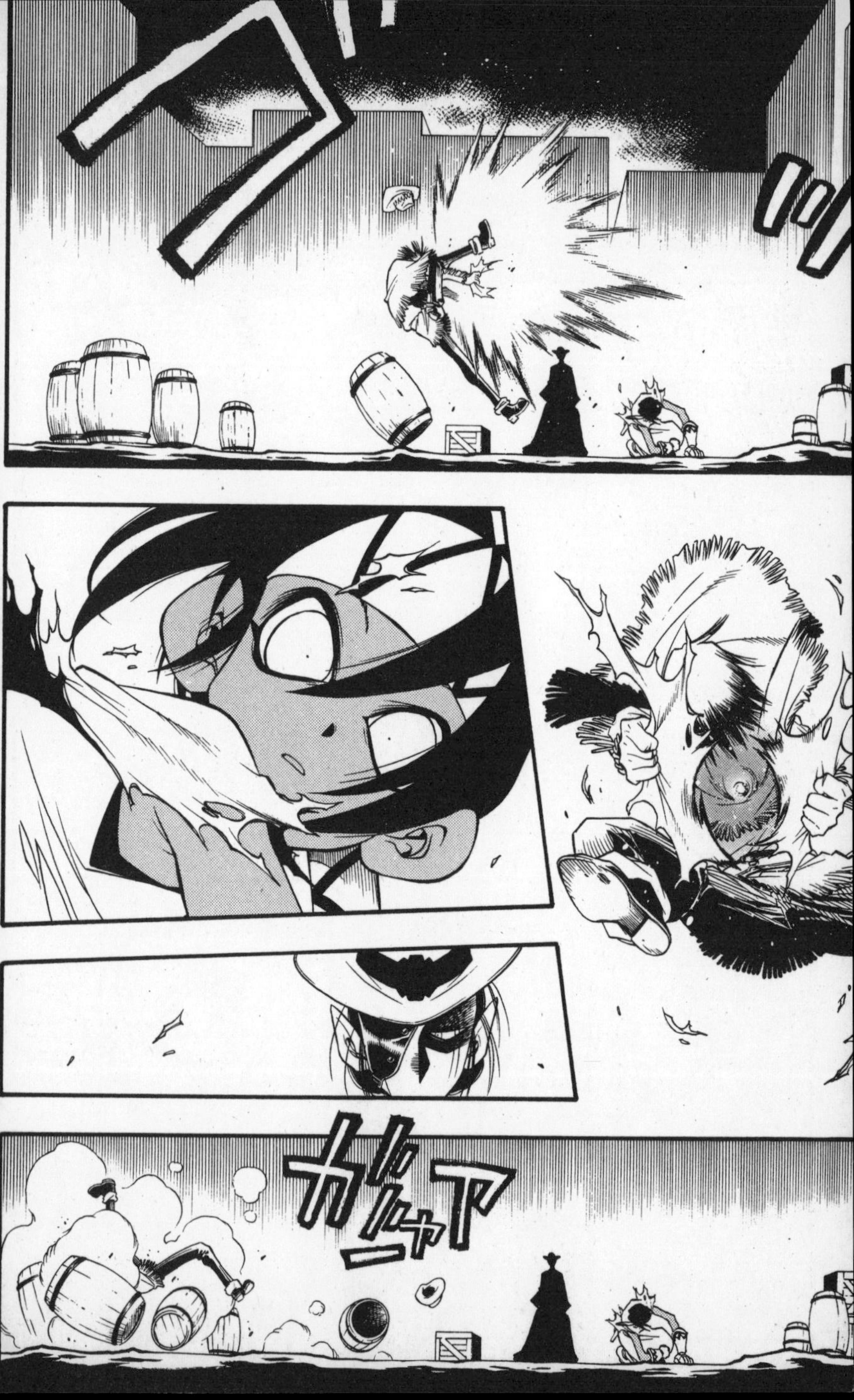
ガシャアー

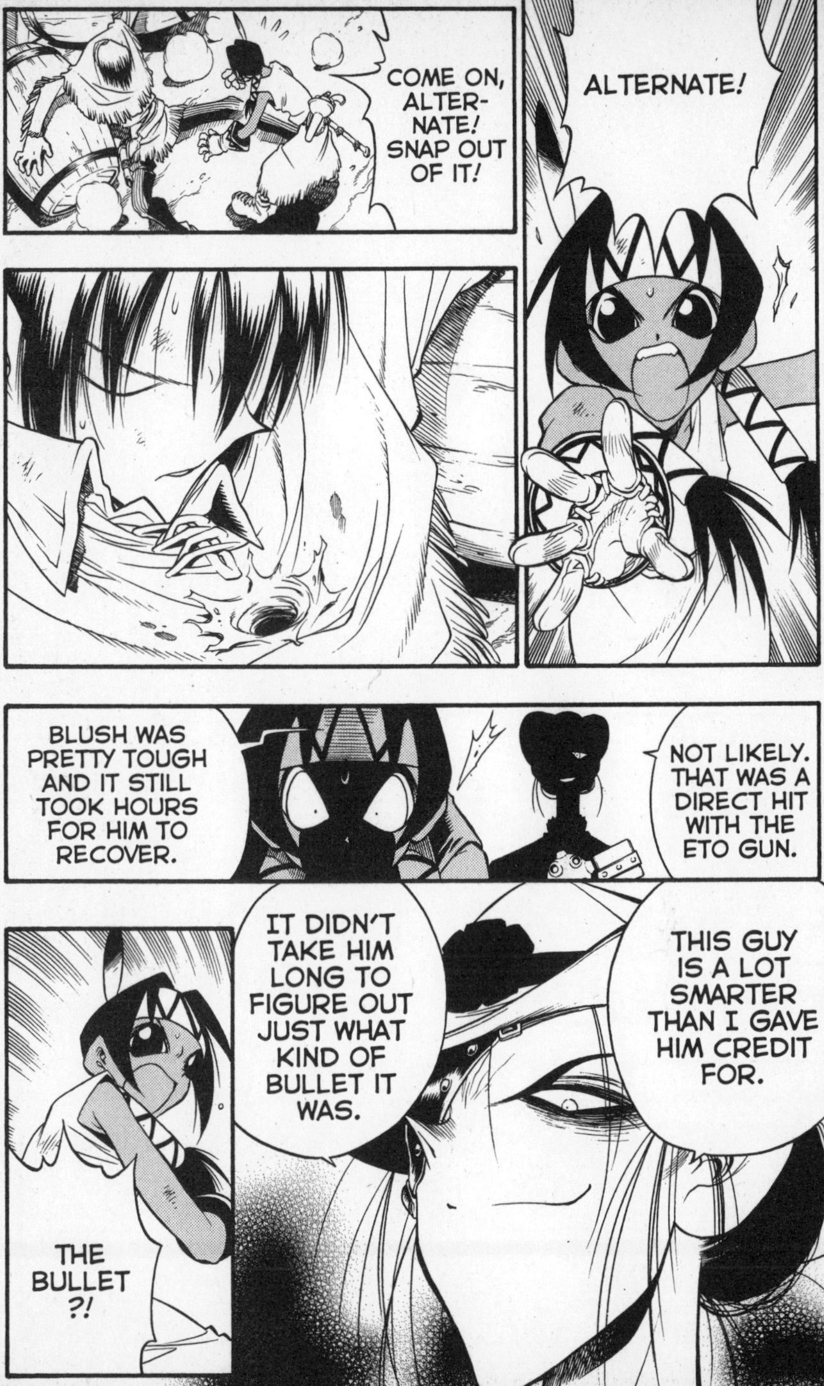
ALTERNATE!
COME ON, ALTERNATE! SNAP OUT OF IT!
NOT LIKELY. THAT WAS A DIRECT HIT WITH THE ETO GUN.
BLUSH WAS PRETTY TOUGH AND IT STILL TOOK HOURS FOR HIM TO RECOVER.
THIS GUY IS A LOT SMARTER THAN I GAVE HIM CREDIT FOR.
IT DIDN'T TAKE HIM LONG TO FIGURE OUT JUST WHAT KIND OF BULLET IT WAS.
THE BULLET?!

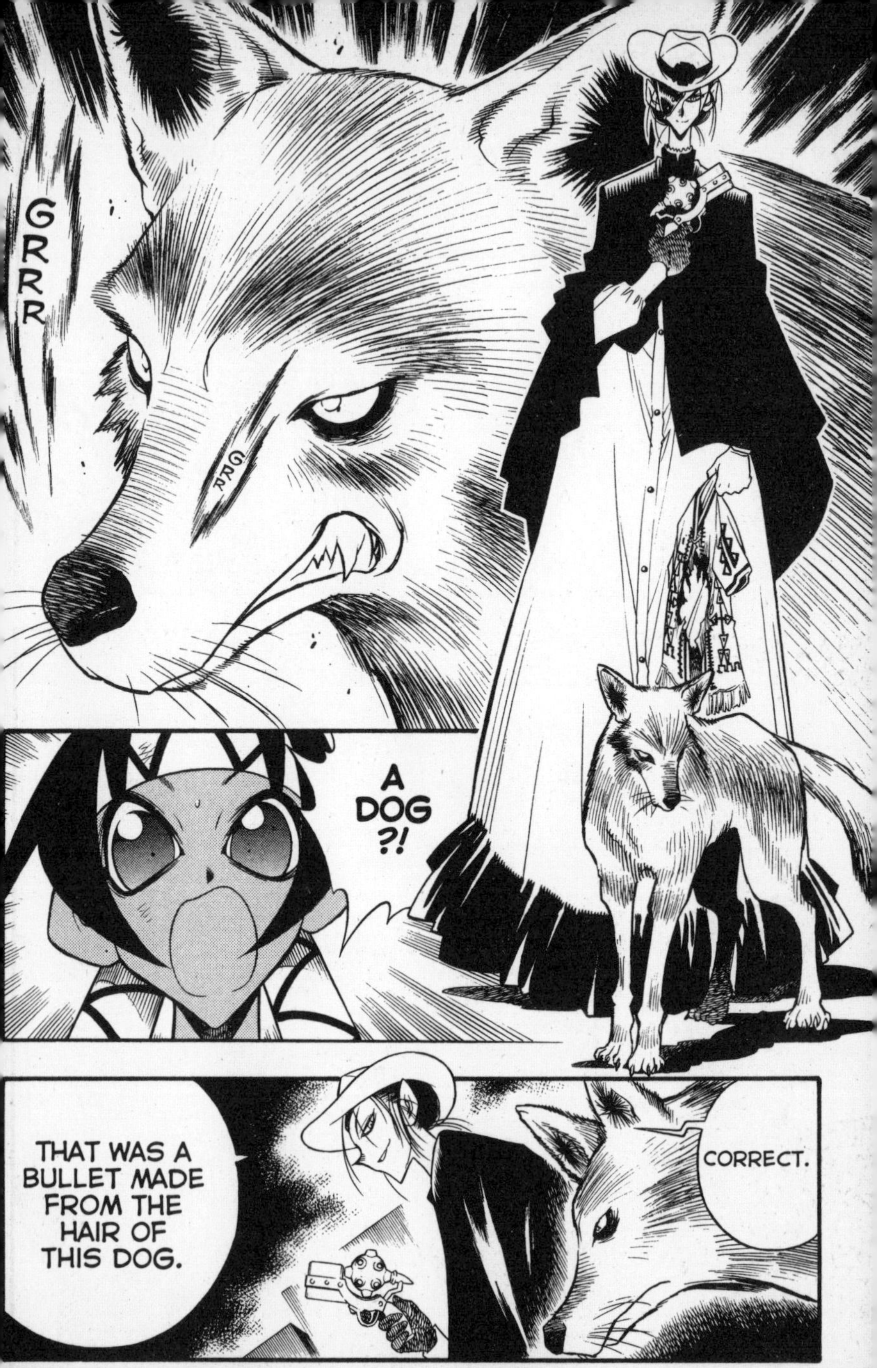
GRRR
GRR
A DOG ?!
CORRECT.
THAT WAS A BULLET MADE FROM THE HAIR OF THIS DOG.

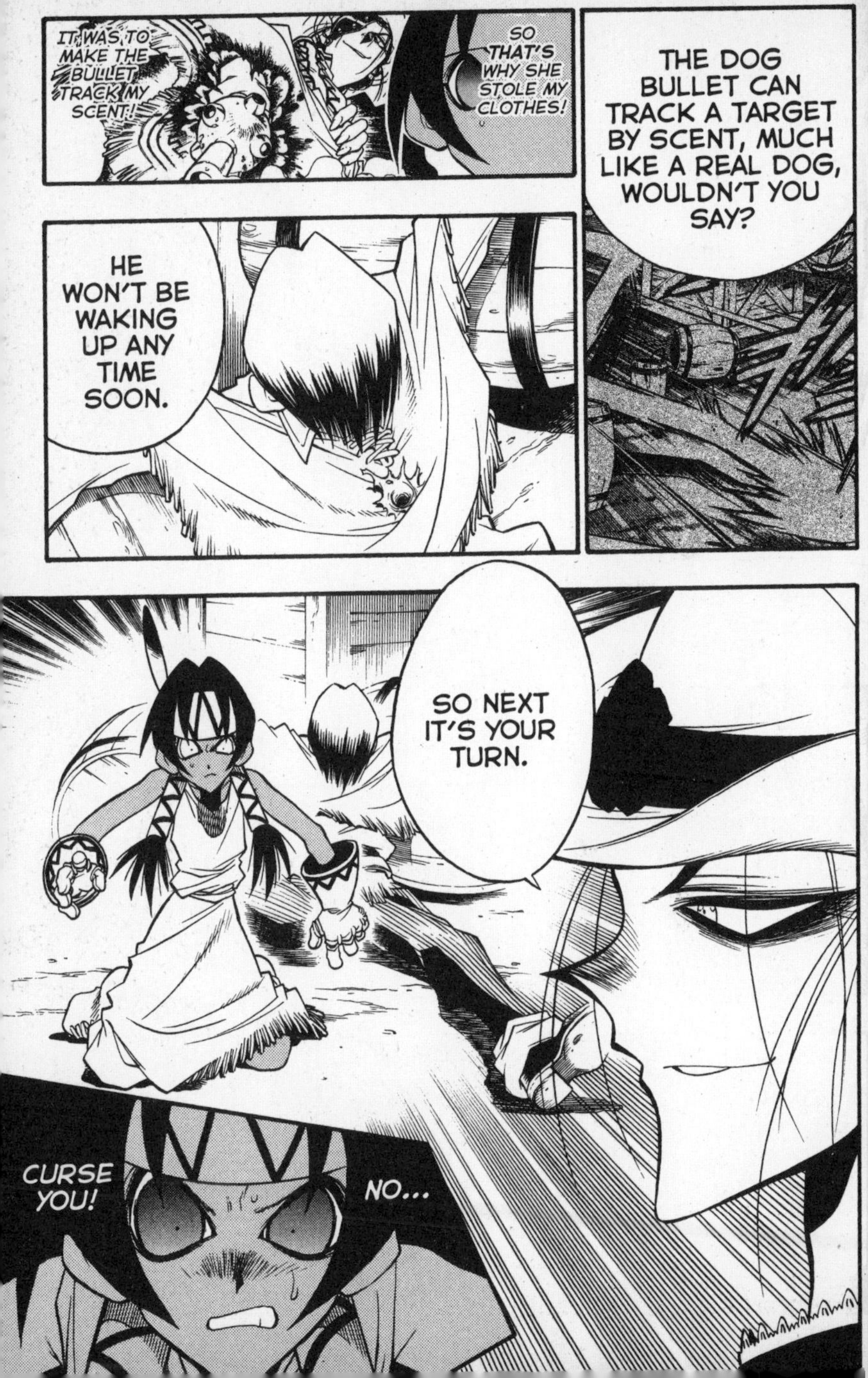
THE DOG BULLET CAN TRACK A TARGET BY SCENT, MUCH LIKE A REAL DOG, WOULDN'T YOU SAY?
SO THAT'S WHY SHE STOLE MY CLOTHES!
IT WAS TO MAKE THE BULLET TRACK MY SCENT!
HE WON'T BE WAKING UP ANY TIME SOON.
SO NEXT IT'S YOUR TURN.
NO...
CURSE YOU!

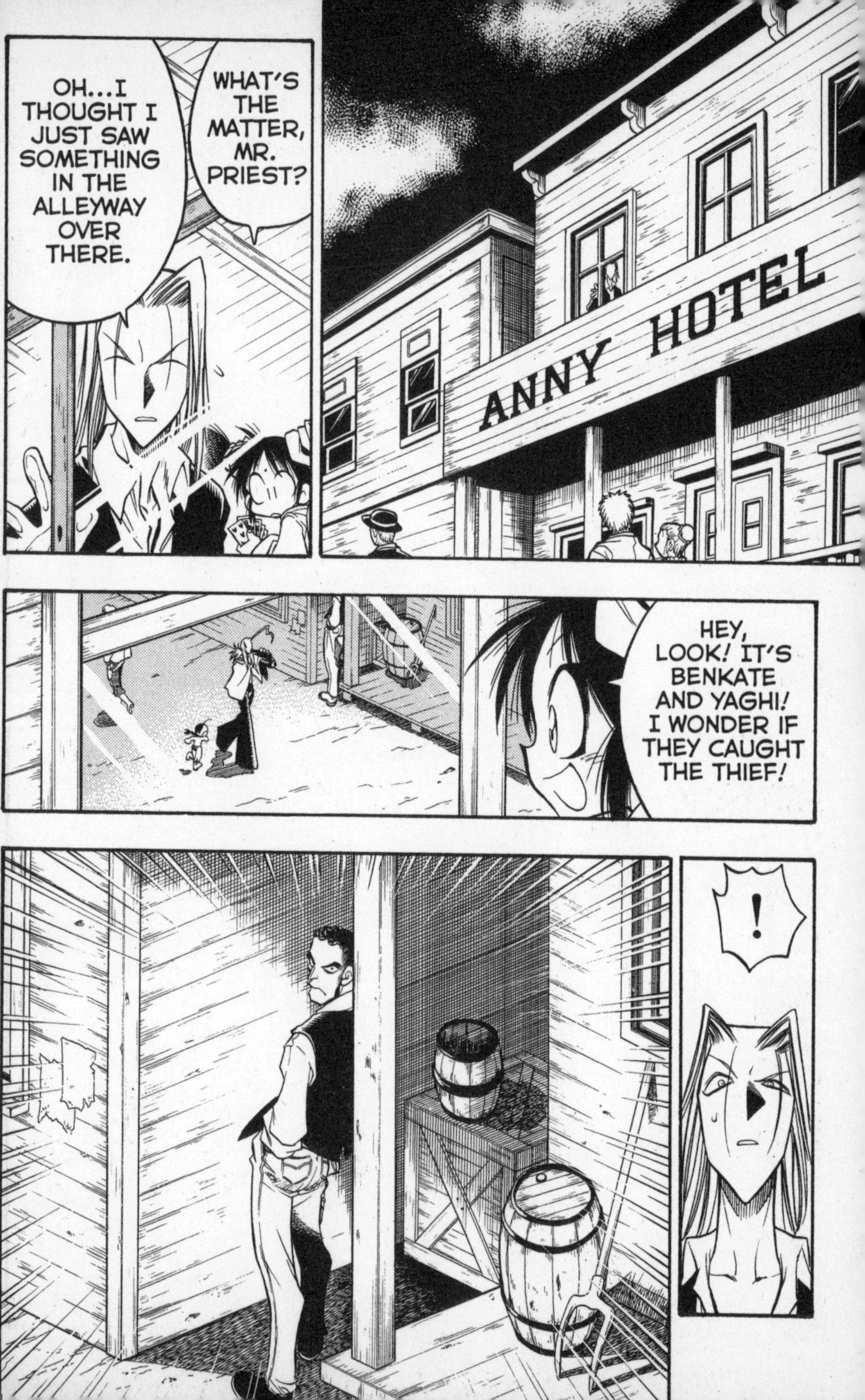
ANNY HOTEL
WHAT'S THE MATTER, MR. PRIEST?
OH...I THOUGHT I JUST SAW SOMETHING IN THE ALLEYWAY OVER THERE.
HEY, LOOK! IT'S BENKATE AND YAGHI! I WONDER IF THEY CAUGHT THE THIEF!
!

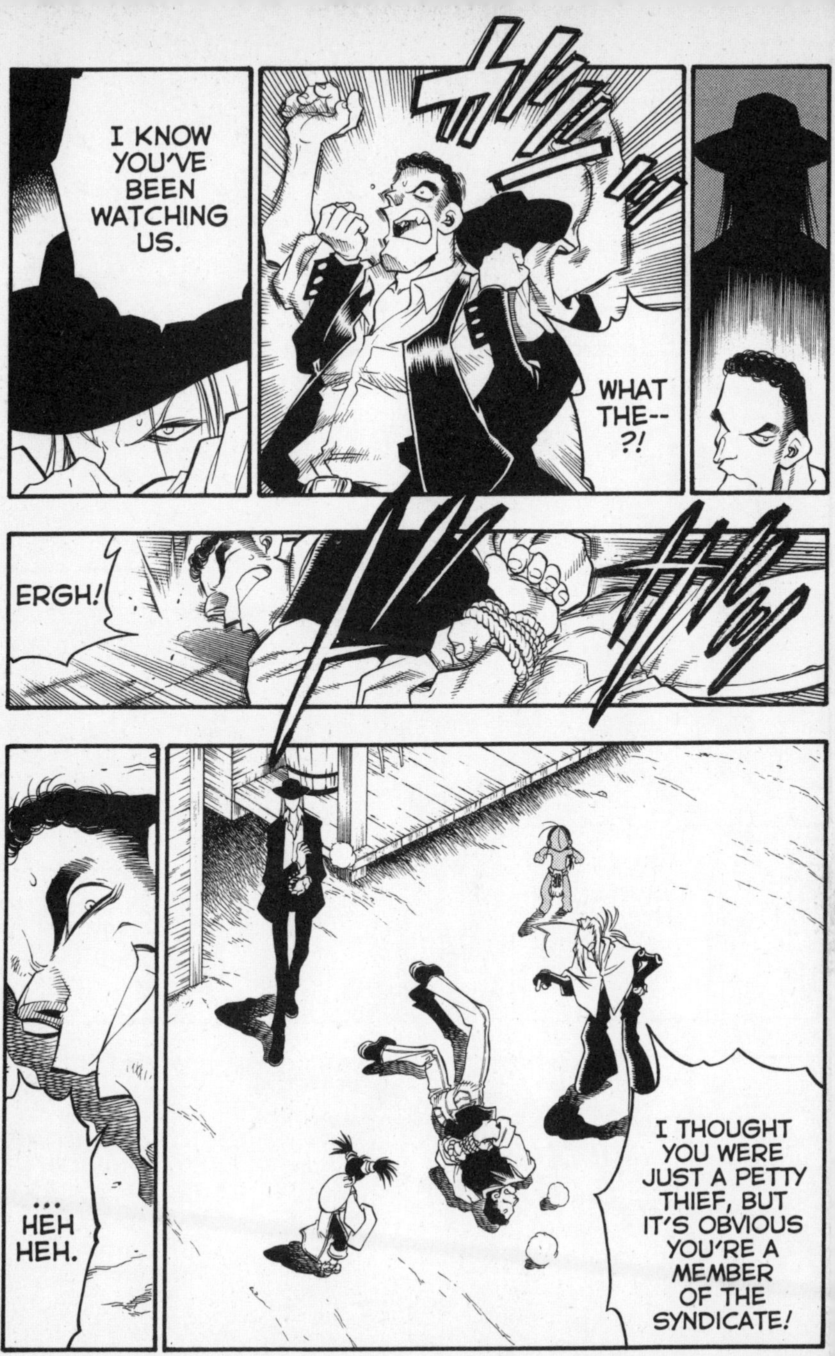
WHAT THE-- ?!
I KNOW YOU'VE BEEN WATCHING US.
ERGH!
I THOUGHT YOU WERE JUST A PETTY THIEF, BUT IT'S OBVIOUS YOU'RE A MEMBER OF THE SYNDICATE!
... HEH HEH.

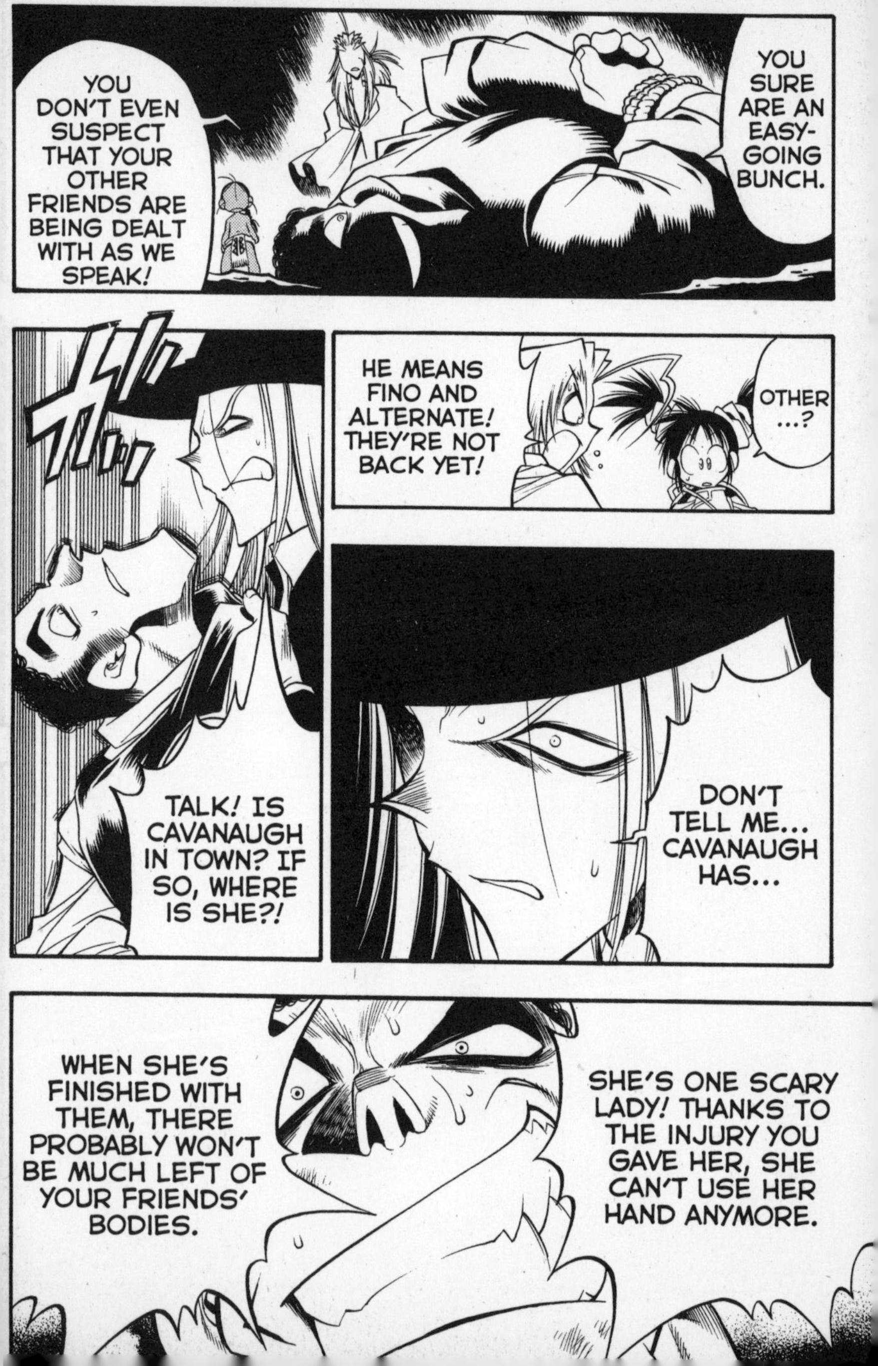
YOU SURE ARE AN EASY-GOING BUNCH.
YOU DON'T EVEN SUSPECT THAT YOUR OTHER FRIENDS ARE BEING DEALT WITH AS WE SPEAK!
OTHER ...?
HE MEANS FINO AND ALTERNATE! THEY'RE NOT BACK YET!
DON'T TELL ME... CAVANAUGH HAS...
TALK! IS CAVANAUGH IN TOWN? IF SO, WHERE IS SHE?!
SHE'S ONE SCARY LADY! THANKS TO THE INJURY YOU GAVE HER, SHE CAN'T USE HER HAND ANYMORE.
WHEN SHE'S FINISHED WITH THEM, THERE PROBABLY WON'T BE MUCH LEFT OF YOUR FRIENDS' BODIES.

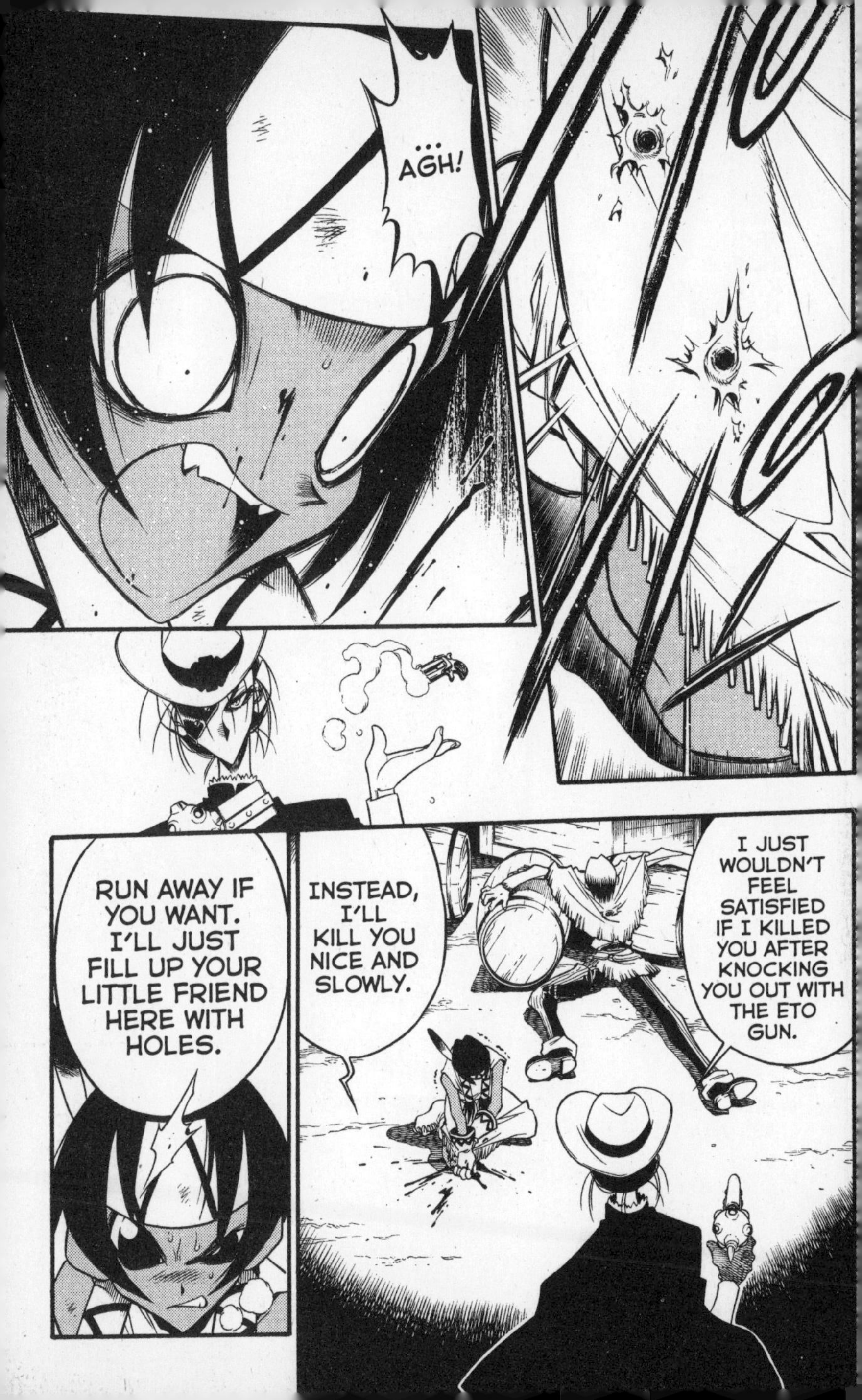
...AGH!
I JUST WOULDN'T FEEL SATISFIED IF I KILLED YOU AFTER KNOCKING YOU OUT WITH THE ETO GUN.
INSTEAD, I'LL KILL YOU NICE AND SLOWLY.
RUN AWAY IF YOU WANT. I'LL JUST FILL UP YOUR LITTLE FRIEND HERE WITH HOLES.

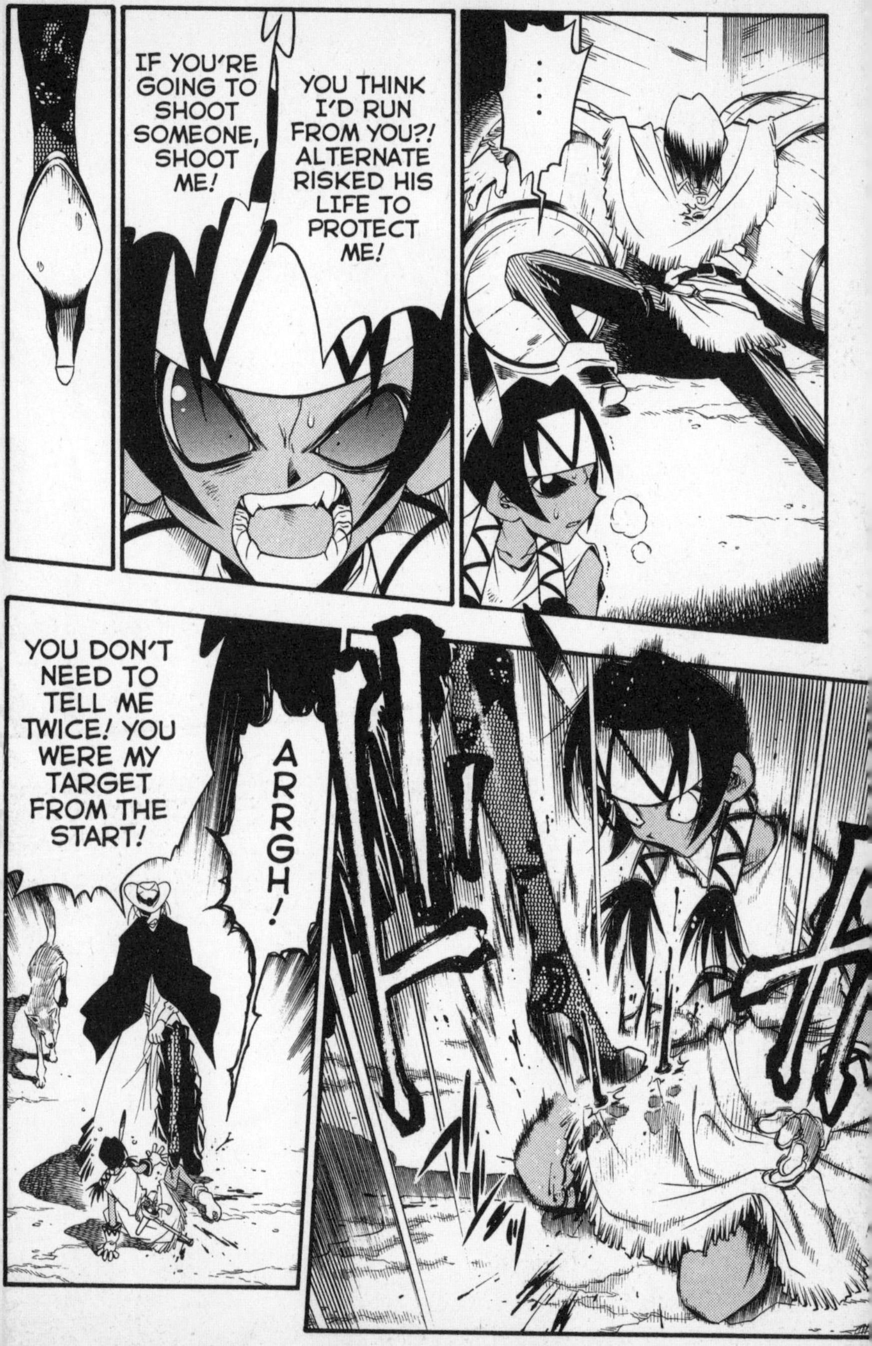
....
YOU THINK I'D RUN FROM YOU?! ALTERNATE RISKED HIS LIFE TO PROTECT ME!
IF YOU'RE GOING TO SHOOT SOMEONE, SHOOT ME!
YOU DON'T NEED TO TELL ME TWICE! YOU WERE MY TARGET FROM THE START!
ARRGH!

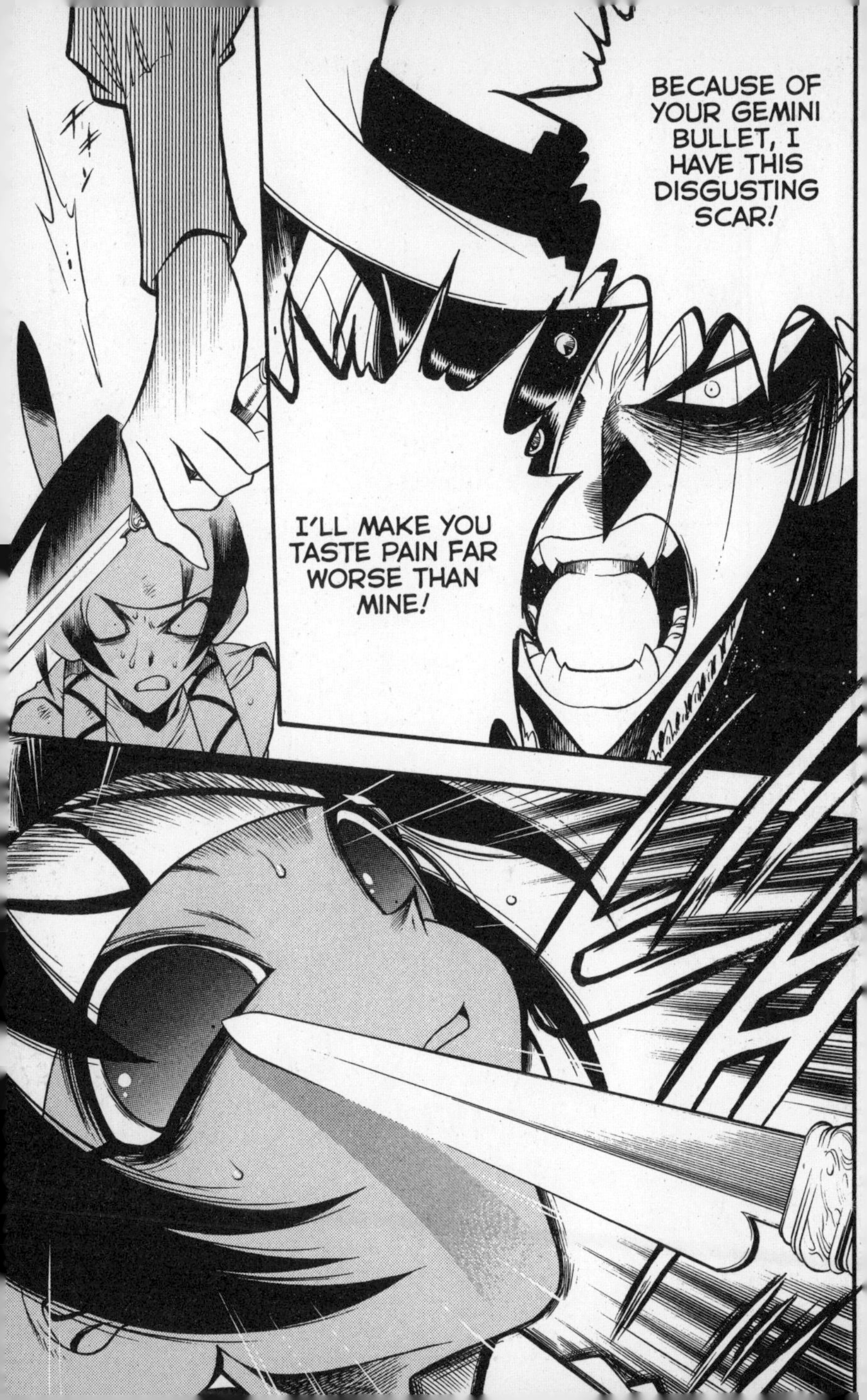
BECAUSE OF YOUR GEMINI BULLET, I HAVE THIS DISGUSTING SCAR!
I'LL MAKE YOU TASTE PAIN FAR WORSE THAN MINE!

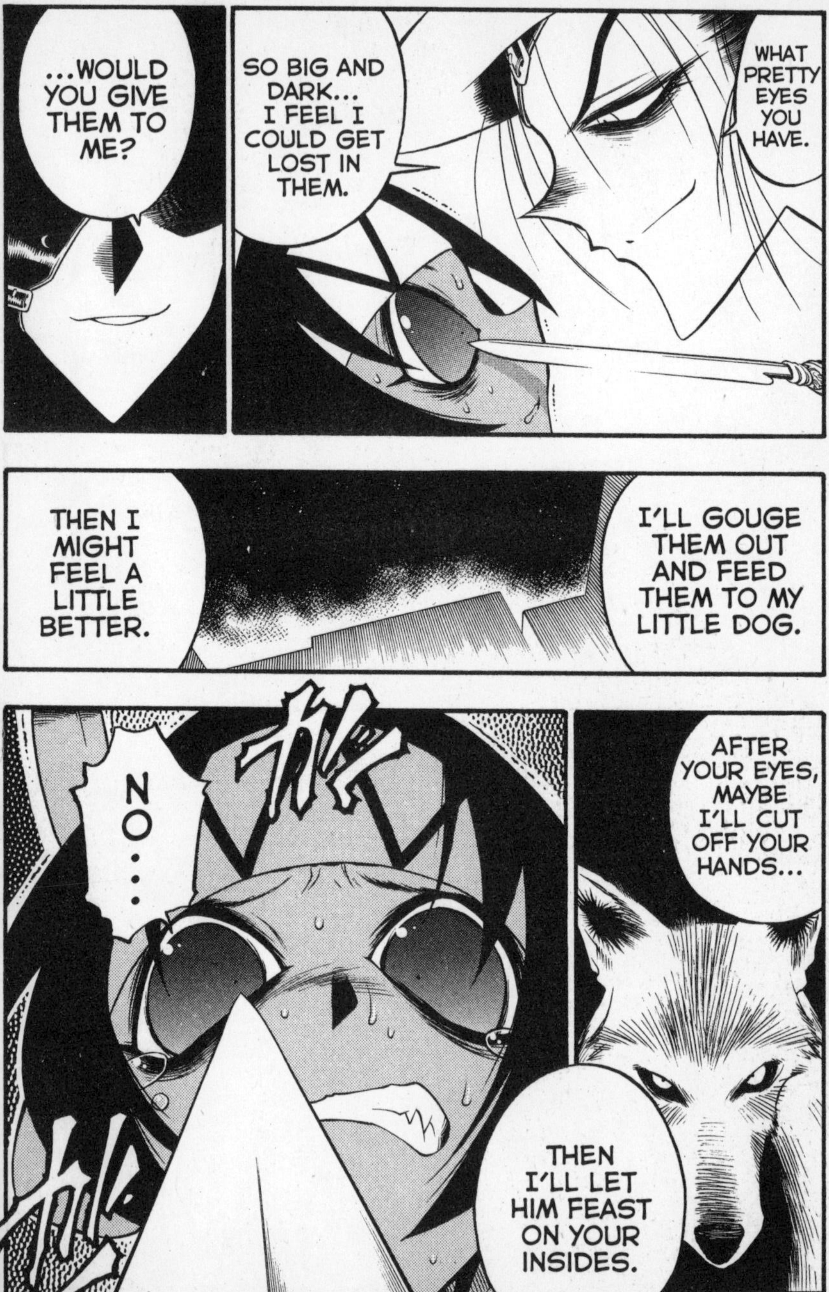
WHAT PRETTY EYES YOU HAVE.
SO BIG AND DARK... I FEEL I COULD GET LOST IN THEM.
...WOULD YOU GIVE THEM TO ME?
I'LL GOUGE THEM OUT AND FEED THEM TO MY LITTLE DOG.
THEN I MIGHT FEEL A LITTLE BETTER.
AFTER YOUR EYES, MAYBE I'LL CUT OFF YOUR HANDS...
THEN I'LL LET HIM FEAST ON YOUR INSIDES.
NO...

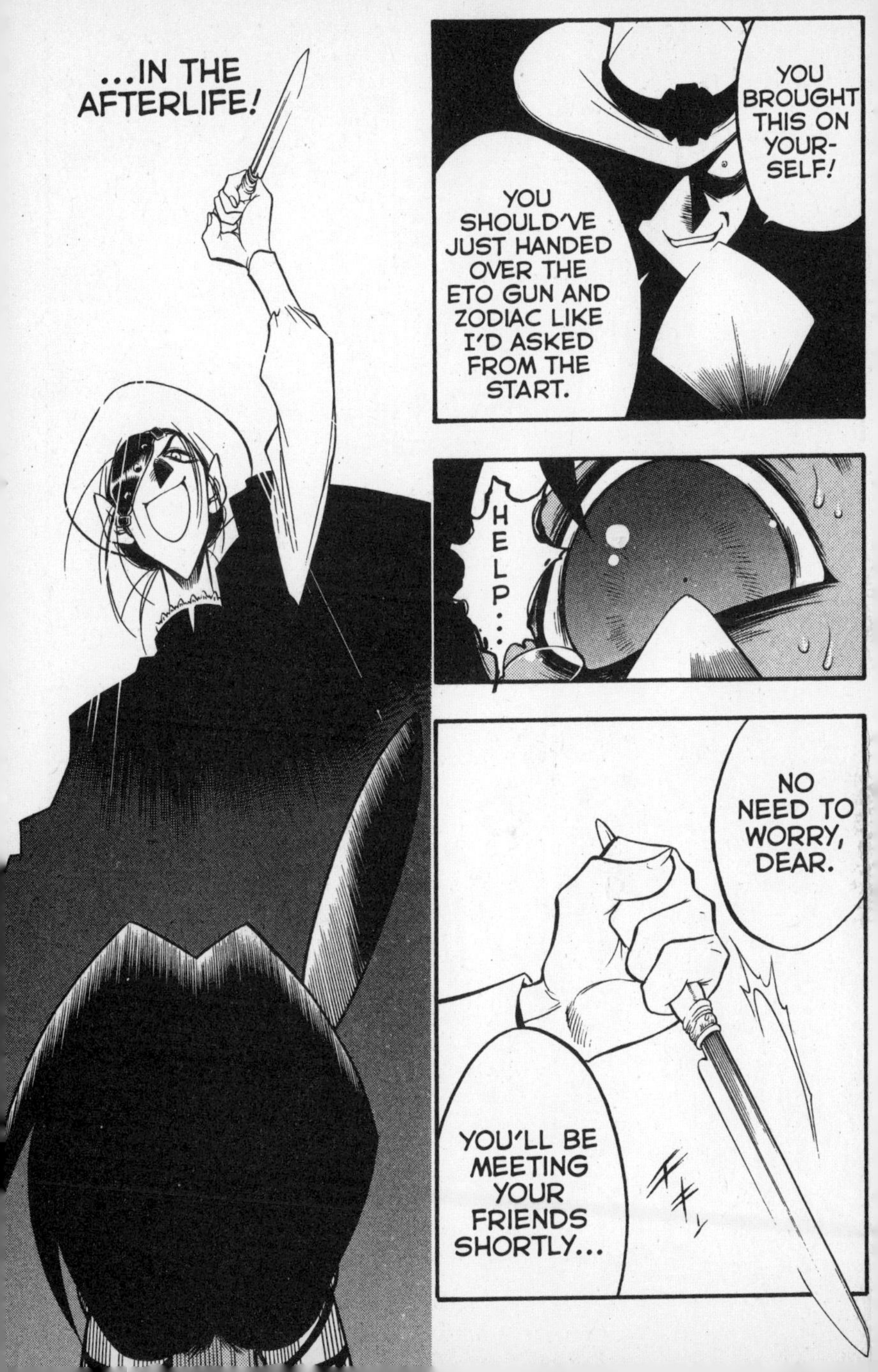
YOU BROUGHT THIS ON YOUR-SELF!
YOU SHOULD'VE JUST HANDED OVER THE ETO GUN AND ZODIAC LIKE I'D ASKED FROM THE START.
HELP...
NO NEED TO WORRY, DEAR.
YOU'LL BE MEETING YOUR FRIENDS SHORTLY...
...IN THE AFTERLIFE!

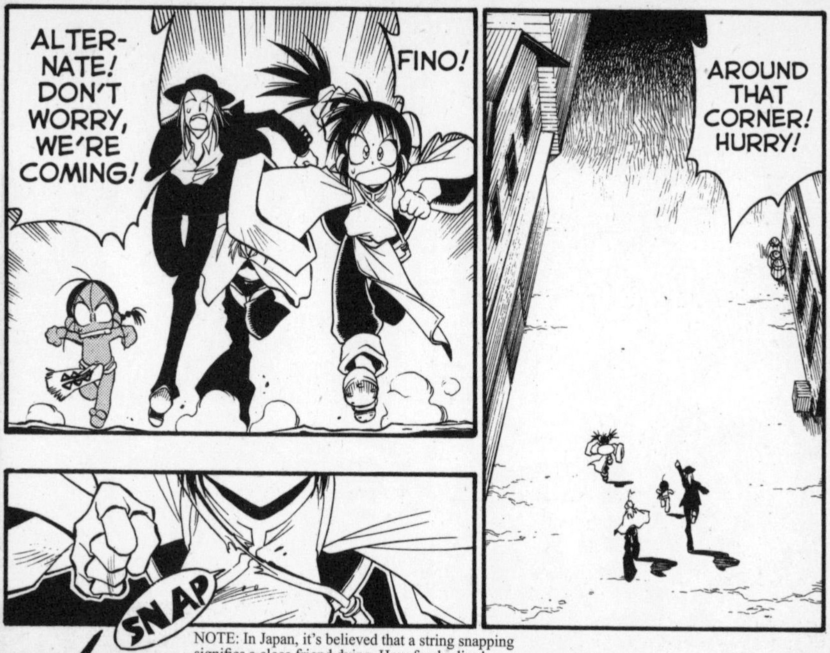
AROUND THAT CORNER! HURRY!
FINO!
ALTER-NATE! DON'T WORRY, WE'RE COMING!
SNAP

NOTE: In Japan, it's believed that a string snapping signifies a close friend dying. How foreboding!

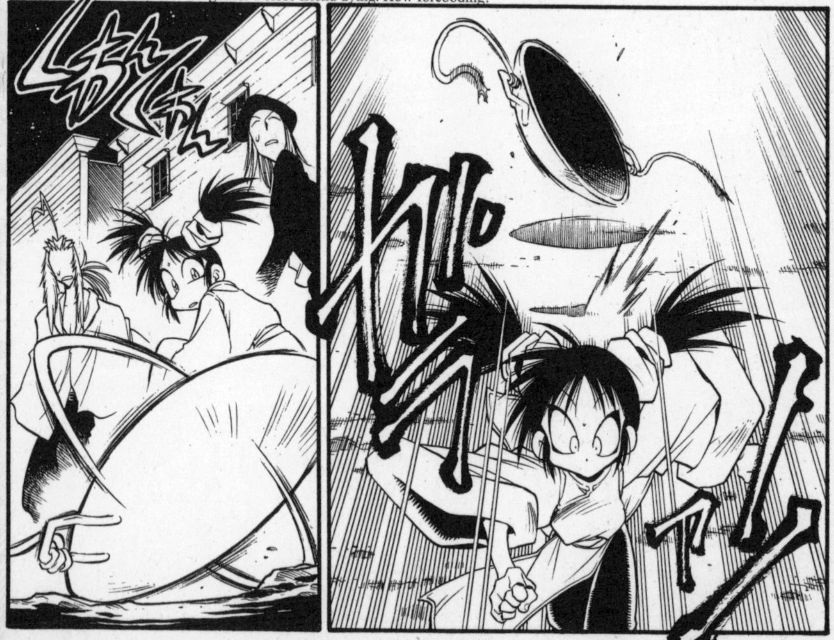

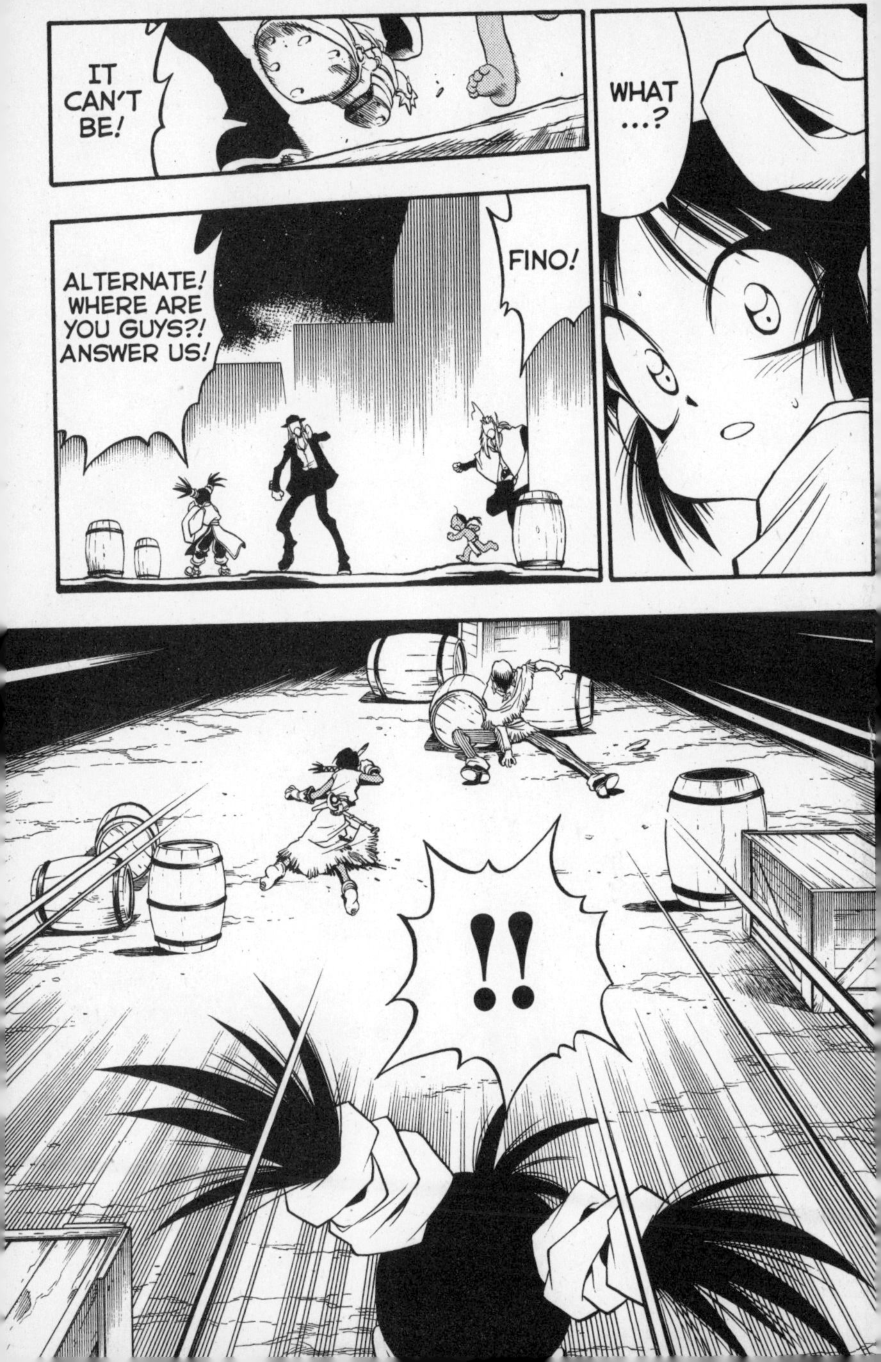
WHAT ...?
IT CAN'T BE!
FINO!
ALTERNATE! WHERE ARE YOU GUYS?! ANSWER US!
!!

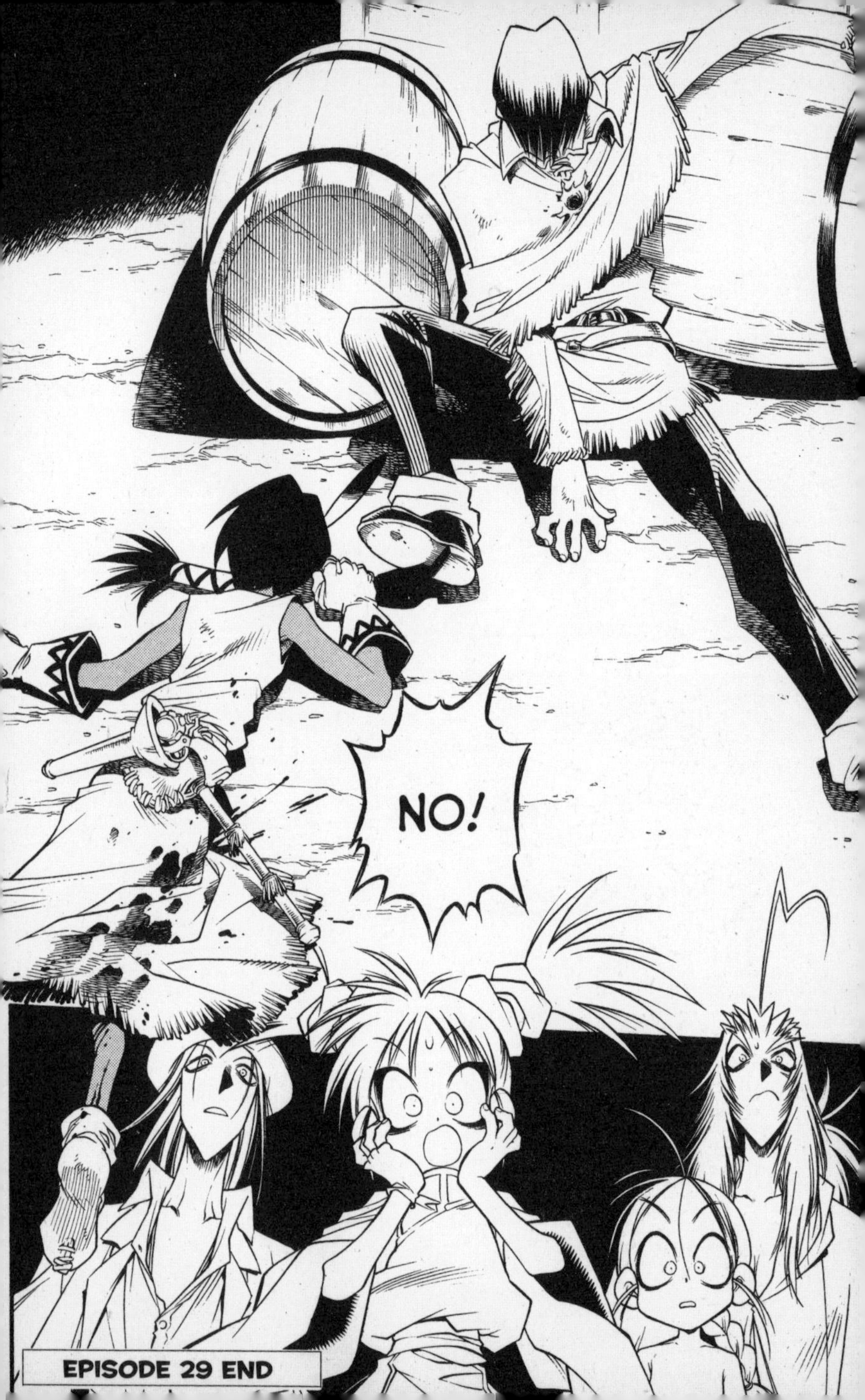
NO!
EPISODE 29 END

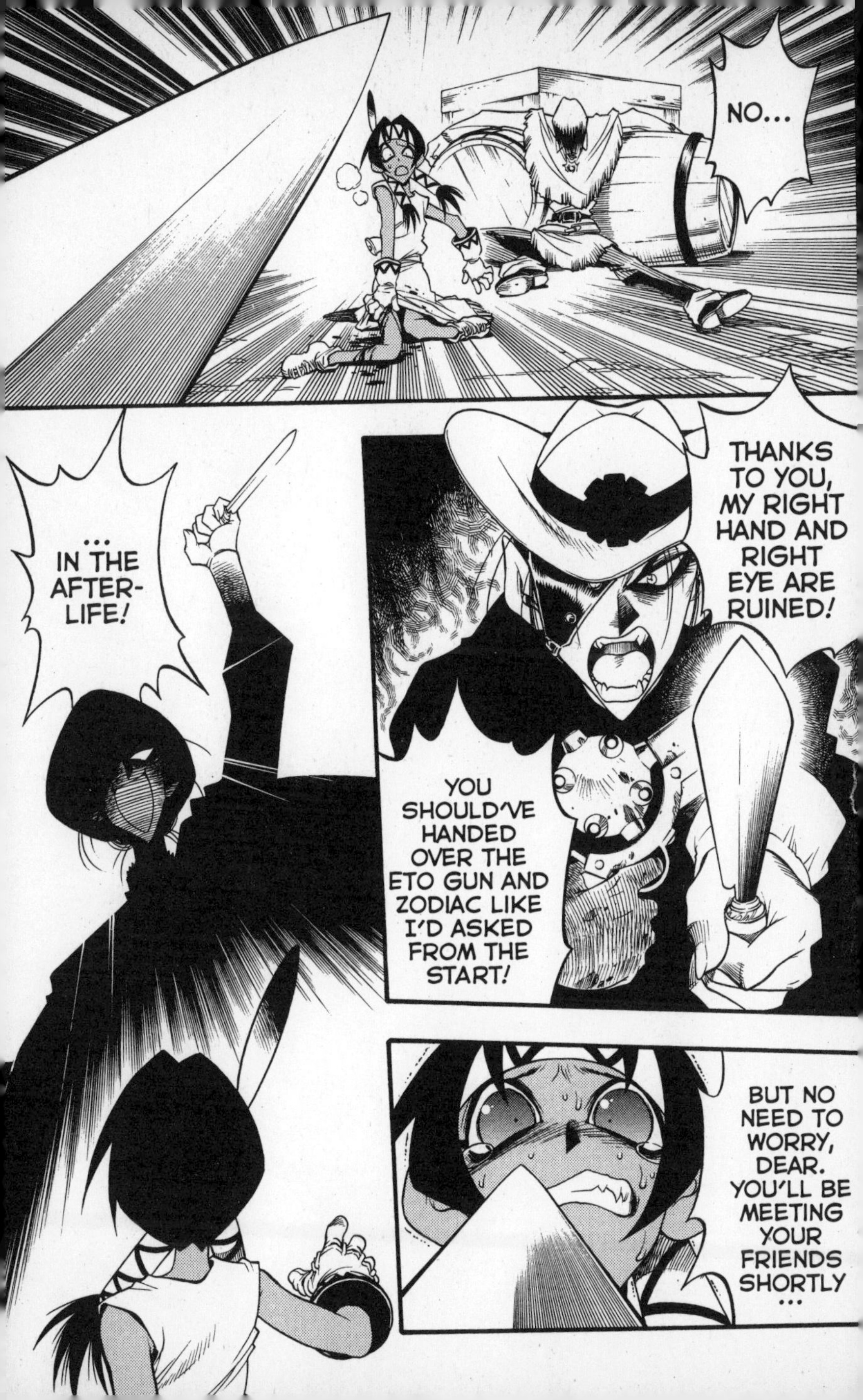
NO...
THANKS TO YOU, MY RIGHT HAND AND RIGHT EYE ARE RUINED!
YOU SHOULD'VE HANDED OVER THE ETO GUN AND ZODIAC LIKE I'D ASKED FROM THE START!
BUT NO NEED TO WORRY, DEAR. YOU'LL BE MEETING YOUR FRIENDS SHORTLY...
... IN THE AFTER-LIFE!

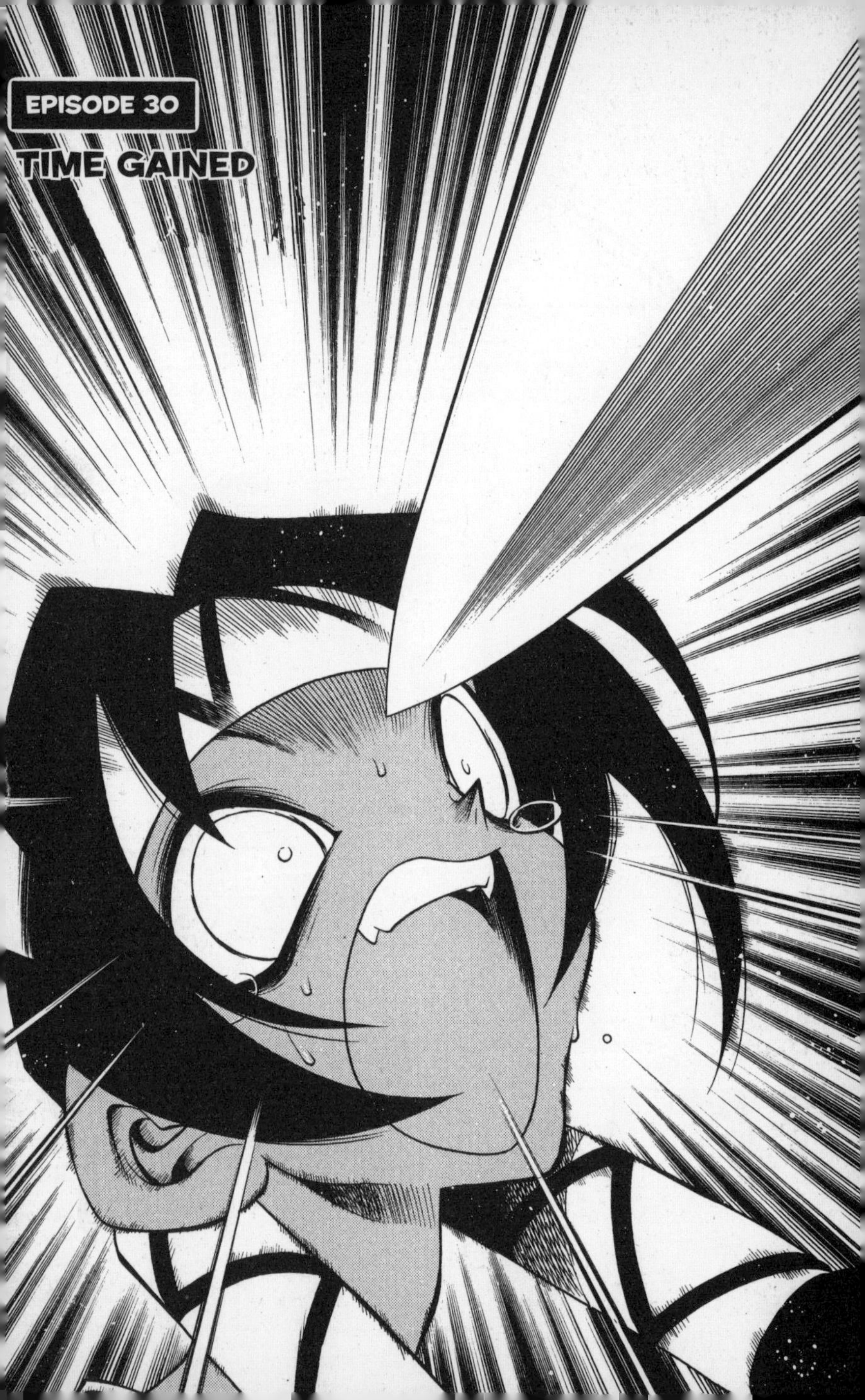
EPISODE 30
TIME GAINED

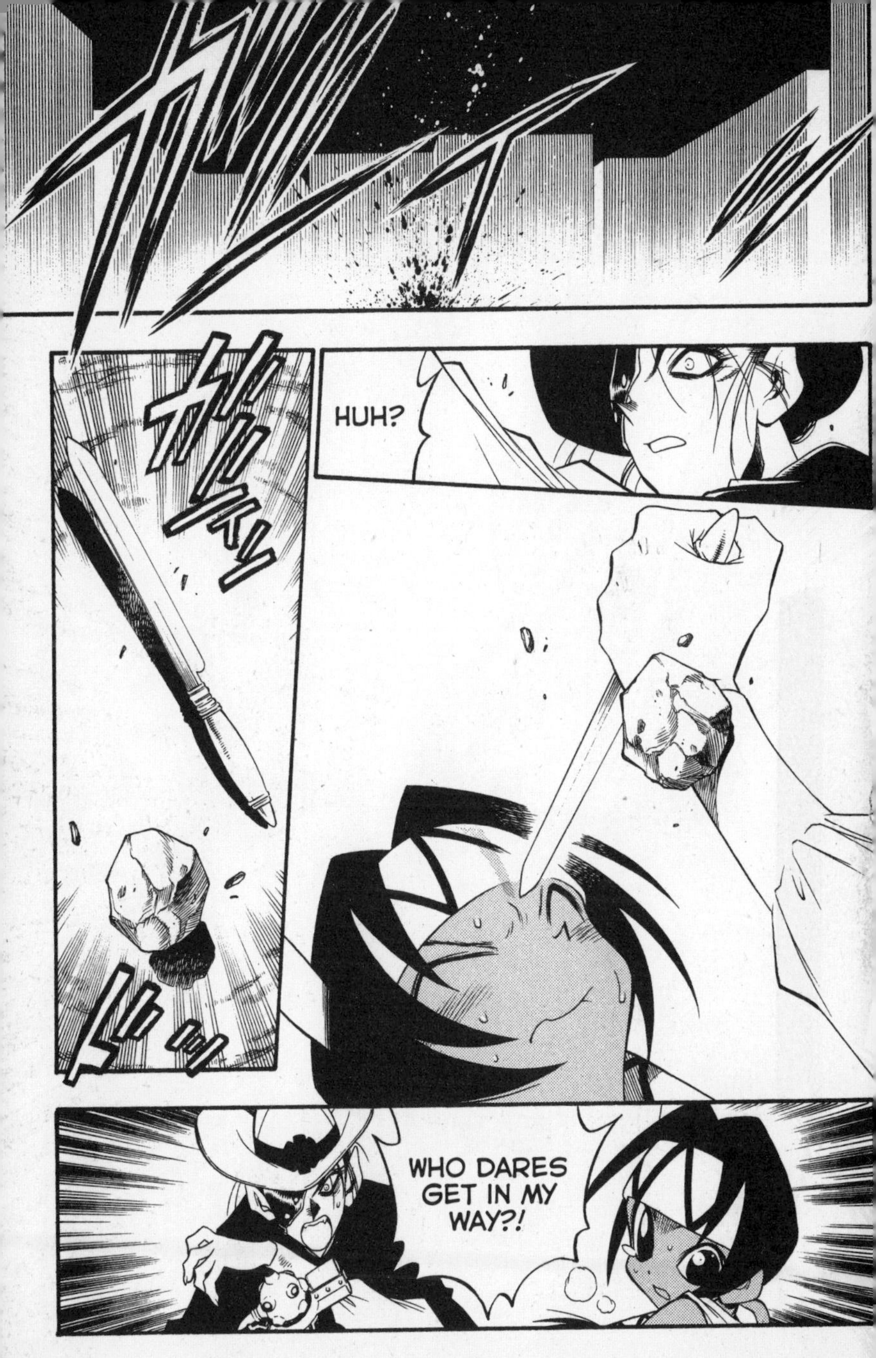
HUH?
KY
WHO DARES GET IN MY WAY?!

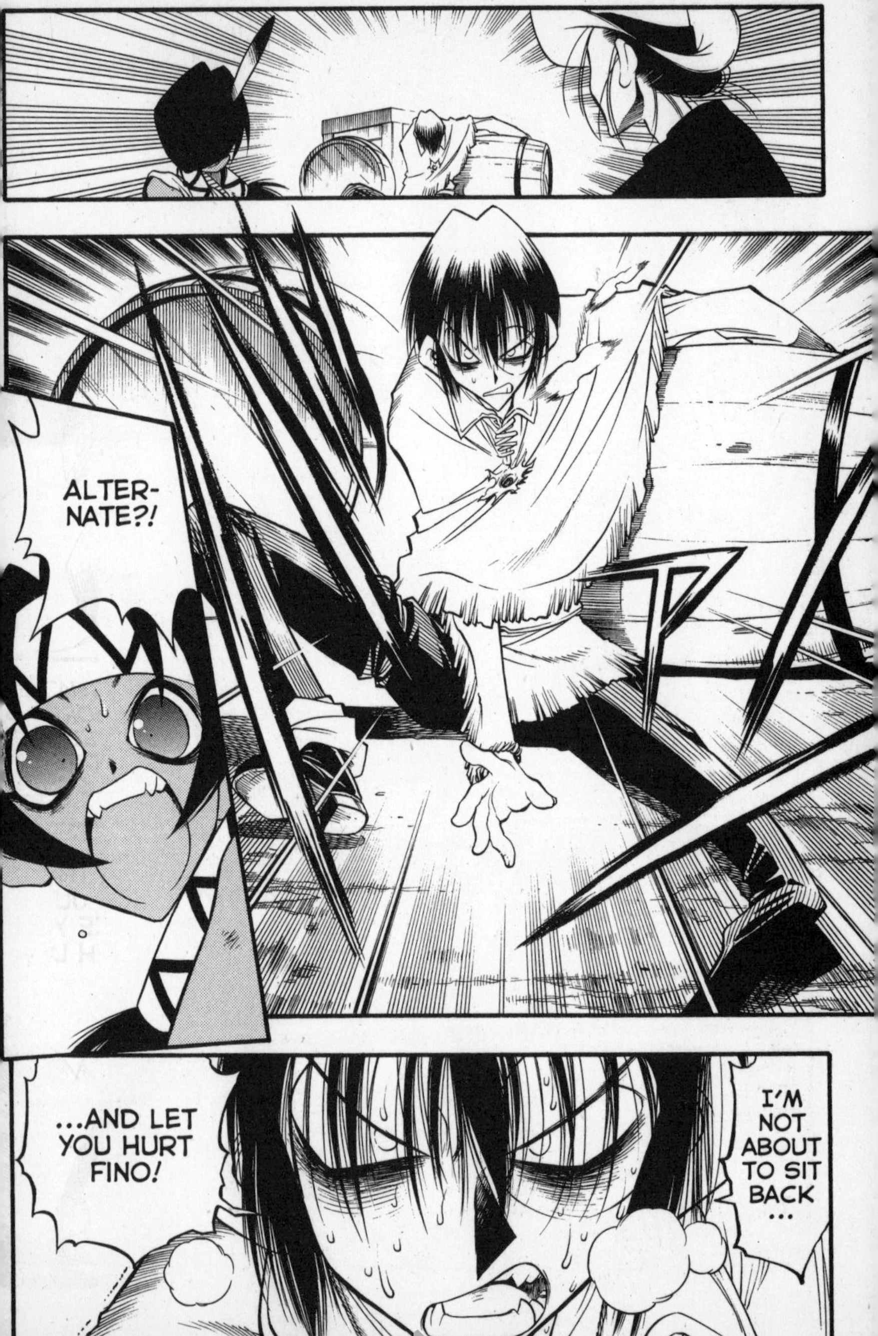
ALTER-NATE?!
I'M NOT ABOUT TO SIT BACK...
...AND LET YOU HURT FINO!

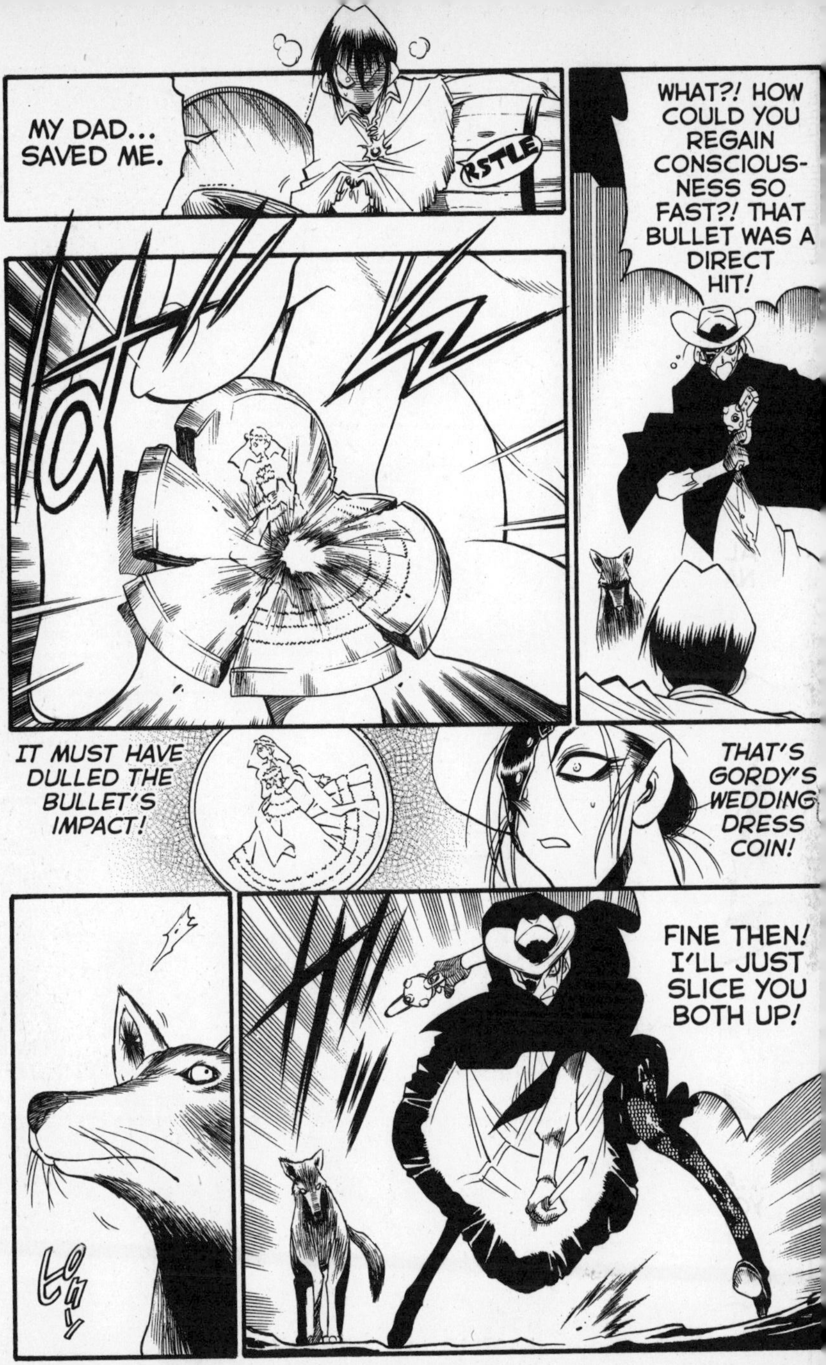

WHAT?! HOW COULD YOU REGAIN CONSCIOUSNESS SO FAST?! THAT BULLET WAS A DIRECT HIT!
MY DAD... SAVED ME.
RSTLE
THAT'S GORDY'S WEDDING DRESS COIN!
IT MUST HAVE DULLED THE BULLET'S IMPACT!
FINE THEN! I'LL JUST SLICE YOU BOTH UP!
ピクッ

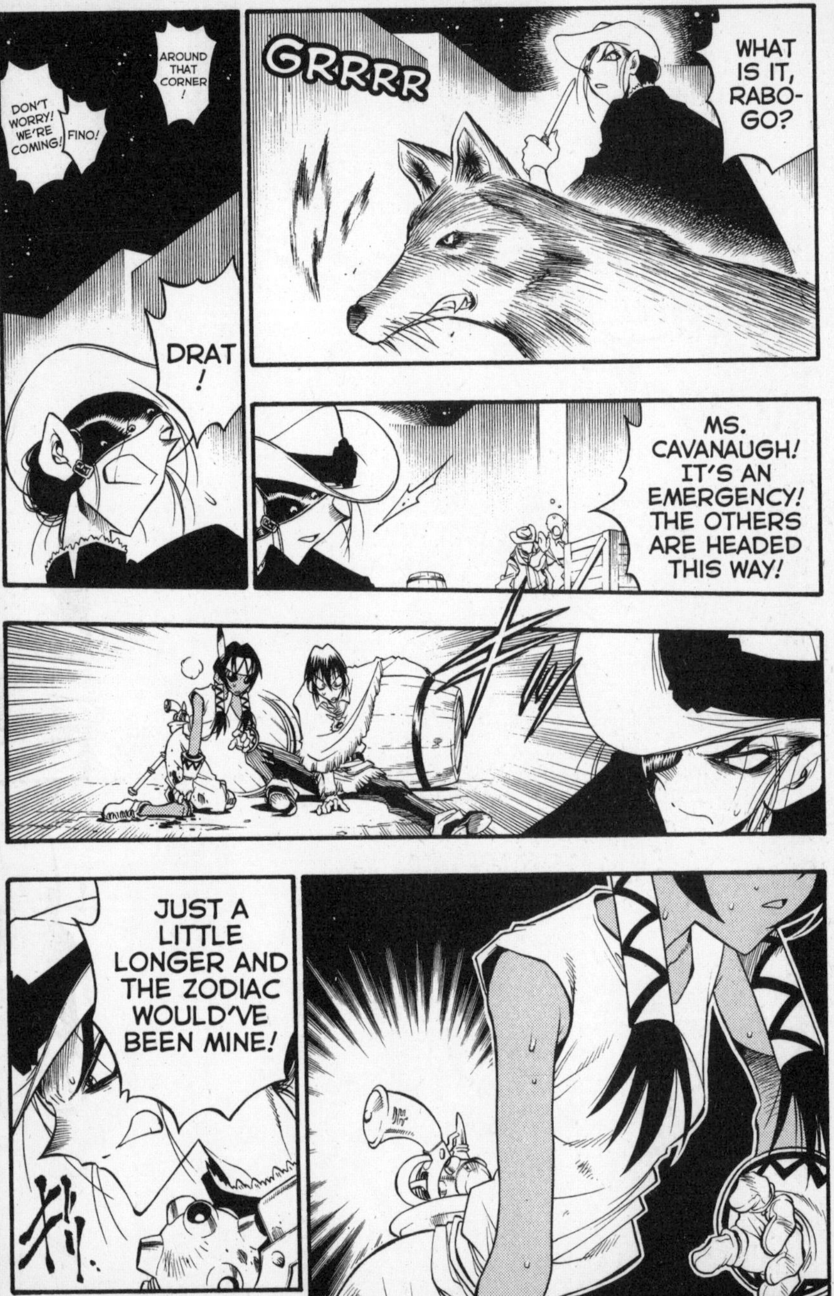
GRRRR
WHAT IS IT, RABOGO?
MS. CAVANAUGH! IT'S AN EMERGENCY! THE OTHERS ARE HEADED THIS WAY!
AROUND THAT CORNER!
FINO!
DON'T WORRY! WE'RE COMING!
DRAT!
JUST A LITTLE LONGER AND THE ZODIAC WOULD'VE BEEN MINE!

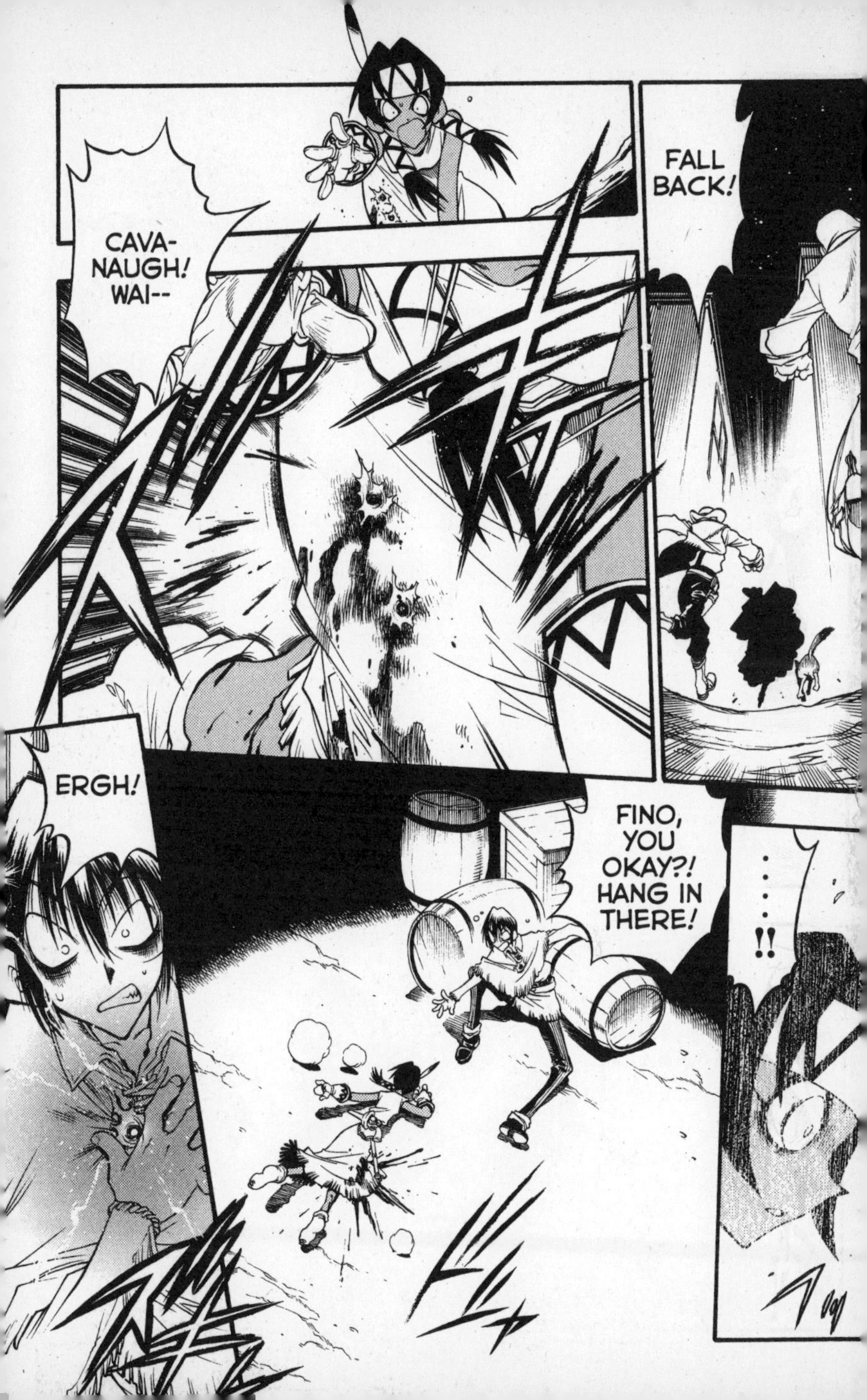
FALL BACK!
CAVA-NAUGH! WAI--
.....!!
FINO, YOU OKAY?! HANG IN THERE!
ERGH!

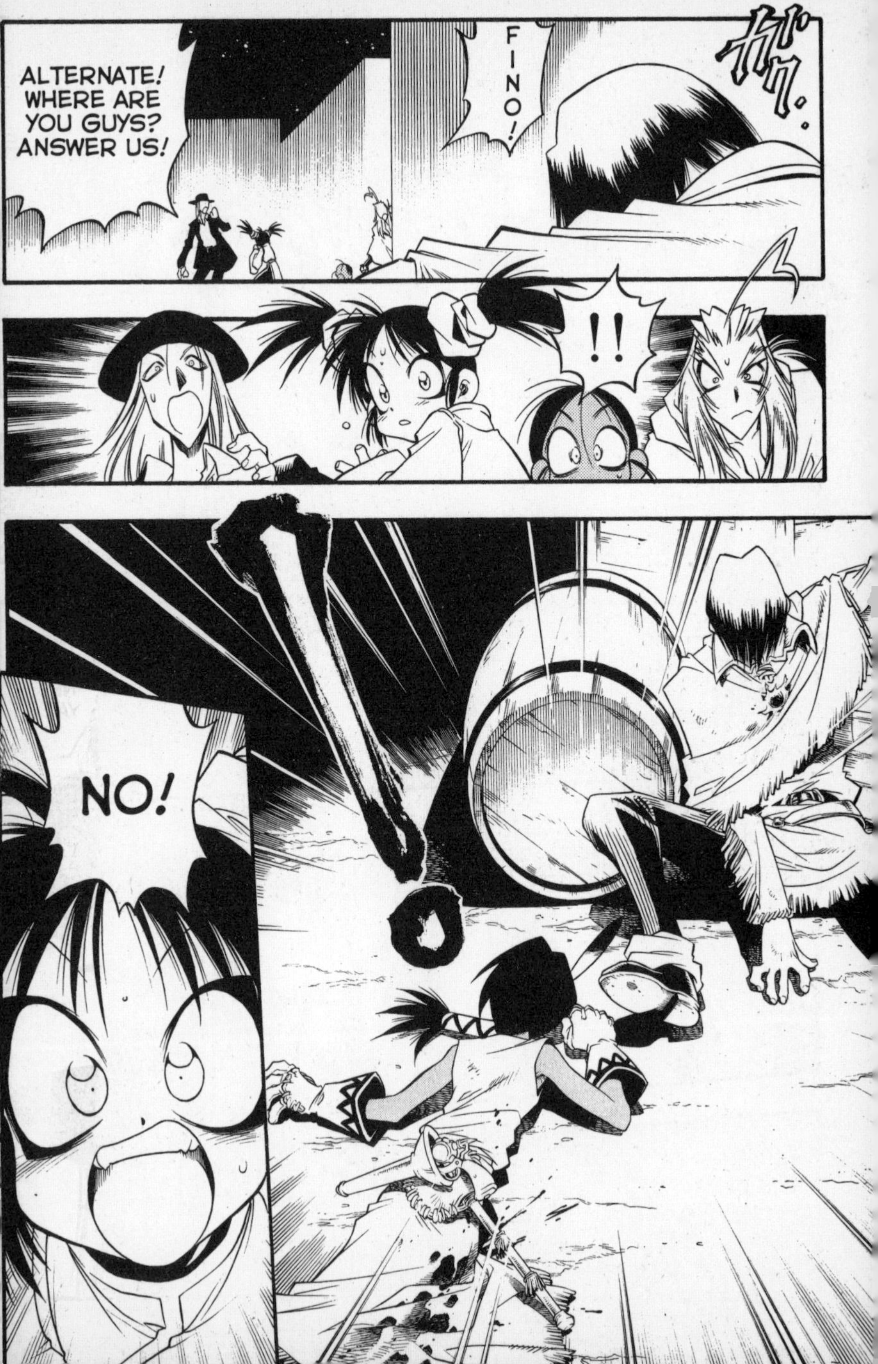
FINO!
ALTERNATE! WHERE ARE YOU GUYS? ANSWER US!
!!
NO!

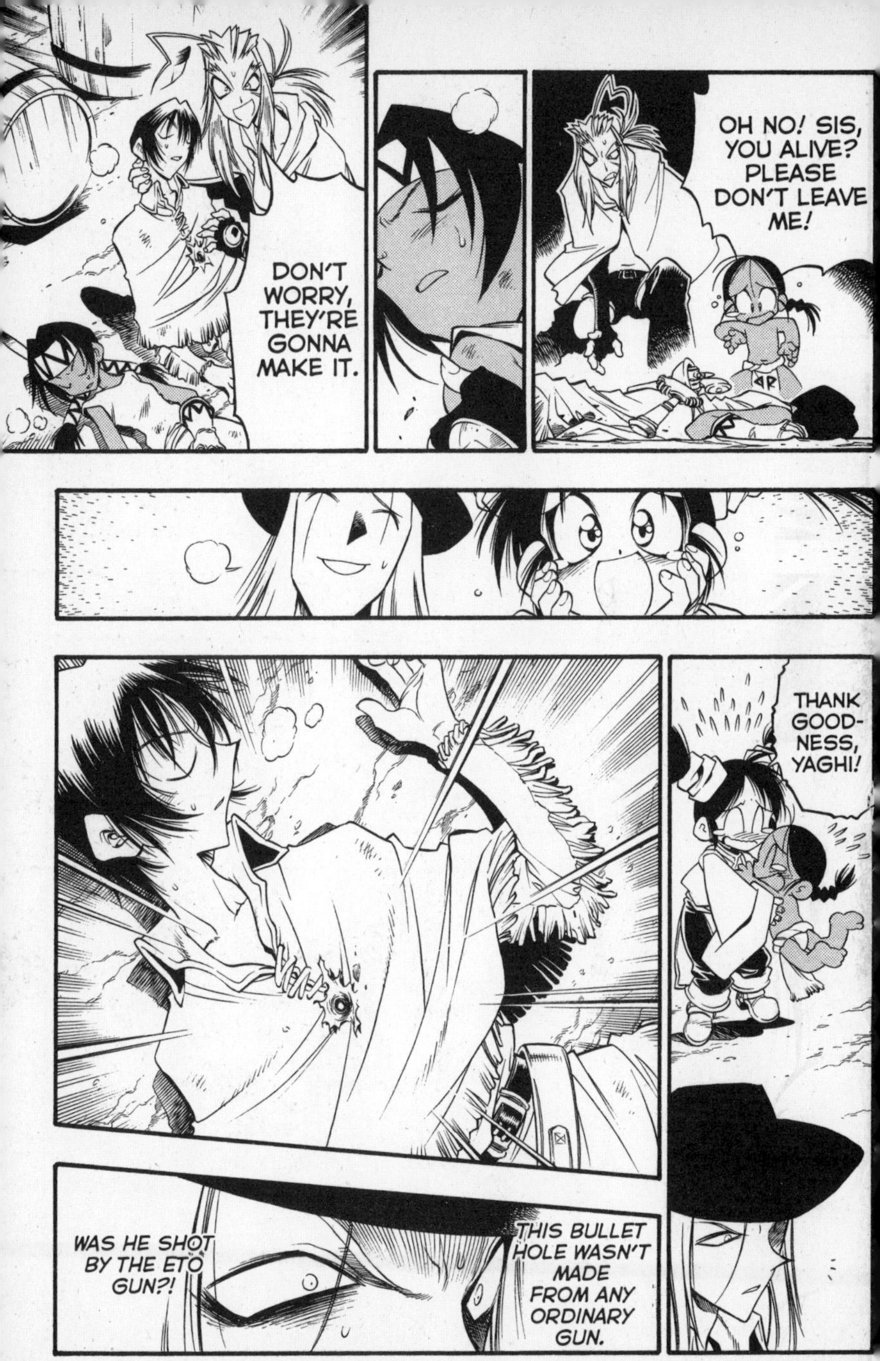
OH NO! SIS, YOU ALIVE? PLEASE DON'T LEAVE ME!
DON'T WORRY, THEY'RE GONNA MAKE IT.
THANK GOOD-NESS, YAGHI!
THIS BULLET HOLE WASN'T MADE FROM ANY ORDINARY GUN.
WAS HE SHOT BY THE ETO GUN?!

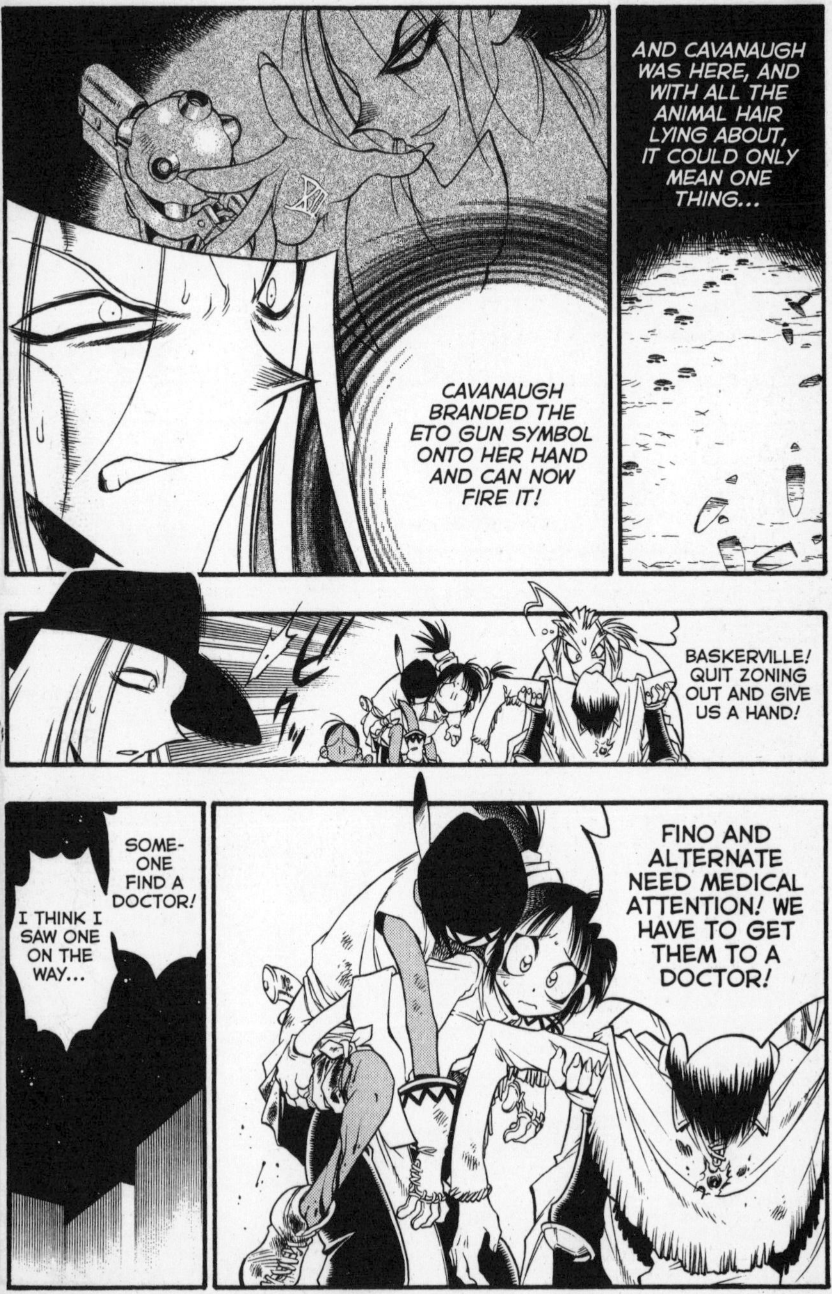
AND CAVANAUGH WAS HERE, AND WITH ALL THE ANIMAL HAIR LYING ABOUT, IT COULD ONLY MEAN ONE THING...
CAVANAUGH BRANDED THE ETO GUN SYMBOL ONTO HER HAND AND CAN NOW FIRE IT!
BASKERVILLE! QUIT ZONING OUT AND GIVE US A HAND!
FINO AND ALTERNATE NEED MEDICAL ATTENTION! WE HAVE TO GET THEM TO A DOCTOR!
SOME-ONE FIND A DOCTOR!
I THINK I SAW ONE ON THE WAY...

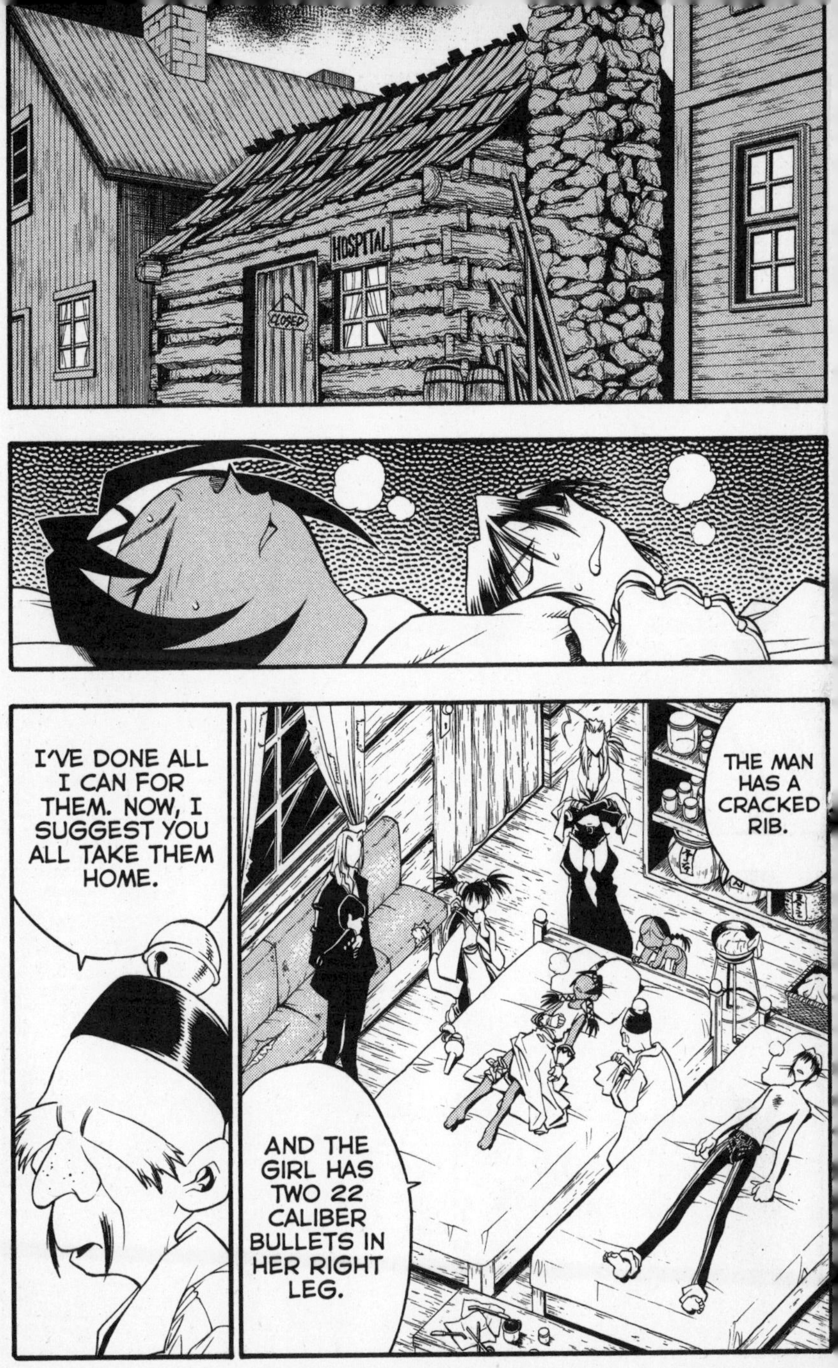
HOSPITAL
CLOSED
THE MAN HAS A CRACKED RIB.
AND THE GIRL HAS TWO 22 CALIBER BULLETS IN HER RIGHT LEG.
I'VE DONE ALL I CAN FOR THEM. NOW, I SUGGEST YOU ALL TAKE THEM HOME.

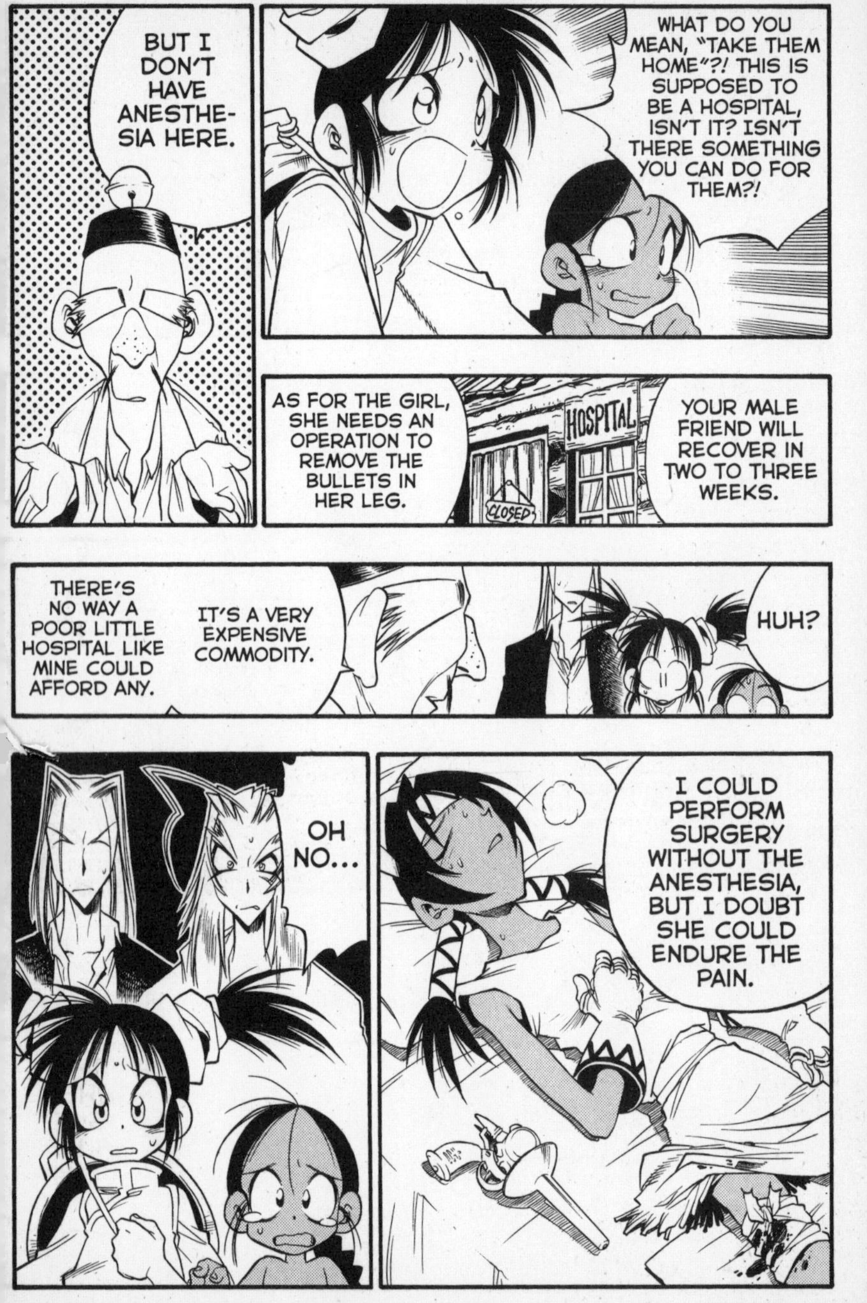
WHAT DO YOU MEAN, "TAKE THEM HOME"?! THIS IS SUPPOSED TO BE A HOSPITAL, ISN'T IT? ISN'T THERE SOMETHING YOU CAN DO FOR THEM?!
YOUR MALE FRIEND WILL RECOVER IN TWO TO THREE WEEKS.
HOSPITAL
CLOSED
AS FOR THE GIRL, SHE NEEDS AN OPERATION TO REMOVE THE BULLETS IN HER LEG.
BUT I DON'T HAVE ANESTHE-SIA HERE.
HUH?
IT'S A VERY EXPENSIVE COMMODITY.
THERE'S NO WAY A POOR LITTLE HOSPITAL LIKE MINE COULD AFFORD ANY.
I COULD PERFORM SURGERY WITHOUT THE ANESTHESIA, BUT I DOUBT SHE COULD ENDURE THE PAIN.
OH NO...

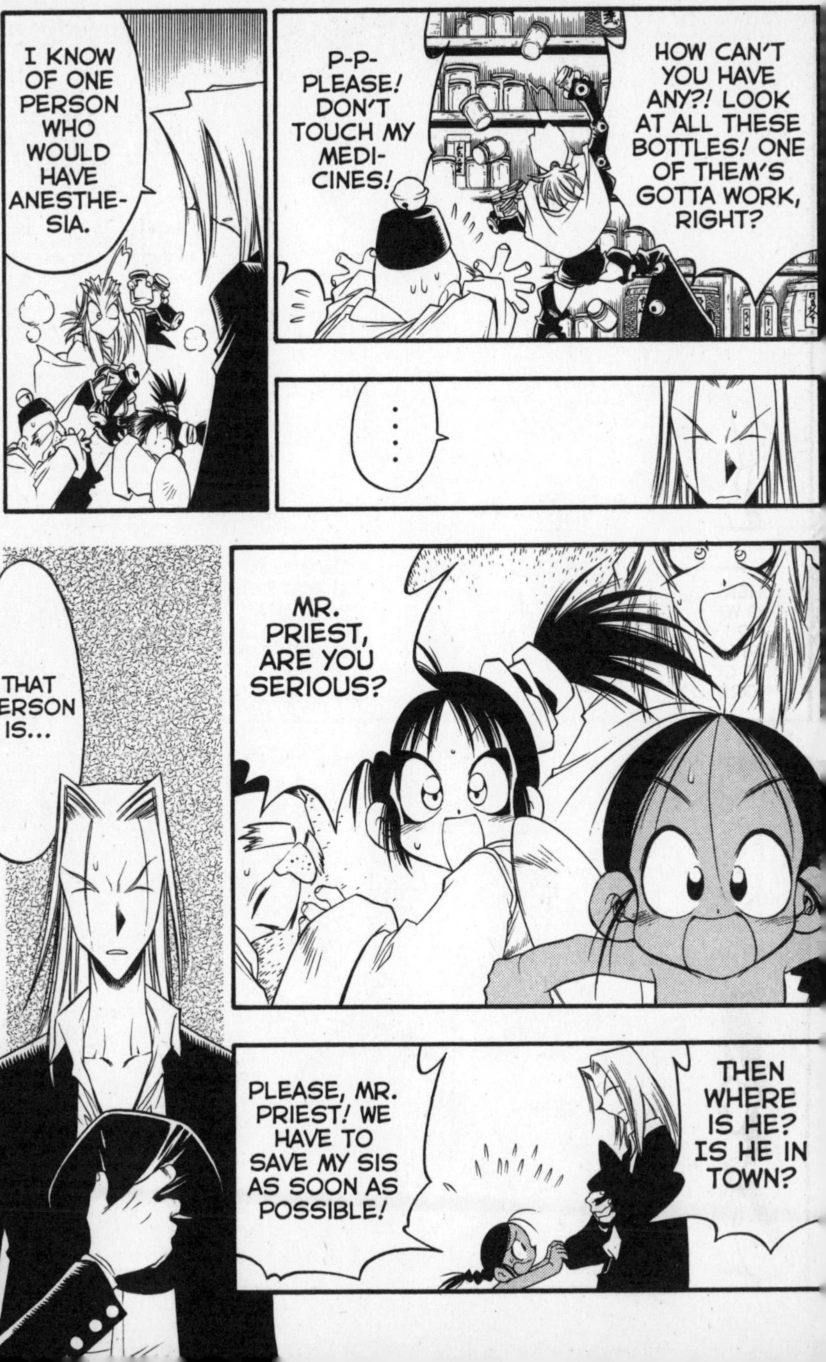
HOW CAN'T YOU HAVE ANY?! LOOK AT ALL THESE BOTTLES! ONE OF THEM'S GOTTA WORK, RIGHT?
P-P-PLEASE! DON'T TOUCH MY MEDI-CINES!
....
I KNOW OF ONE PERSON WHO WOULD HAVE ANESTHE-SIA.
MR. PRIEST, ARE YOU SERIOUS?
THEN WHERE IS HE? IS HE IN TOWN?
PLEASE, MR. PRIEST! WE HAVE TO SAVE MY SIS AS SOON AS POSSIBLE!
THAT PERSON IS...

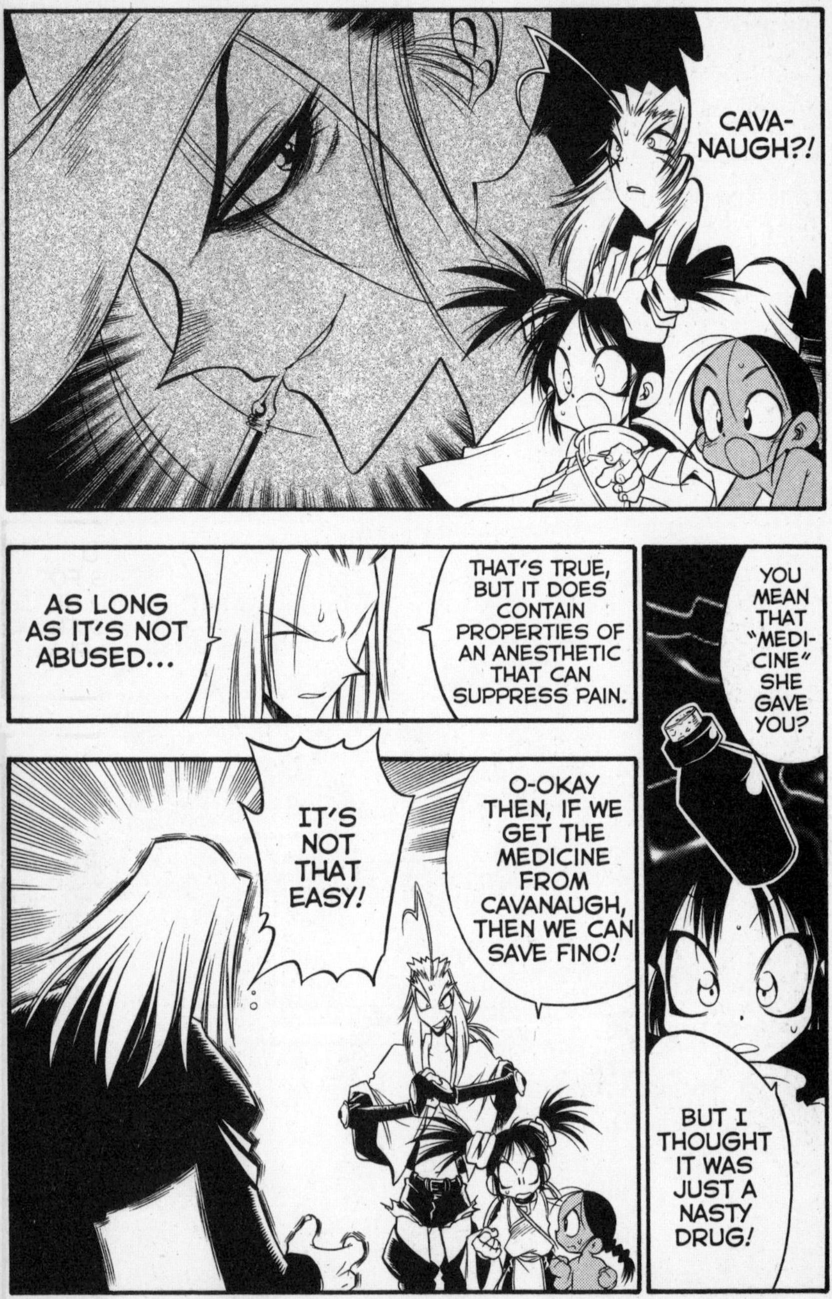
CAVA-NAUGH?!
YOU MEAN THAT "MEDICINE" SHE GAVE YOU?
BUT I THOUGHT IT WAS JUST A NASTY DRUG!
THAT'S TRUE, BUT IT DOES CONTAIN PROPERTIES OF AN ANESTHETIC THAT CAN SUPPRESS PAIN.
AS LONG AS IT'S NOT ABUSED...
O-OKAY THEN, IF WE GET THE MEDICINE FROM CAVANAUGH, THEN WE CAN SAVE FINO!
IT'S NOT THAT EASY!

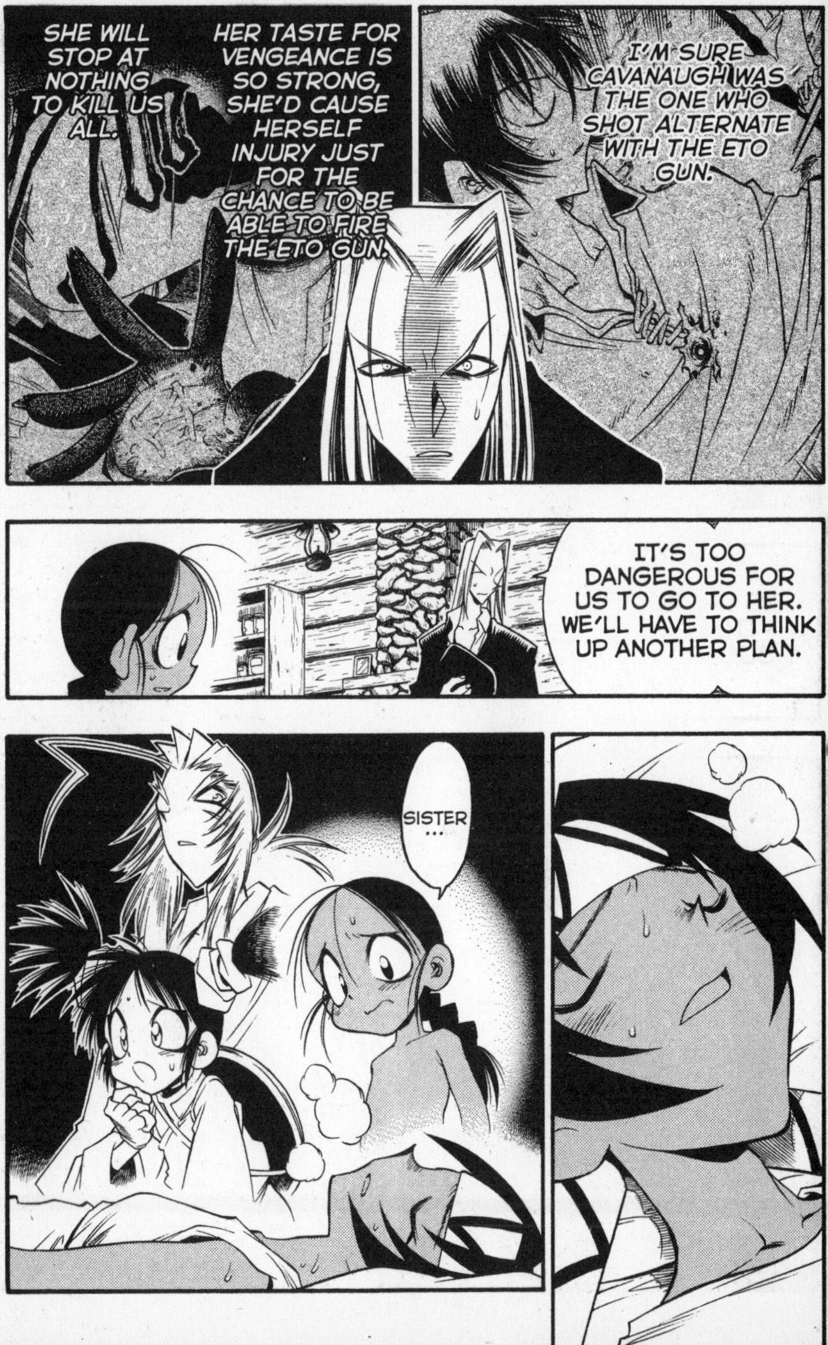
I'M SURE CAVANAUGH WAS THE ONE WHO SHOT ALTERNATE WITH THE ETO GUN.
HER TASTE FOR VENGEANCE IS SO STRONG, SHE'D CAUSE HERSELF INJURY JUST FOR THE CHANCE TO BE ABLE TO FIRE THE ETO GUN.
SHE WILL STOP AT NOTHING TO KILL US ALL.
IT'S TOO DANGEROUS FOR US TO GO TO HER. WE'LL HAVE TO THINK UP ANOTHER PLAN.
SISTER...

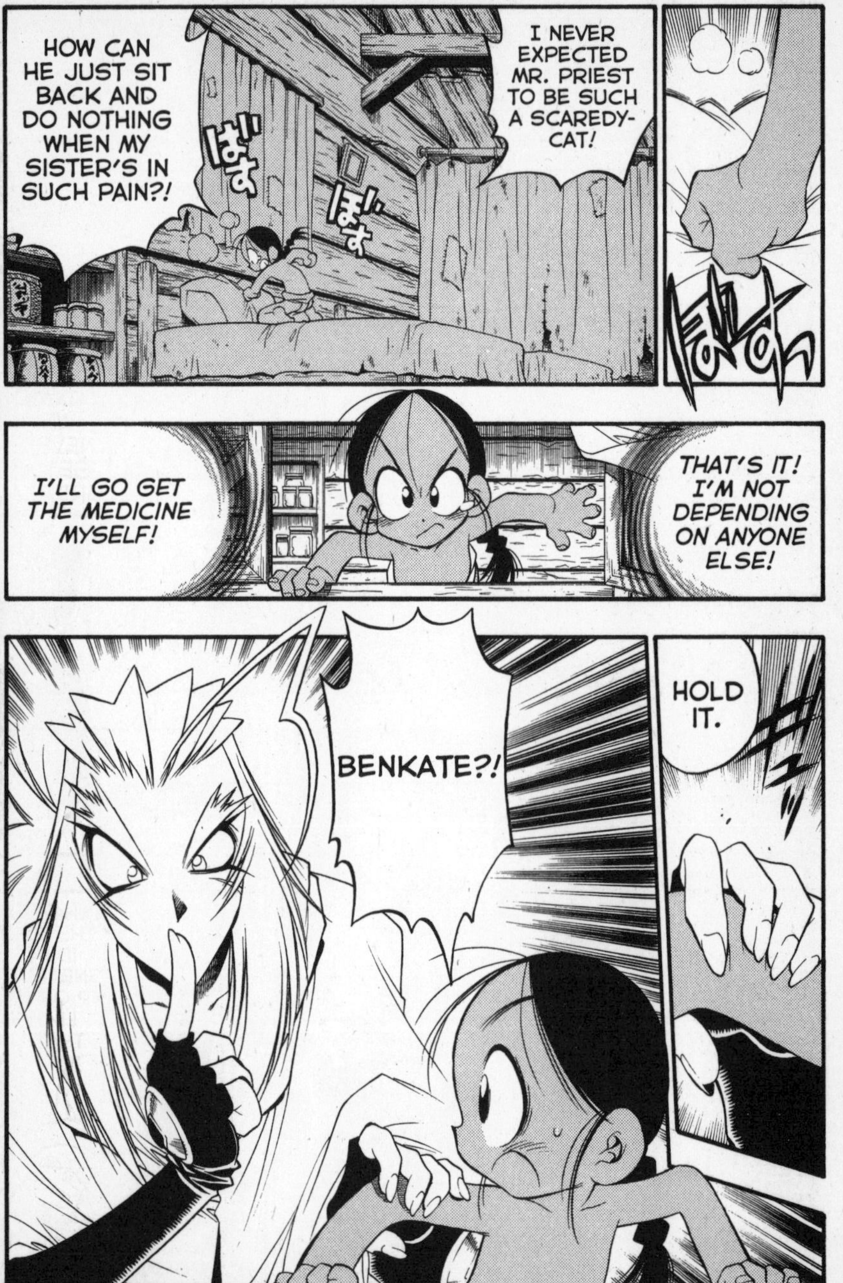
I NEVER EXPECTED MR. PRIEST TO BE SUCH A SCAREDY-CAT!
HOW CAN HE JUST SIT BACK AND DO NOTHING WHEN MY SISTER'S IN SUCH PAIN?!
THAT'S IT! I'M NOT DEPENDING ON ANYONE ELSE!
I'LL GO GET THE MEDICINE MYSELF!
HOLD IT.
BENKATE?!

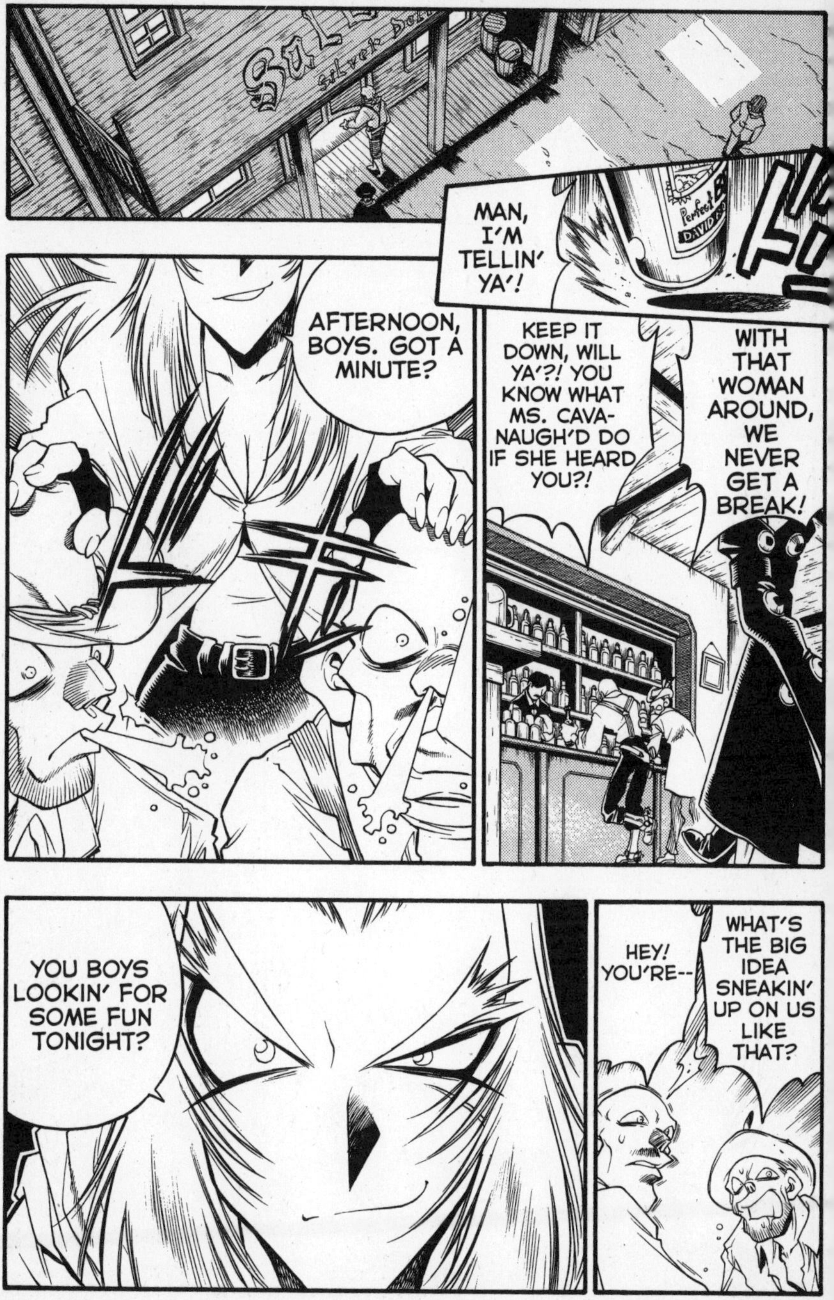
MAN, I'M TELLIN' YA'!
WITH THAT WOMAN AROUND, WE NEVER GET A BREAK!
KEEP IT DOWN, WILL YA'?! YOU KNOW WHAT MS. CAVA-NAUGH'D DO IF SHE HEARD YOU?!
AFTERNOON, BOYS. GOT A MINUTE?
WHAT'S THE BIG IDEA SNEAKIN' UP ON US LIKE THAT?
HEY! YOU'RE--
YOU BOYS LOOKIN' FOR SOME FUN TONIGHT?

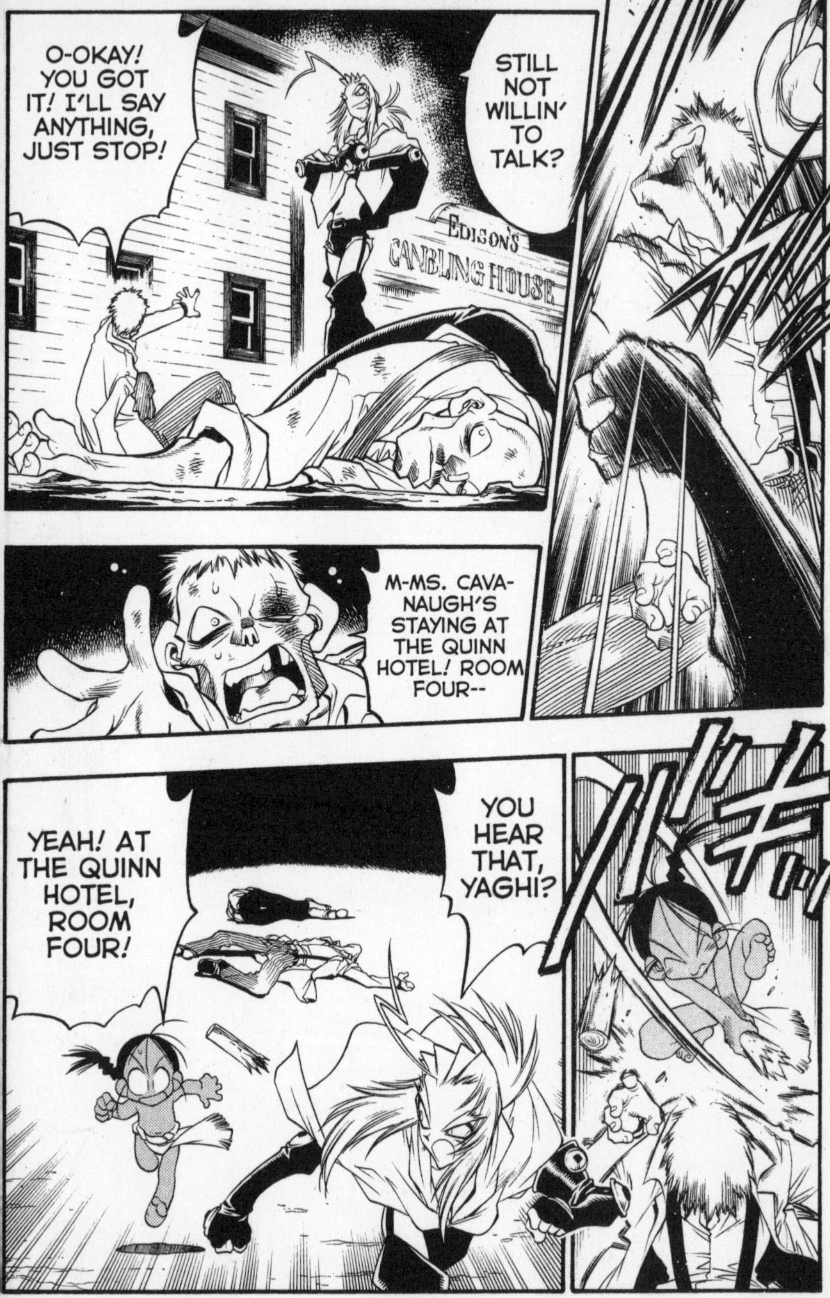
STILL NOT WILLIN' TO TALK?
EDISON'S
CANBLING HOUSE
O-OKAY! YOU GOT IT! I'LL SAY ANYTHING, JUST STOP!
M-MS. CAVA-NAUGH'S STAYING AT THE QUINN HOTEL! ROOM FOUR--
バキッ
YOU HEAR THAT, YAGHI?
YEAH! AT THE QUINN HOTEL, ROOM FOUR!

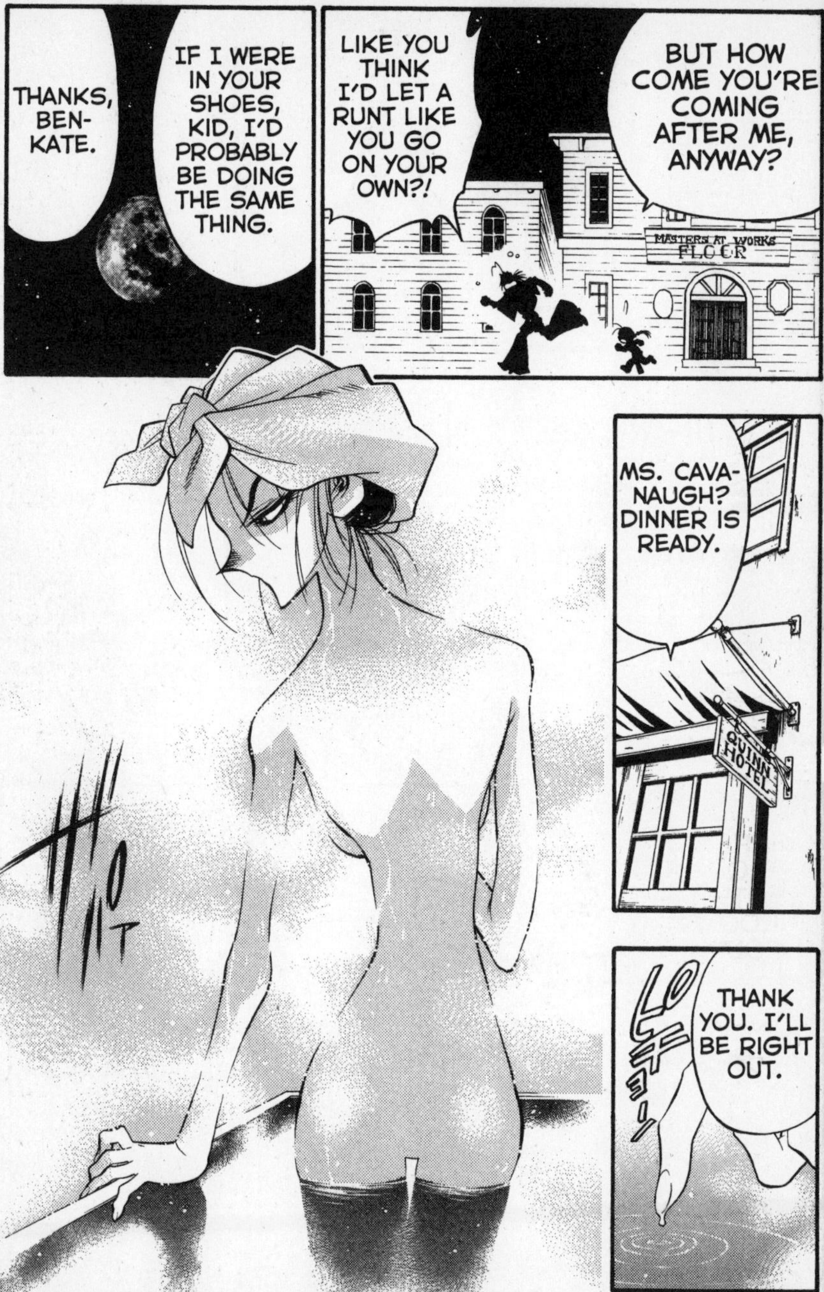
BUT HOW COME YOU'RE COMING AFTER ME, ANYWAY?
LIKE YOU THINK I'D LET A RUNT LIKE YOU GO ON YOUR OWN?!
MASTERS AT WORKS
FLOOR
IF I WERE IN YOUR SHOES, KID, I'D PROBABLY BE DOING THE SAME THING.
THANKS, BEN-KATE.
MS. CAVA-NAUGH? DINNER IS READY.
QUINN HOTEL
THANK YOU. I'LL BE RIGHT OUT.

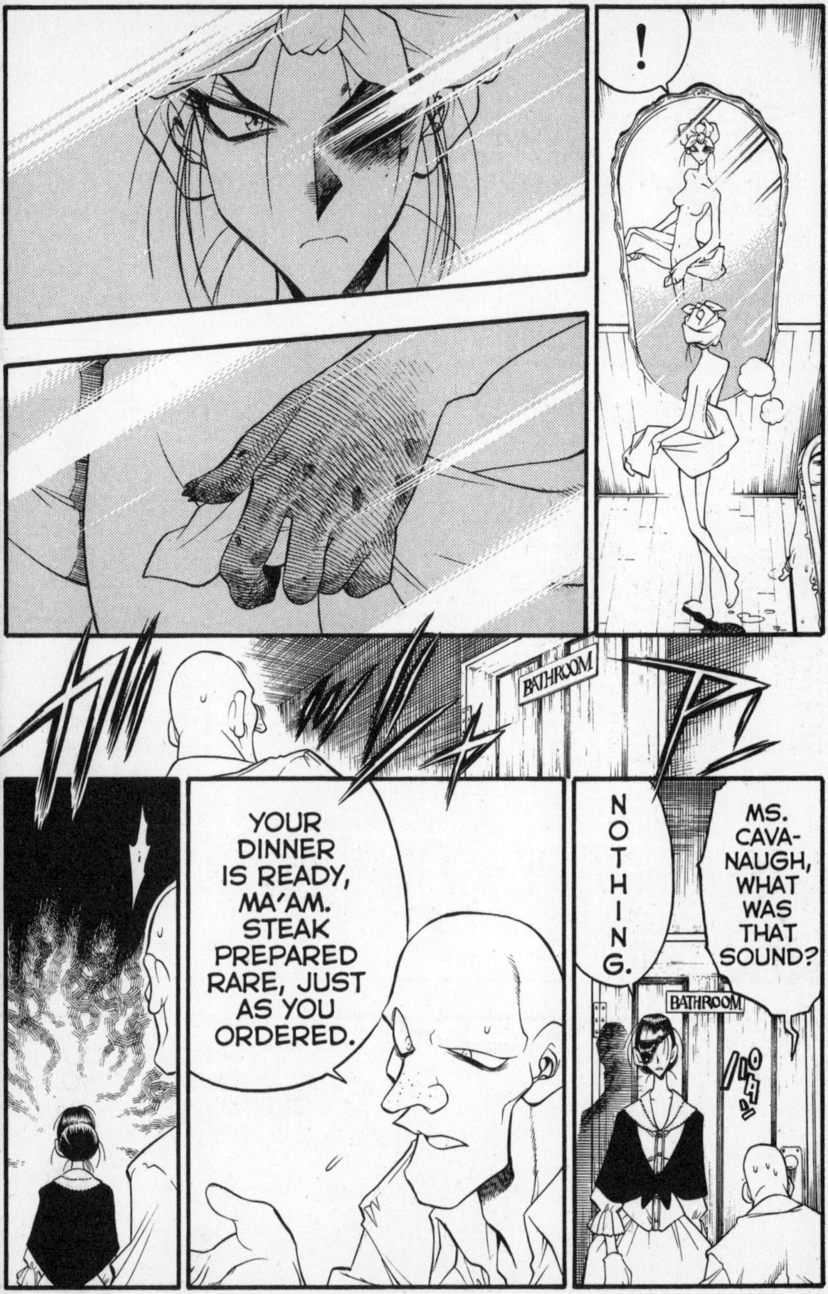
!
BATHROOM
BATHROOM
MS. CAVA-NAUGH, WHAT WAS THAT SOUND?
NOTHING.
YOUR DINNER IS READY, MA'AM. STEAK PREPARED RARE, JUST AS YOU ORDERED.

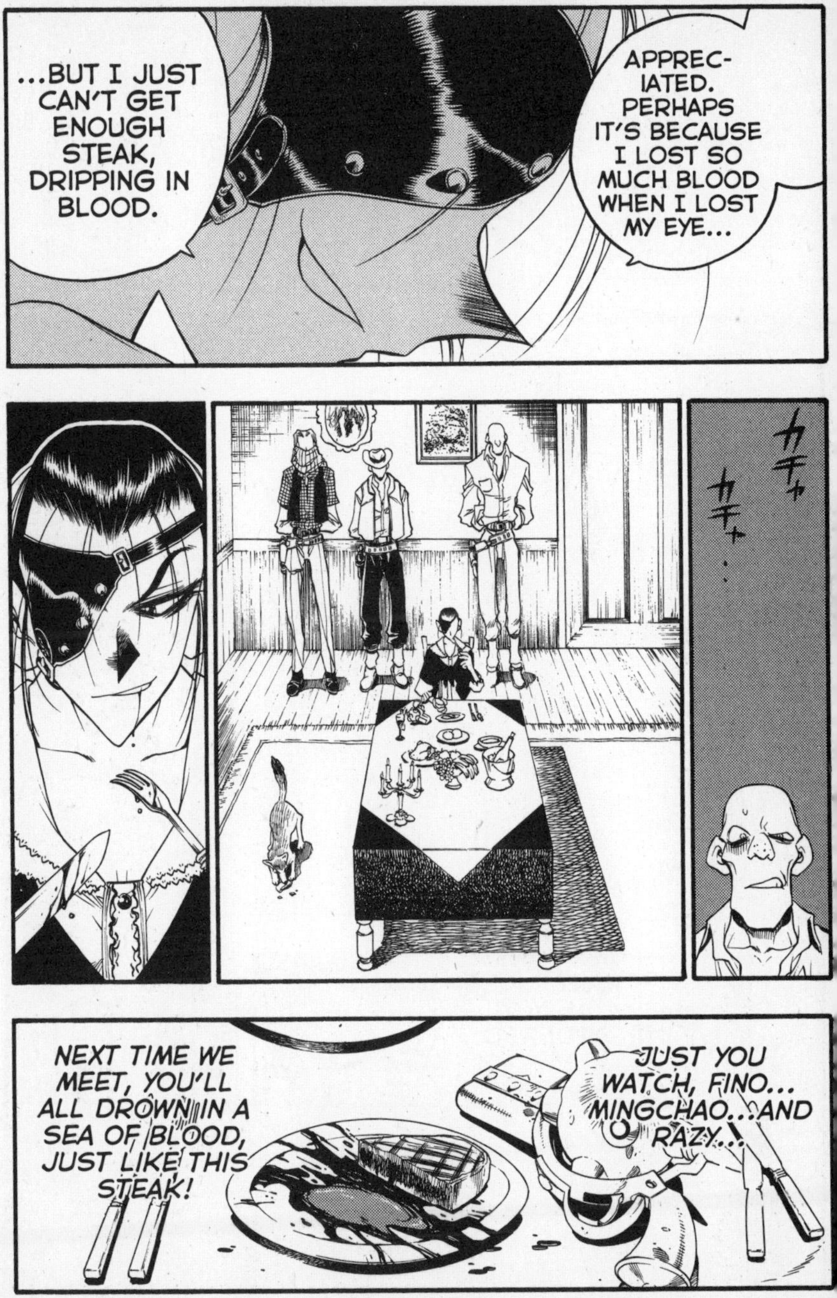
APPREC-IATED. PERHAPS IT'S BECAUSE I LOST SO MUCH BLOOD WHEN I LOST MY EYE...
...BUT I JUST CAN'T GET ENOUGH STEAK, DRIPPING IN BLOOD.
カチャ
カチャ...
JUST YOU WATCH, FINO... MINGCHAO... AND RAZY...
NEXT TIME WE MEET, YOU'LL ALL DROWN IN A SEA OF BLOOD, JUST LIKE THIS STEAK!

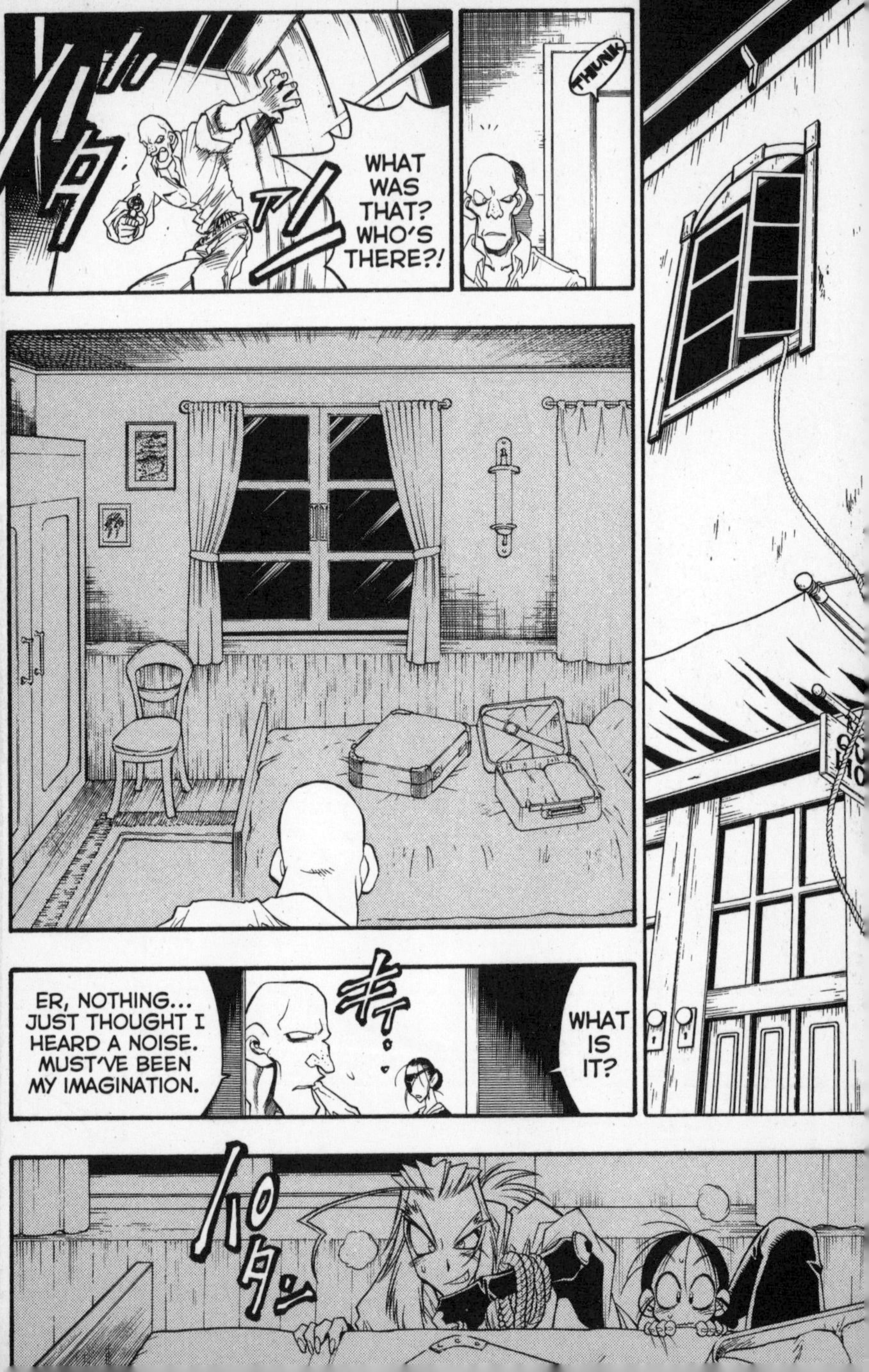
THUNK
WHAT WAS THAT? WHO'S THERE?!
WHAT IS IT?
ER, NOTHING... JUST THOUGHT I HEARD A NOISE. MUST'VE BEEN MY IMAGINATION.

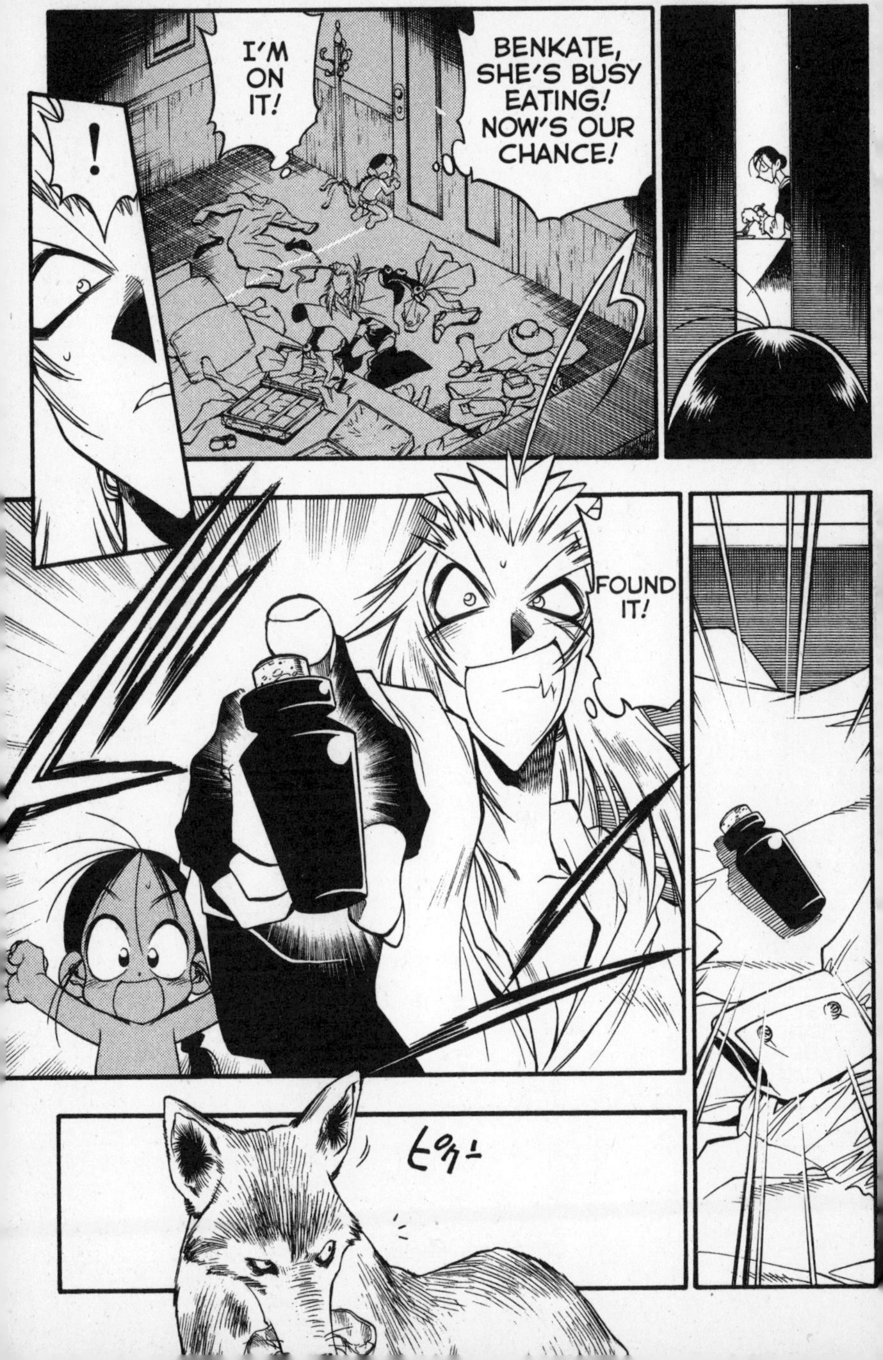
BENKATE, SHE'S BUSY EATING! NOW'S OUR CHANCE!
I'M ON IT!
!
FOUND IT!
ヒクッ

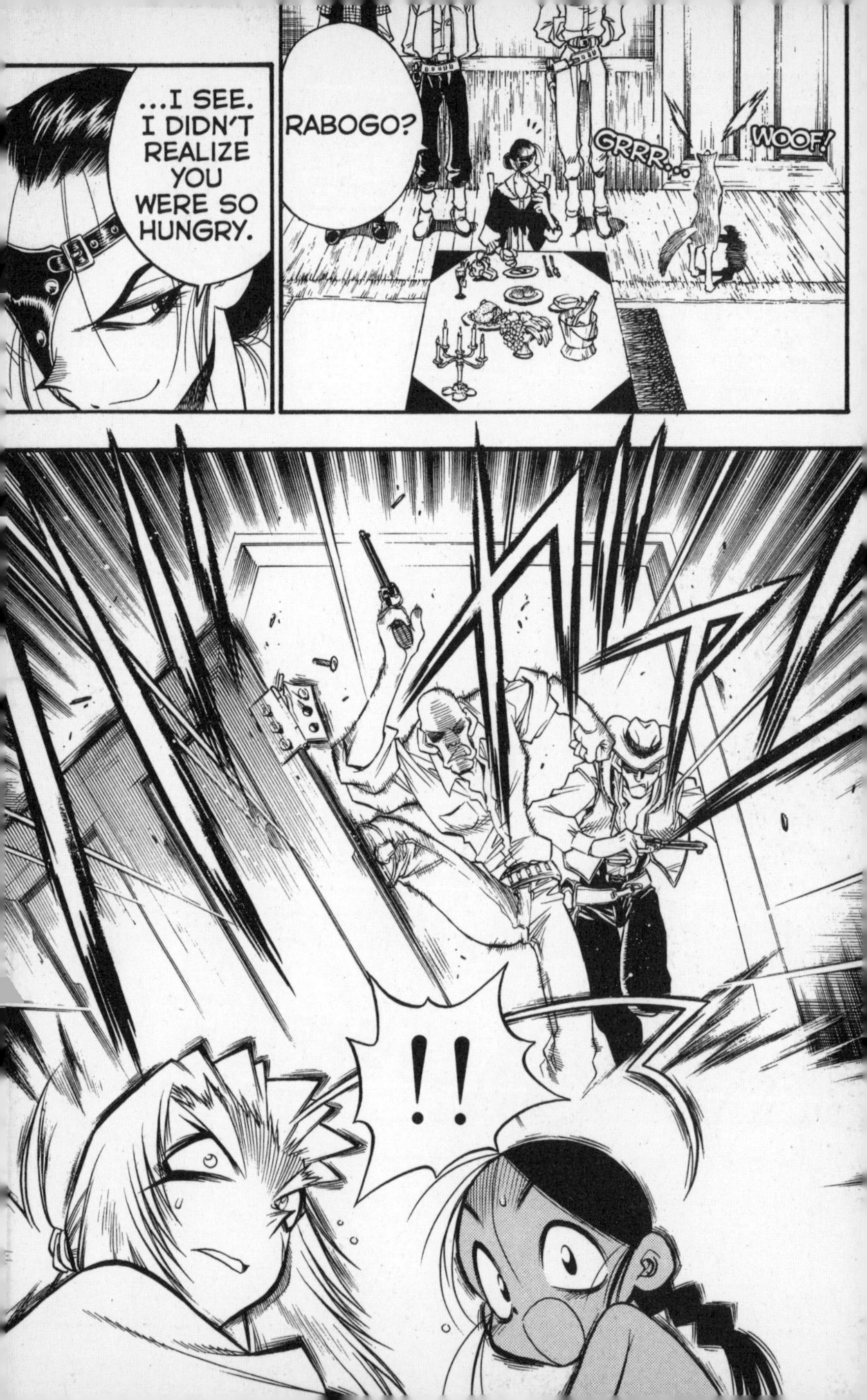
WOOF!
GRRR...
RABOGO?
...I SEE. I DIDN'T REALIZE YOU WERE SO HUNGRY.
!!

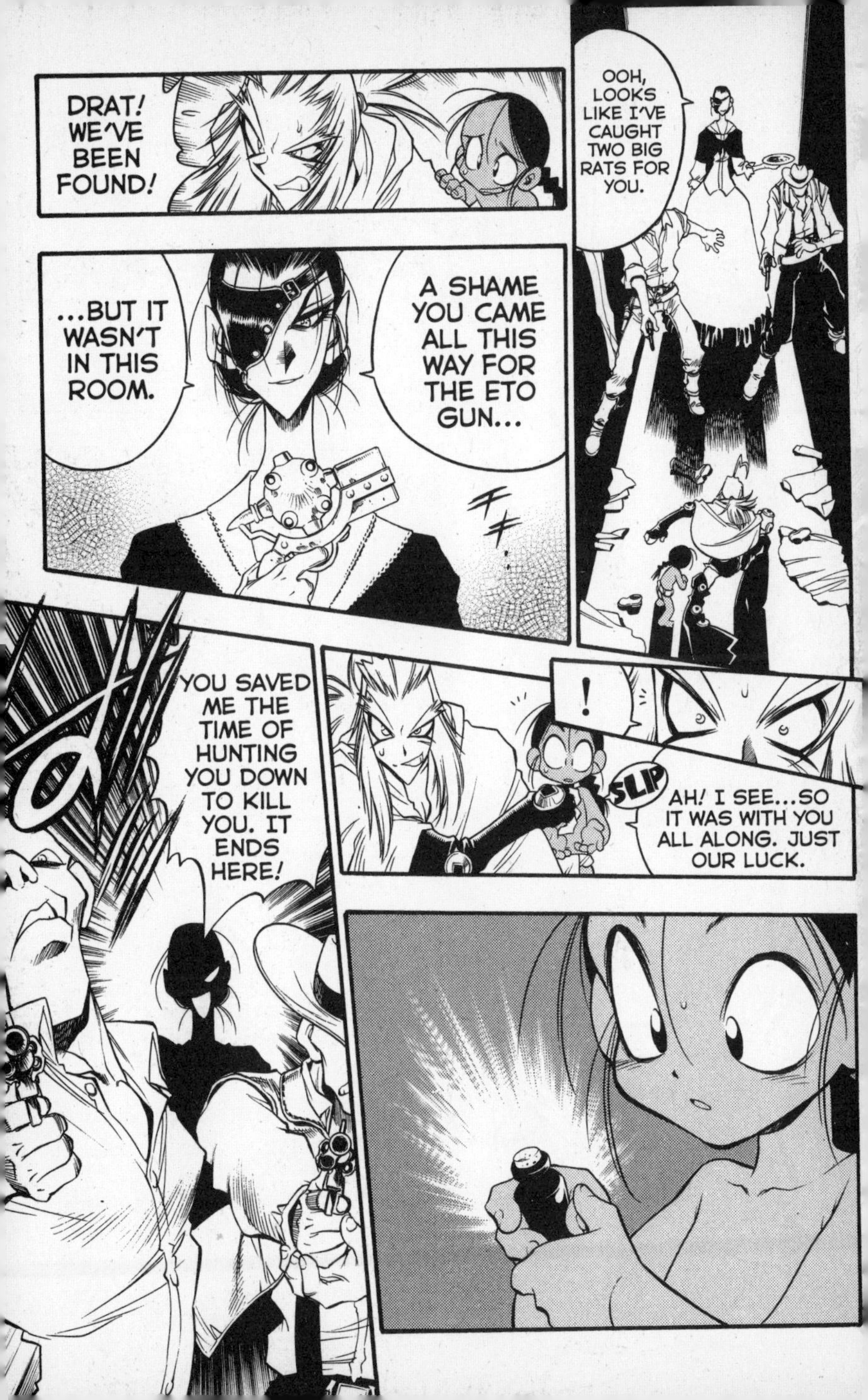
OOH, LOOKS LIKE I'VE CAUGHT TWO BIG RATS FOR YOU.
DRAT! WE'VE BEEN FOUND!
A SHAME YOU CAME ALL THIS WAY FOR THE ETO GUN...
...BUT IT WASN'T IN THIS ROOM.
!
AH! I SEE...SO IT WAS WITH YOU ALL ALONG. JUST OUR LUCK.
SLIP
YOU SAVED ME THE TIME OF HUNTING YOU DOWN TO KILL YOU. IT ENDS HERE!

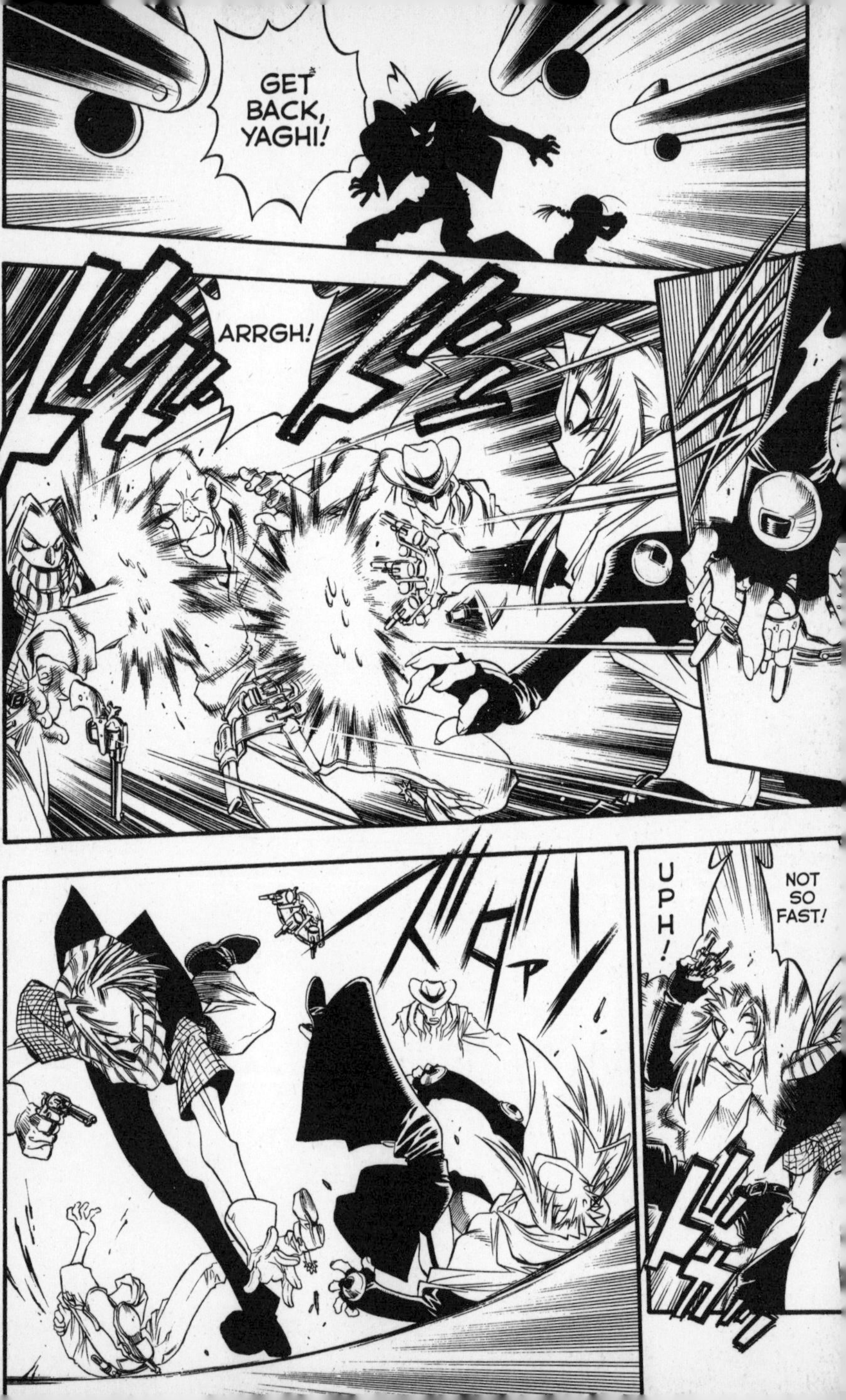
GET BACK, YAGHI!
ARRGH!
NOT SO FAST!
UPH!

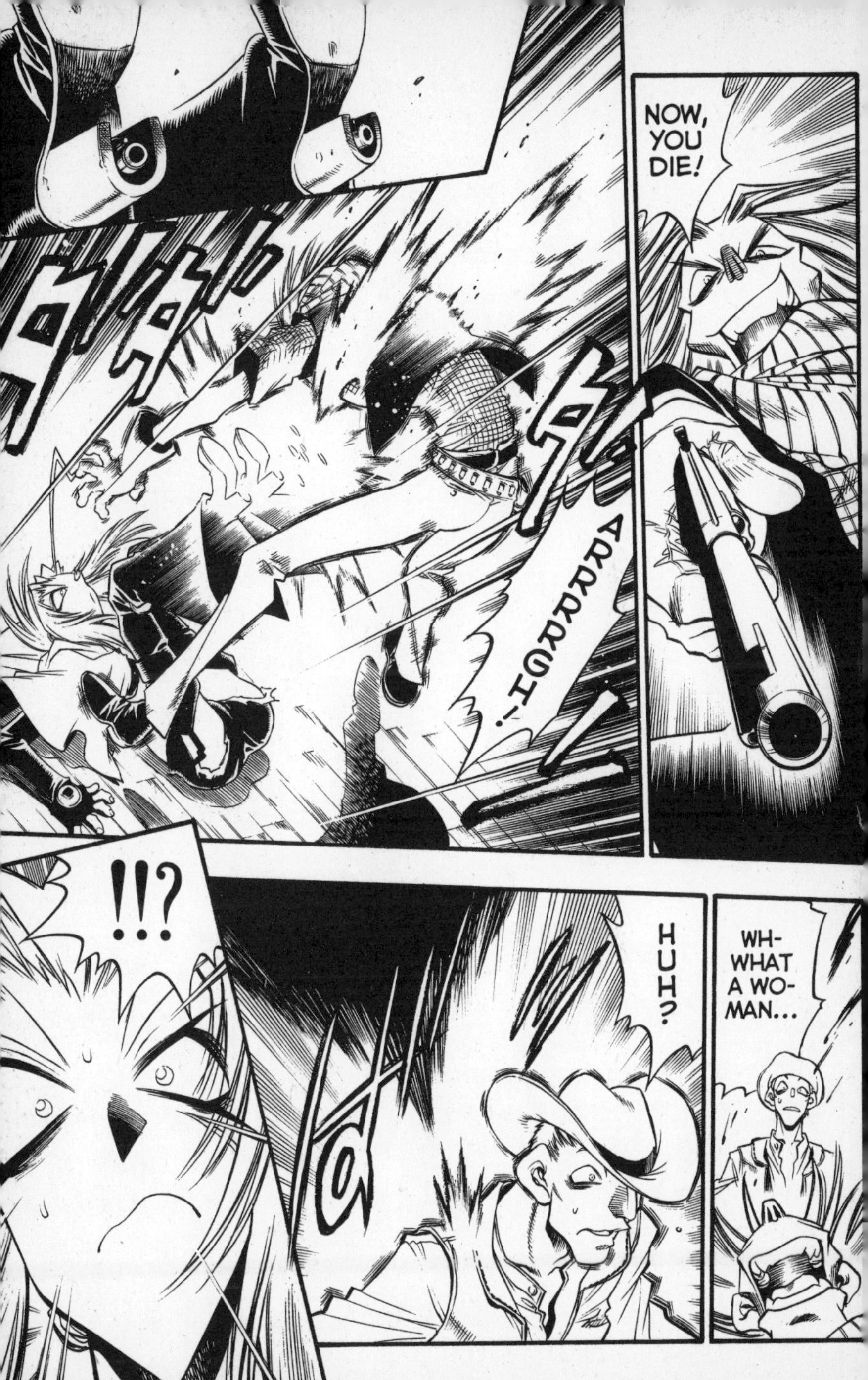
NOW, YOU DIE!
ARRRRGH!
WH- WHAT A WO- MAN...
HUH?
!!?

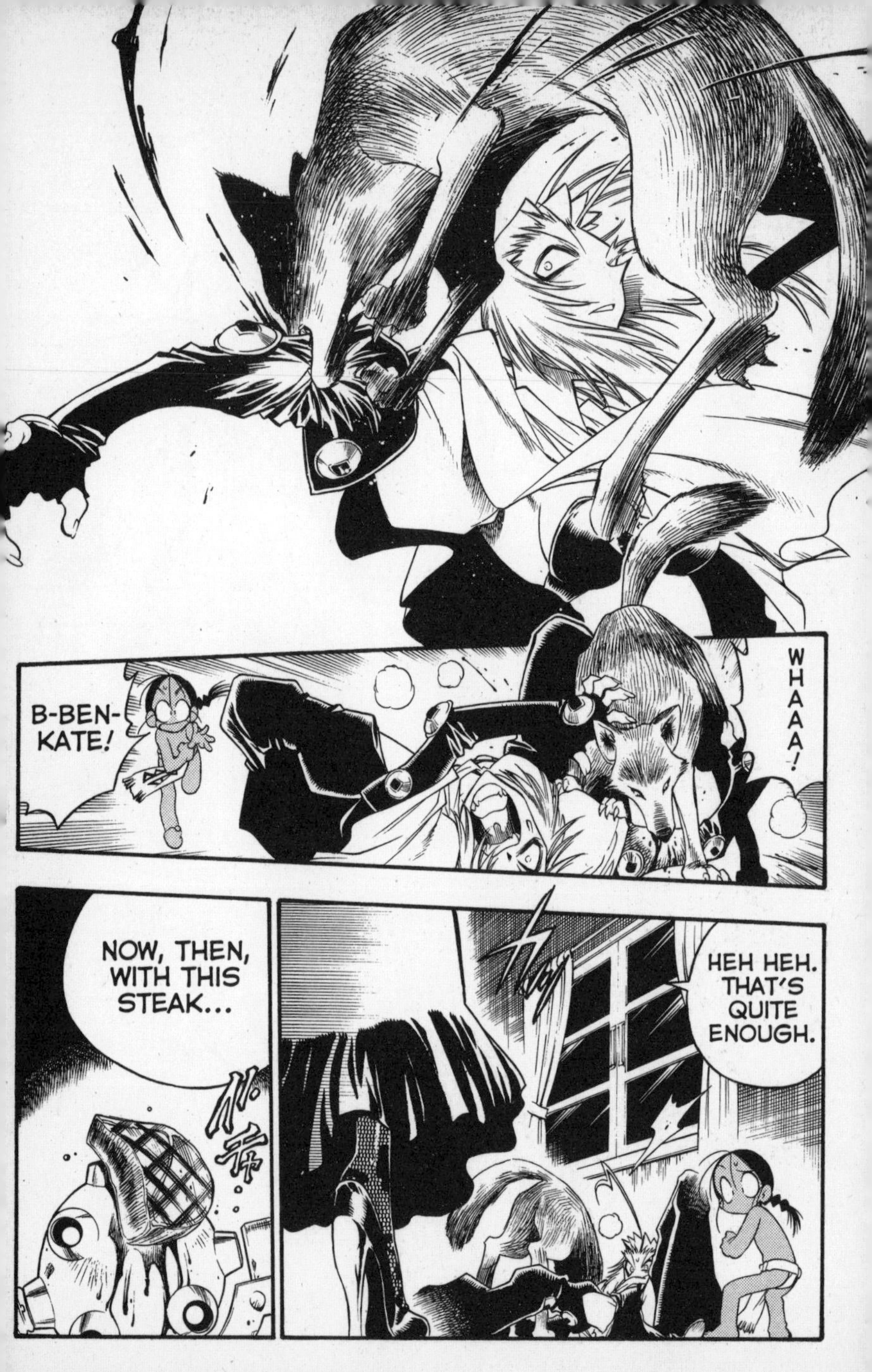
WHAAAA!
B-BEN-KATE!
HEH HEH. THAT'S QUITE ENOUGH.
NOW, THEN, WITH THIS STEAK...

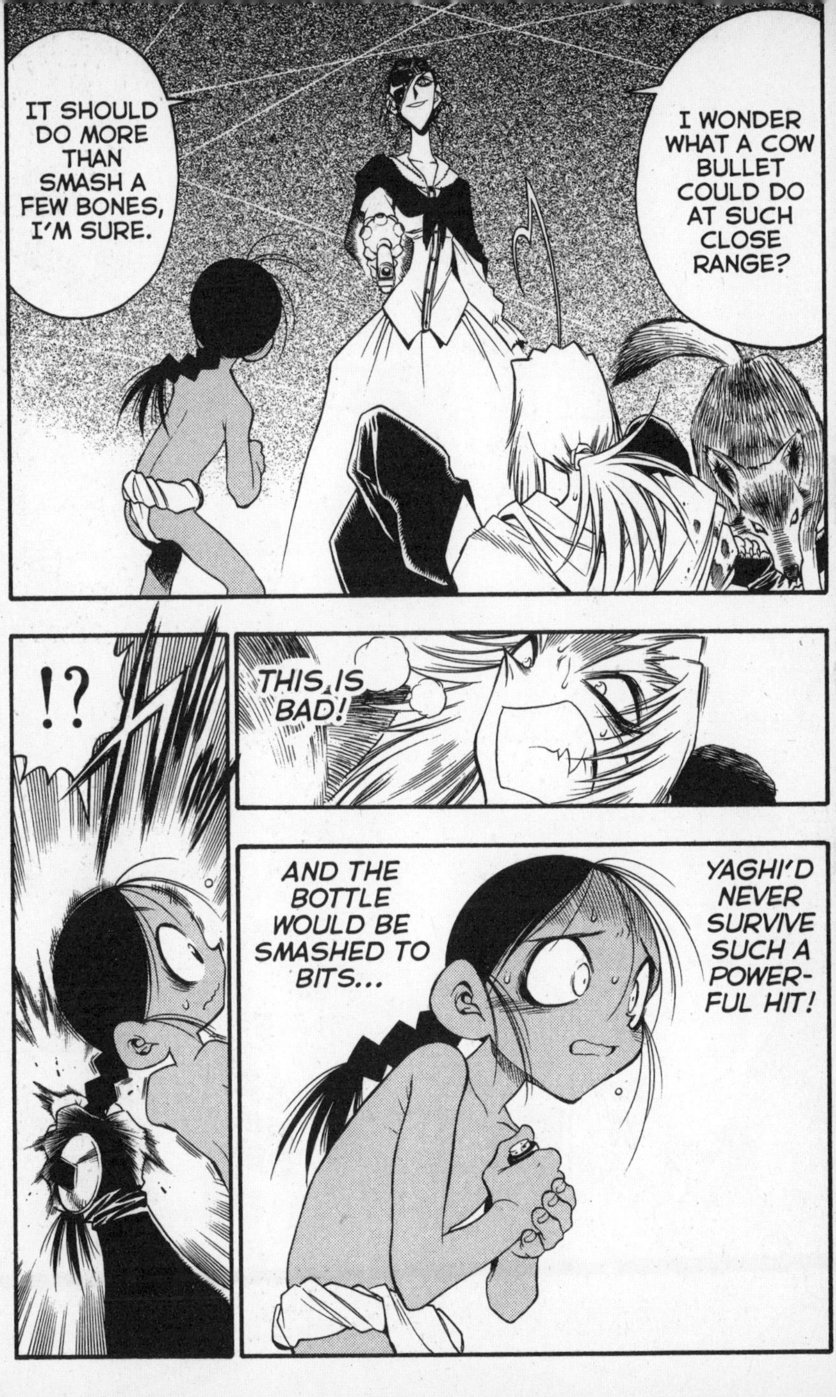
I WONDER WHAT A COW BULLET COULD DO AT SUCH CLOSE RANGE?
IT SHOULD DO MORE THAN SMASH A FEW BONES, I'M SURE.
THIS IS BAD!
YAGHI'D NEVER SURVIVE SUCH A POWER-FUL HIT!
AND THE BOTTLE WOULD BE SMASHED TO BITS...
!?

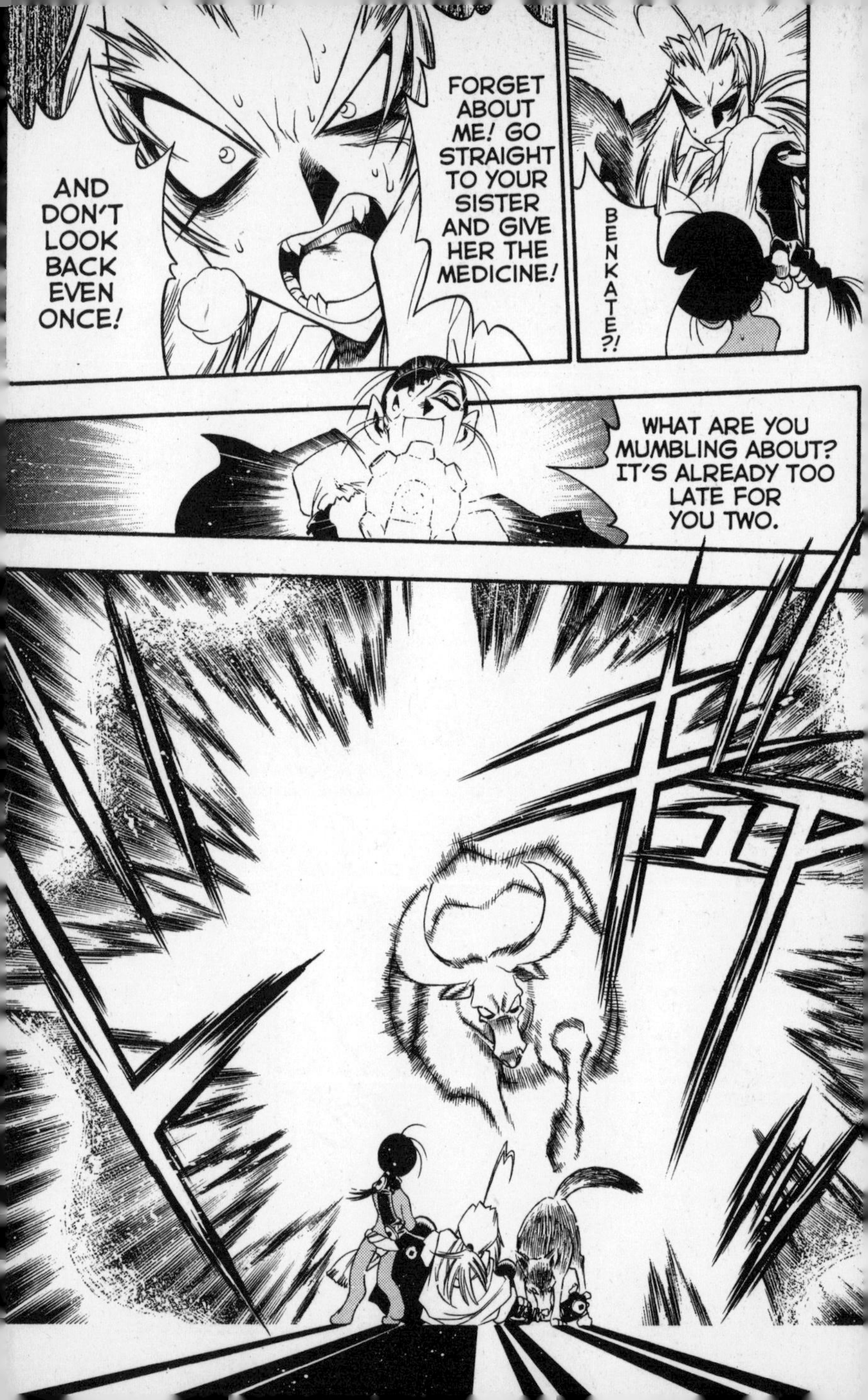
BENKATE?!
FORGET ABOUT ME! GO STRAIGHT TO YOUR SISTER AND GIVE HER THE MEDICINE!
AND DON'T LOOK BACK EVEN ONCE!
WHAT ARE YOU MUMBLING ABOUT? IT'S ALREADY TOO LATE FOR YOU TWO.

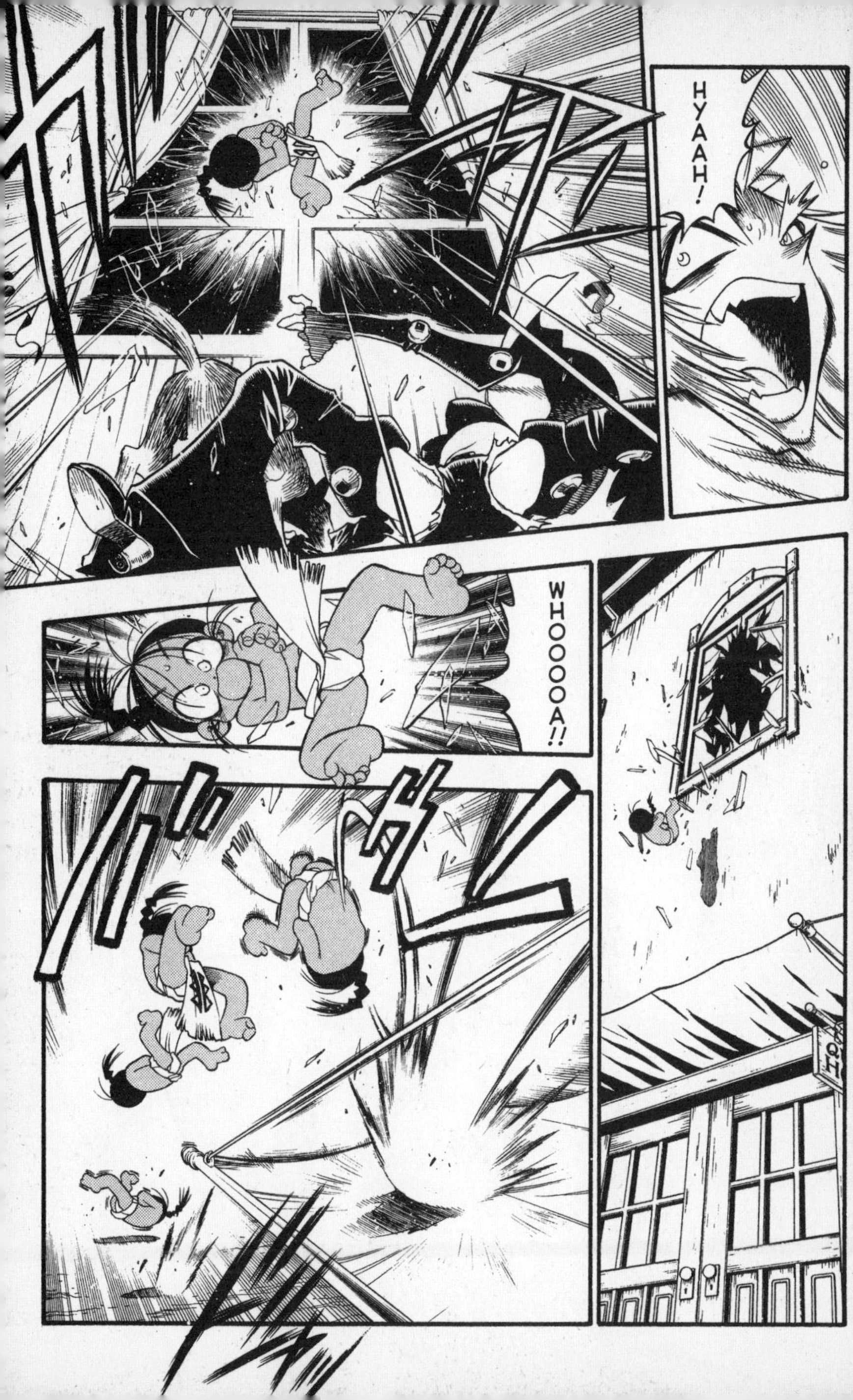
HYAAH!
WHOOOOA!!

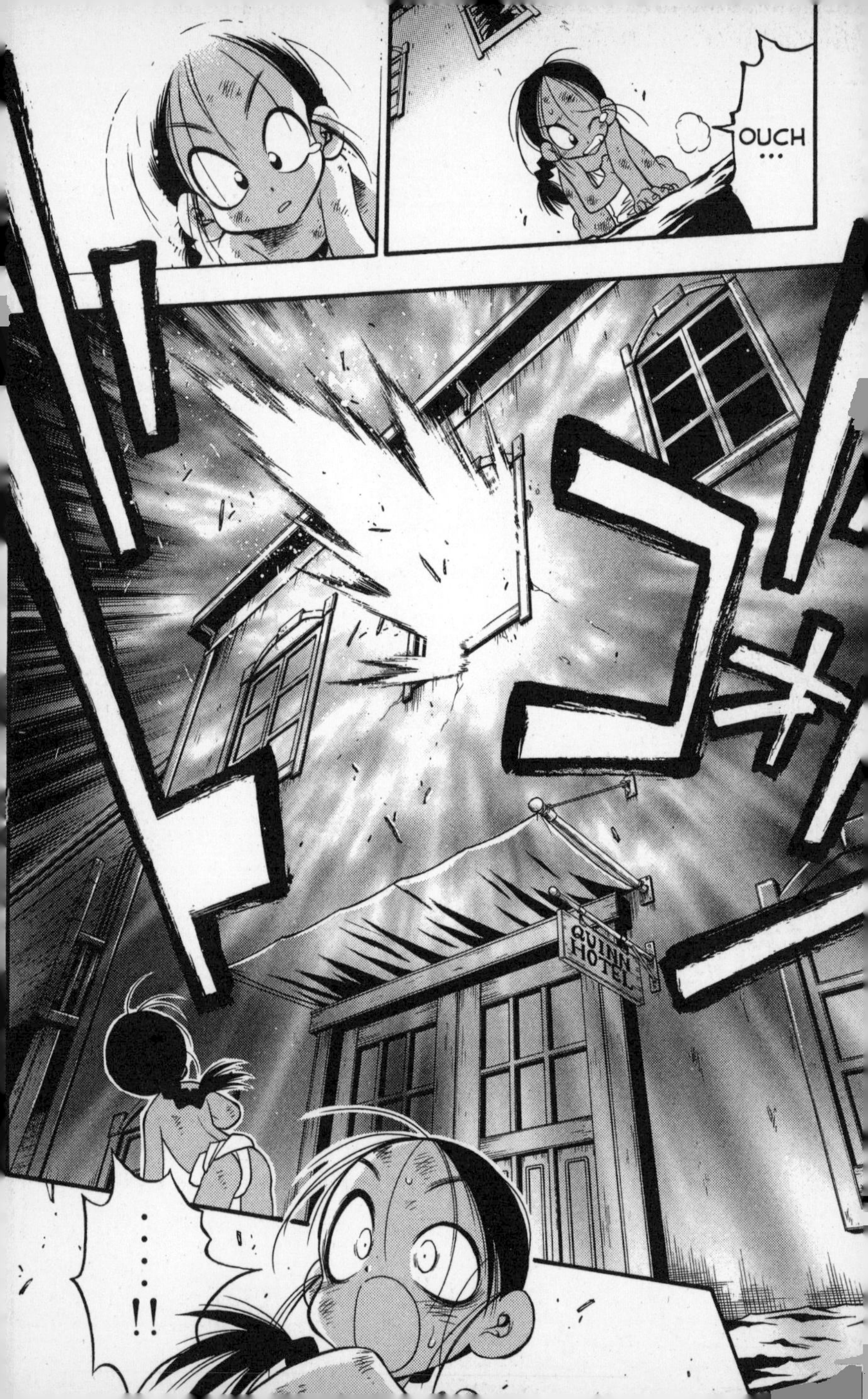
OUCH ...
QUINN HOTEL
......!!

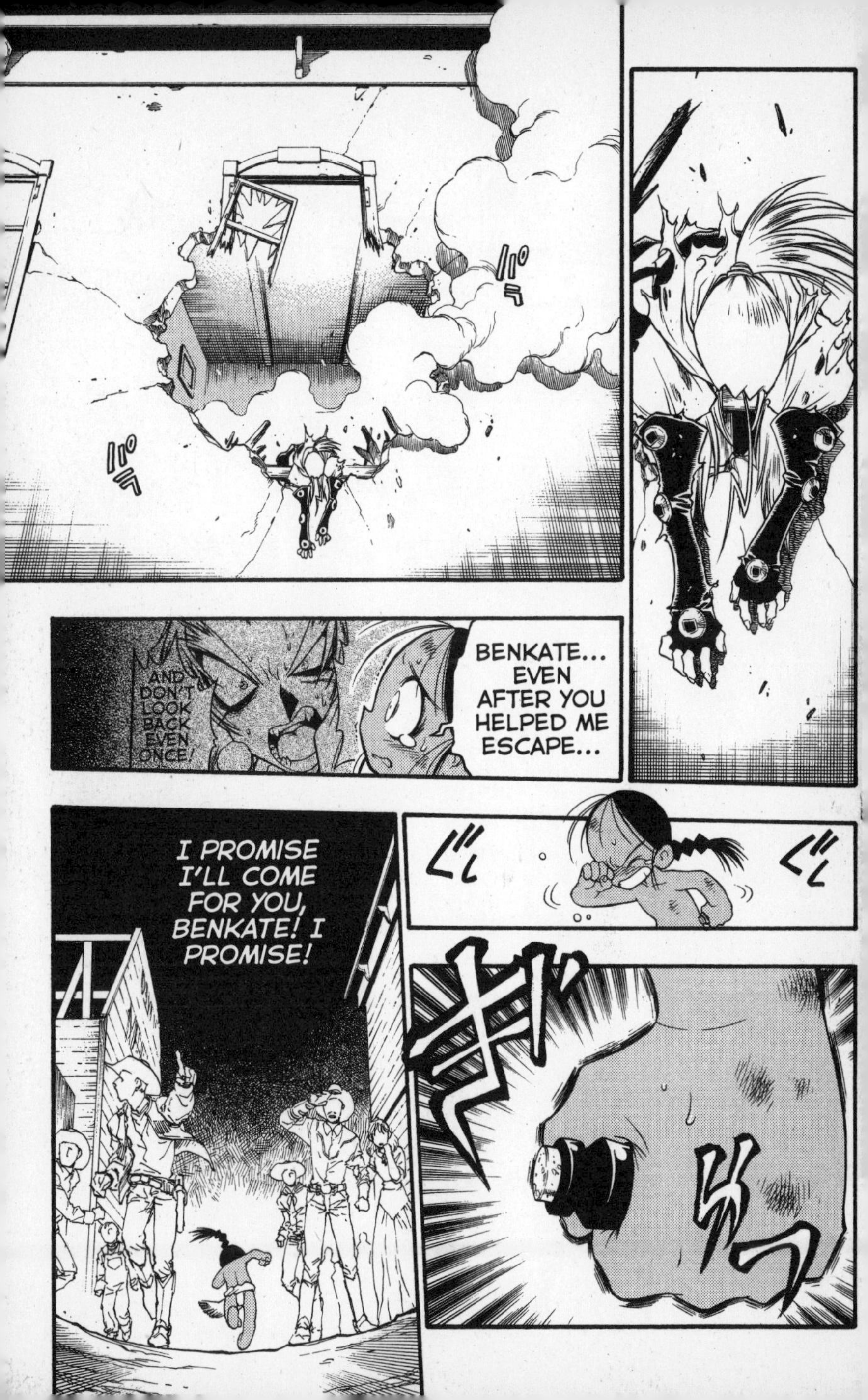
BENKATE... EVEN AFTER YOU HELPED ME ESCAPE...
AND DON'T LOOK BACK EVEN ONCE!
I PROMISE I'LL COME FOR YOU, BENKATE! I PROMISE!

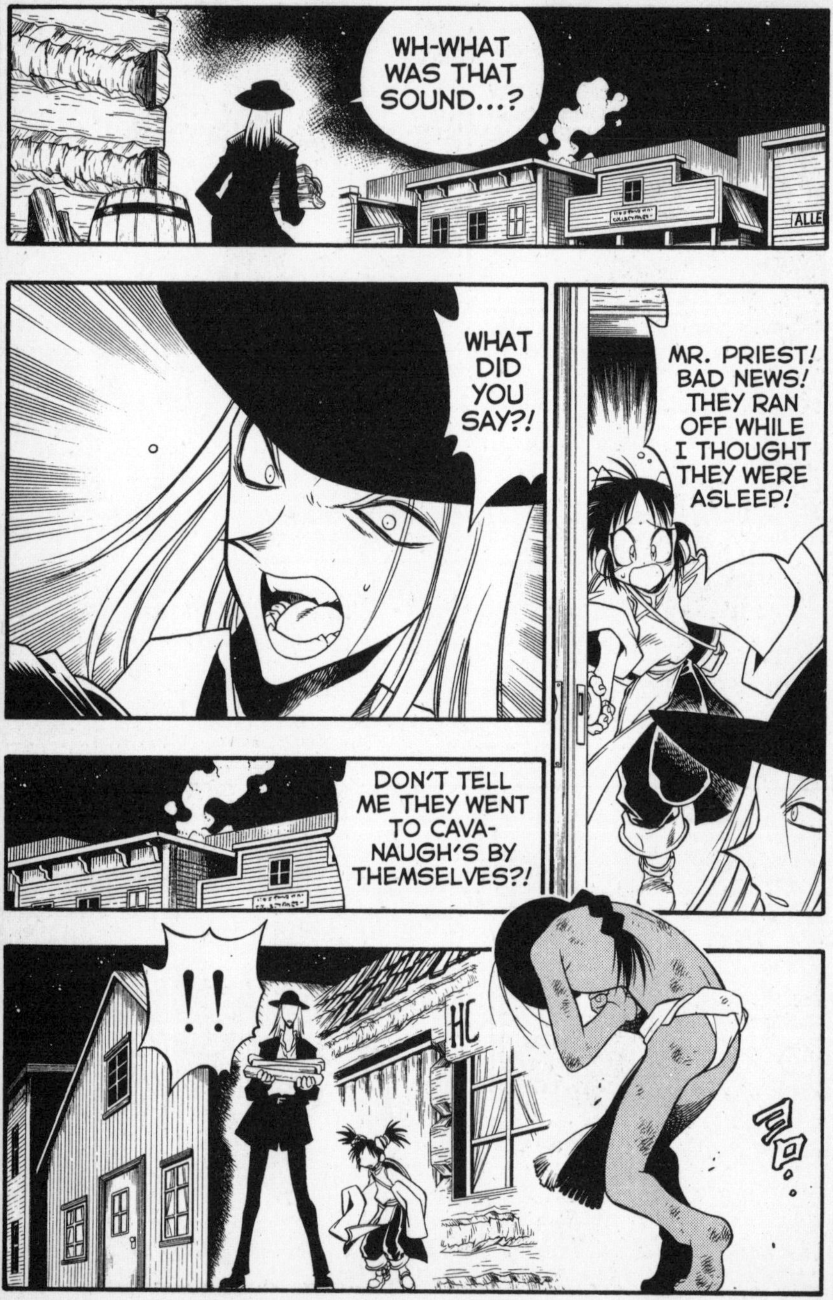
WH-WHAT WAS THAT SOUND...?
MR. PRIEST! BAD NEWS! THEY RAN OFF WHILE I THOUGHT THEY WERE ASLEEP!
WHAT DID YOU SAY?!
DON'T TELL ME THEY WENT TO CAVA-NAUGH'S BY THEMSELVES?!
!!

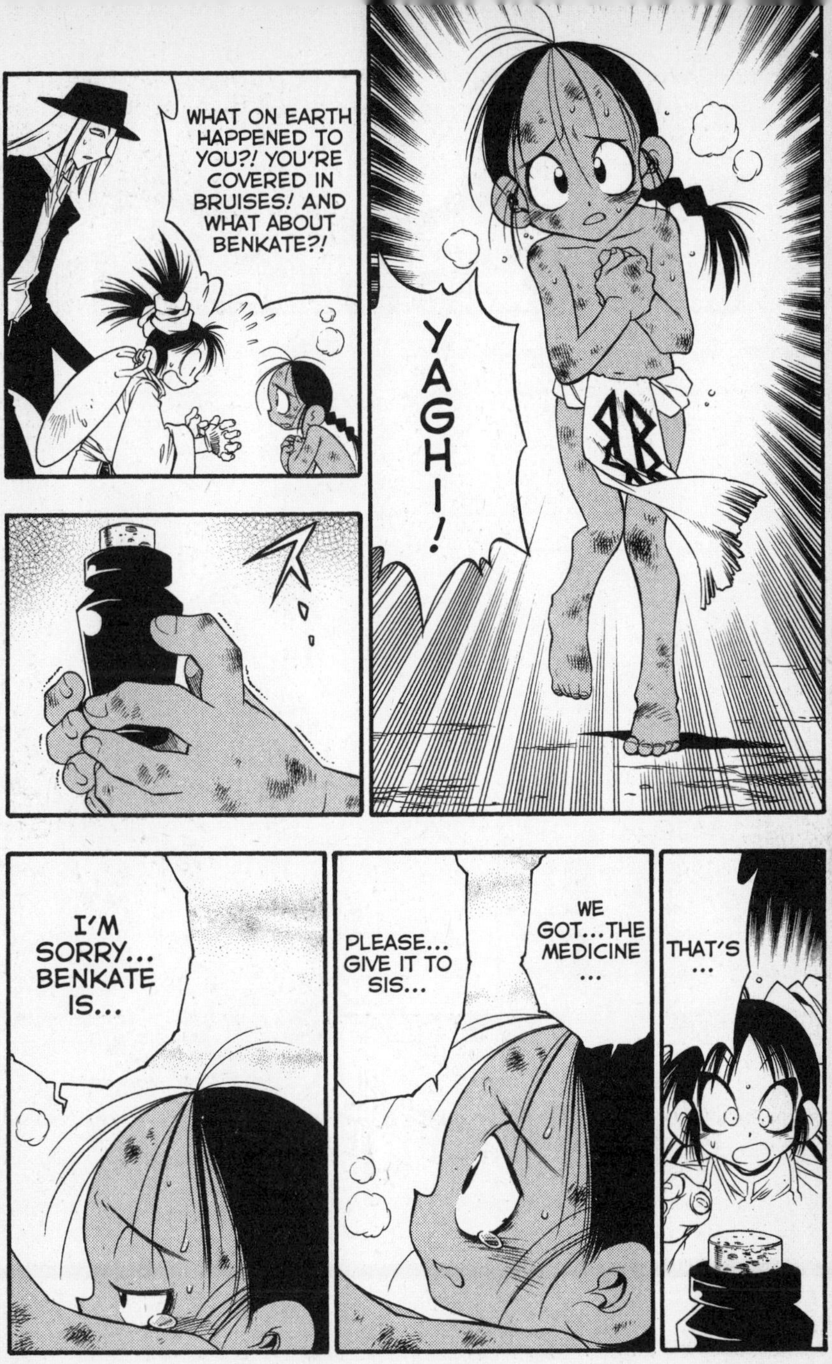
YAGHI!!
WHAT ON EARTH HAPPENED TO YOU?! YOU'RE COVERED IN BRUISES! AND WHAT ABOUT BENKATE?!
THAT'S...
WE GOT...THE MEDICINE...
PLEASE... GIVE IT TO SIS...
I'M SORRY... BENKATE IS...

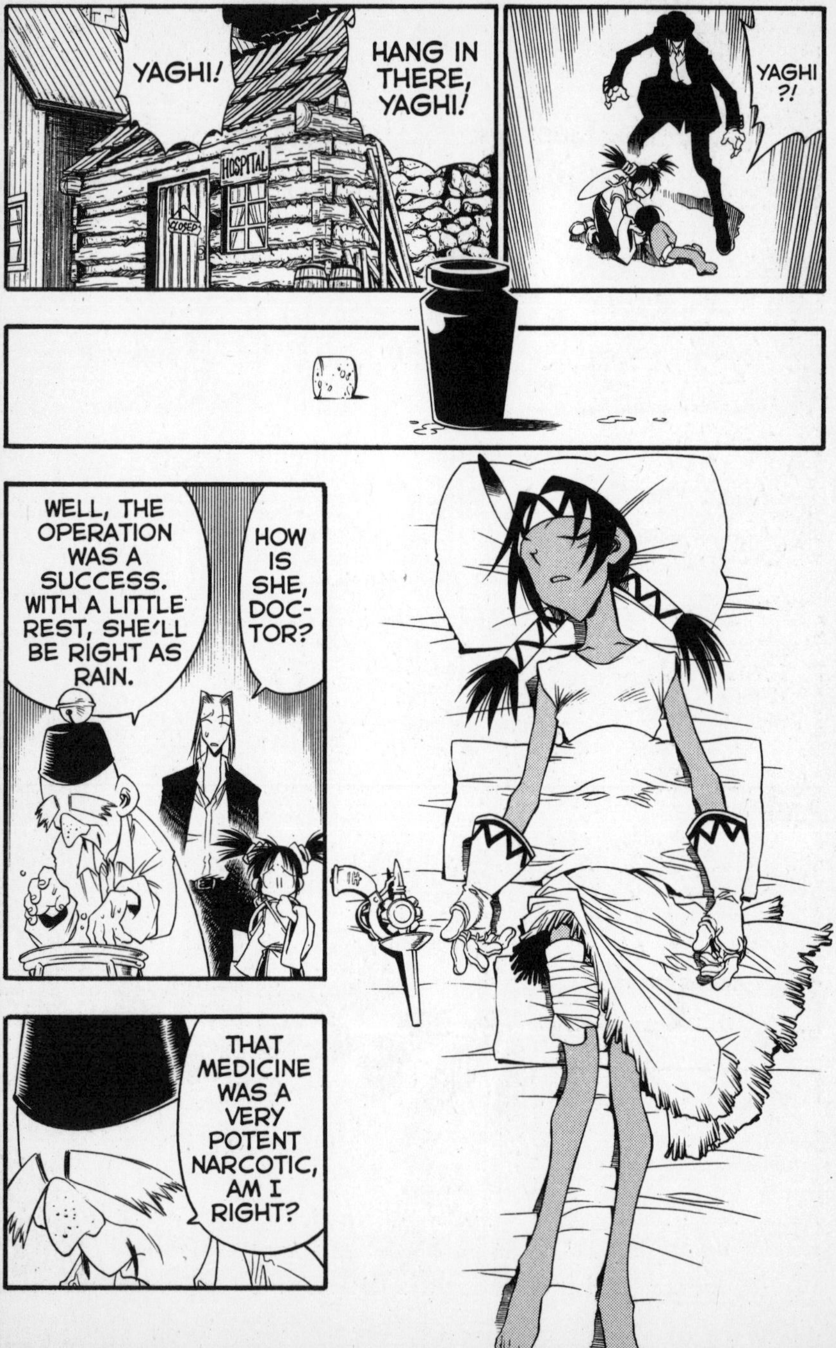
YAGHI ?!
HANG IN THERE, YAGHI!
YAGHI!
HOSPITAL
CLOSED
HOW IS SHE, DOCTOR?
WELL, THE OPERATION WAS A SUCCESS. WITH A LITTLE REST, SHE'LL BE RIGHT AS RAIN.
THAT MEDICINE WAS A VERY POTENT NARCOTIC, AM I RIGHT?

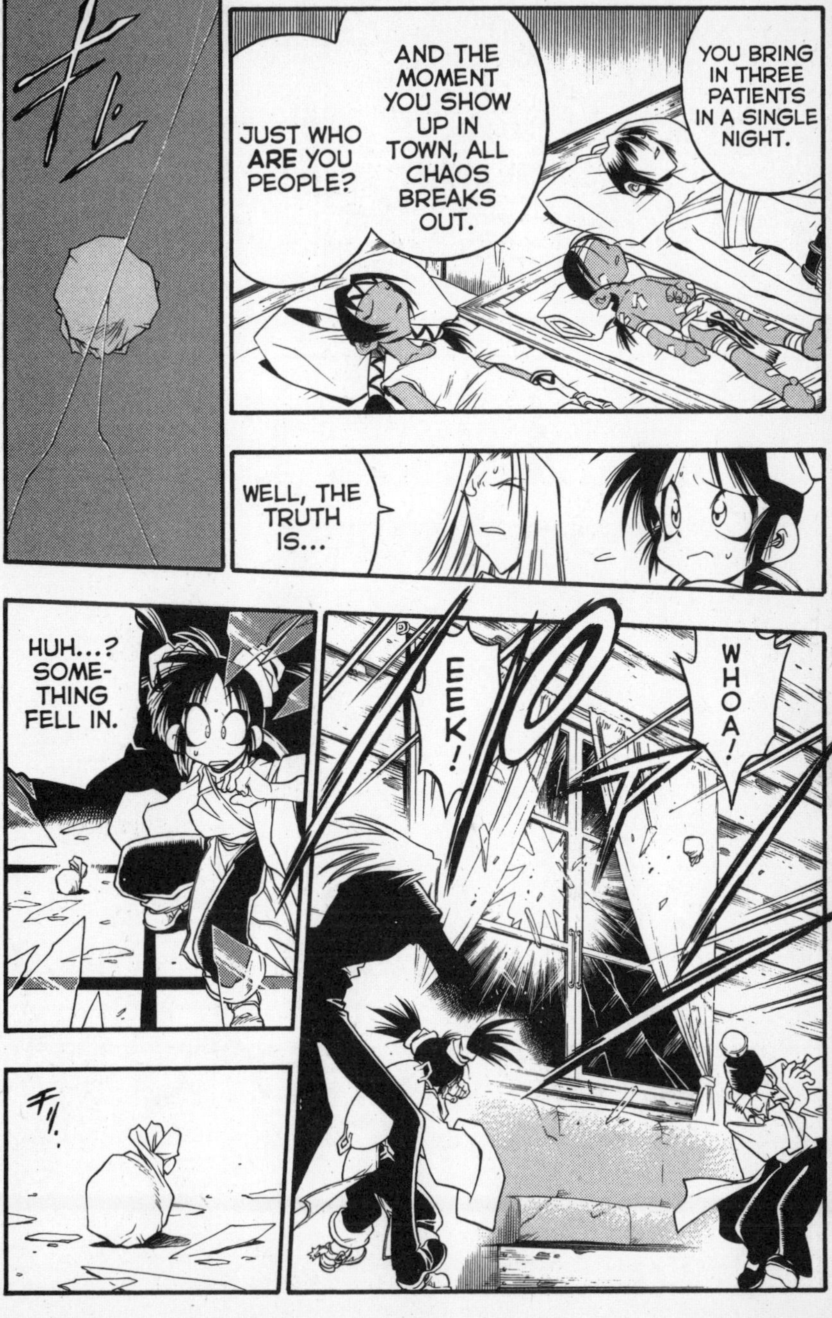
YOU BRING IN THREE PATIENTS IN A SINGLE NIGHT.
AND THE MOMENT YOU SHOW UP IN TOWN, ALL CHAOS BREAKS OUT.
JUST WHO ARE YOU PEOPLE?
WELL, THE TRUTH IS...
WHOA!
EEK!
HUH...? SOMETHING FELL IN.

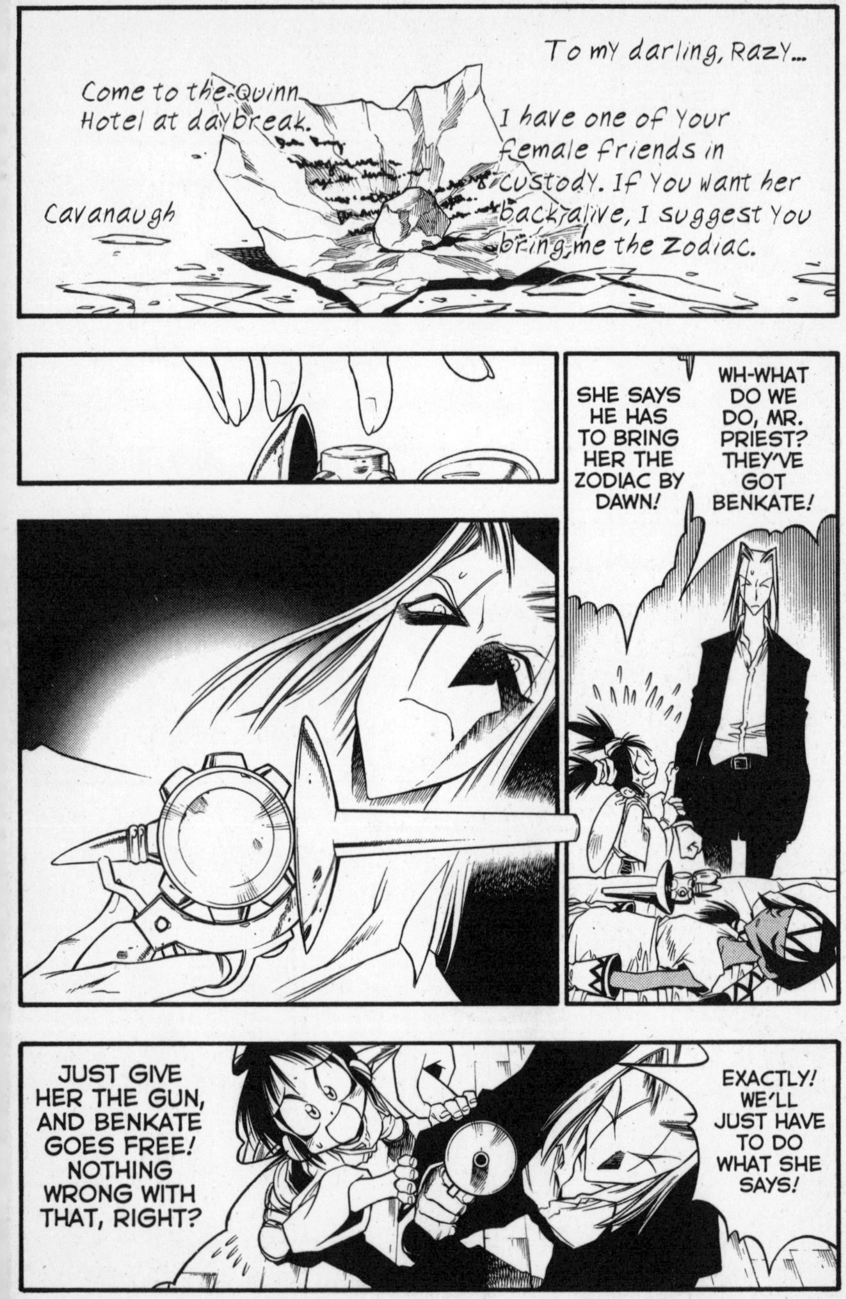
To my darling, Razy...
I have one of your female friends in custody. If you want her back alive, I suggest you bring me the Zodiac.
Come to the Quinn Hotel at daybreak.
Cavanaugh
WH-WHAT DO WE DO, MR. PRIEST? THEY'VE GOT BENKATE!
SHE SAYS HE HAS TO BRING HER THE ZODIAC BY DAWN!
EXACTLY! WE'LL JUST HAVE TO DO WHAT SHE SAYS!
JUST GIVE HER THE GUN, AND BENKATE GOES FREE! NOTHING WRONG WITH THAT, RIGHT?

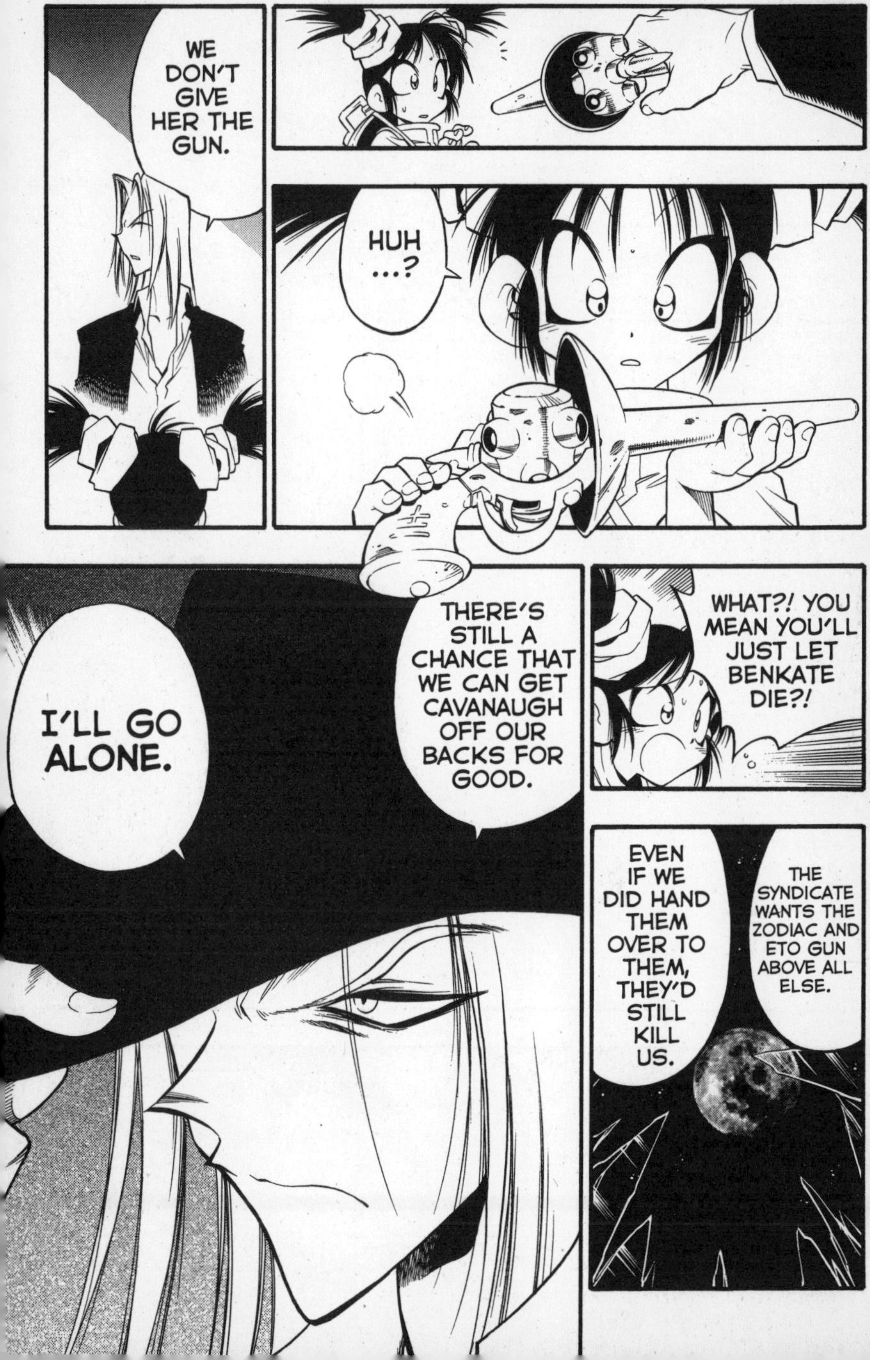
HUH ...?
WE DON'T GIVE HER THE GUN.
WHAT?! YOU MEAN YOU'LL JUST LET BENKATE DIE?!
THE SYNDICATE WANTS THE ZODIAC AND ETO GUN ABOVE ALL ELSE.
EVEN IF WE DID HAND THEM OVER TO THEM, THEY'D STILL KILL US.
THERE'S STILL A CHANCE THAT WE CAN GET CAVANAUGH OFF OUR BACKS FOR GOOD.
I'LL GO ALONE.

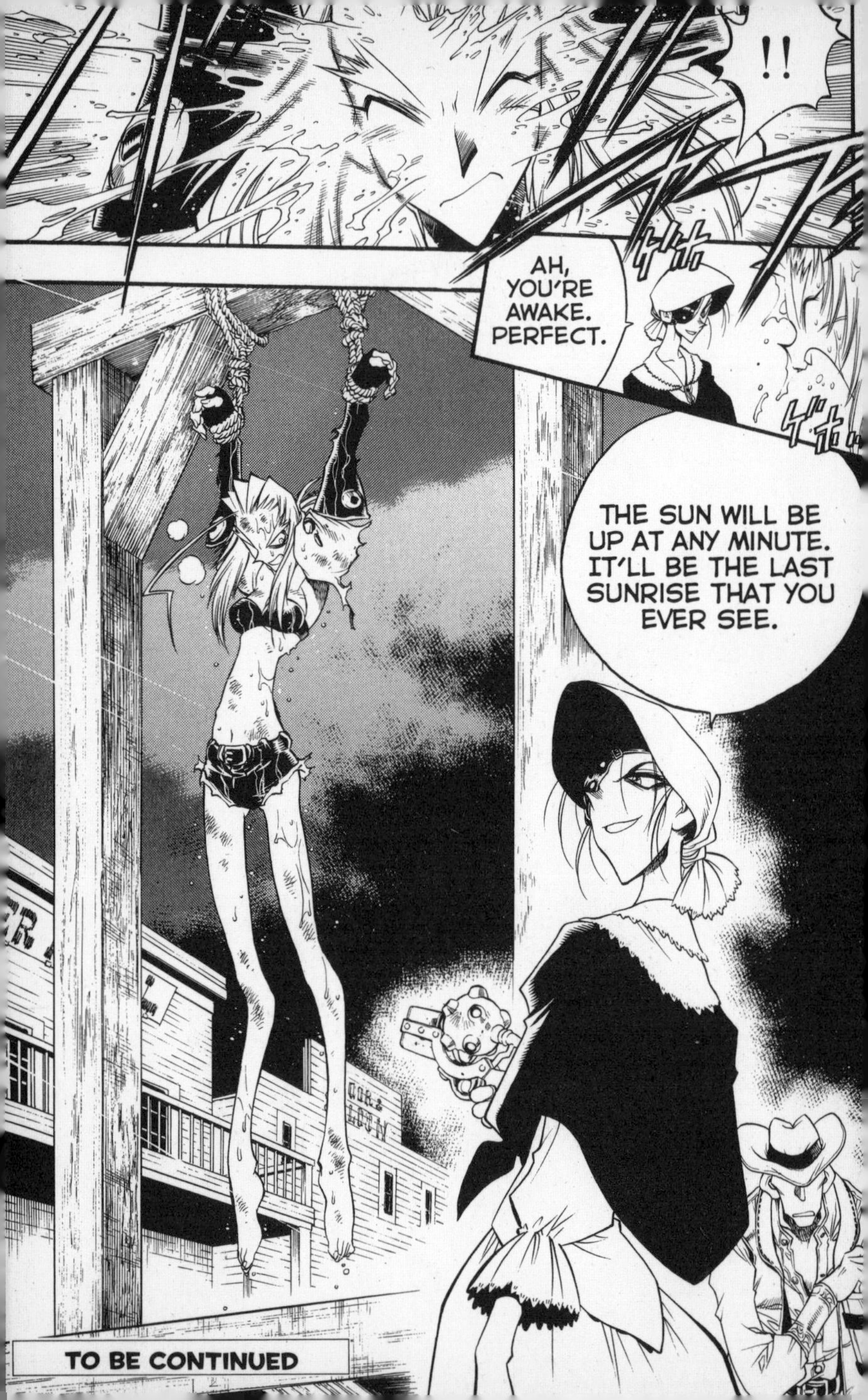
!!
AH, YOU'RE AWAKE. PERFECT.
THE SUN WILL BE UP AT ANY MINUTE. IT'LL BE THE LAST SUNRISE THAT YOU EVER SEE.
TO BE CONTINUED

This was volume seven! It's a lucky number, isn't it?

To everyone that encouraged me in all the mediums that I've tried my hand at, thank you so very much! I'll keep trying my hardest!

Tow Nakazaki

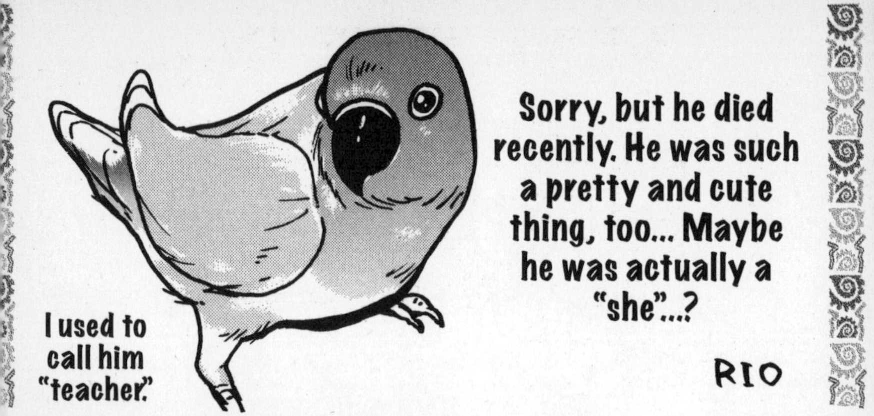
Sorry, but he died recently. He was such a pretty and cute thing, too... Maybe he was actually a "she"...?
RIO
I used to call him "teacher."

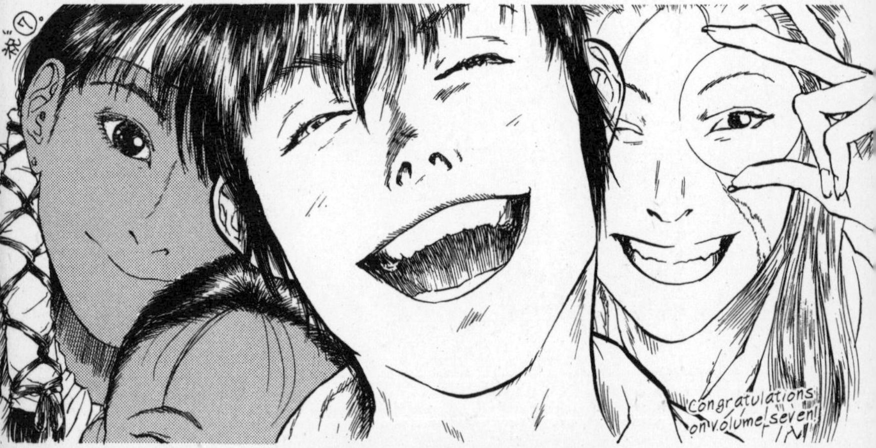
祝⑦
Congratulations on volume seven!

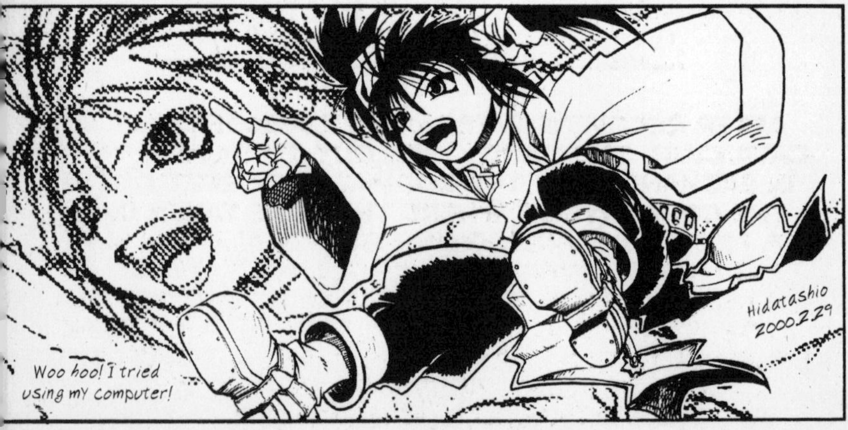
Hidatashio 2000.2.29
Woo hoo! I tried using my computer!

NEXT TIME IN...

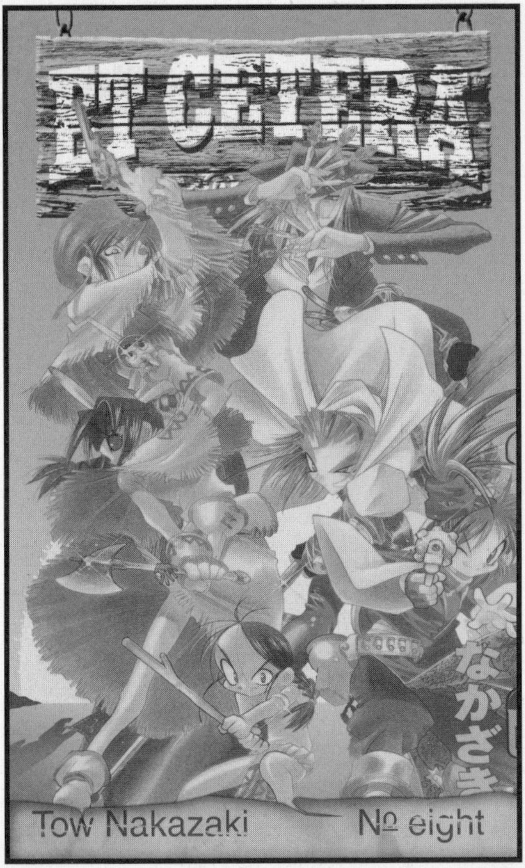

Tow Nakazaki
№ eight

AFTER RECOVERING FROM THE DAMAGE DEALT BY CAVANAGH, THE GANG GOES OUT TO SAVE BENKATE IN EXCHANGE FOR THE ZODIAC. THEY REST OUT IN THE COUNTRYSIDE WHERE THEY ARE TAKEN IN BY A FRIENDLY BEAR-LOOKING FATHER AND HIS SICK DAUGHTER, CORNELIA, WHOSE LITTLE TAVERN IS THREATENED BY A HONKY-TONK LAWYER. LATER, BASKERVILLE REALIZES THAT THERE IS SOMETHING STRANGE ABOUT CORNELIA'S SICKNESS. WHAT IS ITS MYSTERIOUS CAUSE, AND HOW IS THE ORGANIZATION INVOLVED?

TOKYOPOP SHOP

WWW.TOKYOPOP.COM/SHOP

Ayumu struggles with her studies, and the all-important high school entrance exams are approaching. Fortunately, she has help from her best bud Shii-chan, who is at the top of the class. But when the test results come back, the friends are surprised: Ayumu surpasses Shii-chan's scores and gets into the school of her choice—without Shii-chan! Losing her friend is so painful for Ayumu that she starts cutting herself to ease her sorrow. Finally, Ayumu seeks comfort in a new friend, Manami. But will Manami prove to be the friend that Ayumu truly needs? Or will Ayumu continue down a dark path?

LIFE
Volume 1
Keiko Suenobu

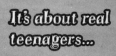

It's about real teenagers...

It's about real high school...

It's about real life.

STOP!

This is the back of the book.
You wouldn't want to spoil a great ending!

This book is printed "manga-style," in the authentic Japanese right-to-left format. Since none of the artwork has been flipped or altered, readers get to experience the story just as the creator intended. You've been asking for it, so TOKYOPOP® delivered: authentic, hot-off-the-press, and far more fun!

DIRECTIONS

If this is your first time reading manga-style, here's a quick guide to help you understand how it works.

It's easy... just start in the top right panel and follow the numbers. Have fun, and look for more 100% authentic manga from TOKYOPOP®!